# IN PURSUIT OF EQUITY

# IN PURSUIT
# *of* EQUITY

*Women, Men, and the Quest for Economic Citizenship in
20th-Century America*

ALICE KESSLER-HARRIS

OXFORD
UNIVERSITY PRESS

# OXFORD
## UNIVERSITY PRESS

Oxford    New York

Auckland    Bangkok    Buenos Aires    Cape Town    Chennai
Dar es Salaam    Delhi    Hong Kong    Istanbul    Karachi    Kolkata
Kuala Lumpur    Madrid    Melbourne    Mexico City    Mumbai
Nairobi    São Paulo    Shanghai    Singapore    Taipei    Tokyo    Toronto

*and an associated company in*
Berlin

First published by Oxford University Press, Inc., 2001
First issued as an Oxford Unversity Press paperback, 2002
198 Madison Avenue, New York, New York 10016

www.oup.com

Oxford is a registered trademark of Oxford University Press

Library of Congress Cataloging-in-Publication Data
Kessler-Harris, Alice.
In pursuit of equity : women, men, and the quest for economic citizenship in 20th-century America /
by Alice Kessler-Harris.
p. cm.
Includes bibliographical references and index.
ISBN 0-19-503835-5 (cloth) ISBN 0-19-515802-4 (pbk)
1. Women's rights—United States—History—20th century.
2. Women—Legal status, laws, etc.—United States—History—20th century.
3. Women—United States—Economic conditions—20th century.
4. New Deal, 1933–1939.
5. United States—Social policy. I. Title.

HQ1235.5.U6K475    2001    305.42'0973'0904—dc21    2001034611

Book design by Adam B. Bohannon

1    3    5    7    9    8    6    4    2

Printed in the United States of America
on acid-free paper

*For Emma and Molly*

# CONTENTS

# ACKNOWLEDGMENTS

Like all books, this one has been, if not quite a collective project, then close to it. I am delighted at last to have the chance to express my thanks to the many people who have counseled and helped along the way and to the institutions that supported my research and writing. My first debt is to those who provided financial support that brought with it precious time to research and write. At an early stage, a fellowship from the John Simon Guggenheim Memorial Foundation provided the space to rethink the parameters of this project; the Center for Social History at the New School for Social Research (then directed by Charles Tilly and Louise Tilly) generously housed me during that period. I wrote most of the manuscript during two years of research leaves offered by Rutgers University and with the help of a glorious semester at the Swedish Collegium for Advanced Studies in the Social Sciences (SCASSS) in Uppsala, Sweden. I also benefited from two short-term residencies at the Institute for Social Research, Oslo.

For more than a decade now, I have been blessed with wonderful graduate students from whom I have learned as much as I have taught. I want particularly to thank those who participated in this project by providing research assistance. At Rutgers, Kimberly Brodkin, Sarah Dubow, Rebecca Hartmann, Beatrix Hoffman, Colleen O'Neill, Mary Poole, Lisa Phillips, and Stephen Robertson were invaluable. At Columbia, Martha Jones, Lisa McGirr, and Jung Pak were particularly helpful. Leah Aden resourcefully aided with final details. Jennifer Brier and Rebecca Kessler hunted up distant archival sources.

I have relied heavily on the good offices of more archivists than I can count. I thank them all, and I want particularly to single out Kathy Kraft at the Schlesinger Library, without whose goodwill and perspicacious energy this book would have been much poorer. Lee Sayres has since left the George Meany Memorial Archives, but while she was there, she proved an adept guide to those resources. I am grateful, too, to Jim Strassmaier at the Oregon Historical Society for providing tapes of interviews with Edith Green and for making sure that I got answers to some key questions. Frances Hart, executive secretary of the EEOC in Washington, D.C., facilitated access to the papers in the EEOC secretariat and made my work there pleasant. Social Security historian Larry DeWitt provided posters, photographs, and information on several crucial occasions.

The often astute criticism of audiences in several countries has participated in shaping my perceptions of the American scene. I particularly appreciated early conversations at the Institute for Social Research in Oslo and with faculty and students in the history and economic history departments at the University of Stockholm and at Sweden's Arbetslivcentrum, where I tried out some of the newly formed versions of these ideas. I thank the participants in seminars at Melbourne, Deakin, and LaTrobe universities in Australia, where Renate Howe and Brian Howe led me through the labyrinth of social policy. For opportunities to discuss my work, I am grateful to participants in seminars at the Bella von Zuylen Institute at the University of Amsterdam, Aalborg University, the University of Bergen, and the Technische Universität in Berlin. At SCASSS, I was lucky enough to find Ann Oakley, Jean Maracek, Christina Florin, and Ulla Wikander. Their daily conversations and persistent questions forced me to refine many an idea.

My former colleagues in the history department's Gender Group at Rutgers provided extraordinary camaraderie and many intellectually stimulating moments. I want especially to thank Deborah Gray White, to whose repeated challenges I hope I have adequately responded, and Dorothy Sue Cobble and Bonnie Smith, themselves extraordinary scholars and models of generous collegiality. The Institute for Research on Women at Rutgers provides a rare intellectual harbor. I particularly thank directors Cora Kaplan and Bonnie Smith and the members of the Seminar on Women in the Public Sphere, including most especially Judith Gerson and Barbara Balliet. I benefited from opportunities to present ideas and papers at the Columbia University Seminar in Twentieth-Century Society and Politics and in the Feminist Interventions series of Columbia's Institute for Research on Women and Gender.

Over the years, I have enjoyed many fruitful conversations with others who are engaged in working out the complicated and intersecting relationships of women and gender. I thank Linda Kerber, Gro Hagemann, Yvonne Hirdmann, and Blanche Wiesen Cook for their intellectual companionship and willingness to offer acute criticism. I am grateful to Ida Blom, Elizabeth Faue, and Barbara Hobson for pointing out moments when my own analysis wasn't sharp enough and for sharing their own thoughts with me. Ira Katznelson provided an important critique at a crucial moment. Ruth and Al Blumrosen kindly agreed to be interviewed about the early days of the EEOC.

Some of the ideas for this book were worked out in articles that appeared in different form in *The Journal of American History, Southern California Review of Law and Women's Studies*, and *Schweizerische Zeitschrift für Geschichte*. I am especially grateful to David Thelen and the participants in the workshop on transnational history at the International Institute for Social History for their trenchant criticism. Linda Kerber and Kathryn Kish Sklar, my coeditors of *U.S. History as Women's History*, helped to clarify the argument that appeared in that volume and became a part of chapter 3.

Ulla Wikander has shared her own work with me and read most of this manuscript in its evolving forms. I have learned much from her often extraordinary insights. Eileen Boris, Annette Igra, and Nancy Cott read the entire manuscript, helped me to clarify some critical points, and saved me from a few embarrassing errors. Martin Fleischer and Amy Swerdlow read parts of the manuscript and pushed me into important revisions. This book began as an idea worked out with Sheldon Meyer, whose faith in it lasted for more years than I want to count. It has come to fruition under the guidance of Peter Ginna, whose trenchant critiques encouraged me to turn it into a far better manuscript than it would otherwise have been.

I would never have finished this book without the love and partnership of Bert Silverman. He has read every word, more than once; offered cogent criticism, which I sometimes didn't want to hear; and sustained me when I lost faith in the project. He has fed me books, articles, ideas, and food; and he has photocopied without complaint. I thank him for all these things and much more that I cannot say, but most of all for his joyous capacity to engage with the world in which we live.

# Introduction

I n 1937, the United States Supreme Court sustained a Georgia law that allowed women to pay a lower poll tax than men.[1] This was quite fair, argued the majority, "in view of the burdens necessarily borne by them for the preservation of the race." Convinced that marriage and childbearing were the normal conditions of women, the majority argued that women's taxes would, in any event, be paid by their husbands. A law that distinguished between men and women thus quite reasonably benefited men as well as their wives. In 1948, the Court approved Michigan's prohibition against women working as bartenders unless they happened to be the wives or daughters of male bar owners, who could be expected to protect the morals of their kin.[2] Justice Felix Frankfurter, speaking for the Court's majority, thought Michigan's desire to exclude "wives and daughters of non-owners" from an occupation that might "give rise to moral and social problems" so reasonable that "to state the question is in effect to answer it."

Neither of these decisions seemed particularly problematic at the time it was made. Until late in the 1960s, and perhaps even after, most men and women tended to agree that the normal order of family life properly subsumed women within its boundaries, rendering their needs and desires as well as rights and obligations secondary to those of husbands and children. Positioning women (even those with neither husbands nor children) as family members accounts for many of the economic institutions and practices we recognize as traditional: the sexual division of labor; disparate wages for male and female jobs; the feminization of poverty; protective labor legislation for women only; women's dependence on government welfare. For many years, and to many people, these practices did not appear to be unfair or unjust. Just the opposite. Each sustained a comforting vision of family life and social order. If they deprived women of economic equality and hindered their access to full citizenship (including their capacity to speak and write freely, to acquire education, or to run for political office), this, too did not appear to most people to be unfair. After all, treating women differently provided them with a valuable protective umbrella to which men could not lay claim. Or so it seemed.

And yet when the federal government began, in the 1930s, to legislate an array of social benefits and tax incentives designed to ensure economic security for the American family, it attached its most valuable benefits not to families but to wage work. Tying benefits like old age pensions and unemployment insurance to jobs affirmed the status of recipients as independent and upstanding citizens and delineated the secondary positions of those without good jobs or any at all. Work, wage work, had long marked a distinction among kinds of citizens: intimately tied to identity, it anchored nineteenth-century claims to political participation. But when the federal government linked wage work to tangible, publicly provided rewards, employment emerged as a boundary line demarcating different kinds of citizenship. Casual laborers, the unskilled and untrained, housewives, farm workers, mothers, and domestic servants all found themselves on one side of a barrier not of their own making. Their own benefits not earned but means-tested, classified as relief, not rights, many protested what seemed an artificial division and demanded inclusion. Their voices were quickly stilled.

The idea that some people (generally women) would get benefits by virtue of their family positions and others (mainly men) by virtue of their paid employment marks the commitment of the United States to its version of the welfare state. Unlike many other industrialized countries, America chose to distribute what the British social theorist T. H. Marshall called the rights of "social citizenship" on the basis of work rather than as a function of residence or citizenship. The distinction had a reciprocal logic in the 1930s. At a moment in time when most women married, when 85 percent of all families boasted a single male breadwinner, and when all but a handful of marriages endured for the (admittedly shorter) lifetimes of the partners, demographic patterns reinforced traditional notions of families as appropriate locations for security. In a world infused by irregular work and persistent unemployment, popular opinion had it that the security of the family relied on the regular wages of its head, who was more than likely to be male. That assumption—or desire—elusive though it was, opened to male heads of families a range of special benefits, which were typically identified as normal. Inscribed into a network of government policies, expectations about male wage earning legitimized long-standing calls for a "family wage." And beginning in the 1930s, a range of mostly male job holders found themselves eligible for special pension benefits and for special consideration when they were unemployed. After World War II, these expanded to include greater access to credit, lower mortgage and income tax rates for some male household heads, and special rights to jobs. These privileges are just a few of those that define economic citizenship: the independent status that provides the possibility of full participation in the polity.

Yet a general consensus did not mean, even in the 1930s, that ideas about what was fair remained uncontested. Danish political scientist Gøsta Esping-Andersen describes as inevitable the tendency of social policies to function as an "active force in the ordering of social relations," and this seems to have been the case in the United States.[3] When the structure and form of social benefits could militate against economic citizenship, many people who did not fit an idealized demographic profile found themselves without resources. They included never-married women with and without children and parents to support; widowed, divorced, and deserted female heads of families; and intact African-American and other poor families whose male heads could not find jobs or earn sufficient wages to feed their households. Their numbers increased over the following decades, perhaps ironically stimulated by the greater availability of means-tested benefits. At the same time, in a trend accelerated by the influx of women into the hungry World War II workforce, married women who took jobs found themselves in an anomalous dual position as family members with paid employment. Those who claimed social benefits that accrued to the fully employed seemed to be violating the standards of an employment-based citizenship. As mounting numbers of women in dual roles challenged the convenient configuration of female-family and male-paid-work, women began increasingly to notice, and to question their exclusion from, the prerogatives of economic citizenship. By the 1960s, tax breaks, benefits, and employment privileges tied to gender and marital status no longer signified fairness quite as readily as they once had. As the capacity of gendered differentiation to generate consensus on social policy diminished, and then became the subject of attack, what once seemed fair came to be perceived as rank discrimination.

This book aims to explore how particular ideas of fairness became embedded in American social institutions in the twentieth century. It investigates how these institutions came to reflect claims to normalcy and to shape them. It argues that gender—racialized gender—constitutes a central piece of the social imaginary around which social organization and ideas of fairness are constructed and on which social policies are built.[4] And it tells the story of how gendered habits of mind—which I sometimes call "the gendered imagination"—framed discussions of what was possible and shaped the boundaries of the politically plausible. I do not argue here that gender is the only, or even the most important, source of legislative change. Instead, I suggest that, at a moment in time when the federal government assumed greater authority over the distribution of resources, gender constituted a crucial measure of fairness and served a powerful mediating role. Appeals to gender could enhance the public appetite for some policies and silence resistance to others. They legitimized, rationalized, and justified policies that could and did serve many other ends, including maintaining a stratified and racialized social order and undercutting radical threats.

In using gender, I follow in the footsteps of a generation of feminist historians who have distinguished the system of ideas around which the social relations of the sexes are constructed from the subjective experiences and individual or collective actions of men and women.[5] In this view, gender is a system of thought and a category of analysis, comparable to class and race. Like class and race, it informs how people imagine their worlds, conditions their expectations, and restricts or expands their options. Gender seems to me always to contain hierarchical racial and class components just as the reverse is always true. I cannot imagine a gender system that is not already racialized nor one that is not rooted in class; but then neither can I imagine a class system that is not already gendered and rooted in race. But the complex and frequently messy interaction of these components is historically circumscribed. Because gender is constructed within families and in the workplace, by and around the sexual division of labor, it is a continual and changing process rather than a static entity. This book is not so much about women as it is about the power of gendered worldviews (often deriving from efforts to preserve a particular prerogative of masculinity that serves the interests of significant groups of women as well as men) to construct the circumstances of history by shaping the parameters within which people see.

I came to these issues out of my work on *A Woman's Wage*.[6] In that book, I puzzled over the power of cultural meanings (like the assertion that women worked for "pin money") to shape the wage. Taking off from the skepticism of some institutional economists about the untrammeled power of markets, I investigated how culture influenced the contents of men's and women's pay envelopes. I argued, for example, that culture explained historical variations in male/female pay differentials—differentials that did not vanish even as the need for female labor grew. It illuminated wage differences among women, like the negligible pay of African-American women who worked as domestics at the turn of the century despite their short supply. In each case the differences embodied some notion of fairness or equity that lay beyond a simple economic calculus. Often, when it came to differences between men and women, the notion was clearly articulated, as, for example, in the century-long belief that men deserved a "family wage." But what was fair sometimes appeared patently unjust. Women who supported families rarely earned a family wage, nor did very many people propose to give them one. Unattached men felt entitled to it even when they were not supporting anyone else.

It seemed to me that this male sense of entitlement in jobs and wages permeated economic life, reflecting and perpetuating the social organization of families, labor market opportunities, and the relationships of men and women in and outside the workplace. It also participated in configuring and sustaining crucial systems of cultural representation such as individual liberty, self-reliance, and the ethic of success by which we measure ourselves as a people and as a nation. For example, individual liberty, conceded to be a fundamental value for men in the United States, has not always or necessarily been the highest good for women. Ideals of service and sacrifice to children, parents, and spouse have often been thought to render liberty for women irrelevant and women's search for individual rights "selfish." Under this rubric, many Americans and their legislative assemblies have felt free to treat women differently from men in many respects: refusing them the right to vote, to serve on juries, or to receive economic and social benefits in the same ways as men.

Political scientists and philosophers trace the origins of this particular gender system at least as far back as the seventeenth-century Enlightenment, which established the natural equality of all individuals and their right both to govern themselves and to contract to delegate this right if they chose to do so. But, as philosopher Carol Pateman describes it, most contract theorists believed that only men possessed "the attributes of free and equal individuals."[7] They took for granted the natural subordination of women, a trade-off that allowed them to challenge the God-given authority of kings while maintaining conjugal order. Men's right to familial authority and the governance of their own households, sanctioned by the marriage bond, accompanied and justified male political participation. Adapted by the new American republic, these ideas located the criteria for male independence first in property ownership and then in an income sufficient for a working man to maintain himself and his family. While the formal qualification for voting was largely gone by the mid-nineteenth century, workers nevertheless continued to associate the capacity to support a family and to acquire the services of a wife with independent political participation. In the United States by the late nineteenth century, this wage, sometimes called a "fair wage," became the substantial grounds for male citizenship.

But to whom was it fair? Many conventional white nineteenth-century American women accepted the notion that men had superior claims to economic property even as the dissident or outspokenly opposed found themselves accused of subverting family and social order. Lack of economic equity for women in the marketplace, while it could be unfortunate, was not necessarily perceived as unfair even by women. An early nineteenth-century skilled mechanic articulated his perception of the crude balance in gendered economic rights. Women's efforts to sustain families, he declared, were "actually the same as tying a stone around the neck of her natural protector, Man, and destroying him with the weight she has brought to his assistance."[8] Nineteenth-century American reformers who lamented the fate of starving seamstresses joined the sewing women in demanding higher wages rather than an expansion of job opportunities. And the Boston sewing women who, in 1869, complained that men were poaching on their turf claimed that they would willingly give up their jobs if they could be assured of acquiring good homes.[9]

Many nineteenth-century women's rights advocates believed that expanding the practical rights of women within the family would meet the demands of fairness more readily than throwing them into the labor market. By granting property and inheritance rights to married women, assigning divorced women custody of their own children, and giving married female wage earners the right to keep their own earnings, they hoped to provide the economic assurance that husbands would not or could not secure. In this scenario, the labor market was a fall-back position, which would provide good jobs for women who lacked male support. To be sure, there were always dissenting voices. The British feminist Mary Wollstonecraft and the philosopher John Stuart Mill demanded equal and practical education for women. French feminists like Olympe de Gouges and Jean Deroin fought for the right to vote and the right to work, which they conceived as integrated objectives. Their work and ideas were known to American women's rights advocates like Frances Wright and Elizabeth Cady Stanton.[10] These and others, including the Grimké sisters, Charlotte Forten, Virginia Penny, Charlotte Perkins Gilman, and Emma Goldman, are well-known examples of men and women who conceived economic independence as the foundation of political voice and ultimately of political equality for women. Persuasive as these voices were to a few women, most contemporaries judged them aberrant and sometimes abhorrent conceptions of gender. To us, these persistant voices point up the remarkable resilience of constraining habits of mind.

Even to those aware of gender injustice, projected solutions created new problems. Turn-of-the-century African-American women, who fully participated in maintaining their households and communities, found themselves excluded by racism from political participation in campaigns for women's rights. Their white feminist allies created racial and class barriers that ignored the interests of black and working-class women.[11] Before World War I, working-class feminists debated the relative importance of political rights for women as opposed to greater economic security. And into the 1920s, historian Nancy Cott tells us, different kinds of feminists disputed bitterly over whether economic equality was an appropriate goal.[12] Relatively few self-styled feminists in that decade, most of them white and privileged, challenged traditional gendered understandings or eagerly advocated the route of absolute economic independence. Many women, including leaders like Eleanor Roosevelt and Women's Bureau chief Mary Anderson, who called herself a "practical feminist," rejected untrammeled statements of sexual equality like that embodied in an equal rights amendment to the Constitution for fear that they would eliminate the special labor laws that protected the personal and family well-being of the wage earners among them.

Angry disagreements among different kinds of feminists reveal the sometimes perverse operation of class and race in conceptions of gendered equity. While poor and middle-class women of every race sometimes successfully reached across the class divide, white women rarely overcame the barriers of race to articulate a common interest in family and women's issues.[13] But everyone who advocated women's equality grappled continually with race and class issues. Among African Americans, the force of racial injustice often dimmed the glare of gender injustice and led African-American men and women to adopt a rhetoric of masculinity that paralleled that of white society. With respect to domestic life, men of both races who aspired to middle-class status shared dominant ideas about wage work and measured family respectability by the presence of a non-wage-earning wife. Men's aspirations to control their domiciles and household property (though far harder to achieve among African Americans) crossed racial lines, as did their sense of entitlement to the sexual and household services of wives. Across the racial divide, men sought to control their own labor and aspired to economic mobility and self-realization. If none of these was readily available to poor men of any race or ethnicity, stringent occupational segregation made them even more difficult for black men to claim. In their absence, the gendered relations and practical expectations of men and women within most black households and communities differed dramatically from those of middle-class white families. These differences created an exclusionary barrier between black and white women that sometimes melded the political interests of blacks with women and sometimes created divisions among women of different class and racial groups.[14]

In the story that follows, I explore how tradition and culture, and especially the deeply intertwined ideological and practical relationships of race and gender, helped to shape conceptions of fairness that found their ways into twentieth-century law and social policy. We now understand how public commitments to the male-breadwinner family produced different kinds of social rights for men and women. These differentially distributed commitments, as many scholars have shown, participated in the evolving process of forming what the British social theorist T. H. Marshall calls social citizenship. I have begun to see the absence of another, more hidden form of citizenship, which I call economic citizenship, as influential in explaining the continuing disadvantaged position of women. Marshall, whose work provides a touchstone for issues of citizenship, offers three categories of citizens' rights: civil, political, and social. In the economic sphere, he contends, "the basic civil right is the right to work, that is to say the right to follow the occupation of one's choice in the place of one's choice." Tracing the struggle to claim rights to work against the power of custom, of guilds, and of a deeply rooted apprenticeship system that limited certain occupations to particular social groups, Marshall argues that by the early nineteenth century "this principle of individual economic freedom" had become axiomatic in the Anglo-American world, required as much as anything else by the demands of a market economy.[15] But subsuming economic rights into the civil arena obscures their interactive influence on political and social citizenship.

If democratic citizenship was closely tied to earning, then the right to work constituted a rather precarious guarantee even for skilled free white men, and none at all for women of any race. In some sense it is no right at all. As the political philosopher Jon Elster points out, it has no equivalent in the construction of citizenship. Classical political rights like freedom of speech and religion are, as Elster notes, "largely negative, in the sense that they protect the individual from interference by others or by the state."[16] The right to work, in contrast, is a positive right, not enforceable by legal mandate but implicit in the expectations inspired by an emergent nineteenth-century democratic decision-making process. The distinguished Swedish social theorist Walter Korpi calls such rights "proto-rights." They are generally not enforceable by state power but "norm-based" and socially reinforced.[17]

For whom, then, were rights to work sanctioned? Marshall thought individual economic freedom, accepted as axiomatic by the early nineteenth century, was shared by "all adult members of the community—or perhaps one should say all male members, since the status of women, or at least of married women, was in some important respects peculiar."[18] And American courts persistently applied the notion as if women's liberties fell into a different category than those of men. Under the equal protection clause of the Fourteenth Amendment, the Supreme Court repeatedly and fervently upheld rights to work for what it called "all" citizens when it meant the rights to be held by males. The right to work in legitimate occupations, it declared in a pathbreaking 1915 decision, "is of the very essence of the personal freedom and opportunity that it was the purpose of the Fourteenth Amendment to secure."[19] And yet for two generations after, it restricted women's access to that right. Senator Robert Wagner thundered popular faith in the notion when he declared: "The right to work is synonymous with the inalienable right to live. ... It has never been surrendered and cannot be forfeited."[20] Yet with respect to women, the idea that such restrictions were "an offence against the liberty of the subject" dueled with the widespread belief that the liberty of women could and should be curtailed if it menaced the health of the family. While rights to work for men could be counted among the fundamental sources of citizenship under liberal theory—a deeply rooted gendered prerogative—the notion that a public interest inhered in restricting women's work-related rights persisted in custom and law well into the 1960s.

Since Marshall's day, many of the political and civil rights denied women have been granted, but the one he called basic, "the right to follow the occupation of one's choice," still remains the subject of informal as well as formal contest—which is why constructing "work" as the passport to certain social rights produced dramatically different paths for different citizens. Not only has women's economic freedom never been accepted as axiomatic, but, with respect to the rights meant to accompany it, the limited freedoms available to all women were further restricted by marriage and motherhood—and by treating unmarried females in the workforce as if they were potentially married and mothers. When employers' devices like differential wages and occupational segmentation by sex have proved insufficient, workers have resorted to more informal strategies to enforce customary understandings of sex boundaries. These include refusing to mentor female trainees, negative job assessments, and sexual harassment on the job. The public interest in social order manifested in regulating (by custom as well as law) women's work-related rights remains vested in women's real or imagined family lives. In this sense the use of the family to justify and rationalize women's disadvantaged workforce position functions as a set of ideological and material blinders that limits women's access to the full range of economic life and shapes the nature of male as well as female economic experience.[21] As Carol Pateman, drawing on Marshall, suggests, given the paramount duty of the citizen to work, restrictions on women's opportunities in that sphere have assigned women to a secondary citizenship based on their roles as family members and have kept them subject to male domination.[22]

A wide variety of political theorists have chimed in to reinforce the idea that without economic independence, vested for most people in claims to jobs, and acknowledged as the social right to work if not as a claim to a particular job, political participation remains a chimera.[23] This has been especially true in the United States, where many rights that are elsewhere the universal entitlements of citizens, including old age pensions, unemployment insurance, and medical care, have been vested in each citizen's record of work. "We are," in the words of political scientist Judith Shklar, "citizens only if we 'earn.'"[24] Norwegian political scientist Helga Hernes tells us why this is crucial: despite their high level of social rights, Norwegian women could not achieve political power; that began to come only when their economic rights changed.[25] American labor leader Samuel Gompers put this another way when he testified before Congress in 1898: "A declaration of political liberty which does not involve an opportunity for economic independence is a delusion."[26] Owen Young, chairman of the board at General Electric during the 1920s and much of the 1930s, reframed the equation: "Here in America, we have raised the standard of political equality. Shall we be able to add to that, full equality in economic opportunity? No man is wholly free until he is both politically and economically free; no man with an inadequate wage is free."[27]

What about women? The language of economic citizenship captures the full complexity of their exclusion, not merely from jobs but from the range of access routes to citizenship prohibited by their real or imagined cultural locations. Economic citizenship has sometimes been used to identify workers' capacity to control their work situations through workers' councils and other forms of industrial democracy.[28] I use it more broadly to suggest the achievement of an independent and relatively autonomous status that marks self-respect and provides access to the full play of power and influence that defines participation in a democratic society. The concept of economic citizenship demarcates women's efforts to participate in public life and to achieve respect as women (sometimes as mothers and family members) from the efforts of men and women to occupy equitable relationships to corporate and government services. Access to economic citizenship begins with self-support, generally through the ability to work at the occupation of one's choice, and it does not end there. Rather, it requires customary and legal acknowledgment of personhood, with all that implies for expectations, training, access to and distribution of resources, and opportunity in the marketplace.

Theoretically, revaluing family roles (and reducing their dependence on female labor) could provide the respect and the resources necessary to define a person as a competent actor in the public arena. Ideally, espousing economic citizenship should not diminish caregiving as an equally enabling access route to democratic participation. In practice, the historical record reveals moments when the collective efforts of women have developed an ideology of caring into a successful politics that enhanced community life and ameliorated disadvantaged working and living conditions. I am thinking here of the social feminists of the early twentieth century—women like Jane Addams in the United States and Sweden's Ellen Key. But individual women have not generally achieved public power for their caring roles, and while proclamations of the value of motherhood and family commitment have extended social rights, they have done little to provide the ground on which economic citizenship has been realized. In modern democratic societies prevailing beliefs in the sanctity of the market make access to it the only practical route to empowerment as citizens.

Because it is predicated on the economic independence of every individual, economic citizenship can be restricted as well as enhanced by social citizenship. Indeed the two are often at odds. For example, policies that enhance motherhood may offer social rights while closing paths to economic citizenship. This happened in the United States when mothers' allowances, pension rights for widowed housewives, and stipends from the program of Aid to Dependent Children required female parents to restrict their access to the labor market or suffer a loss of benefits. It continues to occur when recipients of some social rights lack the kinds of services (adequate day care, efficient public transportation, safe streets) that enable full labor market participation. At the same time, economic citizenship requires a range of gender-encompassing social rights, including most especially a fully integrated labor market that permits, but does not assume, domesticity for either sex. It provides a language to describe and revalue these particular rights. One can imagine, for example, government policies that treat women as individuals, not family members. Such policies might (and in some countries already do) include individually based income taxes, social benefits based not on marital status but on individual records, and mortgage credit for single parents. They might also include sharing the costs of child birth and child rearing; equalizing parental responsibility for children's financial and social well-being, and eliminating discriminatory gendered protections in the realms of employment, education, and political participation.

For the U.S. Congress even to imagine such an agenda (which in the year 2001 it began to do) bespeaks the enormous transformation in popular sensibilities about fairness and equity that has occurred in the United States since the early twentieth century. That is not to say that, given their childbearing functions, women's acquisition of full economic citizenship does not also require moving yet further: toward a greater public investment in social goods and services, including first-rate custodial care for children, public housing, health care, and public transportation. Our failure to approach these issues suggests the continuing contest over gendered equity that still consumes us despite the dramatic changes that have already occurred. By historicizing the change—watching as ideas of fairness alter—we can begin to understand resistances to, and the evolution of, the idea of economic citizenship.

To trace the ways that these changing ideas of fairness challenged existing policies and produced new ones, I have chosen to examine not outlying thought but the mainstream. I look at how the concept of gender shaped definitions and state actions, how it was reciprocally altered by state interventions, and how it was sanctioned by state efforts. I try to show how polices that appear neutral on their face emerge from deeply embedded belief systems that accentuate particular politics, how they play themselves out in ways that inform these policies and the politics that surround them, and how ideas of gender are in turn shaped by the discussions as well as by the policies themselves. If gender constitutes part of what Frank Parkin calls the "meaning system" that informs how we construct policy, the process inevitably alters the rules that frame our lives.[29] The moments of negotiation on policy construction are historically specific and ongoing. I try in the pages that follow to capture some of the key conversations and to assess their importance. I examine the narratives that accompany dramatic moments in the legislative and judicial history of social policy to observe the sometimes subtle ways that social meanings are incorporated and disseminated. Because so much of the practical discourse around changing gender roles has taken place in the chambers of judges and legislatures, I make extensive use of court documents, including judical decisions and briefs, and of government hearings and records. I use these documents not so much to track legal changes as to elucidate shifts in the language that describes gender roles and to reveal the gendered imagination. In so doing, I try to follow the evolution of the ideas that emerge in influential social policies. Generally, I focus on the central actors—the labor union leaders, the government commissions, the men and women who thought they spoke for Americans—hoping to discover subtle distinctions in meaning that may account for the ways in which policies that seem alike on the surface perpetuate quite different and equally influential national self-images.

In chapter 1, I outline the particular gendered conception of rights to work that emerges in the turn-of-the-century United States and persists during the economic depression of the 1930s. In the early twentieth century, newly adopted social policies like protective labor legislation for women only tended to institutionalize and reward familiar gender patterns. Protective labor legislation channeled popular conceptions of social order (men in the workforce and women in the home) into rules and regulations that affirmed the sexually segmented structure of the labor force. As we shall see, this effectively reinforced family relationships; not coincidentally, it expanded the expectations of consumers and focused racial antagonisms as well.

As in many other Western industrial countries, in the United States women were key players in the debates over labor legislation. According to one formulation, they may have played a greater role in the United States than elsewhere because in the early twentieth century a relatively weak American state encouraged the growth of powerful women's organizations with important political clout.[30] The historical evidence suggests that women, as well as sympathetic men, utilized their wits and resources to claim special rights for women, not to increase women's political or social rights but to enhance their roles as mothers and family members. It demonstrates that middle-class women acting in their own individual and class interests, sometimes in alliance with trade unionists, succeeded to an unprecedented degree in providing state-based "maternalist" legislation designed to protect the roles of working-class and poor mothers.[31] For their efforts, they won minimum wages and maximum hours for wage-earning women, mothers' pensions for widows with children, maternal health clinics, and other rights, obligations, and benefits granted to women as mothers and wives. Some historians believe that this separate women's legislation provided blueprints for the federal legislation of the 1930s. In so far as that is true, it is perhaps because it so effectively affirmed prevailing notions of equity in both the family and the labor market. As effective as maternalist legislation was in ameliorating immediate needs, it granted women social rights based on traditional gendered images of work and family. As everyone agrees, these new rights reinforced women's identification with motherhood, creating what the British theorist Ruth Lister calls "mother-citizens" to distinguish them from citizens who benefited from work-derived benefits. The privileges of the "father-" or "husband-citizen" constitute the other side of this coin.[32]

In chapters 2 and 3, I pursue changing conceptions of fairness in the unfolding social policies of the New Deal period. I pause at length in the depression because the development of national welfare systems—using *welfare* in its broadest sense—has exercised such a powerful influence in the modern world, encompassing the lives and influencing the expectations of ordinary people in every industrial country. In the United States, the transfer of authority and voice from state governments to a federal bureaucracy beginning in the 1930s provides a pivotal moment for charting gendered habits of mind and observing how they shift over time. In order to illuminate the broad influence of what is considered fair, I have chosen key policies in which women were not the particular objects of legislation, and sometimes only its peripheral subjects: these include fair labor standards and unemployment and old age insurance. We will see in these chapters how ideas about which wage earners constituted "workers" shaped the differential access of all citizens to important social benefits. Because the conception of "work" encompassed primarily the jobs done by white males, that of "worker" excluded black men almost as fully as it omitted employed women of any race. Yet, through higher prices, all the excluded contributed indirectly to paying the costs of these special benefits without accruing the social rights they conferred. Ultimately, then, the racialized and gendered language of work created inequities, isolating the excluded, placing them in dependent positions in relation to the state, and devaluing their rights.[33]

If I am less interested in why certain policies were adopted than in how they took on particular shapes, it is because so much good work on the practical politics of policy making provides the opportunity to take a different tack. Social scientists like Anna Orloff, Theda Skocpol, and Steve Skowronek, attempting to explain the differences among welfare states, have demonstrated that distinctive administrative and political structures account for why some nations managed to pass social legislation while others failed.[34] In their view, previous state policies, the interests of entrenched bureaucracy, and the structures of political parties explain how particular policies are adopted. Within the United States, the work of Edward Berkowitz, Colin Gordon, and Jill Quadagno, among many others, has effectively illuminated the informal as well as the formal political pressures that produced now familiar outcomes.[35] This work takes for granted the cultural and ideological roots of policy, rather than interrogating them. I want here to expand the lens—to see how even seemingly neutral policies like unemployment and old age insurance acted out gendered assumptions and to watch how these assumptions broke down in the postwar years.

Others have looked closely at how legislation primarily affecting women in their roles as mothers emerged in this period and expanded their claims to social citizenship. Together scholars like Joanne Goodwin, Linda Gordon, and Gwendolyn Mink have made it possible for us to see how some provisions of the Social Security Act reinforced traditional patterns of women's dependence and affirmed racial divisions.[36] The insight of Barbara Nelson, who first coined the notion of a "two-channel" state, is particularly important in revealing how little this legislation spoke to economic citizenship.[37] Nelson argues that the sharp division into means-tested and work-related policies adopted in the 1930s established long-lasting patterns in which assumptions about men's provider roles contributed to women's continued dependency. Until the passage of the 1996 Personal Responsibility Act, which eliminated the "welfare" assumptions of the 1930s, these scholars show, welfare created a particular pattern of rewards and discouragement that effectively regulated the family lives and labor market behavior of mothers in line with patriarchal expectations. I have gratefully built on this work and much more as I seek to discover how commitment to a particular gendered vision has informed ideas of what people can and ought to do.[38] And yet I seek to turn it on its head, altering our perspective from the rights denied to women when they are deemed to be primarily attached to the household to those that are meant to accrue to men and women as part of the obligation to engage in wage work.

Chapter 4 explores the notions of fairness embedded in early federal income tax policy. It focuses on the discussion of a mandatory joint income tax for married couples that consumed much energy in the 1930s and 1940s, and finally achieved a compromise resolution in 1948. The discussion captured a sharp division between those who assumed that male-headed families constituted a desirable norm and those who preferred more flexibility in their definitions of family. And it enables us to see how readily words like *breadwinner*, *household*, and *family* assumed political meanings.

Chapters 5 and 6 turn to issues of equal employment policy in the 1950s and 1960s and the reframed discussion of women's rights that emerged after World War II. In this period of rapid and dramatic change in women's workforce roles, older notions of protection for women workers began to crumble and occupational segregation by sex became the target of attack. We observe how the battle for access to jobs generates sharp divisions over gender roles and how a bitter debate over the meanings of independence and equality comes to a head. We watch how, informed by the African-American movement for civil rights, a new consensus emerges among women leaders. This uneasy alliance, which encourages women to drop claims to gender difference, produces powerful political arguments for equality but only faltering public commitment to the social changes that gendered equity implies. Not everyone was convinced, even by the early 1970s, that what was fair (politically necessary) was socially desirable.

Yet in some ways the language of the early 1970s, by revealing the transformative potential of open access to economic citizenship, also suggests a new and perhaps more effective phase in the campaign to achieve it. Michael Walzer provides a powerful example of how this worked in nineteenth-century China. When Taiping rebels wanted to revolutionize their culture, he tells us, they simply demanded access for women to the civil service exams. They knew that "if women are to take the exams, then they must be allowed to prepare for them: they must be admitted to the schools, freed from concubinage, arranged marriages, footbinding, and so on. The family itself must be reformed so that its power no longer reaches into the sphere of office."[39]

The lesson should not be lost on us. For generations, American women lacked not merely the practice but frequently the idea of individual economic freedom. Neither most men nor most women could fully conceive a gender-encompassing form of individualism; nor could they imagine a right to work that was not conditioned by gender. In the early and mid-twentieth century these gendered habits of mind, these notions of fairness, were inscribed into the social policies that have framed our lives. They were then, and still remain, contested. But no one who has lived through the end of the twentieth century would argue that the gendered imagination remains what it once was. Our own social policies, like the proposals of the Taiping rebels, have carried a complicated and continually changing set of messages, which have themselves participated in the changes that engulf our lives. Uncovering the web of discourse in which they have been embedded may be a first step toward admitting women to full economic citizenship and ultimately to altering the meaning of democratic participation. This book tells a tiny piece of the story of how gender has shaped the rules by which we live and leads us into the moment of change in the 1970s that exposed an outdated gender system and placed women on the threshold of economic citizenship.

# CHAPTER 1

# The Responsibilities of Life

Robert F. Wagner, distinguished senior senator from New York, chair of a duly constituted subcommittee of the Committee on Banking and Currency, and political midwife to much of the labor legislation of the Roosevelt years, opened the hearings on the Full Employment Act of 1945 with an appropriately inspiring statement. Quoting his own words from a 1930s debate on a bill to legislate a thirty-hour workweek, he declared that "the right to work is synonymous with the inalienable right to live" and then added, "Whoever believes in this right to work, believes in it for every adult who is looking for an honest job at decent pay."[1] The bill's cosponsor, Senator James Murray of Montana, concurred. "No thoughtful American," Murray insisted, "would deny that every man or woman in the country who is willing to work and capable of working has the right to a job."[2]

Yet the bill that was then offered up immediately qualified this inspiring and generously inclusionary rhetoric. The draft introduced first into the House of Representatives and then the Senate declared that "all Americans able to work and seeking work have the right to useful, remunerative, regular, and full-time employment, and it is the policy of the United States to assure the existence at all times of sufficient employment opportunities to enable all Americans who have finished their schooling and who do not have full-time housekeeping responsibilities freely to exercise this right."[3] *All Americans*, the bill said, except students and those with "full-time housekeeping responsibilities." Senator Abe Murdock of Utah challenged the exceptions. He objected, he said, to excluding "the housekeeping, the housewives" (making it instantly clear that seemingly neutral language could not disguise the sex of those to be excluded). To leave them out would "impose an indignity ... on one of the very fundamental labors of the Nation. ... I certainly would not want to deprive the housewife of any opportunity that is open to any other American." Quickly

Murray took exception. For his part, he did not expect or want to "take the housewives out of the homes and put them into industry or other employment." Neither did Murdock. Still, he did not want to compromise principle by excluding them altogether: "I do not think that we should make an exception of any class," he argued. "They are all entitled to the same opportunity. If they are in the house today and want to get out tomorrow, in my opinion they should enjoy exactly the same opportunity as any other American." Murray would not back off. Refusing to drop the clause, he insisted that he would not want to "put ourselves in the position of advocating that everyone was going to work in American industry, because that would be impossible."[4]

Why not, then, simply limit the right to work to those "able to work and seeking work," as one legislator proposed? That ought to ensure that women with housekeeping responsibilities would not imagine themselves included. Senator Joseph C. O'Mahoney of Wyoming resisted. He had chaired a special postwar planning committee that concluded that the war had drawn housewives "who otherwise would not have been employed, who would have preferred to stay at home," into the labor force. Now he insisted that the bill's sponsors had added the exclusionary clause because they "did not want to give rise to the inference that this measure was intended to maintain at Government expense employment for people who ought to be in school or who ought to be at home helping to raise families, to make sure that we were not undertaking by a Government program to break up the family." When Murdock confessed he shared those aims with his colleague, O'Mahoney persisted. They had added the language, he explained, to fend off charges that they wanted "to guarantee at the expense of the Government the employment of persons who need not be employed at all and who ought to be left free to do as they see fit."[5]

The bill's advocates now found themselves in a dilemma, called on the carpet for transgressing democratic principles by denying one group of persons "exactly the same opportunity" as other Americans. To them the exclusion of housewives resonated with common sense, validating popular sensibilities about the appropriate distribution of responsibilities for men and women. And including them would have been, as Murray put it, "impossible." From a practical perspective the economy couldn't handle it; it would break up families. No, including housewives would undermine the good life for everyone. Similar tension between women's demands for economic inclusion and broad claims to democratic participation had shaped the course of other national histories. France had twice witnessed social movements on behalf of women's rights to work: once during the French Revolution, when Olympe de

Gouges lost her head for claiming women's full economic and political participation; and again in 1848, when women demanded that their briefly
acknowledged rights to jobs receive recognition by a grant of the right to
vote. Before the turn of the century, an international women's movement
fought for the integration of women into the labor market while socialists
resisted. The United States in the 1920s witnessed a continuing struggle
between "equal rights feminists" who claimed an absolute right to work and
more moderate social feminists who agreed to restrict economic rights to
preserve traditional families.[6] But whatever the arguments about rights to
work in feminist circles, common experience and popular understanding
affirmed male prerogatives.

This chapter traces the gendered nature of rights to work as they emerged
in late nineteenth-century ideas around masculinity and the family. It
describes how these putative rights came to mark the independent status that
provided entry to fuller economic citizenship and signaled access to the political process. And it suggests how, in consequence, rights to work became carefully gendered, a corollary of widespread beliefs in the ideology of family and
in the necessary privileges of the male breadwinner in whose justice women
and men concurred. I argue that by the early twentieth century few people
believed that women had rights to work in the same sense as men and that, as
a result, women's constitutional liberties were severely circumscribed.
Women, in the eyes of many, deserved state protection for fair and equitable
treatment *at* work (equal wages, suitable working conditions, reasonable
hours) precisely because they possessed few rights *to* work. In the first half of
the twentieth century, persistent beliefs about the gendered right to earn
helped to structure the labor market in ways that restricted women's job
choices, fostered the adoption of new corporate welfare strategies that benefited male-headed families, and ultimately shaped the direction of social policy in the 1930s. Though these belief systems sometimes wavered (with regard
to single women and among African-American women, for example) and were
often challenged, their practical effect was to restrict women's access to economic citizenship. This applied to white and black women, privileged and not
so. To the senators who could not imagine government supporting the rights
of housewives to jobs, the idea that women should have the equivalent of civil
rights—an equal chance in the competitive market with the possibility of displacing men—still seemed antithetical to conceptions of a gendered social
order that revolved around family life. And whatever a woman's particular circumstances, she would find herself constrained by ideas that she was powerless to control and that profoundly influenced the legislative agenda.

## The Mere Fact of Sex

No sphere of life was more jealously guarded by the late nineteenth-century working man than his relationship to wage work.[7] His ambition threatened by the loss of entrepreneurial opportunities as capital consolidated, his skill devalued by the relentless ascendancy of new machinery, a working man measured his worth by the dignity of his job. Outside the workplace, a skilled craftsman could hold his head high in the political arena; inside it, he retained his manhood as long as he could evoke discipline and solidarity among his fellow craftsmen.

To defend their rights to work, men organized collectively around notions of solidarity and brotherhood, advocating a notion of free labor that was both racial and patriarchal.[8] "Free labor" was built on a concept of independence in which skill at craft work was equated with a manliness that would preserve self-respect while workers earned wages and that promised ultimately to release them from wage labor. It embodied a conception of male prerogatives rooted in an ordered and comfortable family life that relied on female labor at home. Its moral authority rested on its power to distance itself from symbolic and actual slavery by setting dignified terms of labor. It utilized these constructs to develop a conception of equal rights for white male workers that was to guarantee effective self-representation and provide the basis for the perpetuation of a democratic republic. The idea of free labor thus embodied both the elusive privileges of whiteness and the notion of separate spheres for men and women. It derived economic power from its restrictions on labor imagined as neither white nor male. This included not only African Americans (enslaved as well as free) but recent immigrants from places like Ireland, and later Italy and most of southern and eastern Europe. The idea also explicitly excluded women, even wives and daughters, from wage work.

Neither in nineteenth-century liberal theory nor in practice did slaves of either sex or women of any race hold property in their own labor. The labor of slaves, male and female, belonged to their owners. Free women of every race were conceived as wives and mothers; their labor belonged to husbands and families. Both engaged in subsistence as well as wage labor without acquiring what more privileged men understood as "rights to work." Neither was expected to participate in the polity in the same sense as white men; nor was their wage work expected to lend itself to "head of household" status, with its implication of independent political judgment. Indeed, central to the male conception of republicanism was an ordered family life that incorporated male dominion over wives and children. In men's eyes, the wage labor of free women, where necessary, ought to be dignified and to provide self-support, but it was not expected to lead to independence and self-sufficiency. Rather, just as men's free labor was predicated on their capacity to support families, so women's was assumed to sustain the family labor of men. Both racial exclusion and male gendered privilege participated in maintaining white solidarity, and both sustained the proto-right to work. Since the measure of manhood lay in self-sufficiency and independence, white men closely guarded their employment prerogatives. For if women's wage work competed with that of white men or threatened to undermine men's wages, it simultaneously challenged men's access to citizenship.[9] White women, who expected to participate in the polity through their menfolk, increasingly shared the expectation that any wage work women did would be a response to economic necessity and in subsidiary positions.

By the late nineteenth century, the courts weighed in to defend the independent and presumably self-sufficient actor who possessed the right to compete freely in the economic marketplace. If, as T. H. Marshall had put it, the worker's capacity "to engage as an independent unit in the economic struggle" was among the most basic of civil rights, and essential to a market economy, then the defense of individual freedom not only rationalized the absence of state protection but required it "out of respect for his status as citizen."[10] American courts presumed that workers had the power to protect themselves, and for much of the nineteenth century, men and women, black and white, sold their labor and negotiated the fiercely competitive marketplace of work without hope of positive government intervention.[11]

These circumstances, generally described as "freedom of contract," precluded many forms of worker combination and collective action as well. Except when public health or safety warranted rare exceptions, late nineteenth-century workers of all kinds were said to possess at least the theoretical right to contract freely with employers to sell their labor for as many hours a day, under whatever conditions, and at as low a price as they wished. The poor bargaining position of workers, as other commentators have noted, pitted the hungry stomachs of the many against the inexorable demands of industry for cheaper and more flexible labor, leaving workers virtually defenseless. Still, the elusive promises of escape from wage labor into self-employment or of occupational and economic mobility based on wit and talent left many convinced that fairness would be satisfied by a genuinely laissez-faire stance on the part of the state. In the late nineteenth century, the American Federation of Labor, the major organization representing associations of skilled workers, developed a philosophy called "voluntarism" that eschewed government intervention and celebrated working men's abilities to sustain their individual well-being by strategies of collective activism and bargaining.[12]

How did women expect to compete in this male world of mobility and contest? For the most part they didn't. A typical early twentieth-century urban white working-class daughter might know that she would have to earn wages for several years before marriage and then sporadically thereafter. But she could expect, or at least hope, that some part of her working life would involve caring for her own home and family. Like men, she assigned gendered meanings to "rights to work." When working-class men used the term (and they frequently did), the concept implied dignity, the capacity to support a household and family, the possibility of upward mobility, and a status that justified political citizenship. Working-class women rarely used the term to apply to themselves. They did have job-related expectations, including access to reasonable jobs at reasonable wages and under conditions that facilitated domestic lives. Middle-class women, the college-educated, and those with professional aspirations had ambitions that extended further, but many would have ceded the right to earn a living (as opposed to the opportunity to do so) to the unmarried. Though women were often flung into the labor force—as part of the struggle for domestic survival—the routes to glory were with few exceptions closed to them.[13] To be sure, many women supported themselves and their families through their own entrepreneurial abilities: numbers of female printers, milliners, graphic artists, dressmakers, and cosmetologists acquired credit and good reputations. But by and large success in the contest for skilled and remunerative work became the measure of masculinity—a jealously guarded male arena. Custom supported men's efforts to monopolize the skilled trades by controlling apprenticeships, excluding women from their trade unions, and limiting loans to start businesses.

The law sustained these efforts. In its most notorious articulation, on April 14, 1873, the U.S. Supreme Court upheld Illinois's refusal to admit Myra Bradwell (already an experienced lawyer) to the bar on the grounds that the right to practice law was not a privilege or immunity of citizenship. States were perfectly within their rights to regulate women's admission to that profession or any other in any reasonable way. Just the day before, the Court had set the stage for this decision by agreeing that a group of Louisiana butchers had no claim to redress because the state permitted a small monopoly to control the trade. Only efforts to exclude African Americans, the Court argued in the *Slaughter-House Cases*, fell within the boundaries of the Fourteenth Amendment. Consistently, the Court held that women could not be covered either.

Justice Joseph P. Bradley, who had dissented from the first decision, concurred in *Bradwell*. He extended the Court's reasoning in language that would be frequently quoted and that explicitly marked gender as a reasonable classification for job purposes. "The civil law, as well as nature herself," he argued, "has always recognized a wide difference in the respective spheres and destinies of man and woman." These differences were reinforced by "the natural and proper timidity and delicacy which belongs to the female sex" and which "evidently unfits it for many of the occupations of civil life." After all, "the paramount destiny and mission of women [was] to fulfill the noble and benign offices of wife and mother."[14]

By the late nineteenth century, a discourse of fairness and a set of informal policies that affirmed the expectations of white men and many white women as well sustained the exclusionary behavior of skilled white men toward wage earning. Employers, like most white men and women, shared a sense of social order that accommodated job assignments by sex as they deferred to racial and ethnic hierarchy. Though the precise jobs open to men or women, or to particular groups of immigrants or people of color, varied from place to place and changed over time, a general, if misguided, sense of fairness influenced the distribution of work and affirmed the claims of the most privileged. Women (six million of them) constituted nearly a quarter of the paid labor force in 1900. They worked as teachers, in factory jobs, in the retail trades, in agricultural work, and increasingly in offices, but by far the largest percentage worked in various kinds of public and private domestic service.[15] Almost 40 percent of female wage earners were either immigrants or the daughters of immigrants; another 20 percent were African Americans. Some engaged formally in the labor market; others participated in less visible work like taking in boarders, laundry, and sewing. Most occupied a restricted sphere, modulated and bounded by racial and ethnic prejudice and by settled understandings about the prerogatives of white male breadwinners that underlined a highly refined sexual division of labor.

This is not to imply that all women were either happy with this state of affairs or resigned to it. Leading voices in the growing women's rights movement protested the constraints on women in the labor market, and documents like the 1848 Seneca Falls Declaration of Sentiments linked economic dependence to the absence of political rights. In the early and mid-nineteenth century, theorists of no less stature than Mary Wollstonecraft, John Stuart Mill, and Friedrich Engels had repeatedly argued that economic independence was a necessary first step to the full participation of women in political society. Mill took for granted the legitimacy of women's claims to jobs, noting in his classic *The Subjection of Women* that achieving "the just equality of women" required their admission "to all the functions and occupations hitherto retained as the monopoly of the stronger sex."[16]

Still, the mainstream of the American feminist movement placed the ballot for women ahead of the struggle for economic independence; even the National Woman Suffrage Association led by Susan B. Anthony and Elizabeth Cady Stanton dissented only briefly before making it their first priority. Their choices were buttressed by the development of an alternative conception of citizenship rights for women located within the family. In this view women's citizenship rights could be extrapolated from the home and rooted in the experiences of mothers and wives. Popularized by educators like Catharine Beecher and reinforced by American suffragists, led by Lucy Stone Blackwell and Julia Ward Howe, the idea that women's political insights and influence would come from their special relationships to domesticity spread.[17] Motherhood, suffragist and minister Anna Garlin Spencer told a convention of her allies, has "fitted women to give a service to the modern State which men can not altogether duplicate."[18] Once they were armed with the ballot, their impact would reflect the morals and values of the idealized home. Influenced by the Swedish social reformer Ellen Key, these ideas expanded to encompass a generation of activists, including Florence Kelley and Julia Lathrop, who believed that preserving and extending the moral virtue and nurturing proclivities of domesticity could and should shape twentieth-century policies.

Legislative and judical efforts to protect and extend domesticity expanded women's rights within families while ensuring that women earned wages only when necessary, and then under circumstances that did not undermine their family commitments. Many states began to modify inheritance laws in the 1840s to prevent the inherited wealth of married women from passing automatically to the control of their husbands, and after 1860, when New York extended its Married Women's Property Act to include earned income, states slowly began to give married women the right to control their own wages.[19] But there was a catch. Often such rights rested on the failure of husbands to perform effectively in the workforce. They relied on a growing conception of husbands as family breadwinners and supporters. As legal historian Reva Siegel notes, the possibility of male misbehavior triggered legislature change. Enforcement occurred when husbands failed in their duty to support wives.[20]

Legislative and administrative intervention produced a rhetoric of respectable masculinity that enhanced the responsibilities of male citizenship, redefining as more manly the male who provided best, and allocating to him the services of dependent wives. The rhetoric strengthened male claims to jobs just as increasing numbers of working men experienced a degradation of skill and a loss of control over the work process. We can watch the ideas of manliness develop in increasing calls for a family wage for men—a wage that would ensure that wives could remain at home. A particular favorite of union men, it became a goal of early twentieth-century mainstream reformers eager to extend to working-class women the privileges of what they called "normal" family life. At the same time, we can observe the states begin to coerce men into fulfilling their provider roles, chasing down and prosecuting errant husbands who refused financial support to wives and children in order to coerce them into keeping their part of an increasingly formal bargain.[21]

Diverse and forceful as the opposing voices were, they remained marginal to common understandings. Toward the end of the century, for example, advocates of women's work like Virginia Penny popularized the notion that without rights to work women would remain economically and politically dependent. Penny wanted to sharpen the sexual division of labor to exclude men from jobs like dressmaking and tailoring and to reserve certain skilled jobs for women.[22] But most reformers remained committed to ameliorating working conditions rather than opening new jobs to women. A little later the social theorist Charlotte Perkins Gilman dismissed the notion that woman's political virtue resided in her domestic role. She concluded her pathbreaking essay *Women and Economics* with a plea to discard what she called the "rudimentary forces" of household organization: "Where our progress hitherto has been warped and hindered ..., it will flow on smoothly and rapidly when both men and women stand equal in economic relation."[23] Anarchist Emma Goldman disputed the possibility that "woman even with her right to vote will ever purify politics." Declaring the independence of women's work illusory, she asked how much was gained "if the narrowness and lack of freedom of the home is exchanged for the narrowness and lack of freedom of the factory, sweatshop, department store or office."[24] Instead, she called for freedom of the soul. Among the six million women who earned wages in 1900, surely some must have wanted more than a guarantee of survival and a chance at genuine economic independence. Rose Schneiderman, immigrant capmaker and trade union organizer, was one of these—but she deplored the difficulty of organizing sister workers who had marriage on their minds.

The tension between women's desires for more remunerative and satisfying workforce participation and the sense of entitlement to jobs that would have pitted men against women seems to have found its most effective resolution in the lives of African-American women. Forced into a highly circumscribed labor market because their male kin often suffered from racist exclusionary practices, they themselves experienced both gender and racial discrimination. Proportionately twice as many married black women earned wages in the early twentieth century as their white counterparts. About 60 percent worked as domestic servants or launderers, but large proportions of African-American women worked as professionals, too, taking advantage of new opportunities to become teachers, nurses, librarians, and social workers—jobs for which their men could not compete. As historian Stephanie Shaw argues, in the black community women's responsibilities as members of a segregated minority united with their efforts to train themselves for effective participation in the public sphere. Wage earning expanded the power of women in the African-American community, but, located as it was within a gendered context that valued family roles, it did not alter broader social sensibilities as to women's claims to jobs.[25]

The discrepancy between the numbers of women who participated in wage work and the widespread notion that women's lives would continue to rotate around the home requires exploration. How is it that so many women of all classes and races sustained an ideology that excluded them from wage work's most lucrative forms even as they continued to seek employment? How is it that both men and women supported a culture that located male prerogatives at home and in the polity in unrealistic conceptions of men's opportunities in the workplace? Ideas about men as real workers and rationales for excluding women, constructing them as marginal members of the labor force, grew in tandem. But the growing number of women workers encourages us to look at the central importance of work in constructing ideas of fairness as well as to reimagine the meaning of fairness for early twentieth-century men and women workers.

These changing notions of fairness appear in the new labor laws adopted at the end of the nineteenth century and in the early twentieth, and in court interpretations of them. Following on the decisions in the *Slaughter-House Cases* and *Bradwell*, state courts had concurred that the privileges and immunities clause of the Fourteenth Amendment did not prevent employers or states from denying women access to jobs.[26] Whether legislatures should be encouraged to distinguish between male and female rights *at* work was another matter. Increasingly, the courts resolved the issue by using rigid (and masculine) definitions of freedom of contract. In the 1880s and 1890s, the courts repeatedly struck down efforts of the separate states to regulate working hours and establish sanitary conditions for all workers on the grounds that they infringed on the theoretical freedom of each individual to negotiate a contract. In 1905, the U.S. Supreme Court aligned itself with this position.

In the precedent-setting *Lochner* case, it firmly rejected legislative efforts to set shorter hours (in this case for bakers) unless the health and safety of workers or the public was at stake.

At first courts were conflicted about whether women's health and safety constituted something of a special case. Beginning with Massachusetts in 1874 and continuing to the turn of the century, a dozen states tried to restrict working hours for women and children. The record of success was uneven: the laws were generally weak; some state courts sustained their laws; others held them in violation of workers' freedom of contract. The Illinois Supreme Court declared a model statute designed by the reformer Florence Kelley unconstitutional in 1895. The statute would have limited women's wage work to eight hours a day. But in *Ritchie v. People of Illinois*, the state court overturned it because it violated "the fundamental right of the citizen to control his or her own time and faculties." "Inasmuch as sex is no bar, under the constitution and the law, to the endowment of woman with the fundamental and inalienable rights of liberty and property which include the right to make her own contracts, the mere fact of sex," the court argued, "will not alone justify the exercise of the 'police power' for the purpose of limiting the right of a woman to make contracts."[27] The opinion, by Justice Benjamin Magruder, precluded the state from using its police power to regulate women. After briefly summarizing the statutes of several states that explicitly granted women access to particular occupations, and certifying that even married women could have such rights, he declared woman "entitled to the same rights under the constitution to make contracts with reference to her labor as are secured thereby to men." Pennsylvania's courts disagreed, upholding similar legislation regulating women's hours on the grounds that "the public good was entitled to protection and consideration" even if the worker's own self-interest dictated otherwise.[28]

This language was consistent with the language the courts used for men. Routinely, they continued to interpret the Fourteenth Amendment as not only permitting men's free agency in the marketplace but requiring it except when public health or morals were at stake. Legislation that attempted to provide protection for men was deemed "insulting to their manhood." The courts, in the words of the constitutional scholar Ezra Pound, considered it "degrading, to put them under guardianship, to create a class of statutory laborers, and to stamp them as imbeciles."[29] With perhaps less ferocity and less consistency, the courts applied the same reasoning to women. When a factory inspector found Katie Mead working in a bookbinding factory at 10:20 one cold winter's evening in 1906, she hauled the employer into court on the grounds that he had violated New York State's law against women working at night. Instead of protecting women, New York's highest court rejected both the charge and the statute. "An adult woman is in no sense a ward of the state," it declared in *People v. Williams* (1907). "She has the same rights as a man and is entitled to enjoy, unmolested, her liberty of person and her freedom to work for whom she pleases, where she pleases and as long as she pleases."[30]

This reasoning, which subjected many women to onerous working conditions, changed sharply in 1908, a dramatic turnaround that reflects the discrepancy between earlier decisions and public perceptions of fairness. For three decades, between 1874 and 1908, while courts equivocated about the special position of women, state legislatures, pressured by reformers and sometimes labor unions, continued to pass restrictive and protective labor laws that acknowledged women's vulnerability to exploitative working conditions and the value of their dual roles as mothers and wives as well as workers. In February 1903, Oregon's legislators prohibited employers from allowing women to work more than ten hours a day in laundries, factories, or other places that operated mechanical equipment. A year and a half later, the state labor commissioner cited laundry owner Curt Muller for allowing Emma Gotcher to work beyond the limit. Muller and his lawyers, persuaded that constitutional right was on their side, went to court. Muller, twice found guilty, kept appealing. To defend the Oregon law, the state's attorneys enlisted the help of National Consumers' League (NCL) officers Josephine Goldmark and Florence Kelley, who in turn sought out the well-known lawyer (and Goldmark's brother-in-law) Louis Brandeis. Together with a small army of young social scientists, they researched, compiled, and wrote what would become the first Brandeis Brief: 113 pages of densely packed data demonstrating why women's health and safety was particularly at risk under conditions of overwork.

The brief, which the U.S. Supreme Court approvingly cited in the landmark 1908 case of *Muller v. Oregon*, established a new standard for what was fair with regard to women workers.[31] Disagreeing that the Fourteenth Amendment equally protected the liberty of both sexes, the Court's decision, written by Justice David J. Brewer, held that "this liberty is not absolute and extending to all contracts." A state might, the Court suggested, "without conflicting with the provisions of the Fourteenth Amendment restrict in many respects the individual's power of contract." And since the state had a fundamental interest in women's capacity to rear and nurture children, it could override their liberty and allow protections for women that it had consistently disallowed for men. A woman's "physical structure and the performance of her maternal functions place her at a disadvantage in the struggle for subsistence," rendering her a poor champion of her own liberty. These natural weaknesses along with the disadvantages women faced at work had produced in women such poor health as to impair their reproductive capacities and threaten the future of the race. Working women had too little time for mothering; young women were inadequately prepared for future housework; the well-being of children and families was at stake. Moreover, women lacked many of the benefits of political and civil citizenship that rendered men free agents. The Fourteenth Amendment to the Constitution, which entitled all persons to receive equal protection under the law, did not preclude the court from agreeing that limiting woman's contractual power was reasonable not "solely for her benefit, but also largely for the benefit of all." Like children, women would now be "wards of the state," entitled to receive protection. In *Muller v. Oregon* the Court declared women's freedom of contract illusory—a liberty subject to the state's interest in women's reproductive capacities and in their family lives.

In legal and historical circles, the decision has long been touted because it famously accepted the statistical arguments of Louis Brandeis's brief as an adequate rationale for legal authority to treat women differently. I cite it here for another reason: because it so clearly and unapologetically denied women their status as persons under the law, restricting their rights as individuals in deference to "reasonable" social concerns. Weighing the social costs of women's employment, the Court had opted for a definition of justice that took into account the demanding lives of wage-earning women. At the same time, it denied women a liberty available to other workers, writing into legal precedent a conception of citizenship rooted in motherhood and family life that could and did override women's rights as individuals under the law. Like Bradley's concurrence in the *Bradwell* decision, it acknowledged each state's right to make gender distinctions with regard to employment. But *Muller v. Oregon* also gave the states the authority to make decisions as to liberty of person on the basis of what Felix Frankfurter, who was then a Harvard law professor, approvingly called "the reasonableness of legislative action" and characterized as "the law's graciousness to a disabled class."[32]

Protecting women's roles as mothers was not at all the same as protecting their interests at work and in fact may have had the opposite effect. By formally negating women's property rights in their labor, protective labor legislation affirmed their social rights at the cost of civil rights—denying women what Marshall had called "the right to follow the occupation of one's choice." Because it reinforced the sex-segmented structure of the labor force without regard for individual desire or need or marital status, protective labor legislation altered the relationship of women to the state and gendered the terms of their citizenship anew.

The decision, greeted with widespread enthusiasm, changed the face of industry for women. Convinced of the need to improve the conditions under which women worked in order to sustain better lives for children and families, and imagining all women as mothers, potential mothers, or mothers of the race, a generation of reform-minded men and women agitated for regulation and proscription. With the cooperation of many trade unionists, who believed women workers too weak to negotiate better working conditions through organization, they could and did design a range of legislation to ameliorate some of the most difficult conditions surrounding women's work.[33] Between 1908 and 1917 *Muller v. Oregon* encouraged seventeen more states to pass a spate of labor legislation of all kinds. New laws excluded women from some jobs and defined when they might work at others, for how many hours each day, at what wages, and under what conditions of safety and health. At its peak in the mid-1920s, this body of legislation unevenly covered about a third of all wage-earning women, many of whom achieved tangible benefits in health, safety, and reduced working hours.

The extensive body of legislation, the judicial decisions around it, the stance of social reformers, and the support of trade unions suggest how wage-earning women figured in the assumptions of policy makers. Every state constructed its laws around occupational categories, catching all of the women who worked in a particular arena in a single net, and not incidentally excluding those who fell outside. Even in its heyday, protective legislation excluded many who needed it, including most women of color, domestic servants, and food-processing and agricultural workers. It also failed to cover educated, white-collar, and professional women. At the other end of the spectrum, in the covered jobs, advocates paid no attention to the maternal and marital circumstances of the women whose protection they sought. One might construe this as a willingness (dare one say eagerness?) to restrict women's economic opportunities. Regulation of factory and retail jobs, often held by men and single women as well as married women, applied to all women and only to women. Restrictions on night work, which many reformers thought would benefit all workers regardless of sex, never extended beyond women and applied regardless of a woman's age or family circumstances. While the idea of protection for present and future mothers underlay such legislation, no state included or exempted women based on need, marital or maternal status, or old age.[34]

Measured in terms of symbolic value, women paid a high price for protective legislation. In 1907, New York's high court had knocked down a night-work statute on the grounds that women were free citizens who could not be subject to greater restrictions than men. Eight years later the same court revisited that decision. A woman printer, highly skilled, well paid, and married, had been caught working at night, contravening the state's new law. This time the court retracted. Using the language of *Muller*, it cited "the peculiar functions that have been imposed on them by nature" to conclude that banning women from working at night was "in the interest of public health and the general welfare of the people of the state." Acknowledging that its decision trammeled liberty, the court nevertheless decided that "the state may protect its citizens against even their own indifference, error, or recklessness."[35] So speedily had protecting women in the workforce become the major means of protecting the public interest in motherhood and family life.

There were other costs as well. The dominant maternalist conception that governed the legislation excluded consideration of many strategies that might have eased women's working lives for fear that they would enhance women's labor-force participation. Unlike many European countries at the time, the United States provided few examples of public efforts to develop crèches for infants, effective child care policies, or family allowances.[36] Florence Kelley, perhaps the most prominent advocate of protective labor legislation for women, repeatedly opposed health insurance proposals that would provide wage-earning women with medical benefits for childbirth or mandatory maternity leaves from work because she feared they would tempt women to stay at work and husbands to keep their wives there.[37] Settlement houses and community service agencies that provided child care for poor mothers often excluded married women who engaged in wage labor.[38] Nor did most social reformers protest when corporations began providing such benefits as paid vacations or life insurance only to longtime workers. Why tempt women, perceived as potential if not present mothers, to stay in the labor force? Instead, they promoted policies to enhance the short-term health and safety of women at work and to require shorter working hours.

These policies differed sharply from those then debated in much of Europe. Among British women, as among Americans, there were both those who would have preferred mothers to stay at home and egalitarian feminists who resisted any efforts at labor legislation that did not apply equally to men and women. On the Continent, trade union women and social democrats tended to seek strategies that acknowledged both the rights and needs of mothers with regard to paid work. They could not agree over whether to support legislation that would restrict women's work at night, but they led successful campaigns to provide wage-earning women with mandatory leaves from work during the last weeks of pregnancy and the first weeks after childbirth. Many advocated maternity services as well as family allowances (or mothers' endowments) for the working poor. And some proposed, though they did not succeed until the 1920s in providing, paid maternity leaves from work.[39]

In practice, protective labor legislation reflected a discourse of male prerogative and female dependence that participated in, and perpetuated, a range of public policies that reaffirmed racialized and gendered claims to jobs and citizenship. If all women came before the law as potential mothers, and motherhood vitiated the last vestiges of women's rights to work, then wage work for women appeared as a privilege for the well-off and an obligation for the destitute. For the latter, it marked an invidious status; it was engaged in by the unmarried, single mother, and those whose spouses had failed them. As long as protective legislation was designed only for women, it affirmed the expectation that women would work in their own homes. This expectation continued to shape the labor market well into the 1960s, when most of the legislation's targets agitated for the lifting of restrictions.

Governed by the contemporary sense that wage work for women undermined the well-being of the home, social reformers, many trade unionists, and the public at large assumed they could protect the second only at the cost of the first. The demands of fairness dictated that if women's rights inhered in home and family, then the right to work was a male right. Women trespassed into the world of work to ensure the safety of the most sacred of their trusts: the family. As they did so, most women willingly reserved to men the possibilities of individual upward mobility and gave up precious citizenship rights in return for a promise of family support. The compromise prefigured a bitter contest that pitted married and single women against each other in the 1920s and escalated into a continuing struggle over the distribution of rights in jobs. It also fueled an ongoing conflict between alternative conceptions of citizenship that burst into flame when, in the aftermath of the Civil Rights Act of 1964, women's economic citizenship became a central issue. For the addition of the category of sex reignited a smoldering debate over how to reconcile the public's interest in women's successful performance of family roles with women's individual rights to work, a basic component of economic citizenship.

## A Practical Independence

Far from indicting the champions of protective labor legislation, we should understand the movement to achieve it as a reflection of gendered ways of thinking that stretched into every nook and cranny of the public imagination. We can hear the conversations that ensued in many locations. Following the First World War and into the 1920s, a decade when married women increasingly chose to leave their homes to earn wages, debates over the appropriate distribution of wage work and its impact on family life extended into the halls of Congress. They reveal the limits within which influential people sought to shape discussions of work and gender.

In March of 1920, as the last three states counted the votes that would ratify the women suffrage amendment, the Senate and the House of Representatives convened a joint committee to consider whether the country needed a permanent Women's Bureau. Congress had set up a special unit to serve women in industry during the First World War and funded it annually on a contingency basis. After the war, this unit became the Division of Women in Industry, and representatives of a variety of women's groups, including the National Consumers' League, the National Women's Trade Union League, and others committed to legislative intervention for women, lobbied to turn the temporary agency into a Women's Bureau within the Department of Labor that would provide a continuing source of information on, and advocacy for, women workers.[40] At the same time, many of the same women lobbied for the Maternity and Infancy Act (more popularly known as the Sheppard-Towner Act), which became law in 1921.[41] Sheppard-Towner funded maternity and well-baby clinics whose services were available without means-testing to mostly rural women at government expense. What looks like a two-pronged commitment to women's mothering and wage-earning lives appears on closer examination to be part of the same effort to sustain women's domesticity.

The debate over whether there should be a new Women's Bureau was conducted within an amicable framework: legislators and witnesses at congressional hearings all assumed that women belonged in a special class of workers who lacked rights and organizational strength. Their vulnerability not only subjected them to poor working conditions but threatened social order as well. Everyone wanted the bureau to investigate and report on the conditions of women workers and to formulate standards and recommend policies on their behalf. Trade union leaders like the former glovemaker Agnes Nestor, who testified that "the fact-gathering and policy-making are the big things," agreed with social reformers who sought a Women's Bureau in order to advance women's "opportunities for profitable employment."[42] Julia C. Lathrop, head of the Children's Bureau and one of a large group of influential maternalist social reformers of the period, thought wage-earning women needed the new agency because they were "just coming into the responsible life of the world." They would need special attention in order to give them "a fair deal, in order to make sure that their problems are so met that their solution is in the interest of the women and of society as a whole." Republicans and Democrats shared the consensus. As Iowa's Senator William Kenyon put it, "All of the women in the Democratic Party seem to be for this, and all of the women in the Republican Party seem to be for it." Like most of those who supported the idea of a permanent Women's Bureau, Mary Stewart, executive secretary of the Women's Committee of the National Republican Congressional Committee, wanted most of all an agency that would distinguish the interests of women from those of men—that would provide a voice for women because they "see things in a different way." She saw eye to eye with Henry Sterling, legislative representative for the American Federation of Labor. Not only were women mothers, he told the congressional panel, they needed mothering: "They need a woman or women to look after them, to tell what the trouble is, . . . to tell it from a woman's standpoint, and to do what there can be done to arouse the public conscience for their relief."

The consensus among the respected witnesses who testified on behalf of a new Women's Bureau built on the restricted images of womanhood embedded in the influential *Muller v. Oregon* decision. Carried a certain distance, it promised to protect present and future motherhood; pushed too far, it made unacceptable demands on women's freedom. The delicate negotiation emerged early in the debate over the legislation when Representative John E. Raker, a California Democrat, introduced a competing Women's Bureau bill. His proposal, almost identical to the bill on the floor, contained one crucial difference: a provision that the bureau explore "the influence of industrial employments upon the *subsequent* [my emphasis] home life of wage-earning women." Raker explained both his support for a Women's Bureau and his modification in language that echoed *Muller*. "The delicate character of a woman," he argued, "is such that it is incumbent upon us to look out for them, and I believe it is one of the principal things in any legislation to so protect the women and girls that when they leave that work, they leave it with strong, healthy minds and bodies, so that they may do their functions as American citizens and contribute to the vitality of the coming generations." Raker believed that protecting women's "functions as American citizens" required legislators to place the long-term consequences of women's wage work ahead of their health during their wage-earning lives. This, he insisted, was the heart of his legislation. As he explained it, the importance of these investigations lay in "the fact that 99 per cent of all these young girls go out from these various places of business and eventually become our mothers, and will add to the strength of coming generations." He wanted language that would explicitly empower the bureau to investigate women workers "2, 5, and 20 years, after they have left work." The new agency should, in his view, be encouraged to go into women's homes, evaluate their children, and judge how women's years in the workforce had affected their growth and development.

Most legislators, like Representative John MacCrate of New York, preferred to leave the restrictions on women implicit. Aware that "a great many women do not want a man" ("and we do not blame them for that," he added), he sought a less coercive consensus around motherhood. "May I suggest," he offered, that monitoring "the welfare of women in industry would also include her home life and the effect upon maternity . . . if you say, as it does here, 'upon *all matters* pertaining to the welfare of women in industry' that gives you almost unlimited scope, because as to her home life, if she will become a mother it includes what effect it will have upon motherhood: I submit that all those problems are embraced in the words, 'all matters.'" Raker would not be appeased either by general language or by a formulation that did not explicitly address the impact of wage work on future motherhood. Nor would he settle for MacCrate's suggestion that "it is the women now in industry we are interested in in order to provide that they shall have a subsequent home life." He wanted to "benefit the woman after she leaves her work, as well as while she works." The rest of the group balked at this extension of government power. Raker's interpretation, declared Representative Ira Hersey of Maine, had doomed the clause he wanted.

If legislators held the line against John Raker's efforts to immerse women's working lives in a domestic future, still the majority continued to imagine women as mothers and focused on the relationship between women's work and motherhood. Lathrop (and all of the maternalists who testified) shared this assumption, neatly eliding the differences between women and mothers. "Now especially," Lathrop told the committee, "when women of this country are going into industry in increasing numbers, it is necessary for us to know whether the conditions under which they work are the conditions under which the mothers of this country ought to work." Now especially? Eight million women worked for wages in 1920; of these fully a quarter were married with husbands present, and at least 15 percent more were widowed, divorced, or separated from their spouses. Hardly the delicate creatures of Raker's imagination, virtually all of these women, and many of those who were single, already had family responsibilities. More than a third of married African-American women worked for wages, double the proportion of white women, and two thirds of them worked in service jobs of one sort or another. More than half of all female workers were over twenty-five years old; 20 percent of them were married, and an equivalent number were adult heads of households. A quarter of the industrial workforce was female.

These growing numbers explain something of policy makers' concerns for saving women for families; they justify the mind-sets of those who did not wish to imagine women workers as individuals with the same rights as men. Julia Lathrop fielded a series of questions from members of Congress that suggests the depth of their fears. Could not the existing Children's Bureau headed by Lathrop do the work of the new Women's Bureau? she was asked. Might the new bureau be placed within the aegis of the Children's Bureau? One committee member confused Lathrop with Mary Anderson, who directed the still existing, but impermanent, Division of Women in Industry; another mixed up the wartime Women in Industry Service with the Children's Bureau. Lathrop and Anderson vigorously asserted the different missions of the two units, and both emphasized that only separate agencies could adequately represent women's dual roles. "The interests of women as wage earners are not the interests of children," insisted Lathrop in a statement the more astonishing because she felt she needed to make it. "Women are adults, they are citizens, they are able to contract, they have learned how to secure legal redress and their legal rights, whereas children are in a state of tutorage." But they were not quite workers in the same ways as men, acknowledged Anderson as she fended off a suggestion that the Bureau of Labor Statistics be given the responsibility for women. "Because there is a difference in the problems of women in industry," she testified, "it is necessary to have a special bureau to look after women."

What exactly were these differences? And who were the women for whom Anderson and her colleagues spoke? Anderson had worked for eighteen years in a shoe factory, then spent another seven organizing before she made her way through the National Women's Trade Union League to become the spokesperson for wage-earning women. The factory worker of her imagination was someone with "special needs," with double demands on her energies, a "wage-earning wife and mother."[43] She was neither delicate nor dependent, but she was subject to a double day and therefore to overwork and fatigue. For these women, Anderson believed in providing what she called "industrial justice": practical benefits rather than abstract rights. The discussions around the creation of the Women's Bureau paralleled these concerns, leaving little room for conceptions of individual rights for women. They anticipated that women would marry and that their interests would be better served by adequate incomes and reasonable working conditions than by high expectations.

*Mary Anderson directed the Women's
Bureau in the Department of Labor from
1920 until 1944.* COURTESY, NATIONAL
ARCHIVES AND RECORDS ADMINISTRATION.

Certainly nobody focused on issues of identity and satisfaction, even of skill or promotion.

But regarding women's domestic roles as the primary justification for government intervention in women's working lives left to men the moral claim to the sphere of work. This was, as Mary E. McDowell, head of the University of Chicago Settlement, reminds us, part of a more general confusion about the changing gender sensibilities of the moment. "Where is the normal?" she asked rhetorically. Now that emigration (which had provided young female factory hands for so long) seemed to be slowing down and manufacturers were pressuring women to stay in factories, now that women had proven they could operate lathe machines as well as ironing presses, she wondered how to answer what she called "the very great and serious question" of where women belonged in industry. "Have they a legitimate place?"[44]

Male workers eagerly participated in staking their claim. American Federation of Labor (AFL) legislative representative Henry Sterling told congressmen that the AFL did not have a woman's division because the National Women's Trade Union League (which had turned to legislation in despair at the AFL's refusal to cooperate with them) served that function. Though he pitied the deplorable conditions under which women labored, Sterling dismissed the idea that some AFL unions might have organized them: "The union could not do anything about it. It was a union of men." And he sharply distinguished the needs of women from those of unionists. "The women in industry are in a deplorable condition," he asserted, "and they need the woman's influence and the woman's touch and the mothering that women can bring them that men can not."

The irony was that the AFL and female advocates of the Women's Bureau did not disagree on the moral imperatives. Fathers who provided for families needed good jobs with family wages so that women would not need to work. Those who did would require good job opportunities at reasonable wages as well as government intervention to ensure society's interest in the health and well-being of their children. Such maternalist policies, consistent with the desires of many working men and useful in resolving the immediate economic hardships of many married women, deprived women of opportunities to compete for jobs, education, and apprenticeships that grounded feminist struggles for economic independence.

The feminists who opposed these policies of female protection saw issues of fairness and justice from a different perspective. Led by Alice Paul and committed to equal rights for women, they insisted on women's rights as individuals without regard to family or marital status. Some, like Charlotte Perkins Gilman, had already anticipated these positions, rejecting domesticity as women's only alternative and insisting on economic independence. Like Olive Schreiner, a South African theorist well known in the United States, Gilman rooted her arguments in the Darwinian idea that optimal social evolution demanded maximal contributions from everyone, including women. Around the First World War, such opinions congealed in the practical efforts of feminists like Henrietta Rodman to design housing that could accommodate cooperative cooking, child care, and laundering. They were embodied in the life-styles of some women like Crystal Eastman, who promoted the idea of "marriage under two roofs." Rodman was more explicit about her purposes than most of her friends: "Feminism," she insisted, "does not demand that every woman should be a wage earner; but it does demand that no woman who desires to be a wage earner shall be prevented from doing her work because she has taken up the other responsibilities of women, such as marriage and child bearing."[45]

As Rodman suggests, independent wage earning seemed the logical next step, an intrinsic part of the feminist agenda. It continued a tradition of liberal theory rooted in individual rights that tied economic independence and political participation to the requirements for full citizenship, and it dangled the prospect of individual achievement and economic rewards that would enable women to participate fully in the political sphere newly opened to them. Equal rights feminists, as they came to be known, advocated an equal rights unencumbered by special laws for women. But to obtain what the masthead of the *Equal Rights Journal* called "a man's chance, industrially" meant that women would have to give up the benefits and protections owed to motherhood and painfully acquired through two decades of legislation.

Many women viewed marriage and maternal roles as insuperable barriers to the kind of wage earning that would yield independence, and demanded instead that the workplace accommodate the practical constraints of women's mothering and child-rearing responsibilities. Social feminists, including the women around the Women's Bureau and in most of the well-known women's organizations, shared with a growing number of working men the assumption that men, who derived many of the benefits of citizenship through work, would pass them on to women in their families. In this view, women who undertook paid work in order to sustain homes derived greater or lesser legitimacy as a consequence of their needs: unmarried single daughters, women alone, working mothers, potential mothers, Negro women workers—all were to some extent entitled to consideration as workers. Married women workers who had husbands capable of supporting them occupied marginal positions. But this left unanswered McDowell's question. Where was the normal? The Women's Bureau would fight for decent treatment for women while at work, including shorter hours, more healthful working conditions, more job opportunities, and equal wages when women did the work of men. It would also acknowledge a hierarchy of rights to work in which those with the greatest need to provide had the largest stake. Their position reflected a wide-ranging cultural affirmation of women's domestic roles.

If the equal rights feminists feared that such a vision of women would denude economic opportunity of all meaning, social feminists argued that motherhood deprived most women of effective workplace opportunity. Mary Anderson and many social feminists or maternalists would later dismiss the claims of equal rights feminists as "theoretical" rights, which mattered little against the practical difficulties of women at work. Theoretical feminists, in their judgment, "persistently ignore facts, clinging devotedly to abstractions," while the more moderate feminist "sees and works with facts." Above all things, warned Anderson, " 'rights' must be interpreted for women workers as something concrete, and we must start with the world where it is today."[46] Since industry treated women workers badly, the argument went, and men had already achieved much of what women wanted, protective labor laws that applied to women only would "remove a handicap."

On the face of it, social feminists held the moral high ground. Anderson wanted to benefit women directly by reducing wage differentials between men and women, enhancing women's hours of rest and leisure, and removing women from night work to make time for child care and family life. She claimed what might be called social rights in work. In contrast, those who claimed individual rights to work subordinated their families to individual satisfaction and threatened to deprive needy women and male breadwinners of jobs. They deserved, the social feminists thought, to be labeled "selfish."

Anderson's deputy, Mary Winslow, captured the ambiguity of the Women's Bureau position in an early pamphlet that enables us to see how these ideas translated into practice.[47] In an address before the National Conference of Social Work she affirmed the needs of married women in industry. The country needed standards against which to measure their working conditions, she argued, among them consideration for the needs of industry, of the family, and of the individual. Measuring the gains against the losses in each category, she concluded uncomfortably that she really had no answer as to whether married women should be employed or not. Every gain seemed to produce a loss: a significant contribution to income was inevitably accompanied by a loss of services to the family. The supervision and presence of the stay-at-home mother might result in malnutrition and economic deprivation for children. She could not, she concluded, draw up a balance sheet. The bureau would continue to study the problem with the hope that a conclusion would emerge. But she was optimistic nonetheless. "We shall find that the problem of the employment of married women is taking care of itself," she wrote, if we "make it possible and usual for the normal married man to support his family according to a decent American standard of living."

Outside the halls of policy makers, there seems to have been more room for disagreement. By the 1920s, many ordinary people accepted the idea that while single women would often be required to support themselves, married women whose husbands benefited from a family wage ought to stay out of the labor force. Otherwise they threatened to compete with men and to undermine male wages. Governed by a "moral economy" of need, some men and women protested the acquisition of jobs by those who did not need them, while others affirmed the belief that fairness demanded access to work for all women as individuals, independent of need or marital status. Maurine Greenwald's careful study of Seattle workers during and just after World War I reveals that white working women and men held a complicated range of ideas about the grounds on which women should be entitled to work.[48] Supporters of married women's rights to work were sharply divided. Some argued that women's contributions could increase the family's standard of living; others, echoing the ideas of feminists and demonstrating familiarity with some leading feminist thinkers, claimed that justice and equality dictated fair access to jobs for women. Of course, people disagreed about what constituted "need" and what figure provided a reasonable living standard, but whatever the threshold, as long as prevailing opinion maintained that married women held only conditional rights to work, many married women would be discouraged from earning wages. As long as women were imagined as potentially married, and as long as rights to work were vested primarily in a family rationale, women's expectations of the labor market would be constrained.

An equivalent range of views seems to have existed among African Americans, fiercely complicated by the racial prejudice that denied many black men the economic opportunity to be adequate breadwinners. African-American women, who engaged in wage labor at double the rate of white women, had different expectations of work, rooting their rationale in the absolute necessity to be prepared for wage labor even when they did not undertake it, as well as in a mandate to serve the black community. About half of all married African-American women earned wages in 1920, compared to less than a quarter of white women. Unlike their white peers, married professional women rarely questioned their obligations to work, nor the practical necessity of combining home and work.[49] Nor, of course, did the vast majority of wage-earning African-American women who worked in menial jobs. Among all wage-earning African-American women, three quarters found jobs as farm laborers, laundresses, or domestic servants in the first part of the 1920s.

Rarely did white social reformers pay attention to the conditions under which black women worked; they neither posed the arguments of a disadvantaged motherhood on their behalf nor agitated for coverage of the poorest jobs under the spreading umbrella of protective labor legislation. The few white maternalists and social reformers who paid any attention at all saw black women less as models of economic independence than as demonstrations of the negative effect of wage work. From the perspective of the mostly white policy makers whose conceptions of social order shaped public policy, the poverty of black women in and out of the labor force vindicated (rather than called into question) the maternalist strategy of seeking women's rights within the family and in greater economic opportunities for men.[50]

These conditions called attention to racial discrimination, and particularly to the absence of jobs for black men, rather than to equality for women. Under the circumstances, notions of fairness resided in undermining racial prejudice rather than in expanding opportunities for women's wage work. While integrated women's groups like some units of the YWCA agitated with limited success for the inclusion of African-American women in education and training programs, as well as for desegregating some white women's jobs, many

African-American organizations of the period advocated women's home roles rather than greater workplace opportunity. Marcus Garvey's influential black nationalist movement argued that women should give up their jobs in order to sustain the masculinity of their partners.[51] After 1925, the Brotherhood of Sleeping Car Porters, a highly successful labor organization, actively discouraged wives from working, its members sharing with their wives an ideology of masculine providerhood and female domesticity that closely resembled that of skilled white trade unionists as well as of middle-class whites.[52] African-American female social reformers did not disagree with the effort to develop jobs for black men.[53]

From both ends of the economic and racial spectrum, in ideological as well as practical terms, marriage, childbearing and child rearing appeared incompatible with a commitment to wage work. Several well-known novels reveal the extent to which the dilemma occupied the public mind. Dorothy Canfield's *The Home-Maker* features a temporarily disabled husband who provides the excuse for his anxious and obsessive wife to get a job. In the interim, he discovers that, unlike her, he enjoys taking care of his three children, and she finds a rewarding career in retail sales. Neither wants to resume old roles. But so great is their fear of public disapprobation that they tacitly agree to hide his recovery so that he can continue to work at home while she earns the family wage as a department store executive.[54] In Dorothy West's *The Living Is Easy*, the African-American wife of a successful businessman tries so hard and so manipulatively to bring her daughter and her extended family into respectable and nonearning status that she eventually destroys the source of the family's fortunes.[55]

Fiercely opposing perceptions of how to achieve justice for women produced a politics of legendary antagonism. For three years, champions of equal rights for women, represented by Alice Paul's National Woman's Party (NWP), discussed with social feminists the idea of combining special protections for wage-earning women with a constitutional affirmation of women's citizenship.[56] Ultimately they balked at drafting an amendment that exempted special laws for women. When, in 1923, the NWP introduced the first Equal Rights Amendment (ERA) into Congress, it included no clause to exempt special legislation for women workers. Social feminists could not imagine supporting an amendment that they believed would destroy all their years of hard work. The NWP (the same group that forty years later would successfully instigate the addition of the word *sex* to Title VII) would not back down. The continuing demand for an ERA pushed the two groups into irreconcilable enmity, each side claiming that its goal of economic independence for women was being jeopardized by the other.

The story of the long struggle for an equal rights amendment has often been told.[57] In it, prevailing images of women as homemakers managed to overwhelm the strongest arguments of the National Woman's Party and its allies. The NWP speedily found itself marginalized and on the defensive. True to the instinct that dominated its creation, the Women's Bureau took the lead in developing policies that made it easier for women to earn wages, but it did so in the context of marriage and family life. Before suffrage, its officials had described labor laws as necessary hedges against women's weakness; afterward they proffered them as foundations to enable women to compete more effectively. To prove that protective labor laws did not harm women, the Women's Bureau conducted a lengthy examination of their effects on women's job prospects. At the victory conference to unveil its findings in 1926, and in the influential pamphlet that quicky followed, the Women's Bureau made the case that women had benefited far more than they had suffered. Fewer than sixty thousand women (of more than eight million then employed) had lost their jobs as a result of legislation.[58] And these, it argued, should be willing to sacrifice for the good of the whole group.

## A Man-Run Company

If shared understandings of the fairness of restricting women's rights to work were widely dispersed, they were neither universal nor uncontested. Yet they were supported by employers in formal and informal ways and firmly lodged in a continuing rhetoric of economic independence that remained the prerogative of males. We can find them in the crude sex segmentation practices of employers before the First World War, and we can see how they resided in the new management techniques that reached their heyday in the 1920s. Scientific management, corporate welfare programs, and the new field of personnel management inspired by human relations experts together reveal how readily, seemingly naturally, employers made use of the gendered imagination and attempted to inscribe it into the behavior of employees.

In the years just before and around World War I, a few managers and some labor relations experts came to believe that labor and capital could live in harmonious unity by adopting ideas of scientific management. Relying heavily on the ideas of Frederick Winslow Taylor, they became convinced that productivity could be increased and the rewards to both labor and management multiplied by increasing efficiency and reducing labor turnover. To do this, employers sought to find what Taylor called "first-class" workers—those suitable for particular jobs. At the heart of scientific management lay the idea that an individual worker, appropriately trained and monitored, and allowed a generous share in the productivity gains, would produce best. The new manager weeded out the inefficient worker, the one "naturally unfitted for his chosen work," and sought to "promote each worker to the highest notch he is capable of in his chosen life work."[59] In this context, male and female workers occupied different spaces in the imaginations of managers and workers alike.

Few employers adopted the full range of Taylor's ideas, but many subscribed to the idea of training and nurturing suitable workers. To find the best worker for the job, enlightened employers enlisted the new science of personnel management to streamline hiring practices, a task they undertook with more or less extensive psychological inventories and informal interviews. The leading experimenters in personnel policy, including such giants of production as Ford, General Electric, and Westinghouse, as well as smaller manufacturers like H. J. Heinz and the Joseph Feiss Clothing Company of Cleveland and retailers like Filene's of Boston, assumed that men and women wanted different things from work and adapted hiring and training policies accordingly. They tried to determine whether potential employees possessed appropriate masculine and feminine characteristics for the jobs at hand as well as the appropriate virtues for each sex. By the 1920s, these practices had invaded the offices of the insurance and banking industries.[60]

Taylor had assumed that productivity gains would be shared with workers; in practice, however, most employers returned little if any of the cost savings to employees and, if they paid attention to the resulting dissatisfaction at all, tried to ameliorate it by applying a range of "welfare" techniques derived from historical experience and refined by accommodating them to the supposedly more scientific findings of human relations experts. Their strategies affirmed gendered expectations in the workforce that may not have differed dramatically from those of earlier generations but were certainly more formal. Many employers introduced showers, cafeterias, English language classes, clubhouses, and medical services for all workers. Men got sports clubs and family picnics, designed to build loyalty. Women benefited from lounge areas and sewing or cooking classes along with occasional dances and summer camps. By the 1920s, some companies offered more valuable amenities such as paid vacations, pensions, and life insurance to skilled men. These typically incorporated longevity requirements that effectively barred women from benefits.[61] To ensure a stable workforce, some large companies offered loans for home ownership to male heads of families. General Electric (GE), which like many firms asked women to resign on marriage, restricted pensions to those with twenty years or more of service, while group life insurance policies were at first available only to men.[62] Women received social services, rest periods, and lunchtime recreation instead: sociability rather than security.

Welfare programs could become important adjuncts to creating gendered solidarity among workers. Some employers hoped, through them, to increase productivity. At the Ford Motor Company, managers relied on a happy home life to support steady work habits and reduce labor turnover. In 1914, the company offered its famous five-dollar-a-day "profit-sharing plan" (nearly doubling the wages of the least skilled workers) to those who met its criteria for good citizenship. These included married men living with, and properly supporting, a nonworking wife and children. Single men over the age of twenty-two were eligible if they had thrifty habits and lived in good homes. To ensure their continued worthiness, all workers were subject to stringent reviews of their domestic living arrangements and personal habits, including thrift, temperance, and appropriate respect for family life. The company did not generally hire married women with able husbands, but women could earn the advantageous five-dollar rate if they had "an immediate blood relation totally dependent" on them. All other women, like single men under twenty-two, found themselves ineligible for the high wage. Since factory jobs were, at the time, among the best of blue-collar options for white women, we can imagine that despite pay and benefits significantly lower than those of men, most accepted the differences uncomplainingly. The distinctions contributed to developing a manly spirit among workers.[63]

More subtle policies carried equally powerful messages. Gerard Swope, GE's president and the originator of its unique welfare programs in the 1920s, later acknowledged that some of its policies had been less fair than he had at first thought. He had persuaded male workers to take life insurance, he wrote in an illuminating 1931 article, by arguing that "we wanted people in our organization who were serious-minded, though young, and who would recognize their responsibilities as members of society." GE made the offer initially only to male employees less than forty-five years old who agreed to salary deductions that would partially pay for it. I pass over the issue of whether men accepted the life insurance because it was a good deal or because they feared that not being "serious-minded" would increase their chances of being laid off to note the unusual clarity with which Swope conceived the gender bias. "Our company," Swope later wrote, acknowledging the error in his decision to exclude women, "is a man-run company, possibly unfortunately, and there was a difference in opinion among us as to whether the women would come in.... Our theory was that women did not recognize the responsibilities of life and were hoping to get married soon and would leave us."[64] When the women were asked whether they were willing to have an insurance premium deducted from their pay, 73 percent eagerly accepted the program.

Assumptions about gendered expectations embedded in corporate welfare policies are the more frightening since they seemed so little susceptible to change. For example, Swope admitted that his expectations of women's behavior were unfounded. "To illustrate how wrongly we sometimes conceive the mass psychology of people and especially of women," he wrote, "in certain of our departments our managers said that the women would not take insurance but they would take the pension. As a matter of fact, from a recent study of these figures, it has been found that women seem to recognize their responsibilities to their families even earlier and more seriously than the men. They have taken insurance even before completing a year of service with the company."[65] Yet GE continued to fire these women when they married, and Swope will return to our story as an architect of New Deal social policies that persistently assumed women had few responsibilities.

The most progressive employers deeply believed that ensuring male employees a modicum of economic security along with a rational and dignified work experience would not only fulfill their obligations to build good citizens but would generate increased profits and damp the fires of radicalism as well. This assumption echoed labor's conviction that manliness and democratic participation required both dignified work and the capacity to support a family. Workers, in their own view, deserved not only adequate incomes and decent housing but assurances that their widows and surviving children would be cared for. A few companies tried to meet this goal by supporting orphanages or industrial homes where women could be adequately employed and children educated to become the next generation of workers.[66] Others found work for widows. A sprinkling of companies acknowledged men's provider roles in other ways, by supplying housekeepers to help out if wives became ill, for example, or setting up "little mother's clubs" to teach girls the values that would make them good future homemakers and, not incidentally, to train their parents as well. These interventions may have been the exceptional acts of a few remarkable companies, but from an ideological perspective and without exaggerating either their number or their material impact, they demonstrate the close integration of employment policies with expectations for gendered citizenship.

Occasionally companies that relied extensively on women workers initiated more inclusive hiring and welfare policies. For example, the Endicott Johnson Shoe Company in Binghamton, New York, employed about 4,500 women in 1927, half of them married. They were attracted to the company, according to historian Gerald Zahavi, by the easy work and excellent benefits. Until the mid-1930s, the company provided recreation, medical, and health benefits to the families of male and female workers alike. It sometimes distributed work that could be done by married women at home, and, though it refused to provide day care for children, company president George F. Johnson did contribute to the support of community day care facilities.[67] In contrast, southern textile mills in the North Carolina Piedmont attracted female labor by providing time to nurse babies, clean house, prepare meals, and even supervise children from factory windows.

Welfare policies blended with the new sensitivity to human relations in the workplace unwittingly generated by more frequent applications of efficiency techniques. On the shop floor, industrial psychologists explored the impact of lighting, rest periods, and sociability on rates of production and attempted to relieve monotony that reduced output. The largest and perhaps best-known effort to sort out these effects comes from a lengthy series of experiments in human relations conducted at the Hawthorne Works of the Western Electric Company in the late 1920s. Researchers there noticed the influence of workers' mental attitudes, or "reveries," on their levels of production and set out to explore the issue further. Their data, largely the voices of men and women workers, inadvertently reveal how the ideology of work is gendered in particular ways. They suggest how deeply rooted among ordinary white men and women was the conception that women's rights inhered in their family lives rather than in the workplace, how functional this notion was, and how difficult it would be to dismantle.

The Hawthorne works, located in Chicago, manufactured telephone, wiring, and switching equipment for its parent, employing thousands of workers to do a range of relatively routine jobs that required manual dexterity and speed. Dissatisfied with the output of workers and influenced by the human relations movement in industry, personnel managers there began a series of experiments with workers to see what factors influenced productivity rates. The original company experimenters, Donald Chapman, Clarence Stoll, Homer Harbirger, and, later, William J. Dickson, were soon joined by Elton Mayo, Felix J. Roethlisberger, and a team of researchers from the Harvard Business School. Over a six-year period, this group consulted on ways to extend the original exploration, a study of the effect of lighting, to research into the attitudes of workers. Their search began with first one and then another small test room and led finally to an extensive interview program conducted by plant supervisors.[68] I turn to these conversations now to see what they can tell us about gendered attitudes toward work in the late 1920s.

The first and longest-lasting experiment, the Relay Assembly Test Room (RATR), set up by management in April 1927, consisted of five young women (ages eighteen to twenty-eight) whose repetitive but demanding jobs involved putting together telephone signal switches that would eventually relay calls from one cable to another. Of the five women originally selected, two were replaced about nine months after the experiment started. With the exception of a few months in the fall of 1932, when one worker briefly left, the new team of five "girls" remained together until February 1933, when the company was forced by the depression to abandon all experimentation. This group more or less cooperated with management as their working conditions altered, their output steadily rose, and the economic depression around them deepened.[69] Other small groups of workers participated in shorter experiments. One of these, the Bank Wiring Test Room, established in November 1931, consisted of nine men and no women. It lasted barely six months, disbanded after the workers horrified management by regulating their own pace of work and thus restricting their output.

In apparently sharp contrast to the behavior of men, the women, after a short period of adjustment, increased their production dramatically. Management praised the women for cooperating, and their room quickly become a model test. The apparent difference dissolves on examination, however. As Richard Gillespie has pointed out, in both cases men and women were doing what seemed to be in their fundamental self-interest. The women, paid at a relatively high rate according to their group output, understood that increasing their production could only increase their total wages. They had been promised protection against the typical cuts in rates of pay if the quantity of production increased. The men had not only been made no such promise, but they continued to be paid by the piece at the same rate as workers in the larger section to which they belonged. Fearful that the rate for the job would be cut for all workers if they produced too much, and deriving little immediate benefit from putting out more work, they whiled away hours if it suited them. Asked by an interviewer if he was aware that others would be laid off if he produced too much, one worker replied, "That only stands to reason doesn't it?... Suppose the fellows in the test room could increase their output to seven thousand. I think some of them can. That would mean less work for others."[70] The structure of the wage provided males with incentives to restrain production; a more collective structure for women, and one that did not threaten their sister workers, encouraged them to enhance theirs. In the end the men, whose exercise of power violated managerial conceptions of work, lost their favored places. The women kept theirs.

The researchers, who failed to see women's control over their work, described the men as obstinately resistant to change, while they believed the women were simply immune to it, even "to the experimental changes."[71] They attributed the women's continuously high production to many factors, of which the high level of wages was one. Roethlisberger and Dickson's book *Management and the Worker*, which provides the original and most comprehensive account of the experiments' results, describes the "girls" in this and other test rooms in great detail, recording menstrual periods and in-depth information about their home lives, but pays no particular attention to their wages, though it is clear from the recorded comments of the "girls" that the dramatically higher wages they earned significantly increased both their production and their eagerness to cooperate with the research process.[72] In the end, Roethlisberger and Dickson credited the high levels of production to "a network of personal relations . . . which not only satisfied the wishes of its members but also worked in harmony with the aims of management."[73] In support of the women's cooperative stance, they cited such factors as their social activities, afternoon tea, and frequent rest periods, overlooking the mechanisms that women used to goad each other to work harder and to spell each other when tired.[74] The informal organization of the men, who were described by interviewers as having "a set of practices and beliefs . . . which at many points worked against the economic purposes of the company," clearly threatened management in a way that the women did not.[75] Did researchers choose to see men and women workers differently?

It appears so. Plantwide interviews provide additional clues to their positions. Summarizing them, Roethlisberger and Dickson offered a disclaimer for paying any attention at all to sex differences: "If . . . it seems that too much emphasis is placed on such things as, for example, comparing comments of men and women, it should be said that such comparisons were made largely because the data were originally filed in this way and not because the investigators thought such comparisons to be of paramount importance."[76] Their odd refusal to explore sex differences in an experiment whose guiding principle was that workers' sentiments, attitudes, reveries, and "psychopathology" influenced their ability to perform at work leaves the historian with some vexing questions.

What Roethlisberger and Dickson do tell us is revealing. When researchers content-coded the 10,300 interviews for frequency and tone, they discovered far more similarities than differences between male and female workers. In fact, among the thirty-seven topics they identified as most frequently discussed, they found male/female differences in only a

*The Relay Assembly Test Room, where the longest-lasting Hawthorne experiment took place.* FROM THE
WESTERN ELECTRIC COMPANY, HAWTHORNE STUDIES COLLECTION, COURTESY OF THE BAKER LIBRARY, HAR-
VARD BUSINESS SCHOOL.

handful, most of them trivial. "Women comment more than men about
*thrift, welfare, overtime, rest periods, fatigue, bogey* [the target rate of produc-
tion], *social contacts, furniture and fixtures.* Men comment more than women
about *tools, trucks, advancement, education, life insurance, and pensions.*" These
differences seemed to the authors "natural" since "man's social status in the
community is affected in no small part by the kind of work he does, and
*advancement* and *education* are closely allied with this preoccupation." But,
the authors held, "woman, on the other hand, is not by tradition the breadwinner of the family, nor is her social status so dependent on her job." From
there, the authors made a leap of faith to conclude: "An easy job, not too
fatiguing, in pleasant surroundings, sufficiently well paid to support herself
or to contribute something to the income of her parents or husband, and
congenial hours which allow her to take part in the activities of the home
seem ... to be the woman's main interests."[77]

Perhaps—but the evidence offered by the authors does not support their
conclusion, nor does the language of the interviews.[78] Like men, women
workers articulate an enormous interest in all things financial: wages are

mentioned more often by women than by men, though women complain about them somewhat less. Women mention the "bogey" more, but men and women are equally divided as to whether their particular rates are fairly set and equally concerned as to whether they are earning enough. Participation in the company's stock purchase plans and other benefit plans is at least as high among women as among men, and perhaps higher. If women are less interested in working overtime to accumulate money, approximately equal proportions of men and women are willing to work night shifts in order to earn extra pay.[79] Most of the differences occur at the margins. More men than women are interested in education, life insurance, and pensions, but the data indicate that neither men nor women are particularly interested in any of them. They fall into the "infrequently" or "seldom" mentioned categories. And women, though they may indeed be more interested in plant furniture and fixtures, "seldom" mention the subjects at all.

In one arena, "advancement," there does seem to be a significant difference, and here perhaps lies the key to the emerging content of the right to work—a content that explains why women, in this period, fought for equal pay for equal work while remaining fundamentally unconvinced that they deserved a chance at equal work.[80] The financial incentive afforded by work was critical for both men and women, but for women it was not tied, as it was for men, to notions of advancement, which in turn served as a surrogate for manhood. In this respect women would always be "boys" in the workplace, and even then, they would not, as Martha Banta puts it, ever be "real boys."[81] Ford, according to historian Stephen Meyer, "considered all women, regardless of their family status, as youths."[82] Mary Gilson, one of the early personnel management counselors, recalled how stubbornly managers and the whole industrial relations field resisted women's promotion to supervisory positions, falling back on negative myths and stereotypes about women's behavior. In southern textile mills, which employed women in large majorities, she lamented that "no woman had a chance to rise to overseership." Managers explained their refusal with ominous predictions of high labor turnover and the high cost of training women. But Gilson thought "the climate of public opinion and the exclusive attitude of men" were far more to blame. Despite her own positive, empirical experience with women foremen, supervisors, and managers, she could not persuade Harvard's Graduate School of Business Administration to admit women.[83] Lacking a future in work, perceived as without ambition, and absent the language of entitlement that permeated the attitudes of male workers, working women would remain boys who would never be granted the status of men. That was, in an economic sense, their advantage to managers. Whatever hope most ordinary working women had was vested in the amount of the wage rather than in the job itself.

It takes very little detective work to ascertain just how readily women might have been discouraged. The lack of incentives for women to get somewhere in the world prompted Ida Tarbell, perhaps the most successful female journalist of her time, to undertake a five-part series of articles that would explore women's job possibilities in industry. "The numbers in executive positions have been so few and so scattered that there has been as general a belief that they [women] were not adapted to industrial supervision as there has been that they were not capable of mastering mechanical tasks," Tarbell wrote in the last of this series.[84] Mary Gilson concurred. Noting the limitations imposed by expectations of marriage and discouraging job possibilities, she commented how "little incentive was furnished to women by a world which spurred men to effort in opening all fields to them."[85]

The encouragement provided to ambitious white men appears in stark contrast to the brick walls that faced women. One example will make the point. Sears, Roebuck, one of the largest retail employers of women, published a booklet in 1930 entitled *Sears Jobs for Sears Men* and addressed "To Sears Retail Employees" that invited "Every man in the employ of our Retail Stores" to be interested in its personnel policy. In language that surely excluded every woman who might have been remotely tempted, it assured "men of ambition" that the company was interested in "its men" and genuinely desired "to give to every man, maximum opportunity for self-improvement and maximum opportunity for promotion."

Small wonder, then, that we find far less tendency for wage-earning women to imagine that they could improve their lives through promotions or job changes. Rather, like the women at Hawthorne, most claimed the need for income as both their justification for wage work and their major interest in it. When women talked about working themselves up, they mentioned higher piece rates on easier jobs. Unlike men, who associated skill and satisfaction at work with recognition accompanied by higher pay, women focused on the advantages of greater incomes. Julia S. was the fastest and most productive of the RATR workers: a young woman who financially supported, and kept house for, her unemployed father and three brothers and consistently goaded her teammates into ever greater effort. She seemed at first satisfied with her work: "Oh, no marriage for me. I'm going to keep on making relays." But later, she delightedly showed her high paychecks to her married sister, proclaiming, "I'm doing what I'm doing for money" and "It's a bum making relays. Honest, I have no more ambition to make relays."[86] She might have resolved the dilemma by seeking a different kind of job—by anticipating some marginal upward mobility—but for Julia, her high income (artificially higher than it might otherwise have been because of her involvement in the test room) served not as a marker of skill but as an incentive to stability and the source, by itself, of pride. It was perhaps the only job she could imagine that would enable her to support her family.

Unlike the women, the men at Hawthorne attached wages firmly to what they called "getting ahead" and expected income and some combination of skill and responsibility to progress in tandem. In the interviews, they referred to opportunities for promotion at about three times the rate of women and agonized about their "chances." They spoke about quitting jobs because "there wasn't much advancement" and complained about "how a fellow has to be here a long time in order to get ahead." "Getting ahead" seemed to be part of the normal expectation of things: "When another job comes along you get rid of the guys that are not good, and the fellow that works hard, does a good job, he stays here. That's the way it always is." Another man commented: "It is human nature to want to keep going on the up and up all the time. . . . The company should . . . always see that a man is given a fair chance to keep rising—going up all the time. His wages should keep increasing too."[87]

A promotion without a pay increase conveyed a dual message to male workers. Most considered it unfair. "What I consider an advancement," explained one male worker pithily, "is when they take a person from one job and put him on another where he can learn more and at the same time make just as much money as he did before, but where a person is taken off of the job paying 45 dollars per week and to be placed on a job paying 25, I consider that a demotion instead of a promotion regardless of how much you are learning." Workers sometimes refused promotions unaccompanied by wage increases, even when they carried the promise of future responsibility. One worker refused a job as a gang boss at a pay cut of twenty cents an hour because, as an interviewer reported, he didn't "think it was fair to ask him to take a cut so that he could get a better job." At the same time, even a relatively good wage, if it remained static, signaled poor promotion prospects. While a woman might have thought her good wage a sufficient achievement, one male, an eight-year veteran who complained of "only making a few dollars a week more than I made when I started to work for the company" grumbled: "I think my chances for advancement are zero minus."[88]

In sharp contrast, factory women believed that getting ahead meant getting out of the factory, or at least off the factory floor. Such jobs did not necessarily pay better, so women who aspired to higher status had to sever the positive correlation between income and status that men took as a matter of course. Julia dreamed of becoming a secretary, but she knew, when the men in her family lost their jobs, that they would need her high wages. She quickly gave up her dreams. One of her coworkers, a young woman in the Technical Branch, plotted her escape into a better job via a secretarial course—without mentioning wages at all. "I feel as though if I can say I'm a secretary and graduate with honors I won't have a hard time getting a job," she told the interviewer.[89] She had her future plotted out: she would work nights to get some experience, then transfer to an office job, perhaps even to one at Western Electric.

These subtle differences around the attitudes of men and women toward work and wages emerged from and helped to maintain a broad array of traditions about manliness and womanliness. When Roethlisberger and Dickson argued that workers were motivated by a "logic of sentiments" to describe the "values residing in the interhuman relations of the different groups," they attributed to employees cherished beliefs around the right to work, seniority, and fairness. Their data suggest not only that these concepts matter but that managers as well as workers use them and that they are differently used by men and women and with respect to them. For the women at Hawthorne, the right to work was not an issue of principle or morality and certainly not an issue of when they would get their housework done or care for their families. Those factors varied for women in different circumstances; rather, their interest in work resided in their capacity to earn as much as they could. If anyone had asked them, they might have replied that their "right to work" was the right to support their homes; that they did not wish to compete with men for jobs but to secure for women a greater certainty that they, too, could earn good wages.

## Marriage: A Defining Condition

In hindsight, this limited view of rights produced predictable consequences. When the depression-generated scarcity of jobs magnified the idea that a fair distribution of work would sustain families, it sharpened the already tense debate over who possessed the right to work. At the same time, it illuminated deeply rooted assumptions about women's secondary status in the workforce. For women, occupations that might have become markers of citizenship legitimized ways of meeting personal and family needs. Every woman now had to prove that her job served that purpose. As we have seen, even the potential of marriage reduced women's claims to training. And among married women (about 15 percent of whom held jobs in 1930), the burden of proof loomed large, for insofar as marriage was widely imagined as providing women and their children with support, it sharply reduced their claims to work.

The deepening depression, with its steep unemployment rates, produced ever sharper contests between the few who considered jobs as individual rights and the vast majority who did not. In the minority were those like the female assistant postmaster who complained to Frances Perkins: "I can't see why if we women are American Citizens why we haven't just as much right to work as anybody."[90] On the other side, most married non-wage-earning women, as well as many single women, believed that "if the wife and mother were not working, the head of the house would of necessity have more steady work, and better pay." Exceptions might be made for those who supported families. That left employers like George F. Johnson, who owned the Endicott Johnson shoe factory, in a dilemma: he thought it unfair to fire his married female employees, yet his efforts to protect them led him into conflict with single female and male employees.[91] Like most working men and women, these shoe workers believed that only women who needed to support themselves and their families deserved jobs, although they conceded that the needs of the economy and of particular industries might create exceptions.

Hawthorne workers expressed similar feelings. Single women working there distinguished themselves sharply from the married, expressed curiosity about why married women would continue to work, required explanations from those who did, and applauded when the company laid off married women in moments of crisis. The married took pains to justify their positions as a product of family need: "If I could make more money on these jobs," declared one woman, "I'd feel better because then I would see some way of getting out of debt. My home needs to be paid for and my husband being out of work makes it very hard for me."[92] These attitudes suggest not so much a moral judgment as a cold calculus about the value of jobs and claims to them. Nor did women workers believe their feelings were unknown to supervisors.

Julia (our speedy RATR worker) repeatedly declared her ambivalence to marriage, insisting that "if you get married you'll have to work anyway." Yet when she heard a rumor that married women were to be laid off she said to her coworkers (a married woman among them), "Well, that's the best thing in the world I've heard them do. Now these poor single girls can have a chance to hold on to a job." When the layoffs failed to tap married women first, Julia's sense of fair play was outraged. "Why don't they lay off people that don't need the money? They always begin with the poor ones first." Julia had little question as to who the deserving workers were: "The office people—most of them—can afford it better than we can. And the way they go about it—say there are plenty of married women working whose husbands are working too. Do they lay them off? I should say no. We single girls first, and fellows too who are supporting families. Gee, they do things a hell of a way here." Despite her clear sense of where justice lay, Julia remained confused about the appropriate relationship of marriage to work; while she thought that if she did marry she would not escape work, she also found the idea of continuing to make relays (which she associated with being single) distressing. Consistent to the last, Julia attacked Western Electric for laying off "a girl . . . who had a family to support." In this respect, she echoed the prevailing feeling that "the company ought to . . . lay off all the married women first. They should keep them when there is plenty of work but I don't think they should lay off a single girl and keep the married women."[93]

Whether the attitudes of workers like these influenced the company, or whether the continuing depression affirmed an already existing belief system, we might never know. But in October 1930, the Hawthorne works began giving six-month leaves of absence to married women. Thirty-nine-year-old Rachel, the mother of a fifteen-year-old, was asked to take such a leave along with other women in her department whose husbands were working. She accepted it without much complaining: "It's a good thing as long as everyone gets it except those that really need a job," she told the interviewer.[94] Women who protested enforced leaves on the grounds that the company had made a mistake got a quick apology.[95] And those who were married and insisted on their jobs adopted defensive strategies to save face in front of their coworkers. A young woman who returned to work shortly after she married, to help pay for her husband's unexpected and extensive medical bills, reported that "I was criticized for coming back to work and I am always getting slams about being money hungry and work to support a man. . . . If they knew my condition they would be more considerate of me."[96]

The attitudes of Hawthorne's workers sustain our sense that conceptions of fairness and equity could fluctuate with economic circumstance. Hawthorne's workers were unlikely to have flirted with 1920s feminist notions that work might support an independent female citizenship. They understood their wage-earning status as necessary to family support, and increasingly, as the depression deepened, they reserved approval of women's wage earning for those who functioned as providers. Marital status, if not a sure sign of eligibility for work, was certainly its most reliable indicator. Married women increased their workforce participation during the depression, but they did so in the context of an emotional discussion as to whether and how their work would affect the work opportunities of men and of single women, as much as their family lives. Nonworking married women wanted jobs for their husbands; single women, for themselves; men of all kinds believed that all men and women who supported families had greater rights to earn than other women. In total, 89 percent of the public, according to one opinion poll, thought married women with husbands should not work.

The 1932 Economy Act, which seemed consistent with these attitudes, pointed up the dangers of discriminating against one group of women. Passed rapidly in a moment of crisis, and with minimal opposition, one clause of the act, Section 213, required that in any reduction of civil service personnel, married persons whose spouses were also employed by the federal government should be dismissed first. The clause was justified as a way to spread jobs around, on the grounds that it was inappropriate for one family to have two jobs while others went without. About 1,600 workers voluntarily or involuntarily left the civil service, at least 75 percent of them women and most of them earning relatively modest salaries.[97] Untold numbers of other women adopted a variety of subterfuges to keep their jobs: they lied, divorced, or lived with partners instead of marrying. Ultimately the clause, in the eyes of many, placed a premium on "fornication and upon illicit intercourse" and thus encouraged moral turpitude.[98]

Taking account of marital status hardly constituted a new employment policy, nor had it gone unnoticed. General Electric and many other firms had long fired women workers when they married; Ford managers considered it their duty to investigate the marital obligations of new workers and preferred to hire males with dependents. Hawthorne workers assumed that jobs should go to those who needed them. In the early days of the depression, social investigator Ruth Shallcross reported that insurance companies, banks, public utilities, and many state governments and municipalities formally restricted the employment of married women, as did other employers on an informal basis.[99] And labor unions, as historian Elizabeth Faue points out, believed "there was undoubtedly something subversive about the number of women continuing to take and hold jobs in a time of unemployment."[100] But when the federal government formally adopted the policy, it placed several principles on the table. At first, the most important seemed to be the challenge to the meritocracy that legitimized the federal civil service. Could a merit system survive if it introduced extraneous factors into merit considerations? Was barring some portion of the married a first step to overriding merit altogether? Though it had by no means treated women neutrally, the civil service had nevertheless been a refuge for educated women.[101] The new policy raised the question of whether, if efficiency, skill, and responsibility were no longer sufficient criteria for hiring and firing, the government could not also adopt other criteria, such as the number of dependents, in addition to marital status.[102] If marriage became the primary reason for dismissing a worker because it signaled financial need, at what point might the government investigate the financial circumstances of every employee to determine whether he or she required an income?

Underlying this problem was the larger issue of whether restricting the rights of married women ultimately jeopardized the rights of all women. Legislators tried to defend Section 213 as gender-neutral, arguing that the clause was designed to spread jobs among families rather than to remove married women from government service.[103] Was it really discrimination against women, asked Representative Frederick R. Lehlback of New Jersey, or could it not be seen as "aimed at two salaries in one household during this era of depression and unemployment?"[104] It turned out on examination that little more than 5 percent of those employed by the federal civil service were married women, and most of these did not have husbands who also worked for the federal government.[105] The attack came to seem symbolic—a way to spread messages about married women's employment rather than to provide jobs for men.

Fearing a widespread attack on all women workers, feminists of all kinds rose to arms. The National Woman's Party took the lead, joined by its subsidiary Government Workers' Council and, at congressional hearings by more moderate social feminist organizations, including the League of Women Voters and the National Women's Trade Union League. Marriage, thought the League of Women Voters, could not be allowed to deprive one group of American citizens, "sometimes men, probably more often women, of the right to compete for positions in the public service."[106] Dorothy Dunn, representing the National Federation of Business and Professional Women's Clubs, argued that "discrimination against married women is a blow to all women who work and to marriage itself," which would "sweep from the ranks of workers women whose only crime was their marital status."[107] Workers, several women's groups argued, should be judged on the basis of the work they did, not on the basis of marital status or even of need. "To dismiss a person merely because he or she happens to have a wife or husband employed by the Government," suggested the National Women's Trade Union League, "is illogical and may penalize the most efficient employees."[108] Need should not be the only criterion for public work, testified the National Educational Association; teaching required the "best talent available."[109]

Still, many workers continued to insist publicly that need alone would justify the law's repeal. Dismissed New York City postal clerks (each of whom had worked for at least thirteen years) believed Section 213 to be "unfair discrimination" and a "flagrant violation of the long established rules of our civil service law." Nevertheless, their protests focused on detailed accounts of "the hardship which this law has imposed upon us." The account included a table outlining the financial responsibilites of each of the dismissed workers, including number of dependents and payments on home mortgages. Their demand to be reinstated was qualified by a request that if that were impossible, then at least they should get their jobs back "upon the deaths of our husbands."[110]

Congress eventually voted to repeal the offending section in 1937, but the events that followed suggest that repealing the law did not vitiate the idea that men held jobs on a different basis from women. The Second World War, as many historians have demonstrated, pulled women into the labor force in ways that affirmed rather than negated their primary commitments to families.[111] Manpower experts called on married women to take jobs "for the duration" and discouraged those with small children from entering the labor force; industrial relations experts successfully fostered continued sex segregation of jobs; human relations consultants advised women to retain their femininity and remember that their families came first. Though many women protested pay differentials and tried to hang on to their jobs, an onslaught of postwar propaganda convinced most to give them back to the returning soldiers who had defended their country in wartime.

It should not surprise us, then, that the sponsors of the Full Employment Act of 1945 so quickly forgot the contributions of housewives and consigned them to the category of those without job rights. The several weeks of debate over the bill covered many hugely important issues. Its opponents charged that the bill smacked of communism; its defenders countered that only full employment would deter socialism. It would put the U.S. government into deficit; it would conflict with sacred commitments to veterans by creating competition for training and jobs; it would deny a capitalist economy the necessary "floating pool of unemployed." Still, the bill's cosponsor Senator James Murray of Montana held fast. "In the days to come," he argued, "I see nothing but conflict and recrimination for capitalism in America unless we provide a program which will insure employment opportunities for all Americans who are able and willing to work."[112]

All the weighty concerns notwithstanding, the issue of who could appropriately be included among "all Americans" could not be quieted.[113] Lewis G. Hines, national legislative representative of the American Federation of Labor, thought the provision unnecessary because housewives would not be "seeking work" in any event. But some congressmen wondered whether that might leave them vulnerable. The questions ranged from the reasonable to the outrageous: "Who is going to make that determination of who does not have full time housekeeping responsibility?" "Suppose she starts her housework at 6:30 in the morning and gets through it by 9 o'clock?" "What if she had domestic servants who did her housekeeping? Would she then be entitled to a job?" Would the bill commit the government to providing a woman with funds to take care of her children "so that she could have less full-time duties at her housekeeping?" There was even a sarcastic suggestion that the bill would require nurses for newborns so that new mothers could go right back to work.

Why the excitement? Excluding women pitted two intertwined issues against each other: protecting men's jobs and expanding the democracy for which the war had been fought. Mindful of the scarcity of jobs that had followed World War I, along with race riots and veterans' discontent, the Department of Labor reminded Congress early on that it would not be possible to meet the expectations of veterans for jobs unless other groups were brought into line. Though it wholeheartedly supported full employment in principle, conceding the importance of opportunity for all meant in practice reframing the expectations of those displaced.[114] Representative Clare E. Hoffman of Michigan pushed Secretary of Labor Louis Schwellenbach into dotting the *i*'s. "In considering this bill and its desirability," Hoffman asked, "should we . . . act upon the theory, that many of those who were employed should go back to the places from which they came and the businesses from which they came before they were induced by these high wages and patriotism and one thing and another to get into the factories?" Secretary Schwellenbach heartily agreed. The administration, he assured congressmen, was as committed as they to the principle that a woman "who does not have the necessity of working, but is just working because of the fact that she had gotten in the practice of it and likes it, . . . should stay home." In his eyes, exempting housewives was superfluous. Assured that this was the general consensus, he joined the chorus by agreeing with Hoffman that, after all, "we cannot all have a factory job with General Motors or Little Steel or Big Steel."[115]

At the same time, the potential exclusion of most women from a bill that, its defenders argued eloquently, was "right in harmony with our democratic ideals and . . . a step forward in putting those ideals into practice" required a certain kind of gendered legerdemain.[116] Many men and women could legitimately ask whose democratic ideals were now being defended. Senator Robert

Taft tried evading the linkage at one point by proposing that the "right to work" was, after all, moral rather than legal. Perhaps it wasn't worth fighting over. Murray would not have it. This was not, he agreed, a "right . . . that they could come into court and file a suit on, but it would be a right or a goal that the Government recognizes—an obligation."[117] Like the Declaration of Independence, suggested a colleague, it was "merely a declaration of policy." Yes, Murray agreed, and therefore the language limiting women should stay.

In the end, the Senate dropped the provision, and by the time the House debated it, the bill had reduced the idea of full employment to a mere shadow. The bill foundered on ideological issues around whether government should guarantee employment. But the heated discussion demonstrates that as late as 1945 no commitment to jobs would be allowed to undermine the prerogatives of families by tempting women to believe that they, too, might benefit from even the most abstract right to work.

Whatever the desires of feminists who advocated an equal rights amendment in the 1920s, achieving the formal political equality guaranteed by suffrage did not pave the way to economic equality. There may have been little unity in the ways in which wage-earning women imagined themselves working in the 1920s and 1930s, but most nonprofessional women still conceived themselves in quite different workforce roles from those held by working men. By the 1940s, the expectations of ordinary women had changed as a result of the war, and the rhetoric of democracy and opportunity loomed larger, but legislative standards remained firmly rooted in the sensibilities of earlier decades. Before they altered, they would have to overcome a legacy of social policies designed to affirm custom and restrict the gendered imagination.

# CHAPTER 2

# Maintaining Self-Respect

L ooking at the range of depression-fostered initiatives around labor and employment policy, one is struck first by how profoundly the expectations of ordinary people altered. Americans moved from staunch opposition to federal government intervention in the lives of most men (but not women) to eager experiments with government mediation of every kind. Newly adopted social policies had many goals, but among the most dramatic were those connected with earning wages and keeping jobs. By the mid-1930s, a newly authoritative federal government had acknowledged a role for organized labor and begun to subject business to a range of restrictive, though sometimes welcome, regulation. To be sure, the federal government had not generally been demurely silent in the face of struggles between business and labor. More frequently than not, it had intervened on behalf of business to still the discontent that emerged when market forces created havoc with workers' lives. And, its own civil servants and railroad workers aside, federal legislative and judicial bodies had resolutely left to the states the task of constructing labor legislation.

That changed in the 1930s when the search for economic security became, in historian Steve Fraser's words, the dynamic force urging "collaboration between modern management and centralized industrial unions."[1] The new administrative state that mediated this process fostered a dramatic expansion of union membership and encouraged labor's participation in every aspect of governmental regulation. The process unfolded over a fourteen-year period of congressional debate and government action around a series of bills designed to regulate employment during the Roosevelt years. While considering, and rejecting, bills to limit the workweek to thirty hours and to set up a European-style system of social insurance for everyone, Congress, as we have seen, acted swiftly to exclude married women from government jobs. It then moved to provide unemployment insurance (and old age pensions) to a limited group of workers and to place a floor under the wages and a lid on the hours of many. The administration reluctantly protected the rights of African Americans with an executive order creating a Fair Employment Practice Committee. Congress, in the end, rejected the notion that government had a responsibility to ensure work for all. By 1946, these seemingly discrete events had congealed into a set of policies that redefined the meaning of work, differentiated the value of various kinds of work, and closely monitored who qualified as a "worker." Not incidentally, the process also precipitated a ferocious debate about the federal government's relationships to ordinary people and introduced new and sharper distinctions among its citizens that were written into the ensuing social policies.[2]

All this took place in a period of dramatic changes in the lives of working people. Confronted by rapidly declining employment rates after 1929—by 1932, about 25 percent of workers were out of jobs—Americans responded by tightening and rearticulating their expectations of the relationship between wage work and family life. Like Julia who worked in the Hawthorne test room, they insisted that those who supported themselves or others deserved priority in the queue for scarce jobs.[3] We have already noticed that, even during the relative prosperity of the 1920s, popular attitudes contested women's claims to jobs, placing them on a different basis than those of men. When high unemployment aggravated these contests, singling out married women as especially undeserving, tough questions arose about how to enhance the claims of family breadwinners on the one hand without denigrating the value of work skills on the other.

Achieving consensus on issues of who deserved employment and who could languish in uncompensated unemployment required some hard decisions, especially around questions of inclusion and exclusion. For the government to regulate working conditions and monitor benefits for those without jobs, legislators would have to agree on, and administrators determine, eligibility. Someone would have to decide who could be described as a "worker" and who didn't fit the picture; what jobs counted as work and what didn't; how many hours constituted full-time work and how few precluded the activity from being called "work" at all. Innovative programs and policies demanded clarifications and classifications, precisely placing individuals in their relationships to paid and unpaid activities of different sorts. Each categorization opened or closed a door to the status, social rights, and economic security that measured progress toward economic citizenship for someone. Not only did benefits and entitlements rest on symbols of belonging, but so, ultimately, did the identities of workers, as well as their self-respect, political participation, and a newly differentiated set of meanings for crucial concepts like breadwinning, manhood, and citizenship.

The social constraints that guided these decisions had many roots, including most crucially ideologies of race and of American freedom and liberty. Historians are only now beginning to understand the degree to which they reflected a fundamental consensus around issues of race.[4] But the new policies were also deeply embedded in a widespread and widely shared set of assumptions about gender. Many scholars have pointed out how New Deal policies divided programs that primarily benefited women and children from those that benefited men. Some parts of the Social Security legislation of 1935, like Aid to Dependent Children and Maternal and Infant Healthcare, for example, provided means-tested benefits governed by the need for immediate relief. They were quickly stigmatized as welfare.[5] But programs that focused on what we have been calling "rights to work" and that legitimized the claims of men and some women to federal government protection, subsidy, and inclusion were also deeply gendered and no less consequential in shaping rules around family life and subsequent access to the perquisites of economic citizenship.

In this chapter, I look at how particular kinds of gendered arguments framed new kinds of employment legislation in the 1930s. Our journey exposes entrenched notions of manliness and masculinity, most visible in the organized labor movement and reinforced by what the British social theorist Raymond Williams has called "the structure of feeling" that ultimately accounts for particular pieces of legislation.[6] I look at three pivotal moments—the struggle over the thirty-hour workweek in the early 1930s, the debate over unemployment insurance and its inclusion in the 1935 Social Security Act, and the adoption of fair labor standards in 1938—to see how gendered arguments influenced the outcomes. Different groups dominated each discussion, and the gendered perspective operated differently in each instance. It never acted alone, nor perhaps as the most important shaping force. But paying attention to its presence reveals something of how, gender served as a crucial enabling force to legitimize new policies and identify appropriate beneficiaries.

## Self-Help Is the Best Help

It was not so much what organized labor wanted as what it did not want that shaped New Deal accomplishments around employment. By the late 1920s, organized labor represented only about 5 percent of American workers, most of them skilled white males. African Americans belonged to a few mainstream unions like the United Mine Workers of America and the Brotherhood of Sleeping Car Porters. If women organized at all, they joined unions in the garment, textile, and incipient electronics industries, where the largest proportions of women workers concentrated. Still, the American Federation of Labor was certainly the most powerful voice of workers, and that gave it a strong voice in labor legislation.

As represented by the AFL, organized workers definitively did not want government intervention even when it seemed to be in their self-interest. Until the early 1930s, the AFL clung obdurately to the idea of voluntarism as it had been developed by its revered longtime leader Samuel Gompers. Voluntary organization—the right of citizens to define and pursue their goals in free association—was both a call for action and a mantra for masculinity. In the first guise, it embodied the economic self-interest of the trade union by assuring members that an investment in collective efforts would bring greater benefits and leave them less vulnerable than government intervention. The labor movement could not tell the unorganized, as one AFL officer put it, " 'If you join our union we will secure certain legislation for you.' We believe that we have to do something which would impress the non-unionist with the necessity for a vigorous, virile, militant organization in the economic field."[7] In the second guise, voluntarism closely wove the liberty of members to pursue collective ends into a pattern that reflected manly identities.

Union strategy assumed that jobs were scarce resources to be distributed and protected by workers in defiance of employers' claims to control them. It invoked American ideals of individualism in defense of organization and constructed solidaristic appeals to labor to preserve its collective self-interest in jobs without fear from, or benefit of, government intervention. Voluntarism presumed that wage earners had the courage, independence, and economic power to protect their own interests. In the best of worlds, that included controlling the supply of labor in order to guarantee its price. Voluntarism's advocates assumed that dignity—a man's dignity—resided in the capacity to do so.[8] Because it relied on the unified strength of skilled workers, partisans of voluntarism freely excluded those who might undermine labor's power, including the unskilled, most people of color, and women.

The labor movement marshaled words like *courage, dignity, self-respect,* and *independence* in defense of workers' liberty and freedom, associating them with manly conceptions of virility and economic power. It recognized that threats to liberty did not come only from policemen's clubs and the rifles of the

National Guard but also from more subtle assaults on workers' conceptions of their own strength. Trade unionists found the idea of government regulation for male workers particularly threatening. They believed that regulation would inevitably privilege employers and undermine the manly character on which collective action rested, turning the worker into a cowardly and subservient creature who would need to go hat in hand to the state for benefits. Fearful of the consequences, the AFL, under Gompers's leadership, consistently opposed even the most apparently benign State interventions out of the fear that they "would build up a bureaucracy that would have some degree of authority or control over all the workers of the state."[9] The federation acquiesced reluctantly to workmen's compensation programs in the 1910s, but it so feared government bureaucracy and administration that it opposed reformers' efforts to introduce even such seemingly desirable benefits as health insurance in the late teens.[10] As the secretary of the California State Federation of Labor put it in a 1932 radio talk, "The American labor movement is founded on the principle that self help is the best help, and that the exercise by workers of their economic power is the greatest and most potent power which they can wield."[11]

At the heart of voluntarism lay a uniquely American version of manhood. Closely tied to American ideals of self-sufficiency and upward mobility, it was rooted in the notion that those who gave up control over their own fate gave up a precious source of liberty and would become lesser citizens. In this respect, the stance of American workers differed from forms of social democracy supported by European labor that encouraged alliances between labor and social insurance advocates. American trade unionists believed "socialistic" programs that created universal entitlements would undermine manhood by producing dependent and cringing males. Unlike some Europeans, who believed they could turn government to the purposes of male providers and their families, American labor leaders profoundly suspected government as the instrument of business and capital. As Gompers had suggested, "for the government to intervene would be wrong and harmful; wrong because such interference is destructive of personal (and inalienable) rights, harmful because it destroys initiative, independence, and self-reliance."[12] Gompers was capable of fulminating at some length about this connection between citizenship and voluntarism. For example, opposing a New York State bill to provide health insurance, he argued, "There is something in the very suggestion of ... this policy that is repugnant to free-born citizens" and that would necessarily produce "a weakening of independence of spirit and virility."[13]

No equivalent inhibition guided the AFL's position on women's relationship to government. As we have seen, many craft unionists supported special protective laws for women on the grounds that women could not organize effectively and that these laws protected male bargaining power and jobs. They shared with social feminists a commitment to maintaining male wages and believed, with them, that employers who took advantage of women's cheap labor would undermine the family wage. AFL leaders acquiesced, as early as 1911, in plans to regulate the hours and wages of women and children in several states; by 1916, the federation ardently supported them. But its motives differed from those of social feminists, who often proclaimed labor legislation for women "an entering wedge" that would ultimately lead to protection for all workers. Powerful voices within the AFL saw it primarily as a way of shoring up the family by discouraging employers from hiring women in the first place while ensuring reasonable conditions for those who did enter the labor force. Regulating women's work also promised men less competition over jobs, sustaining the solidarity and collective bargaining possibilities of men's unions. Labor laws would never do for men, whose faith in collective bargaining embodied the manly force of working men's liberty. Yet both groups could agree on the central importance of family life and of male jobs to sustain it. Consensus on this issue may have enhanced the voice of a relatively weak AFL in national legislative councils.

Many in the labor movement questioned the rigidity of the AFL's stance with its sharp suspicion of anything that smacked of "administration" and "bureaucracy." Even before the depression of the 1930s it was the subject of internal debate.[14] After Gompers died in 1924, and in the face of declining numbers brought on largely by a concerted business and government assault against unions, some AFL leaders demanded government protection for the collective bargaining process. They sought relief from court injunctions against strikes and boycotts and legislation to make yellow-dog contracts (in which workers promised as a condition of hiring not to join a union) illegal. The dramatic rise in unemployment in the late 1920s and early 1930s turned a disagreement that amounted to no more than a hairline crack into a fissure. It was time, thought many labor leaders, to abandon the idea of voluntarism and seek government help for workers. The major women's unions (including Sidney Hillman's Amalgamated Clothing Workers' Union) led the assault, but by the early 1930s hundreds of local unions advocated legislative intervention to achieve a shorter workweek and unemployment insurance.

Of the two, the shorter workweek seemed a more effective strategy for reducing unemployment, but it ran afoul of the federation's commitment to manly liberty. The idea was familiar. Initially eager to extend leisure, and later also fearful of technologically created unemployment, the trade union movement had demanded shorter workweeks for members since the 1880s. In the 1920s, when the average workweek still hovered around forty-eight hours and six-day weeks and twelve-hour days were not unusual, unions occasionally struck for a five-day, forty-hour week. At mid-decade, the AFL began to publicly excoriate industries that would not acquiesce to a five-or five-and-a-half-day week. Technological change, it argued, had increased productivity and profits; the shorter workday would permanently spread employment and extend purchasing power. Though it was proud of its record, the AFL had little clout at the time, and its gains were small. Most businesses remained intransigent, and the idea of dramatically reducing hours did not prove popular. Reformers who joined with the unions to plead for greater leisure for workers produced equally dismal results.[15]

Dramatic and compelling arguments for legislating, rather than bargaining for, shorter hours emerged when unemployment increased during the depression. As joblessness climbed to around 25 percent of all workers, proponents argued for a shorter workweek to force employers to distribute work more efficiently. Accompanied by modest pay protection, this would stimulate consumption by increasing purchasing power for workers and their families. By immediately reducing unemployment, shorter hours would also restore the self-respect of workers. In the long term, they would encourage industry to make more rational use of available workers. These arguments produced some results. As industry tried to avoid the disruption of continual layoffs, it resorted to strategies of reduced working hours. Labor and politicians increased their calls for sharing the work, and local unions urged the AFL to put its weight behind a thirty-hour week. Beginning in the summer of 1932, a "share the work" movement spread among business and popular leaders.

But much of the labor movement deeply suspected the legislated thirty-hour week, even with its promise of increased leisure for workers. To be sure, reduced hours promised a new foundation for individual freedom and human progress: goals at the heart of voluntarism. Yet in the early years of the depression, William Green, successor to Samuel Gompers, continued to believe that moral, not political, clout could achieve the shorter workday. Pressured by local unions to support legislation if not a constitutional amendment, Green stubbornly refused. He willingly pressed the federal government to reduce hours for its own employees, including post office clerks, who still worked a forty-four-hour week; he urged state and municipal governments to follow suit by reducing the hours of government workers; he acquiesced to limiting the hours of interstate transportation workers.[16] Still, he resisted legislation for most private industry. In his view, collective bargaining would achieve a short week at less cost and more quickly than legislation. "It is only through the fighting strength of [the] organization," declared John Frey, secretary-treasurer of the Metal Trades Department, "that you are going to get higher wages and shorter hours."[17]

Within the AFL, however, a growing rebellion supported legislative initiatives. After several years of arguments, and in the face of desperate poverty created by the depression, the issue reached the convention floor. In 1931 and 1932, a torn and bleeding membership revisited the question of voluntarism. "We have come to a point in the history of labor," Delegate Allen of the Twin Cities Federation declared, "when we must of necessity change our previous attitude and opinion of regulation of hours of labor by legislation.... I am not afraid of the United States government; it is bad enough, but it is not as bad as having 11,000,000 men walking the streets looking for work." As delegates debated whether to support a twentieth amendment to the U.S. Constitution mandating a thirty-hour week, their leaders roundly rejected the notion. Legislative processes never had and never would, they argued, achieve the shorter workweek. Instead, they invoked "the great mass of workers" who had "progressed successively from twelve to ten hours, then to eight hours, and now, in many instances, to forty-four or forty hours weekly through the power of their economic organizations."[18]

In these discussions, fear of the legislative quick fix prevailed. "Do you know what it would mean to give this power to the Government to rule the hours of labor?" asked Andrew Furuseth of the Seamen's Union. "How do you know that you will not get twelve hours instead of four hours?" Thomas Donnelly of the Ohio State Federation of Labor pitched in: "You attempt to fix the hours of labor for the working people of America, and just as soon as you do you take away from the adult worker his fundamental inherent right to work one hour, two hours, six hours or eight hours."[19] Green agreed. While he remained convinced that only shorter hours could permanently end unemployment, he wanted the labor movement to negotiate them. Anything less threatened labor's manly honor. "It will ultimately rest upon labor to utilize its economic strength in a constructive and practical way in order to secure this great change," he roared to a standing ovation.[20] For the moment, at least, labor's honor had been saved.

But labor could not long resist. On December 21, just two months after the AFL's annual meeting, Senator Hugo Black of Alabama, a former Ku Klux Klan member, and Representative William Connery of Massachusetts introduced twin bills to forbid the shipment in interstate commerce of goods produced in

*Left: John Frey, a vice president of the American Federation of Labor and advocate of male dignity, in 1928.* COURTESY, GEORGE MEANY MEMORIAL ARCHIVES. *Right: William Green speaking at the AFL convention in 1933.* COURTESY, GEORGE MEANY MEMORIAL ARCHIVES.

any facility where "any worker was permitted to work more than five days in any week or more than six hours in any day."[21] With its ranks disrupted, its position as spokesperson for working people in question, and its own economic self-interest at stake, the AFL reluctantly shifted gears and supported the bill. Even as it did so, its leaders feared for the future of manly liberty. "Personally," John Frey told the Senate hearing called to consider the bills, "I have always been opposed ... to regulating the terms of employment for adult males through legislation. I have believed there was enough of a desire to maintain intelligent conditions ... to work out an adjustment of the problem. I have become convinced that is impossible." Clearly distressed at compromising a cherished principle, Frey continued, "I still think Mr. Gompers was one of the greatest men that this country has ever produced, and I always agreed with his philosophy that free men should work out their problems instead of having the legislature endeavor to do for men what they were capable of doing for themselves; but I have reached the conclusion now we are in a position where men are not capable of doing these things unless Congress says."[22] Philip Murray, then a vice president of the United Mine Workers, picked up the theme. He was driven to support the bill, he said, by the need to "sustain character" among those who would otherwise be idle. Men, he told the committee, "want to keep their economic independence. They do not want to become objects of charity. . . . They seek to maintain their relations as normal citizens toward society."[23] Could they do that if they relied on government intervention? For many labor leaders, confusion over a shorter-hours bill reflected the tensions of a complicated effort to solve the practical problem of unemployment while defending labor's vision of manhood as the last bastion of freedom and liberty.[24]

As labor leaders puzzled over how this new form of legislation might affect organized workers, they faced the additional problem of how to compensate for the lost wages of a shorter workday without regulating wages. "You can't fix the hours of labor by law unless you fix the rate of labor by law" was one typical and categorical reaction.[25] Reducing hours without maintaining wages, as Green and others recognized, might well result simply in sharing the existing wage pool without expanding purchasing power. But regulating wages was if anything worse than regulating hours, for wages were at the heart of the labor contract. Submitting to regulation would reduce men to the level of women and children. On this subject, Green would not budge. He remained, he said, "unalterably opposed to legislative interference with the wages of men."[26] Yet shorter hours without provisions for wage maintenance could be a disaster. For a while the United Mine Workers seemed to have a solution. Why not, Murray suggested, simply extend the ban on shipment in interstate commerce to goods produced by workers who were "denied the right to collectively bargain for wages through chosen representatives of their own"?[27] That kind of provision, thought Henry Warrum, counsel for the Mine Workers, would offer "a fair opportunity for the workers to protect themselves against any deflation of the wages" without having the state protect them.[28] But the principle of voluntarism would not yield. William Green testified in favor of the bill, provided it was not encumbered with a minimum wage provision. Among labor leaders, Sidney Hillman alone disgreed. He clung to the idea that a minimum wage could be helpful. It was a futile gesture. When the session ended, the bill quietly died.

Stimulated by the optimism of Franklin D. Roosevelt's inauguration and hopeful that the wages issue could be resolved, its sponsors reintroduced it in March 1933 without a minimum wage provision. By early April, it had already passed the Senate. Observers now thought some kind of shorter-hours bill had, as historian Benjamin Hunnicutt suggests, "become inevitable."[29] With labor's new backing and the issue of unemployment staring the administration in the face, it seemed like a popular and ready-made solution. Speaking for FDR, Secretary of Labor Frances Perkins publicly announced her support for shorter hours, judiciously, some observers noted, omitting to mention this bill. The administration was not yet willing to take on business interests. As passage in the House loomed closer and business grew increasingly restless, rumors of a compromise around thirty-five hours, or even forty, spread.

Finally the administration balked. It accepted the principle of reducing unemployment by reducing hours, Perkins declared, but wanted to make it "more flexible and workable."[30] In a move she must have known would provoke negative reactions among labor leaders, she proposed a three-member board empowered to "license" a six-hour day in industries that met minimal requirements, minimum wages established by boards that would determine appropriate wages in each industrial sector, enough flexibility to extend the thirty-hour limit to forty in some industries, and a relaxation of antitrust laws where a thirty-hour week was imposed. This was everything that labor detested: a bureaucracy that could exercise discretionary powers over men's freedoms; loss of control over wages; untrammeled influence for industry. Fearing entrapment, the AFL withdrew its support. Among major labor leaders, only Sidney Hillman, whose desire for a minimum wage exceeded his commitment to voluntarism, remained loyal to the administration.

Would the bill have gone down had labor been willing to compromise over the imposition of bureaucracy, had its manhood not been offended by the very idea of a regulated wage? What if labor had swallowed its concern for voluntarism and exercised the power of a countervailing force? Would Congress have overcome business's objections to a rigid thirty-hour provision? We have, of course, no way of knowing. The AFL continued to make a reduced workweek the keystone of its collective bargaining demands until the passage of the Fair Labor Standards Act in 1938. Yet its continuing commitment to the manly qualities encoded in voluntarism restrained its enthusiasm for legislative regulation of hours. Though passage of a thirty-hour bill was never a foregone conclusion, once the proposal no longer fit the gendered imagination of a skittish labor movement, it became less likely.

## Have We Lost Courage?

As the labor movement slowly modified its ideal of independence for mutually supportive workers to accommodate the vast need for help generated by the depression, it faced a challenge even greater than that of legislation to reduce working hours: the task of deciding what to do about unemployment insurance. The favorite remedy of a powerful group of labor relations experts and social insurance advocates, the idea of compulsory, government-regulated unemployment insurance may have been the most innovative product of the depression. It was also, by all accounts, the most contested issue in the Social Security Act of 1935, which provided the foundation of the American version of the welfare state.[31]

To set the stage: President Roosevelt created the Committee on Economic Security (CES) in the summer of 1934 to develop a program to relieve want in the short term and ultimately to provide comprehensive economic security for all Americans. The CES consisted of half a dozen cabinet members, chaired by Secretary of Labor Frances Perkins. Recommendations were to be offered to it by an Advisory Council, which in turn relied on three technical committees, each staffed by expert government technicians and independent consultants brought in from outside. The work of all these people was overseen by Executive Director Edwin Witte, who had trained at the University of Wisconsin with the influential economist John Commons. Witte had been brought to Washington on the recommendation of an old classmate, Arthur Altmeyer, and would surround himself with other Commons students and protégés, all of them in one way or another committed to enacting Commons's agenda. There were a few exceptions. Among the people he asked to join him as a consultant, was an economist and professor of law named Barbara Nachtrieb Armstrong. Armstrong, a California native had, in the course of nearly fifteen years at the University of California at Berkeley law school, become an expert on European social insurance systems with a special interest in unemployment insurance.

In the 1930s, unemployment insurance was the newest and least developed form of social insurance, and it was widely perceived as a cure for persistent poverty. It should have been an idea whose time had come, and there were many advocates for a comprehensive and rational system. At one end of the political spectrum, socialists, communists, and radicals of every variety folded unemployment compensation into wide-ranging proposals to eliminate economic inequality and provide generous government support for the young, the aged, and the ill as well as the unemployed. Protagonists of such plans included single-issue and demagogic visionaries like Dr. Francis Townsend and Father Charles Coughlin. At the other end, conservative voices of small business insisted that the federal government keep its hands off. These groups included the National Association of Manufacturers, local chambers of commerce, and a powerful bloc of southern congressmen, eager to retain the historic division between African-American and white workers that reduced the price of labor in their region and provided a sense of social order. Had these more conservative groups had their wish, the federal government would have given grants to the separate states to reduce the costs of relief without intervening at all in popular definitions of work.

Between these extremes lay more moderate groups whose members searched for stability and social justice within a business-oriented framework. Two—both of them active for a couple of decades—proved particularly

*Edwin Witte, Executive Director of President Roosevelt's Council on Economic Security.* COURTESY, STATE HISTORICAL SOCIETY OF WISCONSIN.

important in setting the tone of public conversations and in the policy debates within the subcommittees of the Committee on Economic Security. The first consisted of reform-minded advocates of social insurance, many of them deeply influenced by European-style programs; the second included proponents of employment stabilization through the cooperative action of government, business, and labor.[32] Among members of the first group, a vision of democratic equality ranked high. Its champions (including Armstrong) believed that human dignity in the modern world required income as a matter of right and sought redistributive mechanisms to avoid want. In contrast, advocates of employment stabilization drew on icons of economic liberty, especially individualism and personal responsibility. They aimed to prevent hardship and to ameliorate poverty only as a secondary goal.

Amorphous and shifting, these positions overlapped, as did those of the diffuse and articulate groups of progressive labor leaders, social insurance advocates, and maternalists. Yet both advocates and antagonists of a new unemployment policy shared a vision of the world grounded in a traditional male-breadwinner family. They disagreed on issues of states' rights, class, and often race, but they shared an understanding of gender, and particularly of the value of the male provider. Informed by common assumptions of how men and women should relate to each other, and sometimes represented by the same people, they channeled the experimental bent of the early New Deal into a forceful and interlocked advocacy of democratic social order reflected in the traditional family.

Yet the two groups bitterly disagreed over how to shape the unemployment insurance program. The spirit of social insurance appealed to the maternalist instinct for state protection of the unemployable, but many male as well as female maternalists objected to the reduced influence of local and state administrations it suggested. In the end, they supported the Commons school partly because it appealed to the CES staff, whose support they needed for the women's and children's programs they primarily wanted. And though the AFL found the Commons program consistent with its voluntarist policy of providing benefits as of right, it found several other elements problematic, among them the inclusion of business in economic planning, the self-policing of employers, and the role of government intervention. These raised the threat posed by bureaucracy to manhood. But social insurance was equally troubling. For in subjecting all individuals equally to potential government supervision and control, it suggested the helplessness of union members and, to some, of the entire labor movement. For the AFL, what appeared to be a choice of technical solutions to a serious economic problem represented far larger conceptions of who was and was not a man and of how the dignity and freedom of workers were to be preserved. We read the tension between the lines of both discussions within the CES and the congressional debates that followed.

Notions of social insurance came to the United States from Europe, where by the 1930s they had been adopted in various forms by several countries.[33] Germany had sickness insurance after 1884, as had Austria, Hungary, Norway, and Luxembourg after the end of the nineteenth century. By 1911, Germany, Britain, and Austria were among the countries that had comprehensive programs that covered such things as work accidents, health care, and maternity costs for poor and working women and provided pensions for the aged and disabled. All these programs incorporated relatively broad coverage of industrial workers. Financed at least partially by general tax revenues, they envisaged an active role for government in improving conditions of employment, as well as a commitment to reeducate and train workers for available jobs. Increasingly in the 1920s and 1930s, as state after state assumed responsibility for economic crises, the best programs came to provide a seamless web of coverage: unemployment insurance, followed by relief, or the dole, to reduce distress when job possibilities faded, and old age pensions for the superannuated.

Most Americans did not become familiar with these programs until the late 1920s, but long before that, they had entered the vocabulary of social reform popularized by two immigrants, Abraham Epstein and Isaac Rubinow. Epstein, truculent and assertive in character, emerged onto the unemployment scene after two decades of work with reform groups. In 1927, he organized the American Association for Old Age Security. From the platform it provided, he argued that the financial problems of old age melded into those of workers in their forties and fifties, who found it more difficult than younger workers to get new jobs when theirs were eliminated by technology or economic downturns.[34] Rubinow, a physician by training before he took a second degree in economics, had a long background in social insurance schemes, including workmen's compensation, industrial accidents, and health insurance, when he turned his attention to unemployment insurance. The author of the most respected argument for social insurance, published in 1913, he had briefly been a vice president of Epstein's Association for Old Age Security, but the two men had a difficult personal relationship and parted company. Rubinow earned his living mostly by consulting.[35] On the CES, their ideas were best reflected by Barbara Nachtrieb Armstrong—of whom we shall hear more later.

Rubinow and Epstein proposed to attack the problem of unemployment by increasing the purchasing power of workers. As Epstein put it, they hoped to "secure the worker and his family against the economic emergencies resulting from the temporary or permanent loss of a job through unemployment, sickness, invalidity or old age." They aimed to "guarantee the wage-earner and his dependents a minimum of income during periods when, through forces largely beyond his control, his earnings are impaired or cut off."[36] To do this, they agreed, would require at least statewide pooling of employer contributions in a single government-supervised fund. Epstein, watching the evolution of the British model, preferred a system that incorporated government subsidies and adjusted benefits geared to the family size of beneficiaries—a preference that would have blurred the lines between insurance and relief. Rubinow sharply disagreed, insisting on the crucial importance of social insurance principles, which required an entirely self-funded system with benefits aligned to contributions from employees and their employers.

Their ideas received their most effective airing during a lengthy debate over the Workers Unemployment and Social Insurance Bill, generally known as the Lundeen bill. Named after Ernest Lundeen, the Minnesota congressman who introduced it into Congress in 1934, the bill was largely drafted by the impeccably credentialed Mary van Kleeck, then director of research for the eminent Russell Sage Foundation. Van Kleeck served as director of the World War I Women in Industry Service that preceded the Women's Bureau of the Department of Labor. She had been a staunch supporter of protective labor legislation for women until, under the influence of the depression, she became more sympathetic to an expanded government role in relieving poverty for all workers.[37] The Lundeen bill provided insurance "for all workers, including all wage earners, all salaried workers, farmers, professional workers, and the self-employed." It guaranteed compensation equal to average earnings, and in no case less than a minimum standard of living.[38] It prohibited discrimination because of age, sex, race, or color, and it specifically included those who worked part-time and in agricultural and domestic or professional work. It covered loss of wages due to maternity, sickness, accident, and old age, and it provided allowances for mothers of children under eighteen with no male support. Costs were not to be borne by payroll taxes but paid for by the federal government out of general revenues.[39] Like other major proposals for social insurance at the time, the Lundeen bill tied benefits to work. Unlike them, it threatened to override gender and racial proscription by defining work capaciously enough to include virtually everyone. Supported by communists, socialists, and other radicals including African-American organizations represented by the National Negro Congress, the Lundeen bill was angrily opposed by almost everyone who supported more moderate unemployment insurance programs, including especially the AFL leadership.

Among the opponents were the disciples of John R. Commons who peopled the Committee on Economic Security. Commons was, in 1934, recently retired from teaching at the University of Wisconsin. His *Institutional Economics* had just been published, and the third volume of his *History of Labor in the United States* was about to go to press. In these books, he elaborated his notions of the economic institutions that sustained a democratic capitalism. Most forcefully, he advocated the notion that workers, like capitalists, were "citizens of industry," each with a stake in prosperity.[40] He conceived the right to work as essential to the exercise of citizenship, for, as he wrote early in his career, "the right to work is the right of access to the land, the machinery, the capital, whose products support life and liberty." And "the rights of liberty and property are the conditions on which personal character and responsibility are based."[41] To this end he supported the collective individualism of the American Federation of Labor, with its deep commitment to liberty earned through the manly freedom to work.

Industry's part of this compact was to provide employment: to stabilize work and ensure its availability. Commons believed that large employers should shoulder the responsibility for seasonal and technological employment fluctuations, arguing with most of his fellow economists that they, after all, caused most unemployment. Given adequate incentives, they could prevent it.[42] Modeling his tactics on those that had successfully produced workmen's compensation laws, Commons began in the period around World War I

*John Commons, University of Wisconsin economist and mentor to a generation of policy makers, in 1934.* COURTESY, STATE HISTORICAL SOCIETY OF WISCONSIN.

"to extend this principle to unemployment. Why not," he asked, "make individual employers responsible for their own unemployment, instead of so-called society?"[43] Pursuing this goal, the Association for the Advancement of Labor Legislation (which he had helped found and which was run by two of his former students, John Andrews and Irene Osgood) persuaded Harvard law professor Louis Brandeis to draft an unemployment compensation bill to be introduced into the Massachusetts legislature in 1916. Brandeis turned the job over to his younger colleague Felix Frankfurter when he was tapped for the Supreme Court, but, as we shall see, he never lost interest in the issue.[44]

We have already met Brandeis as the architect of the successful brief that gave women the protections of labor legislation in 1908. After that feat, he publicly supported health and old age insurance for workers and life insurance to care for their widows and orphans, as well as unemployment compensation. He defended these initiatives in language familiar to both the labor movement and maternalist women's groups. Politically, he argued, the American worker was free, "as far as the law can make him so. But is he really free? Can any man be really free who is constantly in danger of becoming dependent for mere subsistence upon somebody and something else than his own exertion and conduct? Men are not free while financially dependent upon the will of other individuals. Financial dependence is consistent with freedom only where claim to support rests upon right and not upon favor."[45] Brandeis's efforts to achieve social legislation that would both care for dependent women and children and preserve the rights of working men persisted into his Supreme Court years.

Deeply opposed by employer and business groups, the Massachusetts bill got nowhere. In 1921, Commons, in consultation with Frankfurter, refined his notions into a new bill, thereafter distributed to the states by the Association for the Advancement of Labor Legislation. It entirely overlooked social insurance, with its effort to replace lost wages, in favor of efforts to persuade employers to regularize work. The bill (often called the Wisconsin plan because it was passed in modified form in only one state, Wisconsin) embodied two of Commons's favorite principles: first, that responsibility for reducing unemployment lay in the hands of employers, not the government; second, that workers' eligibility for compensation derived from the direct contributions of their employers. No one whose employer did not have a plan would be covered. In contrast to most European industrial states, which envisaged an active role for government in improving conditions of employment, as well as a commitment to reeducate and train workers for available jobs, Commons imagined a far narrower governmental jurisdiction. Rather, he wanted each employer held accountable for his own workers and accordingly argued that each should be assessed at a rate consistent with his own record of success. In Commons's view (and in that of his students who designed New Deal legislation), requiring employers to contribute to a fund to compensate workers would provide the incentive for self-policing. This plan, later called experience rating, mandated higher rates for employers who failed to "stabilize" their workforces than for those who succeeded. Successful employers not only paid lower rates, they could recoup a portion of their original assessment.[46] At the same time, the plan imagined workers receiving only minimal benefits for short periods—no more than enough to tide them over a tough patch.

By the time the debate hit the national agenda in the early years of the depression, criticism of the Wisconsin plan abounded. Advocates of social insurance, Abraham Epstein and Isaac Rubinow among them, believed the Commons plan was no insurance at all: it relied too heavily on employers' goodwill, as well as their prosperity and skill, and its employer-managed reserve funds could be readily depleted in economic downturns. Economist Eveline Burns characterized it as designed "not so much to pay benefits to workers as to provide a mechanism for putting pressure on employers to stabilize employment . . . mainly an incentive taxation device."[47] Yet it remained attractive to many: its conception of governmental jurisdiction elegantly echoed popular American images of freedom, for it eschewed the collective responsibility of social insurance in favor of each employer's individual responsibility to succeed. "I was," Commons tells us, "trying to save capitalism by making it good."[48] And it resonated with the labor movement's conceptions of earned benefits—provided as a matter of right.

To save the fundamental principles of the Wisconsin plan, Commons's former student William Leiserson developed an alternative, which came to be known as the Ohio plan. Leiserson, a professor at Antioch College, working with University of Chicago economist Paul Douglas and Elizabeth Magee, secretary of the Consumers' League of Ohio, invited Rubinow (then living in Cincinnati) to join in as well.[49] Together, they produced a modified plan that accepted much of Commons's vision but bent in the direction of social insurance by proposing pooled funds (for greater security) and joint employer-employee contributions (for larger benefits: fifteen dollars a week compared to Wisconsin's ten dollars, payable for up to sixteen weeks compared to Wisconsin's ten weeks).

Their proposal drew mixed reviews. Social insurance advocates appreciated its effort to share the risks of unemployment by pooling reserve funds, but they disliked the state-based features it retained. Labor representatives applauded its lesser reliance on the goodwill of employers while objecting vehemently to the demand that workers be required to contribute.[50] Once again a well-established sense of manly freedom fueled the labor movement's positions. Aiming at the idea of joint contributions, they asked why employers, who had created the unemployment problem, should be able to get off scot-free (they would, after all, pass costs on to consumers) while workers suffered from reduced wages. They objected to the helplessness of workers placed in this situation. And, even as they applauded the idea of pooled funds, they protested the likelihood that government would collude with a coercive employer to exercise "leverage over employment terms."[51] Employers resented the shared risk of a pooled system, believing it unfair that those who effectively prevented unemployment among their own workers should be required to pay for the poor labor-management policies of inefficient industries. And, they argued, individual reserve accounts could be more effectively managed than huge state funds to meet the needs of industry.[52] Consistently, even enlightened employers who believed some form of unemployment insurance to be inevitable preferred individual employer reserve accounts.

Despite the criticism, the architects of the Ohio plan can hardly be described as radical. They never imagined the seamless systems funded by general revenue then beginning to emerge in Europe. Instead, seeking to accommodate their program to American tropes of self-sufficiency, they rigidly tied employer contributions to wage-related assessments, and compensation to each individual's earned wages. As in the Wisconsin plan, these

*William Leiserson, architect of the influen-
tial Ohio plan for unemployment insurance.* COURTESY, STATE HISTORICAL SOCI-
ETY OF WISCONSIN.

associations provided the legitimacy for covered workers to claim benefits as
"rights," the sine qua non for labor movement approval. And, like the Wisconsin plan, the Ohio plan expected employers, not general tax revenue, to pay all
or most of the freight. Both plans aimed to promote employment stability, so
they limited coverage to those who worked in the primary industrial sector.
Both plans incorporated provisions to charge employers on the basis of their
employment records—experience rating. And both balanced this concession
to employers by guaranteeing the independence of working men through an
administrative apparatus that would "not depend upon the arbitrary judgment of the administrative officials as in poor relief, but on the sole question
whether the risk covered by the insurance system has actually arisen."[53] In
both, then, eligibility for insurance through certain kinds of wage labor would
measure the virtues of citizens, inevitably diminishing the comparative social
rights of those who did not, or could not, regularly participate.

   In distinguishing what kinds of wage work would promote eligibility for
social insurance and tying rights to particular patterns of labor force attachment, both programs conceptualized participation in ways that discounted
the lives of the vast majority of African Americans, members of other minority
groups, and most women. If this was obscured with regard to African Americans by a rhetoric that paid obeisance to the responsibility of industry and the
rights of states, it was crystalline with regard to women. Only relatively large
producing industries (where most women of any color and most African
Americans did not work) could conceivably regularize work or develop the
individual insurance fund necessary to provide even minimal compensation.

Only workers who remained in the labor force for lengthy periods could reap benefits. The idea of regularizing work reflected a notion of rights to work that, we have discovered, explicitly excluded women who were not providers and tacitly dismissed all women as actually or potentially married. Each plan thus promised to extend new citizenship rights to men in particular (largely white) labor force sectors while denying them to other men and to virtually all women in the labor force. Epstein, who grumblingly supported the Ohio plan, cited in its defense the 88 percent of married women whom the 1930 census claimed to have earned no wages: "The American standard assumes a normal family of man, wife, and two or three children, with the father fully able to provide for them out of his own income. This standard presupposes no supplementary earnings from either the wife or young children. . . . The wife is a homemaker rather than a wage-earner. . . . The needs of these families must be considered paramount."[54]

Still, even as the representatives of African-American organizations leveled sharp criticisms at the exclusions embedded in these proposals, most women did not challenge their exclusionary biases. Even when an amalgamated version of the Ohio and Wisconsin plans became the basis for conversations within the CES, and ultimately the root of the unemployment compensation system adopted by Congress, women remained silent. Informed by popular beliefs about the significance of marriage in the lives of ordinary wage-earning women, most maternalists pursued social policies designed to reinforce women's continuing family roles. Instead of fighting for women's rights to work, they successfully placed motherhood at the center of the legislative agenda for women workers and encouraged and sustained prevailing conceptions of women's working lives as adjuncts to the family. Perhaps we should not fault them, for they acted on definitions of family developed through fights for protective labor legislation and won, in consequence, means-tested plans that would enable poor women to care for children without wage work. Their relative failure to address work-related issues not only left the sphere of wage work to men but, arguably, allowed greater scope for the AFL's concern for manly liberty.

To be sure, female social reformers and labor leaders shared with other social activists a commitment to male providerhood. Yet the two groups deeply disagreed over whether government intervention would not simultaneously undermine the self-respect and independence that defined manliness. While maternalists placed great faith in government's capacity to shore up the family, the AFL remained committed to the idea of manly independence. An employer-controlled and government-regulated unemployment compensation plan would vitiate the principles of voluntarism by making, as Gompers had put it, "the means for life and thus liberty dependent on government supervision of the conditions of leaving employment."[55] In support of this idea, successive AFL conventions had voted against government unemployment insurance while supporting private union-employer plans and the thirty-hour week. What seemed like simple justice to many felt to labor like an attack. "You can't have unemployment insurance," declared AFL president William Green, "without agreeing to a set-up that will, to a large degree, govern and control our activities ... then you must be willing to give up some of the things you now possess. You can't have an unemployment insurance plan without registration. You must report, you must subject yourself in every way to the control of the law."[56]

The AFL was no monolith, and pressure from several state federations and local and international unions led it to reconsider its position beginning in 1929. Several years of long and heated disputes within AFL councils and on the convention floor followed. Opponents decried handouts from government and protested cowardly submission to state authority. Did American workers, asked a member of the 1930 executive council, echoing the language of the courts that justified protective labor legislation for women, want to follow the pattern of European schemes "under which the worker becomes a ward of the state and subject to discipline by employers under state authority?" In his view, unemployment insurance challenged the American Federation of Labor to decide whether it "shall continue to hew to the line in demanding a greater freedom for the working people of America, or whether liberty shall be sacrificed in a degree sufficient to enable the workers to obtain a small measure of unemployment relief under government supervision and control."[57]

At issue were three things that overlapped the labor movement's concerns with legislating shorter hours. First was the creation of state bureaucracies that would undermine the principle of voluntarism by imposing what labor called "government supervision." Second was the construction of a fearful administrative apparatus. "Every system," argued the executive council in a report that rejected the idea, "contemplates supervision and control by both federal and state governments and will require registration, not only of the aliens among the workers, but of all workers." Finally, compulsory unemployment insurance would provide employers with power even over the jobless. Any such program, insisted AFL vice president Mathew Woll, would remind a worker constantly "that his employer holds what in effect amounts to at least a temporary veto power over his right to benefits when unemployed." This would, he argued, inevitably increase the power of the employer and lead to "a virtual surrender on the part of the workers . . . of their right to organize. . . . Shall we be content to carry industrial passports because they have a government label?"[58]

Enmeshed in the fear of structures they could not influence or control, AFL leaders offered up a conception of liberty demanding defense by courageous men. Throwing down the gauntlet to the cowards among them who would place their faith in the false promises of government authority, Woll demanded to know if members had "lost courage to the point where we regard freedom no longer as the greatest essential of life and the most necessary element in human progress." Nor did he shrink from religious symbolism: "In return for a slice of bread—a mess of pottage, as it were—the workers are being asked . . . to yield up their birthright, to practically surrender in their struggle for liberty." In this struggle over liberty, family support and personal well-being alike would take second place: "Have we come to that position in our labor movement," asked Vice President Victor Olander incredulously, "that we are about to say that one of the most precious liberties we have . . . must be surrendered forsooth, because our people are hungry and they must eat?"[59]

To combat this strong language, supporters of unemployment insurance constructed an alternative conception of manhood. James Duncan of Seattle's Central Labor Council tried his hand at creating one. Invoking William Green's presidential address, which had demanded a new right, "the right of men to work," he insisted that if the government denied "us the right to work" it "must at least provide some means of feeding our families while we are waiting for the opportunity to work." Unemployment insurance, he suggested, far from degrading a man, would give him "a chance to stand up and say, 'No, I will not go in and work for less than my fellows get. I at least will not starve to death.'" Against the executive council's defense of freedom, liberty, and independence, Duncan, making common cause with social reformers, called for a different form of manliness: solidarity with fellow workers and family provision. "I want men to get the sustenance from somewhere so that they can stand up like real men and say, 'No, I am getting enough to get by on. I don't have to undermine my fellows, I will stick to my unemployment insurance until I can go to work with my fellows and maintain my self-respect.'"[60] Philip Ickler of the Pensacola, Florida, Central Labor Council offered yet another justification for the manliness of unemployment insurance. "I don't believe," he argued, that "we are making beggars out of all who need it. . . . It furnishes at least a little help to keep our fellow workers in the militant fighting spirit."[61]

Would unemployment insurance contribute to beggary or fend it off? Some of the same labor leaders who had enthusiastically promoted legislation on behalf of women could not contemplate its negative consequences for manly independence. Andrew Furuseth of the Seamen's Union is a good example. Friend of Louis Brandeis and enthusiastic supporter of special laws for women, Furuseth mounted a last-ditch resistance to unemployment insurance. After the 1932 convention finally accepted the idea, he rose to articulate what he called his "unalterable opposition." No such law, he declared, had been enacted "as will retain the working man his independence and courage. ... I think you are making a mistake, men.... I can't stop you, but the road you are traveling is the road that leads to the destruction of humanity and the destruction of this nation and of all other nations that can find no other way than to make out of a man a pleading beggar and a man who must go for his goods to others."[62]

By the time Furuseth spoke, the executive council had acted. Overwhelmed by pressure to combat existing unemployment, it reversed its position in November 1932 and persuaded William Green to reverse his. While it decried the continuing economic crisis, and once again repeated its conviction that a thirty-hour week would provide the surest solution to unemployment, it offered the convention an industry-funded plan that it thought members could live with.[63] In withdrawal, President Green tacitly aligned himself with the Commons proposals. "If compulsory unemployment insurance is forced upon our industrial, political and economic life, it will be because industrial ownership and management has failed to provide and preserve these opportunities for working men and women," he told convention delegates.[64] Workers, the executive council affirmed, "are as much entitled to work security, to enjoy the opportunity to work, as the owners of capital are to returns from their investments." Industry's failure should be charged to it by the imposition of compulsory unemployment insurance, paid for by employers alone. It should be "clearly recognized as a legal right earned by previous employment within the state."[65]

But no one was completely happy with this solution, and the executive council continued to be wary that the "right" contained in unemployment insurance be absolute, insisting, for example, that drawing on unemployment insurance not infringe on rights of suffrage or on other civil rights.[66] This would be a new, an added, an "earned" right. "We are going to propose and insist," Green told the AFL's leaders in the fall of 1934, "that Congress and the State legislatures enact unemployment insurance legislation, old age pension legislation, the abolition of child labor, and the development here of a social order that will make for the highest degree of citizenship."[67] The gesture meant little. By then, the president had already convened the CES, and its staff and technical committees were hard at work. William Green, who had a seat on the Advisory Council, remained a largely silent member, leading Edwin Witte to dismiss labor's role in the formulation of the final act. It was not, he wrote later, "a major player."[68] Witte was wrong. As much as anyone, the labor movement had set the terms within which the debate would be conducted.

## A Sieve with Holes

On the table before the Committee on Economic Security in the fall of 1934 was a proposal drawn from the recently tabled Wagner-Lewis bill and reflecting the ideas of Louis Brandeis and the Commons/Harvard axis. Drafted by Paul Raushenbush, Brandeis's son-in-law, and Thomas Eliot, a young lawyer in the Department of Labor, the proposal was based on the Wisconsin law that Paul and Elizabeth Brandeis Raushenbush had drawn up in 1931.[69] Wagner-Lewis proposed a federal tax on payrolls, 90 percent of which would be forgiven (or offset) for employers who contributed to either their own state-supervised reserve accounts or to statewide pooled accounts. The offset, which removed the federal government from a direct relationship to the recipients of unemployment compensation, was meant to avoid questions of constitutionality; it also provided states with maximum discretion to develop whatever unemployment insurance program they wished. Employers' contributions were to vary with the employment records of the employer: those with stable workforces would pay less. Everything else, including the level of benefits, possible employee contributions, and eligibility for coverage, would be determined by the states. It was not a bill that labor could like very much, for it left the states (and their most powerful employers) huge discretion. Yet Green reluctantly testified in favor of it when it was presented to Congress in the spring of 1934. "We believe," he told the assembled legislators, "a man will retain his independence and his manhood better if he is permitted to earn a living." In the absence of jobs "we are inevitably forced to this position."[70] The AFL continued to support it halfheartedly when a modified version entered the Social Security bill.

Other oppositional voices clamored more noisily. Mary van Kleeck protested the limits imposed by unemployment insurance that covered only "a specified group of beneficiaries who join in establishing these reserves." The Lundeen bill, with its tempting offer of general revenues to fund government-sponsored social insurance, had been favorably reviewed by the House Committee on Labor and reported out to the House. Supported by socialists and communists as well as by a wide range of radical groups, it promised to subsidize all wage earners without regard to the work they did. From van Kleeck's perspective, only government could meet the needs of mass unemployment. "The economic system as a whole, through taxation," she wrote in the *New Republic*, "should provide compensation for unemployment." This fundamental difference between most European models and the one before the CES captured van Kleeck's distress: "Rules and regulations are made in advance which exclude all those not involved in the contributions. They exclude, for example, the smaller establishments, and ordinarily they make no provision for the self-employed, including the farmer."[71]

Even within the labor movement Lundeen had many champions, including a handful of international unions like the Amalgamated Clothing Workers of America, the International Ladies Garment Workers Union, the United Textile Workers (the leading organizers of women workers), and the United Mine Workers of America.[72] Thousands of union locals signed petitions in support. But the AFL leadership, terrified by the wide opportunity for government control and Lundeen's vague promises of government subsidy independent of wage work, resisted all efforts at comprehensive social insurance. When a breakaway group of members drafted a resolution in favor of comprehensive social insurance, it was excluded from the organization's 1932 convention. The dissidents testified at congressional hearings the following year, only to be vilified by the AFL.[73] For many reasons, business leaders and the staff of the CES shared the AFL's fear of Lundeen. Their concerns revolved around the bill's failure to distinguish workers from each other, essentially providing benefits to all in the form of relief instead of as an earned right. In the end, Witte welcomed its defeat, attributing it to labor: "Thanks to labor's clear denunciation, the 'thunder' for this measure never became more than a tinpan disharmony, which fooled scarcely anyone."[74]

The debate within the CES therefore occurred within a narrow framework, bounded by the rights of free men on the one side and the family and economic responsibilities of individual workers and their employers on the other. For all that they are difficult to see, the technical differences among committee members, staff, and advisers over which there were fierce fights, reflected various takes on these issues. Bryce Stewart, chair of the Technical Board's committee on unemployment insurance, strongly supported a federal program that would pool employer contributions in state-based accounts, provide for additional government subsidies when necessary, and set uniform standards for benefits, coverage, and eligibility. Stewart had come out of the industrial relations movement, a pioneer consultant to corporations on pension and welfare programs. Still, his desires ran counter to those of Witte and the Wisconsin group, who remained committed to individual employer reserve accounts that would encourage employers to regularize unemployment. As Eliot later commented, drafting the act turned out to be complicated because "the Wisconsin people and Justice Brandeis deeply believed in the principle that employers could be stimulated to regularize employment. . . . To fail to include such a provision would be to wipe out the philosophy of the Wisconsin Act."[75] To avoid a stalemate, Witte encouraged the Advisory Council to consider the issue. It set up its own distinguished subcommittee on unemployment insurance, headed by Frank Graham. That panel, which included representatives of labor, employers, and social reformers, divided. It made clear that any unemployment insurance would be better than none and, by a small majority, endorsed a program with national standards. The CES, guided by Perkins, disagreed. Perkins had returned from a 1931 fact-finding trip to England persuaded that charging each industry the cost of unemployment would do little to prevent the disease.[76] But she feared the political difficulties of getting a national scheme through Congress and remained silent.

The bill that went to Congress suggested a provision very much like that offered by Wagner-Lewis: a tax offset plan in which states could choose the program they wanted to offer. Most advocates of state-based options noted that they preferred them because they limited the federal government's capacity to set uniform standards and in so doing allowed states to have maximum control over how to distribute benefits. They did not generally defend state options on racial grounds, but race clearly occupied their minds. Southern congressmen could not vote for a plan that was racially inclusive, nor one that allowed the federal government to set standards without accommodating racial differences in pay. Business joined southerners on this issue. Most businessmen who had come around to believing in the inevitability of unemployment compensation continued to urge, with the Commons school, that its primary purpose should be to help stabilize employment. They preferred legislation to help them do that, rather than to provide more generous benefits. A state-based program would provide the possibility for individual reserve accounts and was likely to be more sensitive to the experience-rating option that would save them money in the long run. State-based programs suited the needs of women's groups as well. Their influence tended to reside in state bureaucracies, where women leaders tended to be more comfortably ensconced than in the larger federal agencies that seemed to be displacing them. From one perspective, then, political forces eager to retain power in the states jousted with those who sought a national program. From another, a state-based program seemed the most effective way to produce a contributory unemployment system.

But a dense network of personal ties and political commitments also prevented a truly national program from emerging. The state-based idea had originated with Commons in Wisconsin, the home state of Witte and many of the CES staff and the province of the politically powerful Senator Robert La Follette. It was also the pet project of Louis Brandeis, whose daughter Elizabeth and son-in-law (aided by Thomas Eliot) had drafted the Wagner-Lewis bill. Brandeis was inordinately invested in the project. His biographer Philippa Strum tells us that he visited FDR as president about only two matters: the plight of the European Jews and "a federal plan for unemployment insurance." Brandeis asked Elizabeth to let him see a draft of the bill before his visit to FDR, and he is credited with incorporating the idea of a federal payroll tax and state tax offset in it.[77] Frankfurter, intensely loyal to his mentor, in turn had earned the respect of organizations like the National Consumers' League and the National Women's Trade Union League, with which he had worked for two decades. Loyalty to old allies may well have influenced the decisions of these groups as much as any principled preference. And the network of women encompassed Frances Perkins, to whom Frankfurter was attached by past history and sympathy. Perkins had also worked in New York State with Advisory Council member Marion Folsom, the architect of Eastman Kodak's pioneering unemployment insurance program and an eager advocate of individual employer reserves. Perkins's own position may have been ambivalent by the time the bill came to the CES, but she was not ready to eliminate individual reserves and state standards entirely.

When Bryce Stewart tried to challenge the Wagner-Lewis model on its merits, he engendered only controversy. Lacking support from either Witte or Altmeyer, he turned to Barbara Armstrong, an expert on European unemployment insurance, for help. Armstrong, virulently opposed to the Wisconsin plan and unfamiliar with the byzantine network of ties that bound the major actors together, appealed to Frankfurter. "I knew—and nobody that I knew who regarded himself or herself as a respectable economist thought—that Miss Brandeis' views of the individual plant reserve were anything but absurd. Economically speaking, you can't have a reserve of one."[78] Could Frankfurter, with his close ties to Brandeis and his family, talk them out of their position? Frankfurter sent his two top aides to talk to her. She recalled the conversation with despair. Whatever his personal opinions, they told her, he could not intervene; his loyalty to Brandeis prevented it. In the end, the

*Elizabeth Brandeis.* COURTESY, STATE HIS-
TORICAL SOCIETY OF WISCONSIN.

CES endorsed a federal tax offset system that would permit states either to pool funds or to allow individual employer reserve accounts, to assess employee as well as employer contributions, to set their own standards for eligibility, and to formulate their own requirements for distributing benefits. No federal subsidy was included. Shortly afterward, Stewart resigned. The decision was justified by Folsom on political grounds: "If you're going to have a state plan, the states ought to have leeway in it. If you're going to have a national system, then you're going to have a knockdown dragout fight on which type it's going to be."[79]

The maternalist women's groups, most of them supportive of unemployment insurance in principle, weighed in on the side of individual employer reserves rooted in state-based programs. The NCL agreed with the value of each state initiating "its own system of unemployment benefits creating machinery to suit its local needs."[80] Its members tended to be concerned with protecting the purchasing power of the family, rather than with providing insurance for women as workers.[81] And though several who testified at House and Senate hearings objected to the failure of the bill to set uniform standards and benefits for those covered, they did not advocate a federal system.[82] Molly Dewson, whose close relationship with Perkins and whose presence on the Advisory Council might have made a difference, explicitly supported the Brandeis/Commons vision of the role of unemployment insurance in "regularizing employment."[83] On the Advisory Council, four of the five women who might be called maternalists voted for the Wagner-Lewis plan, along with all five employer members. They were joined by only one labor member: Henry Ohl, representing the Wisconsin State Federation of Labor.[84]

Reading through this material, one immediately regrets the failure of imagination among maternalist advocates of mothers' aid, who participated only marginally in these debates and who in the end supported the most limited solutions. The long reach of Louis Brandeis may account for some of their caution. In the spring of 1933, the board of directors of the National Consumers' League called a special meeting to discuss unemployment insurance.[85] Nicholas Kelley sat in the chair. Everyone was there, including Lucy Mason, Molly Dewson, and Pauline Goldmark. Josephine Goldmark, Louis Brandeis's sister-in-law, had been invited as a special guest. Eloquently she summed up the recent history of unemployment insurance, concluding that of the available plans, she much preferred "the Wisconsin law with its provision for House accounts by individual firms because of its pressure on employers to stabilize their own industries." She herself also preferred employee contributions, but she understood that this was very much opposed by labor and that no bill would pass without the support of organized labor. In the heated discussion that followed, Nicholas Kelley played the leading advocate for the pooling system. Mary Dewson and everyone else spoke for individual reserves. With Kelley alone opposing, the board at last voted a resolution "to support state legislation providing for compulsory unemployment reserves, publicly administered and kept in accounts segregated for individual employers."[86] The board seems to have backed off this rigid position in later months, with members preferring any insurance to none and agreeing to support the CES, whatever it finally decided.[87] And though some chapters actively supported the passage of the Social Security Act, the evidence suggests that the most important women's group did not shape the content of this crucial piece of legislation.

Their energy invested in drafting programs for children and for maternal health care, their concern for women largely centered on motherhood, the NCL and its friends focused their energies on these relatively noncontroversial subjects. Katharine Lenroot, then acting director of the Children's Bureau and a member of the consulting staff of the CES, confessed to ignoring it. "I don't recall ever discussing that with her," she said of her conversations with Frances Perkins about the unemployment insurance debate.[88] Maternalists spent their energies on issues relating to security for children, and, indeed, Edwin Witte emphasized their contribution: "Aid for maternal and child service was never once questioned in the executive sessions of the congressional committees or during the debate in the two houses," he tells us.[89] But if maternalists successfully attained the principle of relief to mothers of children, they abandoned employment issues to other actors. In failing to challenge the scope of work-related entitlements and the structure of eligibility for benefits (including the exclusion of household and agricultural workers), they conceded the loss of crucial citizenship benefits. In return, they won what may well have been a pyrrhic victory: the protection of the state for women without male support and for their children. The gendered right to work had exacted a heavy price.

Organized labor, which disliked the flexible provisions that emerged, had little choice but to ally itself with the CES plan. The AFL had backed itself into a corner. Equally suspicious of state bureaucracies and legislatures and of employer influence, and uncertain whether unemployment insurance would cool workers' loyalties to their trade unions, Green had failed to take a strong stand either in the CES Advisory Council or before Congress.[90] He would have preferred, he told the Senate Finance Committee, a plan that filtered contributions through the federal government in order that one entity could more readily impose standards for eligibility and benefits; he deplored the possibility of individual reserve accounts, which failed to provide workers with security; he hoped no state would exact contributions from workers; he thought the payroll tax could easily be raised from 3 to 5 percent so that a more generous benefit might be paid. Most especially, he wanted to ensure benefits sufficiently high to guarantee that labor could maintain its purchasing power.[91] Though the AFL would have preferred to give vastly less discretion to the states (and might have allied itself with African Americans to this end), its commitment to voluntarism bound it to a contributory program. It did not believe Wisconsin employers could or would, given incentives, prevent unemployment, but even in those plans, benefits were offered as of "right." It was more willing to hazard the risks of individual reserves than to fund a program (Lundeen style) with general revenues. Conflating unemployment benefits with relief threatened to dilute the relationship of benefits to contributions and undermine male independence. If unemployment benefits were inevitable, they must be tied to employers' contributions. Everything else was secondary, including what the leadership quickly recognized as the unfortunate consequence of legislative discretion in excluding awkward categories of workers.

Labor had given up a lot to get benefits that sustained male dignity, available as a matter of right, without administrative or bureaucratic discretion. Bounded by a conception of unemployment insurance largely designed to provide incentives for employers to "regularize" employment, the issue of who

*Left: Grace Abbott, member of the Committee on Economic Security, which drafted the Social Security Act, in a 1929 photograph.* COURTESY, LIBRARY OF CONGRESS. *Right: Katharine Lenroot succeeded Grace Abbott as chair of the Children's Bureau.* COURTESY, STATE HISTORICAL SOCIETY OF WISCONSIN.

was appropriately defined as a "worker" assumed paramount importance. Gender was a major constituent in that definition. At every turn it emerged as a dynamic agent—its role, as a Freudian might say, "overdetermined." It participated in the initial conception of which jobs should be "regularized" and which not. Its hand was strengthened by the issues of voluntarism prominent in the labor movement, where notions of masculinity fostered suspicion of government intervention of every kind. It was sustained and enhanced by the attitudes of women reformers whose shared sense of the nature of breadwinning for the family, as well as their personal connections to the Brandeis group, blinded them to possibilities for supporting women's wage work. It fueled continuing issues of coverage and availability that continued to wreak havoc with the desire for uniformity.

Debate over who would be covered revolved around so-called marginal members of the labor force. The original bill applied "federal tax to employers of four or more during 13 weeks of the taxable year."[92] This was altered by the House Ways and Means Committee to ten or more employees in twenty weeks of the taxable year and finally compromised at eight employees over thirteen weeks. Witte comments that the change resulted from the insistence of one congressman who wanted the canneries in his district exempted. The committee also excluded a range of other heavily women-employing sectors, including federal, state, and local governments (clerical workers to teachers), non-profits, agriculture, and domestic service in private homes. To this list, the Senate Finance Committee added orphanages and hospitals. The upshot was the exclusion of 55 percent of African-American workers and 80 percent of all women workers, including more than 87 percent of wage-earning African-American women.[93] Anybody could have seen this coming. Charles Houston, representing the National Association for the Advancement of Colored People (NAACP), warned the Senate Finance Committee that "from a Negro's point of view" the economic security bill looked "like a sieve with holes just big enough for the majority of Negroes to fall through."[94]

Among the exclusions, Witte comments, some "were not advocated specifically by anyone but were suggested by members of the committee. Agricultural labor and domestic services were excluded as a matter of course."[95] Yet University of Chicago economist Paul Douglas, adviser to the Ohio Commission, which developed the Ohio plan, and generally sympathetic to labor, had proposed such exclusions in his influential monograph *Standards of Unemployment Insurance*, published in 1932.[96] There he insisted that some occupations might be excluded, among them agriculture, "on realistic grounds because otherwise the farming interests will preclude passage." He proposed omitting domestic service "on grounds of expediency" and then suggested, as it turned out quite incorrectly, that this would not matter because "there's not much unemployment among household workers."[97] Most members of these groups would in any event have been denied coverage because they worked irregularly and for small employers. Their additional exclusion seems gratuitous, designed, as Diana Pearce suggests, to eliminate anyone whose unemployment was considered to be of his or her own making.[98]

If racial agendas remained buried in the language of state prerogatives and putative administrative difficulties, gendered understandings floated quickly to the surface. The labor movement, fearing arbitrary judgment, had placed its faith in unemployment benefits available as a matter of right. It believed it had won them. When Arthur Altmeyer (then administrator of the Social Security Board) told the AFL convention in the fall of 1938 that the Social Security Act provided benefits "geared to the worker's wages—and benefits that come to him as something earned, to which he has a right, irrespective of his need," he affirmed that unemployment benefits had become an attribute of citizenship.[99] He did not mention that they were differentially available to some workers. When the AFL executive council asked Congress to "separate the functions and services of an insurance nature from those providing public assistance," it acknowledged the value of benefits granted as a right. And when it demanded that waiting periods for unemployment insurance be reduced to a minimal period, it did so cognizant of a fundamental value: that benefits "are to provide security—not to undermine the results of industry and thrift before aid is available."[100]

The actions of architects and policy makers suggest that an unspoken contest over women's rights to work qualified the value of their citizenship from the beginning. For example, assumptions about what constituted "the real labor supply" pervaded the discussion. Consistent with another Douglas suggestion, the bill before Congress excluded temporary and part-time workers. "There are some, particularly women," he wrote, "who wish to be employed for only a few hours per day or per week. Such persons as these are only casual and incidental members of the real labor supply and do not need or deserve the same protection as those who are fully dependent upon industry for employment." Those involved in industry for "at least half of the standard working hours should come under unemployment insurance, but this should not be the case for those who have more than one leg in the home." Finally, he suggested, only those "customarily employed" ought to be eligible for benefits. The required number of weeks worked per year ought to be raised, he thought, "to exclude juveniles, married women and old people" who had "voluntarily withdrawn to their homes" when seasonal work ended. Those who worked only one season a year, he insisted, were not part of the "permanent labor supply."[101]

Such thinking was particularly important in light of the experience-rating provisions of unemployment insurance. As the law left the separate states to decide crucial questions of who should be covered and whether funds should be pooled, it also left them free to decide whether to raise or lower rates according to a particular employer's layoff record. All states eventually adopted such a system, which was designed to (and did) encourage employers to vigorously object to paying casual workers, those fired for good cause, and part-timers. The power of employers was reinforced by the requirement that they sign off before benefits were granted to workers. Not accidentally, the law also encouraged workers to join their employers in limiting eligibility for benefits. Since most employers were expected to pass the costs of unemployment insurance on to consumers or adjust wages to compensate for them, benefits constituted something of a deferred wage. Because the level of the benefits received was expected to be potentially higher if fewer and more consistent workers drew on them, workers had every incentive to help their employers limit the pool of eligible workers. Industry and employed workers thus colluded in the belief that including casual laborers, inefficient workers, part-timers, and so on would incur additional expenses. That these were among the poorest and least secure members of the labor force could not have escaped notice.

They were also disproportionately black, female, and married. Married women, it was thought, could potentially be costly to employers by dropping in and out of work. In a special section devoted to married women, Douglas characterized them as posing a "very ticklish" problem. Acknowledging that women "customarily employed in industry should of course be compensated for unemployment irrespective of whether or not they are married," he suggested that under some circumstances, a married woman might legitimately be excluded: where she was

> customarily supported by her husband's earning, ... had entered industry in order to meet some temporary emergency, and after having acquired eligibility under the act, then retired to strictly family life. Such a person would not in fact be at that time a member of the real army of potential wage-workers and should not, therefore, be a charge upon industry.[102]

Douglas would also exclude a woman who, though she might be a genuine member of the labor supply, "marries, and upon leaving industry claims unemployment benefit although she in fact does not wish to continue in employment." His skepticism about the motives of newly married women extended to all women who followed their husbands to new jobs. If, for example, her old skills were not in demand in the new location, she could be assumed, according to Douglas, to have dropped out of the labor supply. In his view, a woman who sought a job where none commensurate with her skills existed must be misrepresenting a desire for work, and benefits could be legitimately refused.

The long-term effects of these assumptions created precisely the administrative discretion the labor movement intended to avoid and whose absence labor held up as one of the measures of citizenship. When Douglas suggested that the threat of abuse from married women was so great that administrative authorities should be given "specific power to deal with cases of married women and to exclude them if they really were no longer genuine members of the labor supply," he encouraged skepticism as to whether unemployment benefits were earned rights—not conditional upon means testing or spousal support.

Questions as to whether women, particularly married women, constituted "genuine" members of the labor force persisted into the 1950s and beyond. In the immediate postwar period, it looked as if women were a greater proportion of claimants, drew benefits for longer, and exhausted their eligibility faster than men.[103] Rather than attributing these circumstances to their poorer employment prospects, the public perceived women who drew benefits as "cheaters." A 1950 *Reader's Digest* story reported outrage at a court decision allowing a woman to keep her unemployment benefits who had quit her forty-five-dollar-a-week job as a clerk-typist to marry. Under these circumstances, historian Edward Berkowitz tells us, experience rating provided incentives to "keep cheaters from the rolls and keep costs down."[104] Pregnancy and motherhood proved to be equally sticky issues. By the early 1950s, every state could exclude pregnant women from benefits on the grounds that they were unable to work; thirty states disqualified even job-hunting women for a specified number of weeks before and after childbirth. Some states flat-out refused benefits to pregnant women, and in others, pregnant women who quit their jobs might or might not be eligible for benefits depending on how strenuous a job was thought to be and whether the expectant mother was or was not thought willing to take and capable of doing a less strenuous job.[105] Similarly, a mother who refused a job during a particular part of the day for lack of child care might or might not be deemed eligible for benefits depending on whether an appropriate job was available during those hours.

Administrative discretion proved to be the answer, and labor found itself hoisted on the petard of its own gendered assumptions. Choosing to protect images of manhood and independence by limiting unemployment compensation, it discovered that the mechanism for doing that enhanced administrative power. For example, to inhibit what he described as an alarming growth in the numbers of housewives in the labor force, economist Richard Lester advocated protecting relatively high benefits for breadwinners by eliminating the claims of these "intermittent" or loosely attached workers. Why not, he asked, offer different benefit levels for those who had worked longer, who could not claim dependents, or who could demonstrate "substantial attachment" to the labor market; or limit job training only to long-term workers? As late as 1960, the benefit claims of women constituted, in the eyes of one authority, "obstacles to improvement in the benefit levels for more firmly attached workers."[106]

Applying administrative discretion to female claimants, and conditioning their eligibility on marital status or motherhood, ultimately threatened the theory that unemployment compensation was available as a matter of right. Trying to resolve this dilemma, supporters of the system advocated a diverse and inconsistent range of solutions that included removing pregnant women from the labor market altogether by providing them with disability insurance, offering children's allowances to parents who, by using them to pay for child care, could remain at work, and encouraging public investment to distribute additional household conveniences to wage-earning women. None of these solutions got wide attention, although, as we shall see, the tax system did bend in the direction of equity for parents. In their absence, experts continued strident demands for more restrictive administration to ensure that "women who do not want to work or cannot accept work do not get benefits."[107]

If this was not predictable, it could certainly have been anticipated by the bill's architects, who had formulated its unemployment provisions within the Commons school, which laid both responsibility and costs at the doorstep of the employer. The model was tacitly encouraged by the AFL, whose fear of state intervention, conception of work as a restricted good (to be reserved for men insofar as possible), and commitment to a particular kind of family well-being provided political momentum. In this context, a plan that induced employers to prevent unemployment in the existing workforce, that sustained and privileged a particular conception of masculinity, that pitted workers against each other, and that fostered a debate about who was entitled to the rights that accompanied work served to reinforce an existing gendered system. By the mid-1950s, even as eligibility requirements tightened and women continued to be excluded from many benefits, the value of those benefits had begun to rise significantly—widening the gap in gendered economic rights. Waiting periods for benefits decreased; the duration of benefits increased; beneficiaries won dependents' allowances in eleven states (in six of them, only for dependents under sixteen or eighteen).[108] The imbalance continued until the 1970s, and then a shift in the structure of occupations initiated a slow erosion. More part-time and contingent workers, more transient work relationships, more women in the workforce, and more work careers interrupted by family concerns for men and women encouraged policy makers to explore how to expand the system. But even as they debated, the proportions of men and women beneficiaries continued to shrink down to 35 percent of unemployed men and only 23 percent of unemployed women. In May of 1999, President William Clinton offered the revolutionary suggestion that unemployment benefits could legitimately cover workers who took time out to care for a new baby or who required other forms of parental leave from jobs. Enacting that proposal would be a symbolic stride toward attaining equitable economic citizenship for all kinds of people.

## A Foundling Dumped upon the Doorstep

Secretary of Labor Frances Perkins tells us that she pulled the bill that became the Fair Labor Standards Act (FLSA) out of her drawer when she thought the time was right. It had been sitting there for nearly four years, almost since her appointment as the first woman in a presidential cabinet, but she had despaired of its passage after the Supreme Court's 1935 decisions restricting the Agricultural Adjustment Act and the National Industrial Recovery Act had ended the federal government's first experiment with regulated wages and hours. Perkins had a long history of involvement with wages and hours regulations stemming back to her association with the coalition of women reformers headed by the National Consumers' League, whose primary goals included protective labor legislation for women and an end to child labor. She had, the story goes, agreed to head the Department of Labor only after she convinced the president to include minimum wages and maximum hours for workers in his agenda. For her, this was a moral issue of the highest sort. But her efforts had been stymied by the Supreme Court's refusal to extend legislation regulating working hours beyond women and children and its insistence that minimum wages violated the constitutional prerogatives of all workers—even those, like women and children, whom it sometimes described as "wards of the state."[109]

When, in March 1937, the Court unexpectedly overrode its own 1923 ruling against minimum wages and followed up by sustaining the constitutionality of the 1935 National Labor Relations Act, the time seemed ripe. The minimum wage decision had particularly commented on the relationship between wages and hours, noting that denial of a living wage to workers "casts the burden for their support upon the community."[110] Perkins opened her metaphorical desk drawer and offered Congress a bill that forbade the shipment in interstate commerce of goods that had not been produced under a rigorous set of labor standards by workers whose hours were to be specified. The bill proposed, for the first time in the United States, to establish national, not state-based, standards that would cover male as well as female workers.[111]

The bill to regulate labor standards had been well prepared to address the political realities that Congress would face in considering it. Drafted by a group that included the distinguished legal scholar and soon-to-be Supreme Court justice Felix Frankfurter, Labor Department lawyers Tom Corcoran and Ben Cohen, and their former colleague Charles Wyzanski—all of them veterans of the battles in and around Social Security and the thirty-hour week—it was designed to avoid the constitutional pitfalls encountered by earlier efforts to regulate health and morals utilizing the police power provisions of the Fourteenth Amendment. In advance of its introduction, Perkins, her friend Amalgamated Clothing Workers of America leader Sidney Hillman, Senator Hugo Black, and the president himself had discussed strategy. Hillman solicited the support of progressive business leaders like Robert Johnson, president of Johnson and Johnson pharmaceuticals and textiles, who in turn rounded up business support.[112]

To be sure, everyone anticipated opposition. Southern businessmen were bound to plead the lower cost of living in their region as a defense against nationwide standards; farmers and agricultural interests would surely object to including migratory and seasonal workers. But the bill's authors had sought to defuse some of these sensitive political issues by vesting in an administrative board the power to create differential wage rates even within industries in separate sections of the country and to exempt small employers. At the last minute, at the special request of a former head of the Children's Bureau, Grace Abbott, the drafters incorporated a provision to prohibit from interstate commerce goods made by children. Following a recommendation of the Women's Bureau, the bill proposed to regulate homework as well. The stage seemed set.

Introduced into Congress by two sympathetic advocates, Hugo Black in the Senate and William Connery (sponsor of the ill-fated thirty-hour bill) in the House, it was placed on a fast track. House and Senate joint hearings got under way in early June 1937. They were kicked off by a star witness, Assistant Attorney General Robert Jackson, who had developed a strategy to overcome the objections of a Supreme Court widely thought to be the main obstacle to passage. As Jackson explained to Congress, this bill, unlike earlier state efforts to regulate the hours of men and the wages of all workers, was rooted not in the police power of the state to protect health and well-being but in the federal government's authority to regulate interstate commerce. Perkins herself followed up with strong support. She liked the bill, she said, though she objected to the clause exempting small employers, and she wanted an amendment adding a prohibition on goods made in industrial home work. Pushed on the question of whether the minimum pay provisions should apply equally to men and women, Perkins seemed somewhat taken aback but acknowledged that she had assumed they would.[113]

The legislators heard testimony from representatives of women's organizations with long histories of sympathy, especially at the state level, for labor legislation for women. Most, including Katharine Lenroot, head of the Children's Bureau, confined their testimony to support for ending child labor.[114] Lucy Mason from the National Consumers' League and Elinore Herrick, a former director of the New York Consumers' League and regional director of one of the National Labor Relations Board administrative units, enthusiastically endorsed the mechanism for vesting administrative discretion to set wages in a board, and neither took particular issue with regional differentials in wages.[115] At stake for these maternalist social reformers was the principle that the federal government could intervene to protect the health and morals of workers, or, in Elinore Herrick's words, that it could play a role in lifting "oppressive conditions from the backs of toilers."[116]

But amidst the general agreement and carefully orchestrated acclaim, somewhat unaccountably to Perkins and the congressional leaders, many advocates of organized labor, which had at first supported the bill, began to balk. The craft-oriented American Federation of Labor had been burned by the codes adopted by the National Recovery Administration; its leaders believed that the decisions of the National Labor Relations Board favored the industrial unionization of the newly formed Congress of Industrial Organizations (CIO), which the AFL detested. Above all, they found themselves once again resisting the idea of an administrative board—this time one that could intervene in the wage-bargaining process. In particular, the leadership objected to the power of boards to set regional differentials, which they believed would ultimately permit continuing low wages in the South and create competition among workers. The AFL's William Green wanted half a dozen amendments that would guarantee the sanctity of organized labor's newly won collective bargaining capacity or there would be no deal.

The AFL was not alone. On the issue of regional differences, he was joined by John P. Davis, chair of the newly founded National Negro Congress (NNC). The two formed an unlikely partnership. The NNC, an umbrella organization of some six-hundred African-American groups, partly funded by the Communist Party, typically sided with the CIO. On this occasion it feared that a board with discretionary power to set wages would become the tool of southern racists and virulently opposed it.[117] CIO head John L. Lewis, initially a partner in the development of the act, offered only lukewarm testimony. He approved the idea that a worker might get a minimum wage as a fundamental right, but he protested that the bill, in giving discretion to a board to raise that wage, "amounts to a wage-fixing by a governmental agency made in consideration of all the equities involved."[118]

Labor's hand grew stronger when, halfway through the hearings, in June 1937, William Connery died. He was replaced by Mary Norton of New Jersey, a ten-year veteran of Congress and, until she became chair of the House Committee on Labor, a disinterested observer of the bill. But Mary Norton, woman though she was, was neither a member of the network of women reformers nor privy to the thinking of social insurance advocates. She did have special reasons to watch out for the interests of the AFL, stemming from her allegiance to old-time political boss Frank Hague of Jersey City. Hague, as Norton recalls in her unpublished autobiography, telephoned her just before the House debate on the bill was about to begin and warned her that "the AFL had always been friendly to me and that I should not oppose them." As Norton tells the story, Hague threatened: "They are opposed to your bill, and in fact I have been told that you betrayed labor." Fearful of offending her benefactor, Norton quickly contacted Green and persuaded him to intervene on her behalf. But Norton's fear remained palpable. The incident, she tells us, "left me with a deep scar. Frank Hague was the Democratic leader in New Jersey. He wanted and needed the support of the American Federation of Labor."[119] From then on, Norton seemed to walk a tightrope between the administration, which badly wanted a bill to regulate wages and hours, and the AFL, which would accept only a bill that stringently protected the battered remnants of its voluntarist philosophy.

Norton's protectiveness of the AFL's concerns did little to endear her either to the bill's supporters or to the southern congressional interests, who also deeply opposed the bill. Many southern congressmen would have preferred no minimum wage at all because, they argued, even a low minimum would threaten the regional wage differentials from which southern industry benefited. What seemed to be at stake, as Frank Friedel notes, was the South's self-serving belief that its capacity to support its black population would be undermined by raising the wages of black workers.[120] Southern opposition may have made the bill even more important to the president, who, according to historian James Patterson, desperately wanted to take advantage of it as an opportunity to bring southern congressmen into line.[121]

Nor were the social reformers any more sympathetic to Norton's dilemma. The National Consumers' League had committed itself to a nationwide campaign to pass a wages and hours bill. Leaders believed that Norton could destroy their efforts. As the hearings concluded at the end of July 1937, Clara Beyer (assistant director of the Bureau of Labor Standards) wrote to Mary Dewson to complain that Norton "is proving even worse than anticipated. She is definitely opposed to the wage and hour bill and has done all that she could to obstruct it in the committee."[122] Norton, Beyer protested, had cast the deciding vote to scotch the child labor provisions of the bill. But Norton, under pressure from southern members of her own committee, was in fact walking an uncomfortable tightrope, juggling the interests of every imaginable constituency as she tried to satisfy an administration that desperately wanted the bill.

When the hearings wound down, the Senate quickly passed—without the AFL's desired amendments, and with the child labor provision—a bill so disappointing that Green supported its passage only because he believed the House would radically change it.[123] Of the original labor supporters, only Sidney Hillman remained committed.[124] In the House, Norton waged a desperate struggle to unleash the Labor Committee's version from a southern-dominated Rules Committee. It took her three months before she succeeded in scheduling House debate. In the end, the AFL, having failed to get the changes it sought, torpedoed the effort by inviting congressmen to vote to recommit it.

Still the administration persisted. In the early winter of 1938, Perkins and the president leaned heavily on Norton to bring the bill up again, and in the early spring the AFL once again found itself maneuvering to shape a bill that it could live with.[125] It tried a substitute bill, which went down to defeat in the committee, and ultimately persuaded the committee to recommend a modified version of the 1937 plan that the House triumphantly passed. Now Senate conferees balked, insisting that any measure contain some opportunity for regional differentials in wages. Finally, and reluctantly, a compromise bill emerged, to be signed into law on June 25, 1938.

There was much to be said for it, as a start. The legislation incorporated a forty-four-hour workweek, to be reduced in three years to forty, and requiring overtime pay after that. It incorporated a minimum wage of twenty-five cents per hour, to be slowly increased until in seven years it reached forty cents. It permitted no flat regional differences; it required the advice of regional industrial groups before a single administrator could sustain exclusions and inclusions or approve variations in wage rates above the set minimum; it prohibited the shipment of goods made with child labor (formally excluding two hundred thousand children from the labor market); and, in order to discourage paid home work, it applied minimum wages and hours to the manufacture of goods in the home.[126] It also forbade classifications by sex for wage purposes.

If the final, hard-won Fair Labor Standards Act only dimly reflected the hopes of its originators, it starkly captured the gendered and racialized sensibilities that underlay the political battles. It excluded from coverage so many categories of workers that, in the end, its provisions incorporated only 20 percent of the labor force, or approximately eleven million of fifty-five million workers. Among those excluded were not only the by-now-traditional groups such as domestic servants and agricultural workers but workers in the retail

*Mary Norton, congressional representative from New Jersey and chair of the House Committee on Labor during the late 1930s.*
COURTESY, SPECIAL COLLECTIONS AND UNIVERSITY ARCHIVES, RUTGERS UNIVERSITY LIBRARIES.

and service industries and in food processing, packing, and transportation, all government employees and those who worked for nonprofit organizations, and seamen. Women were disproportionately excluded from the bill. It covered only 14 percent of working women, compared to 39 percent of adult working men.[127] African-American women, more than a third of whom still worked as domestic servants in 1935, and African-American men, who constituted 80 percent of agricultural workers, almost completely lacked its protections. Even those theoretically covered by the bill found its benefits scarce indeed. The minimum wage was so low that, working a steady forty-hour workweek, no worker could earn the average weekly industrial wage in any state, even though that average included depression-shortened hours.[128] In the end, fewer than three hundred thousand workers stood to benefit in the first year, with an additional million and a half added in the second and third years.[129] Given the AFL's discomfort, it was perhaps ironic that male industrial workers benefited most: overtime provisions mandated time and a half for hours worked beyond forty a week. Women, generally prevented by custom and law from working extra hours, could not take advantage of this extra pay clause.[130]

Some groups, like the National Consumers' League, viewed the FLSA as a victory of principle. Though disappointed that the act's single administrator gave less authority than it would have liked to state boards, the league took pride in the evolution of federal power to the point where it could regulate wages and hours. National and state leagues had lobbied hard for this bill, which, for all its defects, they considered a valuable foot in the door.[131] The AFL, in contrast, accepted grudgingly the principle of government intervention in the wage relationship, yet took comfort in a minimum wage so low that it could not compete with negotiated bargaining agreements and in its success in fending off a powerful administrative board. Still, many were deeply disappointed. Elizabeth Brandeis blamed the AFL for many of the act's shortcomings. In 1937, she thought, "with strong AFL support a forty-cent minimum wage and a forty-hour week might have been written into the statute." Instead, the AFL had "probably delayed passage of the law for nearly a year and weakened it materially."[132]

What accounts for labor's unenthusiastic acceptance of the idea of fair labor standards and for its belated endorsement of the particular bill that made it through? How do we explain why labor rejected a bill that would have improved the conditions of many far more quickly than the bill that finally passed? And what accounts for the willingness of organized women's groups to settle for a bill that continued to rely on states to provide special protections for women workers? What was at stake here? Like all such policy debates, this one occurred within a many-layered context of meanings. The legislation that institutionalized minimum wages and maximum hours emerged from a series of not entirely satisfactory compromises between prevailing interest groups. It was profoundly shaped, as well, by a particularly powerful set of meanings about work and manhood, crucial to the AFL, and by a shared conception of the meaning of the family that facilitated the final agreement.

The actors in this case include, at one end of the spectrum, a powerful bloc of southern congressmen, eager to retain the historic division between African-American and white workers that reduced the price of labor in their region, provided a sense of social order, and sustained what was euphemistically described as the southern way of life. This group drew strength from small business organized by the National Association of Manufacturers and local chambers of commerce, which continued to insist that the federal government keep its hands off. Had these groups had their wish, the federal government would never have initiated labor standards legislation at all.[133]

At the other end were some of the same maternalist advocates for legislation on behalf of motherhood who had led early campaigns for protective labor legislation for women only and who viewed the FLSA as a crucial step in the campaign for family protection. Some of these women found their way into the new federal bureaucracy, where, in partnership with advocates of social insurance, they represented the belief that increased hours and wages legislation would contribute to ending the depression as well as to ameliorating the lot of the poorest workers.[134] Informed by popular beliefs about the significance of marriage and motherhood in the lives of ordinary wage-earning women, most advocates for women pursued social policies designed to reinforce women's continuing family roles.

The counterweight lay in a sharply divided labor movement whose vision of work (like that of the maternalists) came out of the traditional male-headed family and whose desire to preserve control over good jobs shaped its attitude toward the FLSA. Leaders of the skilled craft workers, who constituted the bulk of the AFL's constituent unions, viewed their diminishing control over skilled jobs with anxiety. Having faced aggressive employer strategies to undermine their power in the 1920s, confronted for nearly a decade with the challenge of mass unemployment, they remained suspicious of government intervention that seemed always to oppose them. Yet they continued to encourage legislative restrictions on women's work and supported efforts to exclude children from the workforce entirely. They had helped to shape social insurance programs that would provide security and rewards for those with demonstrated commitment to labor while preserving at least some portion of their members' manly independence. Now they were confronted with the greatest challenge of all: an effort to infringe on labor's prerogatives in the wage sphere.

After 1935, an increasingly influential minority, led by Sidney Hillman and John Lewis, publicly disagreed with the AFL's voluntaristic philosophy and actively promoted government intervention, instead of resisting it. Having long ago abandoned the idea that organized labor could adequately regulate the labor supply, these leaders of the more inclusionary CIO had a more benign view of the FLSA's effort to regulate wages. Like craft unions, this group feared employer power. Unlike them, it believed that the state could be made to function on behalf of working people. Far from hesitating to support the act as resistance to it developed, Hillman relied instead on the power of labor to influence government enforcement. Joined by dissidents within the AFL (and sometimes by communist-influenced state and local federations) and supported by advocates of social insurance, Hillman alerted the nation's workers to possibilities for broader federal coverage. The act would provide, in his judgment, a "bottom where collective bargaining would start."[135] If Hillman had the ear of an administration eager to find innovative solutions to incipient social unrest, the AFL leadership provided a powerful political opposition on the legislative battlefront. Anxious to provide economic security for workers, the AFL had reluctantly come to support government-sponsored old age and unemployment insurance, but it had consistently opposed wage regulation as a fundamental threat to the liberties of free men. The FLSA's invasion into this territory seemed to many labor leaders to strike at the heart of organized labor, rendering the issue at stake the principle of voluntarism itself, with all it represented in terms of the freedom and liberty of working men.

The background of this struggle lies in the ambivalent position of many state federations of labor toward regulating wages (as opposed to hours) even for women workers. Regulating women's working hours and restricting their job opportunities, as Patricia Brito persuasively demonstrates in an elegant case study of Ohio in the 1920s, could enhance the job opportunities of men.[136] But differential pay rates for women had the opposite effect: threatening male work opportunities by allowing women to work more cheaply.[137] In deference to the horrendously poor pay of most female workers and in an effort to combat the problem of sweated labor, many state federations withheld their opposition to minimum wages for women, preferring to rely on a sex-segregated marketplace to protect men's positions.[138] A few continued to see regulation of women's pay as an entering wedge into the wage relation.

This was the case in Ohio, where John Frey, the iron molder who became president of the Ohio State Federation of Labor in 1924 (and thirteen years later would lead the AFL's internal opposition to the FLSA), frankly opposed any law. Frey, in concert with such women's rights groups as the National Federation of Business and Professional Women's Clubs and the National Woman's Party, argued that minimum wages for women only would disadvantage them ultimately. More important, he believed that they would undermine "our faith, as Trade Unionists, in collective bargaining as the only method by which we will agree to have our terms of employment established."[139] Neither opposition within his own organization nor the efforts of women trade unionists and members of the Ohio Consumers' League could convince him otherwise. The principle at stake was too important: it was too short a step, as some Ohio trade unionists had suggested, from a minimum wage law for women to one that included men and, by introducing the state as mediator, threatened them with the loss of their bargaining power, and ultimately with a loss of their manhood. Now Frey's fear was being realized. The cries of one delegate to the 1924 Ohio State Federation of Labor reverberated in the 1937 AFL convention that debated the wages and hours bill more than a decade later: "I want to remain a free man as a wage earner and not become a subject of the State."[140] The sentiments could have come from Frey himself. It was he, after all, who had declared in the shorter-hours debate his opposition to having legislatures do what free men could do for themselves.

In light of his own commitment to voluntarism, and in the face of its rapid erosion in the 1930s, perhaps William Green should have been more prepared for the virulent opposition of his own organization, but the rebuke he got when the executive committee met after his testimony seemed to take him by surprise.[141] It was affirmed by the convention that met in Denver in October 1937 while Norton was still maneuvering to release the wages and hours bill from the Rules Committee. There, in an explicit jab at Sidney Hillman (who had helped to conceive the bill) and the CIO, Frey (joined by Mathew Woll of the machinists and William Hutcheson of the carpenters) led angry delegates to consider resolutions that proposed to treat with suspicion and subject to "thorough examination" any bill that, like this one, "was not introduced by the American Federation of Labor, neither did officers of the American Federation of Labor participate in its preparation." After considering a resolution that "unalterably opposed ... giving over to lawmakers the power to fix wages," they rousingly approved a committee report that insisted that Green consult with some of the AFL's officers (including Frey) before taking further action on Black-Connery.[142]

Fear of losing the final vestiges of manhood fueled revolt. In an unprecedented resolution introduced by AFL officers, the bill, as it then stood, was described as creating "a governmental agency influencing, and at its discretion replacing, collective bargaining as now carried on by voluntary association of wage earners and their employers." This was a problem, the resolution continued, because "the most essential right of free men is that of voluntary association for lawful purposes, a right upon which the exercise of free speech, free political institutions and of religious organizations have their foundations." Finally, then, the convention was called on to oppose "any form of legislation ... which would in any measure interfere with, supplant or transfer the practice of collective bargaining from organized labor to Boards, Commissions or other bodies established by Federal laws."[143] With the vestiges of voluntarism and its vehicle, collective bargaining, to defend, a chastened Green returned to the battle, bent on getting a bill that respected labor's sense of itself as the last bastion of "free men."[144]

The problem lay with the implications of this stance for attitudes toward women workers. What the AFL called "government control and dictation" had, in the guise of protective labor legislation adopted by the separate states, set the ground rules for the relationship of working women to the state for many years. For many women workers, and certainly for the maternalist social reformers who had devoted their lives to bettering the conditions of working women, voluntarism signified exclusion. Since 1908, they and many male as well as female trade unionists had accepted that government regulation on behalf of wage-earning women compensated for the absence of collective bargaining and provided women more freedom to work than it threatened.[145] To the AFL leadership, treating women as wards of the state with regard to work had been essential to preserving male rights to job competition and supportive of men's family prerogatives. The FLSA's threat to apply what had been a principle of gendered order to all workers threatened to upset a precarious balance. Now the AFL had to try to construct a bill that fiercely defended its prerogative of bargaining collectively while continuing to restrict that process to real and symbolic "men." It would work toward an FLSA that did not dictate to "free men" while flinging its sheltering arms around the unmanly, low-paid, and unskilled, who could, in its judgment, never be organized.

Confusion within the AFL and among its supporters found its way onto the floor of Congress; a persistent undercurrent in the congressional discussions reveals its depths. It appears repeatedly in the insistence of legislators on both sides of the issue that, despite their different positions, each supported organized labor. Its most pernicious effect occurs in the tendency of some legislators (northern and southern) to refer to the wages and hours bill as "an orphan child—a foundling with no father," implying that Perkins, who had invested herself in it, and Representative Mary Norton, who had shepherded it though Congress, were women without virtue. Perhaps Norton let herself in for the extended metaphor by describing herself early on the floor of Congress as the bill's "adopted mother." Glenn H. Griswold of Indiana, who claimed to support a better bill, gleefully challenged Norton to turn the lights on the "face of this illegitimate child, fathered in darkness and born in obscurity."[146] To great applause and laughter, Sam D. McReynolds of Tennessee declared the bill to be

a child born out of wedlock in impractical idealism, abandoned by its repenting parents, and left upon the doorstep of the kindly and gracious gentlewoman from New Jersey, and she, not being satisfied with it, has kept on changing it in an effort to curry favor from labor, proven indifferent to the child, and its self appointed nursemaids have so mishandled the diapers and the safety pins until from too frequent changing the poor child is now suffering from a pernicious skin rash. The result is that its identity would not be recognized by its own parents, if indeed it has any.[147]

McReynolds returned to the metaphor in the spring debate, claiming that "since this orphan child was exhibited before us at the special session last year it has had some growth." Clearly implicating Perkins in its birth and exculpating Norton, he continued, "The brain child of last December was a foundling dumped upon the doorstep of the gentlewoman from New Jersey."[148]

The ongoing discussion suggests that the AFL had caught itself in something of a conundrum. It argued for protecting low-paid workers ("that part of labor unable to protect itself") if doing so would not harm the collective bargaining potential of the labor movement (where manhood was vested). But unlike state-sponsored minimum wage legislation for women only, which was designed to combat sweated labor, a minimum wage for all workers had to be high enough to maintain the purchasing power of families. As one congressman put it, defending the legislation, "All I ask for an American father is that he be paid a wage sufficient in amount that his wife may stay at home and bring up her family and that his children may be educated and that he may set a little aside for his old age."[149]

A wage high enough to significantly increase the purchasing power of recipients led other congressmen to wonder why women, boys, and by implication African Americans needed a minimum at all. After all, as one put it, a minimum wage for a man with three or four children was one thing, but "when you get into the earnings of a single girl, a single boy under 20, perhaps you are hurting an industry in certain sections."[150] Witnesses objected that "girls" would benefit from it.[151] Still others protested that "grandmothers" did not require any higher minimum wage.[152] Congressmen like Robert Luce of Massachusetts echoed the confusion, arguing for the minimum except for *young* women—because they tended to get married or had, in any event, been historically subject to sex differentials.[153] One legislator wanted poultry excluded from the act because "it is the business of the housewife ... a wholesome and proper and happy labor for them ... [which] ought not to be regulated and controlled by bureaucratic officers."[154] Another, eager to exclude newspaper employees, asked, "What are you going to do with the old maid who travels about ... to gather the society items.[?] ... She does not take time away from her regular duties."[155] Of course, all such questions spelled danger for the bill, for, as labor's representatives had testified, to lock in a differential by sex (like one by race or region) would be to undermine the bargaining power of organized workers by ensuring a pool of cheap labor.[156]

As long as it attempted to set a base wage lower than any that a man could expect to earn, the AFL had no effective response to these arguments. Instead it focused its energies on maintaining control of wage setting by proposing to eliminate the projected "board" or reduce its discretion, restrict the kinds of people affected, and minimize the effects on negotiated wages. In other words, it would demand a relatively rigid bill that covered only people who were outside the traditional purview of collective bargaining and whose wages fell below those of every imaginable unionized worker.

Yet now the AFL found itself in bed with an embarrassed and uncomfortable coterie of southern congressmen. Perkins (driven by FDR's concern to get a bill even if it meant conceding something to the South) had already testified for geographical differentials if market conditions warranted them. Hillman, too, had declared himself open-minded on the question of differentials, though he had stated his preference to do without them.[157] The AFL adamantly opposed them, believing that regional wage differentials—allowing the southern states to pay less to workers by virtue of their presumably lower costs of living—might demonstrate the irrelevance of labor's bargaining power, for it would place the discretion of administrative judgment above the weight of collective bargaining. Compromising, organized labor agreed to a minimum wage low enough that it did not challenge the South's desire to maintain what it euphemistically called its style of life. In the bargain, the South won an agreement to exclude all but industrial workers. In practice that meant virtually all African Americans of both sexes.

The maternalist women's organizations faced a different kind of dilemma. Eager to protect the home by regulating women's working conditions, and convinced that sweated labor threatened it, they had successfully sought state wages and hours legislation for women for many years. Grassroots strategies and state-based political networks effectively persuaded state legislatures to adopt various kinds of protective laws for women. After the *West Coast Hotel* decision upholding minimum wages for women, some groups, including the League of Women Voters, argued over whether they should now support wages and hours legislation for all workers. Reluctant to invade an arena about which they knew little, members decided for the moment to hold back.[158]

The National Consumers' League took a dramatically different position. Seizing the moment, it lobbied fiercely for family protection. From their positions in the new federal bureaucracy, its leaders testified to the importance of motherhood and family life in the legislative agenda. But their power base and practical experience remained in the states, as did the protective labor legislation for women in which they were utterly invested. For them what was important was a federal law that did not preclude state action. Not only were they comfortable with boards and with bureaucratic commissions to administer wages but, convinced that the administration would never appoint a female administrator of wages and hours, they believed that continuing authority and influence lay in building regional strength.[159] With this in mind, they created an uncomfortable alliance with southern conservatives, whose demands for regional differentials, while more rigid than those of the women social reformers, sustained the state-centered influence that mater-nalists wanted. Indeed, as Elinore Herrick and others testified, their experi-ence with boards demonstrated a flexibility that negated fears of "dictatorial powers."[160] To maternalists, investing in a system that would operate through a series of designated boards seemed more important than particular limits on wages and hours or inclusion and exclusion, however restricted. And the bill's child labor clause, central to the maternalist agenda, provided an impor-tant reason to compromise. Ready to settle for half a loaf, wanting desperately to establish the principle of government intervention, and believing that cov-erage would spread, the NCL and other women's groups ignored the exclu-sions and the low wage level in order to get a bill, any bill.[161]

The support of women's organizations for state or regional boards posed a serious problem for labor. Given the regional antagonisms, the issue of whether Congress should mandate a single nationwide minimum or whether an administrative board should be empowered to do so became pivotal. Labor objected to the proposal for a five-member board with its power to evaluate and set wage rates, offered in the original and Senate versions of the Black-Connery bill. In its view, boards symbolized labor's potential captivity, raising questions about whether freeborn men should be encouraged to give up their democratic rights. A board empowered to make wage decisions seemed merely a ploy to undermine collective bargaining and to destroy the independence and manly solidarity of the labor movement. These issues shadowed the con-gressional debates, first in December of 1937 and then in June of 1938. As Green expostulated when he resubmitted the AFL's version of the wages and hours bill to the Committee on Labor in the winter of 1938, "Labor, industry and the public are fed up with federal boards."[162]

The language of labor's anxiety framed discussions of the bill in Congress. An administrative bureaucracy would, as one New Jersey congressman put it, "sound the death knell of organized labor by substituting the commands of a federal bureaucrat for collective bargaining." This bill in its present form, remarked James M. Wilcox of Florida, was "the most serious threat to repre-sentative democracy which has been proposed in this generation." Martin Dies of Texas concurred: "No government could be administered wisely and properly," he orated, "when Congress delegates its constitutional functions to bureaucratic boards or to dictatorial administrators."[163] Others joined in, one declaring that whether by "an oligarchy in the guise of a Labor Standards Board or by a king called an administrator," the bill would surely "set up an absolute despotism over the lives and liberties of the working men and women of this nation."[164] The context provided southern congressmen opposed to reasonable pay for African Americans with the oportunity to affirm an unholy alliance with labor, as, for example, when Wilcox opposed the bill because "when we turn over to a federal bureau or board the power to fix wages, it will prescribe the same wage for the Negro that it prescribes for the white man." This just would not work in the South: "You cannot put the Negro and the white man on the same basis and get away with it."[165]

A respectful acquiescence to the common thread of gendered order in the end resolved the special concerns of each group. Labor's concern for voluntarism, maternalists' insistence on family protection, and southern advocacy of regional wage differentiation had a single solution: a minimum wage that would be low enough to accommodate most of the demands of southern manufacturers but would minimize administrative discretion in establishing regional differences. The AFL settled for a base of twenty-five cents an hour rather than the forty cents that had been bandied about. A narrow construction of interstate commerce pleased both the South and labor by exempting many of the same categories of workers as before. In addition to domestics and agricultural workers, the law initially exempted most food processors, the retail trades, clerical and service workers, and all establishments with fewer than eight workers. Excluding huge numbers of workers avoided the complicated task of reconciling sexual and racial wage differentials across regions and protected the collective bargaining process by ensuring, as Green put it, that only those who had no possibility of collective bargaining were included.[166]

The low wage did not particularly trouble maternalists, because far more women would continue to be covered by state legislation than by federal laws. The Supreme Court had ruled in 1937 that states could define who was a person under the Fourteenth Amendment.[167] Many states jealously guarded that privilege. When the architects of the FLSA opted to locate the right to government protection under the rubric of interstate commerce rather than that of the Fourteenth Amendment, they left the forty-eight states free to regulate women's hours and to restrict women's opportunities—and thus continued to subject them to the police power of the state in quite different ways from men.[168] Treated equally only in terms of wages, women still had to fight the battle as to whether they were "persons" under the law—or whether they were equally free to make contracts of their own choosing. But for the moment, maternalists could breathe a sigh of relief.

In the context of continuing state protection for women, the precious equal pay provision takes on a different light. The law forbade classification on the basis of age or sex (although not race) with regard to pay: a victory in principle for women, but one that labor claimed as a practical achievement. Equalizing women's pay at the lowest levels would raise the wage level without harming more skilled men. For labor leaders it confirmed their belief that women were weak links in the collective bargaining process. Since no equality provision was inserted into the restriction on hours, states remained free to cap women's daily or weekly working hours. The continuing occupational sex segregation encouraged by state protective laws affirmed women's special labor force positions and rendered the equal pay provision largely symbolic.

At the same time, while a forty-hour week ultimately set a new standard, it did little to assuage a labor movement that had argued for thirty hours as a way to solve the unemployment problem. Though forty hours accommodated some of labor's demand for increased leisure to provide education, information, and sustenance for the worker-citizen, it also embodied the principle that all men should work.[169] In that sense it might signal something of a turning point. Yet the FLSA hardly made room for expanding the labor force. Most labor leaders, in the CIO as well as the AFL, continued to believe in the marginal position of women workers. Their representatives resisted the entry of additional women, even as they attempted to stretch the umbrella of collective bargaining to all those who already worked.

Unlike compromises that satisfy no one, the final shape of the FLSA enabled all the major players to claim victory. By creating a state-regulated minimum wage that benefited only the poorest and most vulnerable workers, the FLSA turned some men into "wards of the state" in the same sense as women. But it also removed a large category of workers from the collective bargaining process, which became visibly the prerogative of the best men and the last bastion of manly independence. The AFL's final defense of voluntarism came at a steep price for women and for African Americans—who were the largest groups among those whose "unmanly" status denied them coverage or subjected them to a minimum so low as to have little meaning. To skilled workers, this was a small price to pay for an outcome that maintained allegiance to principles that had influenced the AFL's policies since the 1880s. Its resistance won it a short stay for its defense of manliness, as it ensured that fewer men would be tainted by the brush of government protection. Maternalists won a victory for the principle of protection—placing men as well as women under a small but expandable umbrella of federal government regulation. Ironically, even as it opened the possibility for general protection for all, the legislation prefigured the likelihood that in a world where social insurance benefits were connected to paid employment, everyone, including women, would soon seek the particular forms of citizenship offered by the privileged categories of wage work.

# CHAPTER 3

# Questions of Equity

In the spring of 2000, the Republican congressional leadership pro-posed, and Congress unanimously passed, a revision of the nation's Social Security code that lifted restrictions on earnings for people under the age of seventy. The new law allowed every contributor over the age of sixty-five to receive a full old age pension regardless of whether he or she continued to earn wages. Exuberant praise and congratulatory public comments greeted this expansion of benefits in one of the country's most beloved social programs. This, said the *New York Times*, "is one of those exceptional government initiatives that hardly anyone faults publicly," and it quoted a reigning lobbyist to the effect that it was "good labor policy, good social policy and good economic policy."[1] The twenty-two-billion-dollar price tag, commentators noted with satisfaction, would be recouped after barely a decade—offset by a technical change that rescinded higher benefits to those between sixty-five and seventy who remained in the workforce. This bill was not about money; it was about a new consensus, forged during a time of labor shortages, to encourage the elderly to stay at work longer. Yet it cogently invoked a concept of fairness that no one involved in the original Social Security Act would have recognized. "Older Americans," said a Texas congressman, "can work, they want to work and they shouldn't be punished by an outdated law if they choose to work."[2]

The notion that aging individuals who wished to earn wages should be encouraged to do so flatly contradicted the ideas behind Title II of the original act. Drafted by the Committee on Economic Security and passed in 1935, when the nation faced a 25 percent unemployment rate, it aimed to remove people from the workforce, not keep them in it.[3] Its purpose, recalled Barbara Nachtrieb Armstrong, one of the designers, was "not only *to protect the older worker* from no earnings income, but it was also *to get him out of the labor market.*"[4] In Congress, Senator Robert Wagner solicited support for old age insurance by arguing that the best way to make places for newcomers to the labor force was by "making possible the withdrawal of those who are older and less efficient, and who deserve and want a few years of rest."[5] When Representative Fred Vinson suggested benefits for employed workers over sixty-five, his proposal was quickly scotched.[6] Old age insurance, concludes historian William Graebner, after examining this record, was "a piece of retirement legislation ... consciously designed to accomplish ... the removal of older persons from the work force."[7]

In hindsight, old age insurance appears to have been a logical extension of the New Deal's search for economic security. But at the time, it appeared a rather risky business: an unpredictable diversion of funds and energy when the immediate needs of the aging poor demanded instant action. Even before the depression, social analysts had called attention to the precarious situation of "citizens who arrived at economic old age," to use Armstrong's felicitous phrase.[8] When the CES tried to compile figures as to the numbers of people in this group, it concluded somewhat vaguely but persuasively that at least one third had incomes below the mimimum three hundred dollars a year on which a person might barely survive. In some urban areas, even before the depression, three quarters of the aged would qualify for public assistance, if assistance were available.[9] In rural areas, the aging poor were somewhat more comfortable, but overall fewer than 20 percent could live without some form of assistance.

These figures expanded dramatically during the depression, yet little public relief existed. Though by 1930 thirty-five states offered some form of public relief to the aged poor, only 10 or 15 percent of those eligible actually drew any money, and the depression left even the most generous states (Massachusetts, New York, and California) with long waiting lists and no funds. To be sure, a few other forms of support existed. Railway employees benefited from a retirement program designed, for safety reasons, to remove elderly workers. A dozen trade unions had set up joint contributory pensions with employers that in 1930 paid benefits to some thirteen thousand retired members, and a handful of large private employers had created pension programs before World War I. By 1930, some four hundred companies boasted pension programs. Most of these provided meager benefits, at the discretion of the company, and limited them to workers with twenty or more years of continuous service—a near impossible feat for all but the most skilled and valued employees, and one that only about 5 percent of all workers had achieved. All these programs faced financial turmoil as the depression deepened, and some companies simply reneged on their commitments. Half of the destitute aged, the CES concluded, relied on their children, an always precarious resource that became less reliable as unemployment expanded.[10]

The pressing need of old people in the 1930s was for assistance or relief, not insurance. Advocates ranging from Abraham Epstein, whose American Association for Old Age Security proposed federal grants to the states, to Francis Townsend, whose plan to give everyone over sixty-five two hundred dollars a month to spend at will exceeded all others in popularity, stimulated the public to believe that the federal government could and should help the states solve this problem. Over this, there was little controversy. The very first title of the Social Security Act, Title I, provided states with matching grants to give relief to the needy aged and to care for unemployable old people. It replaced the mostly inadequate state-based programs with uniform federal standards and more generous grants than all but a handful of states had been able to provide. But Old Age Assistance came at a price: it subjected recipients to the indignities of means testing, fostering an unmanly spirit of dependency.

Means testing was, in any event, a depression-generated anxiety. By 1935, the United States had already experienced half a decade of family crisis. Couples postponed marriage and babies; they moved in with parents or children; wives who found jobs earned wages while unemployed husbands walked the streets. The lucky found temporary work in an alphabet soup of federal agencies. The crisis called into question traditional ideals of self-sufficiency for men and placed the formerly self-respecting male at the edges of a fearful and feminine dependence.

Social insurance advocates sought to circumvent this anxiety with insurance rather than relief: they sought to prevent destitution and "obviate the necessity of public charity" by protecting family breadwinners against the potential hazards of industrial life.[11] Most European countries had long before acknowledged the need for preventive measures, but they had done so in quite different ways. Bulgaria and Poland, as well as Denmark and Great Britain, had developed noncontributory old age pensions, often requiring proof of residency and citizenship as well as lack of income. Belgium, Italy, Spain, and France had experimented with government-subsidized programs to which workers voluntarily contributed and from which pensions were payable at age sixty, sixty-five, or seventy. Romania, the Netherlands, and Sweden all insisted on compulsory contributions from workers, meant to sustain universal pensions for all citizens who passed a certain age.

In the United States, the idea of government-subsidized insurance ran counter to the American grain, which reified independence and self-reliance. If there were to be any old age insurance program at all, its designers faced a formidable challenge: to remove aging workers from the labor force (which required that they be adequately supported) while affirming the dignity of pension recipients (which required that the program be self-supporting). To solve the labor force problem, policy makers imagined a program tied to work rather than to citizenship. Deciding which workers would be covered, however, created two classes of citizens: those who participated regularly in the kind of wage work where resolving unemployment seemed most important, and those who did not. In 1930, men made up the vast majority of gainfully employed persons (75 percent of the total); about 12 percent of this number were classified by the census as "Negro." But most African-American men did not work in the core industrial sectors, where issues of unemployment and labor force stability mattered most. And while women made up a quarter of all wage earners, their tenuous rights to work led many to assume they had little commitment to wage labor. We have seen how, despite women's own efforts to seek jobs during the depression, public opinion resolutely condemned wage work for those with husbands and fathers who could support them. Through the depression years, less than 15 percent of married women earned wages. Consciously or not, policy makers imagined a program available to most white wage-earning men that would omit "as a matter of course" most African Americans, by virtue of their positions in the labor market, and most women, whose positions appeared derivative of their marital partners.

Efforts to preserve the dignity of beneficiaries participated in the same gendered imagination. In the battle over unemployment compensation, men fought to maintain a sense of themselves as self-sufficient, independent, free, and capable of providing for their families and especially for the dependent women within them. In the struggle for Old Age Insurance (which we now call Social Security) participants deployed gender in more subtle but equally aggressive ways, not only to promote a conception of fairness that relied on the language of male dignity and female dependence but to ensure adequate support for all the aged. Gendered constructs helped to soothe a public increasingly enamored of government-funded assistance (which seemed to some policy makers an appropriate and to others a short-sighted and short-term solution). And they provided the language of family normalcy that convinced reluctant policy makers who remained skeptical of the capacity of an insurance program to solve employment problems without depending on general taxation. Ultimately, gendered conceptions provided the keystone that maintained public confidence in the core old age program and justified its redistributive goals. By providing economic security in particular ways and to particular people, old age insurance defined a new category of economic citizenship; at the same time, as this chapter reveals, it fueled the desires of the excluded for fuller participation. Let us watch that process unfold over the span of two generations.

## Matters of Right

Initial efforts to achieve old age insurance had, as Barbara Armstrong insisted, more to do with unemployment than with compassion for the aged. In the heady summer and fall of 1934, when the notion of social security entered the nation's vocabulary, the big issue was joblessness. In the staff of the Committee on Economic Security, which Edwin Witte headed, finding solutions to the expanding unemployment problem was on everyone's minds. Encouraging aging workers to leave their jobs would certainly be an attractive option, but the consensus had it that the way to do this was by expanding state-based old age relief or assistance.

The notion of doing something else probably came from Barbara Nachtrieb Armstrong, whose maverick role in the councils of the CES we have already noted. An associate professor of labor law at the University of California at Berkeley, she was a longtime student and advocate of social insurance. Just two years before the CES was formed, she had published a powerful book laying out the principles of social insurance. And while she

*Barbara Nachtrieb Armstrong, law professor and influential participant in the debates over what kind of social security the nation would have.* COURTESY, LARRY DEWITT, SSA HISTORIAN, SOCIAL SECURITY ADMINISTRATION HISTORY ARCHIVES.

could not have been called a friend of the chief lobbyists, Abraham Epstein and Isaac Rubinow, she certainly knew them and believed their aims compatible with her own. In 1915-16, she had participated actively in California's ultimately futile campaign for health insurance, and she was an avid student of European social insurance programs. On the strength of these experiences, she had met Rubinow. In the 1920s, she investigated European practices with social insurance, looking especially at the British and German models. She corresponded with Epstein. But she was a relative unknown in Washington. As she declared crisply, she knew "none, nobody" before she came there: not Witte or Altmeyer or Hopkins or Perkins.[12] Independent, not a team player, she arrived in Washington laden with principles and a sense of opportunity.

Asked at first to join the staff as a consultant on unemployment compensation, she was boosted into the chair of the Old Age Security Committee only after J. Douglas Brown, Edwin Witte's first choice, turned down the job. At the time, an insurance scheme must have seemed to Witte only a marginal possibility, and certainly far less important than expanding relief or assistance.[13] Brown, an expert on insurance, could not have wanted to chair a committee everyone thought would focus on assistance. He agreed to work with Armstrong, though, and together with economist Murray Latimer (chairman of the influential Railroad Retirement Board), they used the protective shadow cast by the public controversy over unemployment insurance to conceive what became Title II of the Social Security Act and to orchestrate its acceptance by the Advisory Council and the CES. Like Armstrong, Brown was an advocate of social insurance. Unlike her, he was connected both to Wisconsin and to the social insurance group through his work in industrial relations. Like Latimer, he had worked largely with industrial pension programs. A member of the American Association for Labor Legislation and a participant with Latimer and Bryce Stewart (who became the embattled chair of the Unemployment Compensation Committee) in a prominent consulting group called Industrial Relations Counselors, Brown was well liked and trusted by industrial leaders and the political world. More personable than the "acerbic" Armstong, Brown did the congressional and political footwork.

The three turned out to be a superb team. Each had a different strength: Armstrong brought her knowledge of European social insurance and her devotion to its principles; Latimer contributed his previous work with private pension programs and his position on the Technical Board; Brown offered his integrity, his political savvy, and his personable style. Joined by actuaries Otto Richter and Robert Myers, they set out to imagine what an insurance program

*J. Douglas Brown helped to reshape old age insurance into a plan to benefit families.*
COURTESY, PRINCETON UNIVERSITY LIBRARY, UNIVERSITY ARCHIVES, DEPART- MENT OF RARE BOOKS AND SPECIAL COL- LECTIONS.

for aged workers would look like. For all that they disagreed with most of the CES staff and Technical Board about the importance of insurance, they imagined the world in similar ways, agreeing that "the worker and his family" deserved "a living wage." Like everyone involved in the CES, they sought to relieve poverty by providing relief. That effort, embodied in Title I, was uncontroversial. As much could not be said for old age insurance.

By September of 1934, Armstrong's committee had decisively rejected the possibility of a noncontributory pension system that would cover everyone. Such a system, she wrote, with its "inevitable necessity of proving inadequate income as a conditon for receiving a pension, would be regarded as inflicting a 'poor relief' institution upon the majority of our wage earning group who have not within their own means any hope of saving for individual old age security."[14] While it recognized the need for such a system for the needy, the Old Age Security Committee conceived of it as temporary. Its ultimate aim was to "prevent the old-age assistance getting out of hand" by virtue of a "contributory insurance scheme" that would place pensions "upon a business-like basis and would eliminate all question of individual proof of need of income upon arriving at old age."[15] The two-pronged plan of assistance and insurance was consistent with the commitment to preventing unemployment and with the president's insistence that general tax revenues not be used to support economic security.

Three things distinguished the early version of the insurance plan: its work-related contributory feature based on a payroll tax to be divided between employer and employee and modestly supplemented by government funds; its administrative location within the federal, rather than state, apparatus; and its rather complicated calculation of benefits to take account of the needs of the poorest contributors. Contributions were to be collected by the national treasury, deposited in a trust fund, and distributed by an agency to be set up by Congress for the purpose of administering the plan.[16] The proposal recommended including agricultural and industrial workers, though not domestic workers, public employees, or the self-employed. Armstrong, Brown, and Latimer anticipated that old age insurance would eventually cover nearly all workers. As it spread, assistance would be phased out.[17]

Opposition to the idea of social insurance emerged right at the start and right at the top. Frances Perkins, Witte, and Arthur Altmeyer, the assistant secretary of labor who headed the Technical Board that supervised the policy committees, all balked.[18] Everyone, according to Altmeyer, believed that unemployment compensation "should have top priority" over old age insurance.[19] No one could imagine Congress accepting a second payroll tax; nor could anyone imagine Congress approving a uniform national system without intermediate state intervention. Personal ties figured as well. Witte and Altmeyer's close ties to John Commons and the deep commitments of all three to the Brandeis/Frankfurter nexus led them to favor unemployment insurance.[20] As we have seen, these connections ran deep. Armstrong attributed their lack of enthusiasm for her work to pressure from Paul Raushenbush, Brandeis's son-in-law, and to Perkins's attachment to Thomas Eliot, who had helped to draft the Wagner-Lewis Act and was committed to state-based programs.[21] Brown interpreted their skepticism more charitably: "It wasn't so much that they didn't want old age insurance as it was that old age insurance was a very new idea." Yet even after they came around, right up until the last, Brown recalled, "Witte would have said that if the old age insurance scheme caused the unemployment insurance scheme to face a barrier in the Congress, he would give up the old age insurance in order to be sure the unemployment insurance was passed."[22]

A closer exploration of the resistance to old age insurance reveals a more complicated picture that extended beyond the desire to protect unemployment insurance. Perkins had a long-standing attachment to the women's networks, and especially to Grace Abbott and Molly Dewson. Grace (who for thirteen years had headed the Children's Bureau) and her sister, Edith (a founder of the University of Chicago's School of Social Service Administration), had for years championed government mothers' pensions, maternal and child care programs, and other innovative policies for poor women and their children. Dewson, an early advocate of the minimum wage, had by the 1930s become an influential advocate for women in the Democratic Party. Grace Abbott and Dewson served on the CES Advisory Council. Both were uncomfortable with the concept of a federally based old age insurance system because they thought it privileged male workers and because they did not believe it could provide adequately for the poor. Abbott feared it would undermine the possibilities of a government-subsidized noncontributory system. She believed that means-tested assistance or relief, in contrast, could offer more generous benefits to the indigent old, and especially to the women among them. Not tied to employment, or to husbands and fathers, it promised to serve the needs of women without partners as well as those with irregular work patterns or no wage-earning experience at all.[23] Financed by general taxation rather than by a regressive flat tax or "contribution," it promised greater flexibility than any contributory insurance program then imagined. Edith Abbott apparently so opposed contributions that during a Washington conference on the subject "she left the room because she felt it was unfair to ask working class people to pay anything for their protection and that it should be done out of the generosity of the state."[24] Armstrong recalled that Molly Dewson "was very nasty" about this issue and "thought it very wrong that the employers should put out money for their workers for their old age."[25]

Many of the women's organizations remained silent or rejected the idea at first for the same reasons they opposed a national system of unemployment insurance.[26] Armstrong's insurance program anticipated a federal structure. The influence of organized women centered in state administrative agencies, where assistance was destined to be monitored and administered and which could regulate its amount and distribution. The preferences of many women's groups coincided with those of the southern states, which preferred an administrative apparatus at once more sympathetic to their racial purposes and more malleable than the behemoth federal government. Joseph Harris, Witte's assistant on the CES staff, confirmed this during the congressional debate: "In connection with the old-age pensions," he wrote to a friend, "the sore point has been the negro question, with fear from the Southern congressmen that the Federal Agency would exert control over state action."[27]

Most of those who believed in the principle of old age insurance, and especially those who advocated a European-style, government-subsidized, contributory insurance program for working people, were not in Washington during those late summer and early fall weeks. Abraham Epstein, Isaac Rubinow, and Paul Douglas were excluded, according to Edwin Witte, largely because of their controversial positions on the unemployment insurance issue.[28] Had they been there, they might have argued for Armstrong's partial government subsidy in addition to a payroll tax. Armstrong did consult them, and she paid respectful attention to members of her staff who argued their positions. But in the end, she and the other members of the subcommittee solicited support by tilting the program away from adequate support for all contributors, restructuring it so that it more effectively defended the dignity of men as reflected in their contributions.

Convinced that the president would not support a program that required government subsidies, and that only a contributory insurance program that returned benefits as a proportion of contributions could accrue sufficient legitimacy to make a permanent dent in unemployment, the committee modified its proposal. While a skeptical Witte continued to wonder if workers could possibly furnish, "even through insurance, sufficient contributions to provide ample retirement annuities for superannuated workers," the committee maintained its faith in the importance of individual contributions to the success of social insurance.[29] Brown remembered his feeling: "It should be protection as a matter of right, therefore it should be a contributory arrangement, it should require contributions throughout life, and it should be as automatic as possible."[30] Armstrong waxed equally positive: "If we hadn't made those insured people contributors, i.e., pay regularly toward their insurance so that they would think of it as theirs, they would have no protection against the politicians who periodically would wish to reduce their benefits or even eliminate them."[31] But the committee did debate the relationship between contributions and benefits, ultimately deciding that this was where dignity resided.

To get to that place, Armstrong successfully steered her little committee through two major compromises. The first rotated around the tension between providing adequate support for all beneficiaries and making sure that all contributors received a fair return on their investments; the second, around the issue of eligibility. Both demanded a careful negotiation of gendered priorities.

If old age insurance could not provide adequate benefits, public support for insurance would quickly swing to assistance. Nor would old age insurance succeed in eliminating people from the workforce if it did not support them and their families at least adequately. "Those of us who were more on the academic side," Brown recalled, "knew that the whole scheme was developed to prevent dependency and that therefore we had to have a strong concept of adequacy." Adequacy required redistributing some of the moneys collected by an old age insurance program to the poorest subscribers. But dignity resided in equity—in the conviction that every individual deserved a return consistent with contributions. To provide sufficient income for the poorest contributors while honoring the demands of the best-off for a fair return seemed an actuarial nightmare. Brown ruefully recalled the tussle over the two. Latimer, he remembered, was for equity, a position that emerged from his experience with private insurance plans. Brown opted for a middle path: "We were always caught between the upper and lower levels. We did not want it to get too low because of adequacy. We did not want to go too high since we wanted a self-financing system at that time."[32] Armstrong was more reticent about equity, describing the planners as "thinking of setting up benefits that would be socially adequate, ... but we were also thinking in terms of a contributory system based on the idea that the longer the man contributed, the more he would nearly approximate a heavy percentage of the wage he was losing by retiring."[33]

The conflict was captured in the tussle over whether the benefits of old age insurance could properly be described as an annuity. The object of an annuity, in private insurance, was to provide a guaranteed lifetime income in return for a specified contribution, which would then be returned in annual payments, with interest. Armstrong resisted the use of the word *annuity*, which, she believed, suggested an unconditional benefit, a code for the notion that a contributor would get back what he paid in and one that Brown himself at first adopted.[34] Instead she pointed to the conditional aspects attached to social security benefits: "Retirement means that you've stopped working for pay. It doesn't mean that you just reach a certain age, as you do in a commercial policy, an annuity policy, and you can cash in on your annuity when you get to that certain age.... If you keep right on at your job you are certainly not without income from work and are not eligible for benefits." Using the word *annuity*, she thought, "was confusing to people who then expected what they received in the way of benefits to be automatic on reaching a certain age." In her view, the program was "never meant to propound equity except insofar as what was given in return for retirement had some relation to contributions."[35]

In the end, the language of annuities proved too tempting to resist, its image of dignified insurance too respectable an analogy. As the proposal for old age insurance faced challenges in the fall of 1934, the committee repeatedly emphasized the relationship of benefits to contributions and modified the plan to tie them more closely together. The change justified the concept of annuities. Committee members supported a flat payroll tax that took equal percentages out of every pay packet, up to an agreed limit, and they insisted on equal contributions by both employers and employees. The business members of the Advisory Council (like the members of Congress who voted for the bill) clearly preferred this method of financing. Testifying before Congress, Marion Folsom of the Eastman Kodak Company argued that the worker "doesn't look upon it as a tax. He looks upon it just the same as he would paying his own insurance, and of course it's a right."[36] American Federation of Labor president William Green echoed these thoughts. Sharply opposed to sharing the costs of unemployment compensation, he readily agreed when Brown suggested that employers and employees split the cost of old age insurance. He accepted, Brown recalled, on the condition that "it must not be relief, provided that it was a matter of right. Contributory is a matter of right."[37] The rhetoric reveals that contributions were expected to buy much more than a floor against poverty: they would purchase dignity, ward off the threat of future political intervention, and give workers a voice in running the program. With this in mind, the CES staff committee, later the CES itself, and finally Congress agreed to two conditions: to cap the level of income on which contributions were assessed; and to provide benefits to everyone in a covered occupation, no matter how wealthy, who contributed to the system.[38] In the first round, equity largely prevailed over adequacy. The proposal presented to Congress was routinely portrayed as an annuity.

As the Old Age Security Committee shaped the program into an artefact of male dignity, it found itself policing the boundaries of admission more closely and raising questions of who might be appropriately included. Covering workers with low and irregular contributions threatened the equity principle: their contributions were likely to be too small to provide decent benefits. On these grounds Armstrong's committee excluded household domestic workers; everyone feared the administrative difficulties of forcing housewives to pay taxes on their household helpers. On these grounds, too, agricultural laborers, once included, found themselves shut out. Excluding these two important groups (who together constituted about 16 percent of the employed workforce) apparently did not overly concern the architects of old age insurance. They were, in any event, focused on industrial workers whose retirement would more effectively open jobs to young people. Doubts about the constitutionality of taxing employees of nonprofit groups, states, and municipalities exempted them from coverage, railroad workers and federal civil service employees chose to remain outside because they already had safe retirement programs, and no one felt comfortable taxing the self-employed, for whom some people proposed a voluntary program.

These distinctions recall our discussion of the consensus that surrounded women's limited rights to work and suggest something of its tacit consequences for their economic citizenship. Overrepresented in the excluded jobs, women tended to earn wages only irregularly and at low levels. But their absence went without comment from either the CES or the legislators who later debated the program. Imagined as lacking a commitment to work and as working irregularly, and rarely in the core industrial sectors, they scarcely figured in the debates around equity and adequacy that governed the shape of the final old age insurance provisions; their retirement had little to do with the central imperative of regularizing the labor force. As Arthur Altmeyer later put it, the program was designed "to protect and promote the economic and social well-being of workers and their families," not to provide the basis for "a fundamental reconstruction of economic and social institutions." This was, as Altmeyer perfectly understood, labor legislation rather than poor relief.[39] Still, paying attention to the "adequacy concept" would be the first order of business after the act's passage.

But the CES remained uncomfortable. At a crucial moment in September of 1934, Witte, with Perkins's knowledge, chose to exclude Armstrong's recommendations for a national, contributory old age insurance scheme from his preliminary recommendations to the Advisory Council. Armstrong objected fiercely and finally succeeded in attaching her plan as an appendix. She then sought a consultation with Perkins, who apparently evaded her requests. "Time and again," recalled Armstrong bitterly, "I tried to see her. . . . I was in a position where she should have seen me. No, she was fighting our program. She was not helping it and she did not want it."[40] All through the fall, Armstrong fought off dismissive accusations that her scheme for a federally based program could not pass constitutional muster. In response, she consulted a range of experts on constitutional law, deliberately excluding Frankfurter, to provide convincing support for a program based on the federal government's right to tax.[41]

In October, when Witte once again tried to circumvent her committee's recommendations, an infuriated Armstrong did a brilliant end run around him by leaking them to several crucial business representatives called to consult with the CES Advisory Council. The three key players, Walter Teagle of Standard Oil of New Jersey, Gerard Swope of General Electric, and Marion Folsom of Eastman Kodak, all of them veterans of the National Recovery Administration codes, and all of them knowledgeable experimenters in industrial welfare and pension schemes, responded positively. Armstrong had correctly gauged the temper of business, which vastly preferred a system that made the costs of old age insurance predictable and uniform and that would help them rationalize the costs of eliminating superannuated workers. The Advisory Council chair, distinguished sociologist Frank Graham, subsequently gave his support to a national system as well.

In mid-November, the president read a statement (probably written by Witte) that committed the administration to unemployment insurance and relegated old age insurance to the status of "a second step" that might occur sometime in the future. Armstrong reacted even more strongly. She leaked news of internal opposition to the program to the press, producing a shower of questions that, ten days later, led the president to "clarify" his remarks. He was convinced, he said, that "some plan embracing old age insurance could be evolved for the next Congress."[42] Resentment over Armstrong's devious but effective tactics may account for why, in the wake of the subsequent popularity of old age insurance, most of the major actors barely acknowledge that Armstrong had any role in conceiving it.[43] By Armstrong's account, at the end of the process, she and Witte (to whom she contemptuously referred as "half-Witte") were barely talking to each other.[44]

Yet in the end, Title II proved to be the only effective barrier against more radical proposals. It defused impossibly expensive schemes like that of Francis Townsend to give all old people two hundred dollars a month to spend at will. As Brown said later, "Everyone was scared.... They believed that the only constructive device to kill off the Townsend plan would be a contributory Old Age Insurance."[45] It held out an array of potential social benefits as well. It promised not only to enhance male dignity but to maintain consumer purchasing power by replacing the lost wages of those who retired, to release jobs for young workers, to make the labor market more efficient, and, eventually, to end the high costs of state-based, means-tested old age assistance programs. As an added bonus, drafters promised that it would relieve young workers of the burden of supporting aging parents. All this in a self-sustaining and self-financing cocoon.

## The Hardest Problem of the Whole Thing

No sooner had the Social Security Act been signed into law on August 14, 1935, than issues of adequacy began to surface. The bill provided for a 1 percent payroll tax, payable by employers, to be instituted in 1936 and matched by an equivalent contribution from every employee; benefits would not be payable until January 1942. The lag produced a surplus that, in a depression economy, threatened to exercise a deflationary effect. Most important, the exclusions written into the old age insurance provisions of the Social Security

Act exempted nearly half the working population, evoking questions about its fairness as well as about its capacity to provide for the aged.[46] Because the program did not provide benefits to those who worked intermittently or for only a few years even when they worked in covered occupations, more than three fifths of fully employed African Americans were denied coverage. Sixty percent of the excluded workers were female—in a labor force whose membership was more than 70 percent male. Probably as many as 85 percent of wage-earning black women were deprived of participation and benefits.[47]

At the same time, powerful popular support continued to build for the state-run, noncontributory old age assistance pensions that provided more generous benefits to the needy aged than those envisioned under Social Security for most contributors. Seventeen states had already begun to receive federal subsidies for such benefits under Title I, and California's generous assistance had drawn widespread national attention.[48] Political pressure to change Social Security's old age program came from Abraham Epstein's American Association for Old Age Security, which condemned the inadequate benefits, the absence of support for aged wives and widows, and the assessment of costs to workers. Some came from the newly established CIO, which asked for broader and more generous coverage to be subsidized by general taxation. And some came from the followers of Francis Townsend. Because its object

*From left to right, President Franklin Delano Roosevelt is surrounded by Robert Doughton (North Carolina), Robert Wagner (New York), Frances Perkins, Pat Harrison (Mississippi), and David Lewis (Maryland).* COURTESY, LARRY DEWITT, SSA HISTORIAN. SOCIAL SECURITY ADMINISTRATION HISTORY ARCHIVES.

was to enhance consumption, not regularize labor, the Townsend plan could offer gratuitous coverage for every old person, including those omitted from old age insurance like non-wage-earning women and casual workers.[49] But short of the Townsend program, a sense of entitlement to old age pensions as a matter of justice had spread widely. Everyone knew that even when the insurance program started paying benefits in 1942, they would go at first to only three hundred thousand people, compared to the estimated two million needy elderly who would then be receiving noncontributory assistance.[50]

Good reasons existed for the popularity of the pensions subsidized by Title I's old age assistance. But many feared that if that program succeeded in undermining old age insurance, the damage to the principle of equity would bring the work ethic tumbling down with it. In the judgment of many, continued assistance would be so expensive as to be unsustainable. Witte believed that even a pension of thirty dollars a month to everyone over sixty-five would "doom the present economic system and . . . inevitably lead to a dictatorship."[51] What was to be done? The solution seemed to be to spend the surplus. But how? And on whom? Despite the sharp and purposeful distinctions between adequacy and equity, the principle was violated by the very first set of amendments, which added old age insurance benefits for wives and widows who had not paid for them. No charitable impulse toward women motivated this act; no concern for their poverty inspired it. Rather, Congress added dependent wives and aged widows in order to shore up the legitimacy of a system in trouble. It did this by enhancing the benefits of already covered (mostly white) males to ensure extra income to those who had aged wives to support and extra insurance to those with young children who survived them. These amendments, adopted in 1939, reinforced the prerogatives, self-images, and citizenship rights of some males while reaffirming racialized conceptions of gender. They redefined equity to incorporate more adequate and appropriate provision for some men, infusing the American system of entitlements with the peculiar imbalance from which it has struggled to release itself since the early 1970s.[52]

In the spring of 1937, the Senate Finance Committee pressured the Social Security Board into creating a federal Advisory Council to suggest remedies. In May, when the new Advisory Council, which J. Douglas Brown agreed to chair, was announced, it consisted of twenty-four members. Six represented employers; six came from the labor movement; and twelve were designated as "public" participants, most of them academics and businessmen. On the employers' side, three, including Albert Linton, president of the Provident Mutual Life Insurance Company of Philadelphia, Gerard Swope, president of

*This 1939 cartoon is captioned "The Bride-groom Didn't Show Up."* COURTESY, RICH-MOND TIMES-DISPATCH.

the General Electric Company, and Marion Folsom, had histories of involvement with the Social Security Act and continued to play active roles. All of the business representatives attended regularly and contributed at least occasionally to discussions.

The same could not be said for the six labor representatives, who were only marginally involved, frequently missing meetings and rarely speaking when they did attend.[53] The CIO's Sidney Hillman attended irregularly, often represented by Lee Pressman. Philip Murray, vice president of the United Mine Workers of America and Harvey Fremming, president of the Oil Field, Gas Well, and Refinery Workers International Union, also seldom attended meetings. Behind the scenes, Douglas Brown kept AFL representatives John Frey and Mathew Woll informed, but, as he remembered, "I had to keep explaining things to the AF of L group.... I'd have private discussions with them and say, 'I think it would be a good thing if you came along.'"[54]

Prominent figures from the social insurance community made up the public members. The significant figures included Brown, Witte, Alvin Hansen, Molly Dewson, and actuary William Williamson. All had been major players in the original Social Security Act. Paul Douglas, who had helped to shape unemployment insurance, and Arthur Altmeyer, now chair of the Social Security Board, regularly sat with the Advisory Council. Once again, the John Commons/University of Wisconsin connection predominated. Witte, Altmeyer, Williamson, and A. L. Mowbray shared that connection, as did University of Washington professor Theresa McMahon. The public members included three women: McMahon, social work professor Elizabeth Wisner, and National Consumers' League president Lucy Randolph Mason. Only one of these, Mason, was closely connected with the network of social work professionals identified by Linda Gordon.[55] When Mason resigned before the council's first meeting, she was replaced by Josephine Roche, an old friend of Frances Perkins, a National Consumers' League activist, and an assistant secretary in the U.S. Treasury Department at the time of her appointment. Roche had frequently attended CES meetings in 1934, in place of her boss, Henry Morgenthau.

Together with the Social Security Board and several congressional committees, the Advisory Council worked through the following year and a half to recommend basic changes. Their charge from Congress was clear: they had to recommend a permanent way of dealing with ballooning reserves.[56] They were to do this by beginning old age insurance benefits earlier than the originally mandated January 1942 start-up date and by making them larger. They were to explore the possibility of extending benefits to the disabled, to survivors, and to excluded groups. In the end, the council sidestepped the challenge of significantly extending insurance to most of the excluded groups, including the disabled, domestic servants, and agricultural workers and chose to rely instead on a new and expensive package of benefits for aged wives and survivors to reduce the surplus.[57]

The discussions over these alternatives tell us something about how invisible assumptions about men and women informed an entire network of social policy. For when the council moved toward emphasizing expanding benefits to those already covered, it utilized gender to mediate the conflict between adequacy and equity—a conflict in which women played little role but issues of manliness and womanliness assumed paramount importance. The council's set of proposals served congressional purposes well: relieving budgetary pressures, undermining challenges to the legitimacy of the old age insurance program, and providing more adequate subsistence for some of the aged. It did so by renegotiating "equity" to affirm male dignity. Incorporating the family needs of men into the principle of contributory insurance provided additional benefits for covered men while finessing local demands for an adequate income for the aged even at the cost of equity. The council, as its chairman, Douglas Brown, put it, had adopted "the principle of family protection." [58]

The conversations within the Advisory Council and in Congress clarify the meaning of that principle. The council quickly agreed on pensions for fatherless children—an idea that already had popular support.[59] The Advisory Council adopted the notion rapidly because it promised to significantly reduce the numbers receiving means-tested assistance under both Title I (Old Age Assistance) and Title IV (Aid to Dependent Children) and strengthen the entire Social Security program by providing the illusion that their support was a product of insurance, the provenance of thoughtful and thrifty fathers.[60] Benefits to children, Advisory Council members agreed, should be a "matter of right," in order to avoid "the growth of a habit of dependency among . . . youth" and to sustain "the concept that a child is supported through the efforts of the parent."[61]

The Advisory Council used the same concept of equity for covered men to provide benefits for the widowed mothers of young children. These widows were to have benefits only as long as their children were young. The sums granted, and the restrictions on them, suggest that insurance for widowed mothers was conceived of as a matter of peace of mind for the husband. The widowed mother was to get three fourths of what her husband's pension would have been. The pension was granted as a matter of need, to enable "the widow to remain at home and care for the children."[62] It was to be reduced or eliminated if her earnings exceeded fifteen dollars a month (a tiny sum, even in 1939), thus encouraging her not to try to earn wages. In the likely event a widow's children's reached eighteen before she reached sixty-five, the council recommended that all support end, to be resumed again when she became sixty-five, if in the meantime she had not remarried.[63] A young widow without children lacked any "rights" in her husband's contribution and got no benefits until and unless she grew old without remarrying.

Tying the dignity of men (defined by their capacity to provide) to the virtue of women (their willingness to remain dependent on men and to rear children) proved to be a continuing problem for young and old widows alike. The Social Security Board was fully cognizant of what it called the "widow's gap," noting at congressional hearings that "middle aged widows find it more difficult to become self-supporting." Still, when it agreed it deferred the annuity of an under-sixty-five widow until she reached that age, on the grounds that "there is some likelihood that the widow may reenter covered employment."[64] Its sympathies for widows whose children were grown could not overcome internalized portraits of the family that fully rationalized its position: "They are likely to have more savings than younger widows and many of them have children who are grown and able to help them until they reach 65 years of age."[65]

The conversations within the council and the provisions finally adopted suggest that old age insurance was never imagined in terms of fair treatment to women—a product of the joint efforts of a marriage partnership. Consistent with the notion of sustaining male provision for the family, and over the objections of some members of the Social Security Board, the council voted to eliminate any annuity to a widow who remarried lest it construct a system that, in the words of one member, constituted widows "a prize for the fellow that has looked for it."[66] It recommended a plan that gave a wife no rights at all in the husband's insurance in consequence of his contributions to it, though demanding that she forfeit everything if she remarried clearly violated the equity principle that promised a return for what had been put in. Research director Isadore Falk pointed out that this denial violated the notion that the widow, "during the years when she was married to the insured person, was also accumulating certain rights because the basic rights of the insured person come to her by reason of earnings of which she was a partner." But the council overrode his objection, and Falk backed off. Once a woman was no longer dependent on the earnings of a particular male (dead or alive), the council contended, his support for her should cease, "rendering the woman ineligible whether she is the widow of an annuitant or the widow of a worker who dies before 65."[67] As long as she remained dependent on him, the level of the surviving widow's benefits, like the level of children's benefits, would be tied to the earnings of the deceased male, feeding the illusion that families deprived of a father or husband would nevertheless conceive him in the abstract as a continuing provider.

In the same vein, the Advisory Council, on the advice of the Social Security Board, rejected a hard-fought proposal to reduce to sixty the age at which widows might receive benefits. Altmeyer told the council that the board had "worked for three months on that one problem, which is the hardest problem of the whole thing."[68] Many members argued that it would be a comfort to men if their widows (most of whom in the 1930s would not have earned wages for many years) could draw benefits earlier than men, but in the end the board recommended that the age of sixty-five be maintained for both men and their widows. Once again, equity to men governed the choice. Citing a recent study, it argued that men who married only once were likely to be about the same age as their wives; wide age differences occurred among men who married two or more times, and these were the men who would benefit if their widows could draw benefits earlier. But it dismissed the economic needs of the second group: "Since men who marry late in life are likely to be of a somewhat select economic class, the pension needs of their dependent wives or widows will tend on the whole to be relatively slight. It is chiefly for the couples who married earlier that protection must be sought."[69] Not wanting to aid higher-income men at the cost of those with more modest means, the council rejected benefits for younger widows.

We have no need to guess at the gendered images that sustained these seemingly arbitrary decisions. They pop up everywhere. For example, halfway through its eighteen months of deliberations, the Advisory Council confronted the question of what allowance to provide to aged widows. Should it be half of what their provider-husbands would have received? Two thirds? Three quarters? After several hours of debate over what proportion of a husband's benefit might appropriately descend to his widow, one member thought to ask a question that had escaped scrutiny: "Why should you pay the widow less than the individual himself gets if unmarried?" "She can look after herself better than he can," shot back the group's actuary.[70] But the question would not die. Two months later the Advisory Council returned to the issue. This time the chairman, prodded by one of its three female members, took up the defense. "A single woman" he suggested, can "adjust herself to a lower budget on account of the fact that she is used to doing her own housework whereas the single man has to go out to a restaurant."[71] By now, though, others had joined the fray. When the argument resumed at the next meeting, Douglas Brown tried to end it by painting a portrait everyone could accept. Lower rates for women made sense, he argued, his patience clearly worn thin,

on the principle that it is more costly for the single man to live than for the single woman if she is able to avail herself of the home of the child. A woman is able to fit herself into the economy of the home of the child much better than the single man, that is, the grandmother helps in the raising of the children and helps in home affairs, whereas the aged grandfather is the man who sits out on the front porch and can't help much in the home.[72]

Such homely images shaped decisions that influenced the lives of almost everyone. They appeared at sporadic moments of unguarded conversation. Imagining women as irresponsible, the council voted to remove the original act's lump-sum death benefit to widows. "Such settlements," its minutes recorded, "are likely to be used for many other purposes long before her old age." Women could also be greedy and unprincipled. To avoid what it referred to as "deathbed marriages," the council adopted a clause requiring a pair to have been married and living together for at least a year before the husband died or reached sixty for his widow to be eligible for benefits on his account.[73] No benefits accrued to the woman who married a man over the age of sixty, unless she had lived with him for at least a year before he died.

The imagery became more complicated around the question of whether to increase benefits by providing more to every contributor or by enhancing the benefits of married men. Here the council clearly had in mind the normative 1930s household in which wives earned little or nothing, and it wanted to protect the economic well-being of the husbands who supported them. No one noted that its image failed to account for the more than 15 percent of white and at least 33 percent of African-American households in which women earned regular wages. Rather, members noted that even the original bill had been criticized by social insurance advocates like Abraham Epstein for its failure to include additional benefits for men with aged wives. In 1934-35, the need for equity—for a close relationship between contributions and benefits—had inhibited Armstrong's committee from moving so far toward adequacy as to provide extra benefits for married men. Two years later Advisory Council staff members, including Wilbur Cohen and Isadore Falk, returned to the issue.[74] They claimed that old age insurance would be perceived as more fair if it treated married men with greater generosity.

Albert Linton, president of the Provident Mutual Life Insurance Company of Philadelphia, put the issue on the table in the fall of 1937. Drawing on the British system, in which each member of a married couple received the same basic benefit, Linton proposed to "arrange our benefit schedule in Title 2 so that you will get one amount if you are single and alone and another amount if you have a wife living with you."[75] The assumption of a male annuitant who would require benefits for a female partner pervaded the rest of the discussion: "If you were married and had a wife aged 60 or over—because the average figures show that the wife is usually 5 years younger than the man," Linton specified, "you would receive an additional 50 percent of the primary benefit. If one partner died, the pension would revert to the individual level."

Reactions ranged from puzzled to skeptical. Some questioned why wives, who were not a "contributory group," deserved anything. Others wondered if it made any "difference whether the wife has earned or not." Many expressed distress at the degree to which the proposal bent toward adequacy. Several asked whether adding a means test for those whose insurance was inadequate would be preferable to giving the benefit to all married men. Linton stood his ground. Conceding that a wife "may have picked up some credits along the way" and that she might therefore be entitled to benefits on her own account, he held firmly to the principle that neither her previous earnings nor the husband's need should matter. "If she has not been in industry at all and is married to a man who has been in industry the double benefit is paid just the same as though she had been in industry. It is a scheme by which you assure a certain figure when you are 65." Two months later, this principle was still under discussion. Having agreed that it would increase benefits somehow, the Advisory Council still confronted the question of whether it could do so more effectively by "the method of the wives' allowance or whether by the method of enhancing the individual, whether man or woman, the individual benefits regardless of marital status."[76]

The Advisory Council never doubted that the wives' allowance was meant to benefit husbands. After a long discussion, one committee member complained that the draft being considered "doesn't say supplementary allowance—it leaves the reflection that the allowance is to the wife and not a supplemental allowance on the family set-up"; Altmeyer assured him that "the idea is to write your check for the two unless the wife elected the annuity in her own right."[77] To clear up any confusion, the final language recommended by the Social Security Board explicitly proposed "that the enhancement of early old-age benefits under the system be attained, not by increasing the amount of benefit now payable to an individual, but by the method of paying to a married annuitant on behalf of an aged wife a supplementary allowance equivalent to fifty percent of the husband's own benefit."[78] When, more than thirty years later, the issue came back to haunt what was then the Old-Age, Survivors, and Disability Insurance (OASDI) program, J. Douglas Brown insisted that the Advisory Council had explicitly intended to create "an allowance to protect a family unit" rather than to provide the wife with an individual benefit right. Proof that the payment "was considered a dependent's *allowance* ... and not a true benefit" could readily be found in the proviso that if a wife's earned benefit exceeded the husband's allowance for her, she could draw her own benefits.[79]

The minutes do not indicate that anyone responded in terms of the advantages the proposal offered to wives, widows, or families or of its disadvantages for wage-earning women. Rather, sympathy for the man who might not otherwise be able to support his aged wife governed the discussion. Nor do the minutes indicate that external pressure from any women's groups played a role in these deliberations. None of the three women on the Advisory Council (Theresa McMahon, Elizabeth Wisner, and Josephine Roche, who seems to have been there only rarely) raised a question about gender equity or the rights of women. Neither did Mary Dewson, who attended council meetings as a member of the Social Security Board, on which she actively served during nine crucial months from September 1937 to June 1938. The letters and papers of these four women provide no clues as to their silence on these issues.[80] In the several speeches that Dewson gave in the early days of the debate, there is no more than passing mention of extending benefits to wives.[81] We can speculate that under the historical circumstances the proposals of the Advisory Council offered far more security to the families of covered workers than most women could expect to provide through earnings. Since influential women social reformers had long since accepted that providing security for the family was the most likely way to safeguard women, providing increased individual benefits for all workers would have been an unlikely strategy. With the exception of McMahon, the women engaged in the Advisory Council's deliberations had been involved in some part of the effort to develop state-run welfare systems, and all were more or less hostile to the efforts of more radical feminists to fight for women's individual rights—a battle that would have contributed to negating any perception that the development of the Social Security program might involve an issue of rights for married women.[82] In addition, at least some members of the women's reform network (including perhaps Dewson herself) had become convinced of the need to abandon an earlier strategy of seeking benefits for women only and to focus instead on an integrated system of security.[83] Family benefits would encourage this direction.

If the suggestion to provide dependents' allowances for aging wives appealed to some because it recognized the family responsibilities of men, it appealed to others because it retained equity among covered men by maintaining a relationship between contributions and benefits. This strategy was essential to garnering the votes of southern racists. When Dewson queried the logic of relating benefits for wives to contributions, proposing instead the flat entitlement adopted by the British, Linton's response revealed the deference to current racial divisions and the opinions of southern legislators that had led him to adopt a strategy that reinforced gendered roles: "It is impractical to have a level benefit in this country because of the differences between the colored workers of the south and the skilled workers of the north. A single flat figure for everybody would not work."[84] By establishing the earnings level of the husband first and then calculating the additional sum as 50 percent of his benefit, whatever that was, the system preserved the contributory relationship and yielded a more adequate income for elderly married beneficiaries without transgressing relative expectations of income based on occupation or race.

Though the discussion that followed ultimately resulted in including a wife's benefit in the Advisory Council's proposals, neither female security nor justice to women was at issue. The idea of tying wives' benefits to husbands' wage earning seems to have been as unproblematic within the Advisory Council as the idea of restricting the benefits of wage-earning women to take account of their marital status or dependents. Justification for these differences did not seem like sex discrimination but rather like equity to men and their families. The women involved readily agreed to them. In the Advisory Council's deliberations, the achievement of benefits for wives and widows seems to have been neither the object of female struggle nor the source of conflict between men and women. Rather, the council's deliberations hovered around a limited range of issues involving the extent to which a benefit to men on behalf of their wives retained a sense of equity with regard to each other as well as with regard to family life. The wives' allowance easily prevailed.

In later years, Brown defended the way the 1939 amendments changed the Social Security system. "Apart from its social justification, the introduction of a wife's allowance served the purpose of balancing collections and disbursements in the long-run financing of old age insurance."[85] Brown might have revealed some of the other ways in which the changes undermined the value of women's wage-earning roles. Participants in the 1937 Advisory Council noted approvingly that the sporadic contributions of wage-earning wives, which were never expected to produce benefits equivalent to those their husbands would receive on their behalf, could be captured to contribute to the solvency of the fund. They understood that benefit calculations based on an average monthly wage over a working life advantaged continuous wage earners. As long as equity continued to be measured in gendered terms, adequacy could be achieved only by disproportionately benefiting men's families. To most people, that seemed merely fair. But it obscured a multitude of racial and gendered inequities.

In adopting the program, Congress accepted, with little debate, the relatively rigid definition of the family it demanded. For covered workers the 1939 amendments provided benefits, without means tests, to fatherless children, widowed mothers of small children, and aged wives and widows. It did not extend benefits to the surviving children of covered women or to aged husbands, aged widowers, or widowed fathers of small children. Thus fatherless children might learn the sweet lesson of continuing parental support beyond the grave, and aging wives would continue to be dependent, though on phantom earnings. But motherless children and aged husbands without resources received quite another lesson in citizenship rights.[86]

## They Feel That They Have Lost Citizenship

Three million domestic workers (including two and a quarter million in private households) counted themselves among the women who learned bitter lessons. Like three and a half million agricultural workers, mostly male, they found themselves among the still "uncovered" workers when the 1939 amendments emerged from Congress.[87] In fact, as a group, they had received a slap in the face. Following the Advisory Council's recommendations, Congress incorporated more than a million seamen and bank employees into the old age insurance program. At the same time, it excluded an equal number of mostly female and largely African-American workers by eliminating even the few who had crept under the wire. Three hundred thousand domestic workers in clubs, fraternities, and large households and about seven hundred thousand food-processing workers lost their coverage. But the program contained internal reasons to expand.

When Congress agreed to save the old age insurance system by changing its financing and using the funds generated annually to provide family protection, legislators altered expectations of the Social Security program and provoked a set of new, vaguely anticipated pressures toward universal coverage. Abandoning the idea that each generation of recipients would build a reserve fund that would support its own retirement in favor of a pay-as-you-go system required each generation of working people to subsidize the retirements of its predecessors. The shift turned a program that had originally been perceived primarily as a labor regulation device meant to preserve the dignity of workers who made way for the next generation into something more clearly approximating a promise of economic security freed of its rigid requirement for an equitable return on individual contributions. Adequate insurance for families displaced individual equity as the primary measure of fairness.

The inexorable logic of a system tilted toward adequacy fueled the hopes of policy makers and the excluded that old age insurance could more quickly include everyone and effectively replace the costly and demeaning charity offered by old age assistance. Advisory Council member Paul Douglas warned his colleagues that the changes made there raised the question of why the council could not recommend an "all-inclusive universal system": "If everybody is in from the standpoint of benefits, then everybody is in from the standpoint of contributions, and if there is to be a government subsidy ... for only the industrial part of the population, it is going to be difficult to have the entire population pay taxes for benefits designed for only half of the population."[88] As Douglas noticed, by enhancing the value of social insurance for some groups of relatively privileged wage earners without extending coverage to significant numbers of additional workers, the program, which was now called Old-Age and Survivors Insurance (OASI), created two classes of citizens. For one of these, the "right to work" had become a more valuable commodity, carrying with it significant economic benefits and social rights for which the other half was indirectly paying. A large proportion of this other half consisted of self-supporting women (black and white) and African Americans of both sexes.

Afterward, the implications of these distinctions became clear. For one thing, some survivors benefited more than others. The family benefits offered under contributory social insurance slowly removed most widows and their children from the public assistance rolls.[89] By 1960, OASDI (disability insurance was added in 1941) covered 93 percent of widows with children. Most of these were the dependents of men who had held covered jobs, leaving only a tiny number of children and their widowed mothers to rely on relief, or what quickly became known as welfare. The result was to produce an invidious distinction between those said to have earned benefits as of right and those for whom benefits remained a matter of public charity. Both systems exercised some controls over the behavior of mothers caring for children, restricting the amount of income a mother could earn before benefits were lost and removing benefits on remarriage, but charitable provision subjected women to stringent moral and supervisory controls as well.[90] At the same time, the promise of more immediate and more reasonable provenance for the aged, anchored in their own virtue and thrift, successfully undermined public support for noncontributory old age assistance schemes, which soon suffered from derogatory labels. Because so many of the poorest and least stable workers could not collect Social Security benefits, these changes also made racial exclusion more visible.

For another, women quickly learned the costs of a gender-segregated labor market, and black women learned the bitterest lessons of all.[91] The poorest-paid workers, invariably women and people of color, appeared to have been multiply disadvantaged. As workers, they would see their intermittent contributions captured by an insurance program that excluded them, to be used to subsidize more stable workers. As consumers, they would pay higher prices as employers factored their share of taxes into the prices of goods and services. As citizens, they were not only deprived of the dignity attached to a contributory program, but they were compelled to support a dual system of noncontributory and contributory relief, producing the apparent injustice of some receiving a demeaning "free" benefit while others received a due return on their investment.

Their position speaks to what was most disturbing about the construction of the 1939 amendments. This was not that the architects of the changes operated from such a white, male field of vision, nor that many women did not benefit. Rather, OASI promulgated a conception of equity that reflected a narrow spectrum of experience. To preserve a sense of fairness for some men, the program incorporated a continuing passive and even sacrificial role for many women. Equity for women was rarely in question, and then only as between the wage-earning and the dependent. In hindsight we see how the legislation produced a continuing tension in the expectations of married women, and in the relationships of the married to the unmarried, and pushed those women, some of them domestic workers, who did not fit the web of assumptions into challenging definitions of equity.

The system's planners had anticipated that some part of the contributions of intermittent workers would be captured and returned to beneficiaries. In their imagination, these workers were single women who would soon marry or married women who, though they worked intermittently, would ultimately reap enhanced benefits earned by their husbands. Policy makers frequently articulated these assumptions. With congressional concurrence, the council agreed on the irrelevance of most women's wage work with respect to this new citizenship right. "A married woman whether she works or no," it decided, "will receive an allowance because of her husband's earning." Its intent could not have been plainer. While "a single woman earns her own benefit rights," it concluded that "a married woman who works will not get advantage . . . of her own earnings, as in any case she will receive the 50% allowance for her husband."[92]

The actual situation was even worse. The council fully expected that married women would work occasionally and that their contributions, as well as the early contributions of single women who then married, would be absorbed by the system and help to sustain its financial health without necessarily yielding any direct benefit to the female contributor. There is no question that this was intentional, done, as Douglas Brown told the House Ways and Means Committee that affirmed the council's recommendations, "in order to control the cost of the system. . . . Women, as time passes, will more and more have had industrial or other employment in their early or middle years. They will have more and more credits in their own right, so as they approach 65 they will help build up the financing of these wives' allowances . . . so that they are not a net addition to the cost of the plan."[93] Altmeyer affirmed the intent to fund this new benefit to husbands out of women's contributions: "The additional cost of the widows and the wives," he told a congressional committee, "is not an absolute cost, because those wives and widows would have developed some benefits in their own right."[94] If a wife's own credits as a member of the labor force exceeded those to which she was entitled as a family member, then her family advantage was forfeit. Put another way, if a woman did not function as a stay-at-home wife most of the time, her husband would get no benefit on her behalf.

The effect of this policy on women was unclear, but the hopeful anticipation of the architects was not. It might, thought Brown, have the advantage of discouraging wives from returning to industry.[95] It would "take away the urge to go back and compete with the single women." Yet the availability of Social Security in their own right could also have the opposite effect: stimulating "more of them to come back in industry." While some members of the council deplored its failure to provide equitable treatment to wives who earned wages, suggesting, for example, that "women who work all their lives should have a larger return than those who don't," most symbolically shrugged their shoulders along with Paul Douglas, who declared: "Of course, wives work too." Congress apparently concurred that wives who worked would simply have to sacrifice because, as one put it, "most wives in the long run will build up wage credits on their own account."[96]

The 1939 council that designed this trade-off also aimed to discourage family members from taking advantage of the insurance program. Fearing inflated claims to benefits by women who falsely maintained they had worked for their husbands, Congress excluded "service performed by an individual in the employ of his spouse."[97] Nan Ransone got caught in the backwash. She had worked as her physician-husband's secretary for three years, duly paying her Social Security taxes, until she was ordered, at the end of 1939, to stop. She had a simple question: if she couldn't be covered anymore, would the government refund three years' worth of contributions? Altmeyer politely defused the question: her contributions would remain in her account until her death, he wrote to her senator, and perhaps at some later point she might be able to add to them. But the issue of "forfeited" contributions had lasting resonance, for wives were not the only ones who forfeited their contributions. "Scrubwomen on their knees" fell victim, too, as well as all those who earned less than two hundred dollars a year from a single employer.[98] This hit African Americans particularly hard, as a special 1941 Senate report lamented when it deplored the unfairness to "contributors who fail to qualify because of insufficient employment or low wages. . . . Money thus forfeited by the dispossessed of the act will flow into the insurance fund and from there it will be distributed to workers everywhere."[99]

The architects of the 1939 amendments surely never intended to harm poor women, but the particular ways in which their gendered imagination infused the legislation nevertheless produced negative consequences. In 1940, the male-breadwinner family remained the modal family. Only 15 percent of wives with husbands present earned wages. If countless numbers of others hid the incomes they earned by taking in sewing, laundry, and boarders, still, most white women and men gratefully accepted the derivative benefits offered to wives and widows. Not so for African-American women. As the depression deepened throughout the 1930s, racial segregation made wage work an absolute necessity for many black women, regardless of their marital status. At the same time, gender segregation confined more and more women of color to domestic service jobs, most often in private households. Of the two and a quarter million private household workers in the United States in 1940, about 90 percent were women.[100] A little less than half were African Americans. In contrast, men made up 94 percent of agricultural workers. Yet viewed from the perspective of the prospective worker, the figures take on a different cast. Nearly a third of all black workers (1.6 million men and women) and two thirds of black working women (compared to less than 18 percent of white women workers) were in domestic service.[101] Of the five and a half million African Americans in the labor force in 1935, fully two thirds were excluded from old age insurance because they belonged to noncovered occupations. No constitutional impediments stood in the way of including them, especially after the Supreme Court sustained the Social Security Act on the grounds of the welfare clause. In contrast to agricultural workers, whom farm interests desperately wanted excluded, and unlike some other groups, such as nonprofits, retail clerks, and the self-employed, no large interest group lobbied to keep domestic workers out of the old age insurance provisions of the new law. Race alone united them.[102]

But no one involved with the new social legislation paid any more attention to its racial consequences than to its discriminatory gendered effects. Discussions frequently lumped them together. Over the objections of black leaders in the NAACP, the CES staff committees had recommended omitting domestic and agricultural workers from coverage in 1935 "because of the difficulty of obtaining contributions from irregularly employed persons."[103] Everyone had assumed that the low wages of these groups would not permit them to contribute enough to an annuity-based scheme to warrant the administrative difficulties of including them. Still, the Committee on Economic Security had overridden its staff. Under pressure from Works Progress Administration (WPA) head Harry Hopkins, who hoped to relieve the WPA load, and with Perkins's blessing, the CES sent its proposal to Congress with domestic and agricultural workers included. They were eliminated again by the House Ways and Means Committee on the probably specious grounds that their contributions could not buy sufficient benefits and that in any event collecting their taxes and administering benefits would be costly.[104] Agitation to include both groups continued even as the Social Security Act made its way through Congress. Mary Anderson wrote hopefully that she expected, regardless of what happened to the unemployment provisions, that "all workers regardless of occupation will be eligible to share in the old age benefits of the Economic Security Bill."[105]

Her hopes, of course, did not materialize, and this despite full awareness of the double cost that race would levy. As Abraham Epstein commented, just after the passage of the Social Security Act, the "Negro stands definitely to lose more than his white brother by the enactment of the unemployment insurance and old age contributory insurance plans." Large numbers would be ineligible for benefits, yet "as a consumer the Negro will be forced to bear a full share of the indirect sales taxes imposed."[106] But Epstein, like many others, took no responsibility for the evident discrimination. "Farmers, domestics and casuals were being excluded from the contributory old age pension plan because of the difficulty of collecting the money and administering the plan," he told an NAACP committee, and in any event they would share equally in the noncontributory pension plan. When some black leaders objected to this, especially on the grounds that the plan did not have safeguards against "the abuse of its provisions on account of race, creed or color," Epstein "stated bluntly that the old age security advocates were not seeking to solve the race problem and did not draw a bill with the idea in mind of speeding the solution of the race problem; but that they are interested in securing old age legislation and antagonizing as few persons in the process as possible."[107]

A special 1941 Senate committee report confirmed Epstein's judgment that payroll taxes exacted hidden contributions: "It is obvious that the income which is derived from the employers' tax is ultimately collected from our general consuming public. Thus it must be understood that in the immediate present, one-half the funds being collected are from social rather than from individual contributions." The shared social cost of old age insurance worked a particular hardship in farm states and in the South, the Senate committee concluded frankly, because so many of their workers paid the "nation-wide consumers' tax" without benefiting from the program.[108]

Why, then, did they continue to be excluded? A racialized conception of gender created the double jeopardy of black women. The policy committees publicly cited putative administrative difficulties that stood in the way of enrolling workers employed in single-person workplaces; in private they admitted the difficulties of offending southern sensibilities. In public, legislators repeatedly sought to protect white housewives, whose ability to handle the paperwork they denigrated; at the same time, they labeled household workers as "girls" and fostered disrespect for the occupation. Over more than a decade, they deployed race to exaggerate the differences between household workers and their employers while seeking to attach to each the special attributes of gender.

The NAACP inadvertently participated in this strategy by tying the fate of household workers to that of agricultural workers. It exerted relentless pressure for the inclusion of both groups beginning before the Social Security Act was passed and continuing year after year thereafter.[109] The Advisory Council knew about these efforts but remained unmoved by them. Early in 1937, the Social Security Board alerted its staff to the possibility that "certain labor units, formed under various names," would organize a campaign first among domestic servants and then among farm tenants to bring them into the old age insurance program.[110] The Advisory Council also received numerous letters from church groups and African-American constituencies. "As you know," wrote Adam Clayton Powell Jr., "the Farmer and Domestic Worker is not taken care of under the present set up. This vitally affects our people, for most Negroes are employed along these two lines."[111] By August of 1938, a campaign was in full swing. Roy Wilkins, then assistant secretary of the NAACP, wrote a public letter to President Roosevelt in which he placed the issue of exclusion on racial grounds: "The great bulk of negro wage earners in this country is now excluded from the benefits of the Social Security Act because they are occupied in agriculture and domestic service. Of the five million colored people normally gainfully employed, some three and a quarter millions are engaged in agriculture and domestic service, so that you can realize how important to colored Americans is the contemplated revision of the Social Security Act."[112]

As individuals and as members of organized groups, domestic workers wrote letters pleading for coverage on the grounds of their own work situations and family needs. To most of these letters, the Social Security Board replied with a stock answer: "The Board is wholly in sympathy with extending the Social Security Act to include agricultural and domestic workers and has given the question much thought," it replied, persistently lumping the two predominantly African-American categories together, even as it sometimes separated them from casual labor. It then pleaded administrative difficulties and pledged that the matter would continue to be investigated.[113] But its internal discussions reveal a less cavalier attitude and much sympathy for extending coverage, especially to domestic employees. One of the board's chief staff members, Wilbur J. Cohen, objected that "we ought not to lump together" the two groups and briefly advocated bringing domestic workers "into the system even before any possible consideration is given to the inclusion of agricultural workers and farmers." In his mind, domestic servants were unlikely to give rise to "the political, financial and administrative" problems posed by agricultural workers. Social insurance, he argued, "was in part a method for providing cash income to persons whose flow of money income has been temporarily or permanently discontinued." As such, it was better suited to the largely urban occupation of domestic service than to agricultural workers, who, in popular parlance, could always rely on the produce of the land. Besides, he did not think there was any great opposition among housewives (as compared to farmers) to filling out the forms, and they could afford it.[114]

As it became clear in the deliberations over the 1939 amendments that adopting a pay-as-you-go formula would ultimately require extending coverage as broadly as possible, the wisdom of continued exclusion came into question. In its formal recommendation to the Advisory Council, the Social Security Board still refused to believe that casual laborers and the self-employed could participate but proposed "that the exception of domestic service be eliminated, with a reasonable time allowed before the effective date."[115] Yet ambivalence pervaded its judgment. Altmeyer raised administrative objections to including both agricultural and domestic workers while indicating that the board was "on record as favoring the extension of the benefits of the Social Security Act as rapidly as administrative experience is developed." Nor did the board raise any serious objections on administrative grounds. Though it continued to believe that a payroll tax could not be efficiently collected from a transient group of workers, it held that a stamp system was ultimately feasible. Dewson presented its position to the Advisory Council: "I think that the Board feels it is only fair as fast as we feel we can administer the law that we should take in every one of these excluded groups. The difficulty is in administering the law with domestic workers and with agricultural labor."[116]

The Advisory Council agreed in principle to extending coverage to domestic and agricultural workers as well as to casual laborers, conceding that including five million new poor and female workers would create popular loyalty to the whole Social Security program.[117] It also found the potential cost savings tempting. By removing many aging workers from the assistance rolls, it estimated, adding the excluded groups would actually reduce the combined costs of both programs by 1 or 2 percent. This, according to one actuary, was because "you are obtaining taxes which do not pay them a benefit in the same proportion so that there is economy in it." The Advisory Council also acknowledged the increased incentive to the excluded groups of the survivors and disability benefits being contemplated. After all, "in covering farm labor and domestics, the offering of not merely wives' protection in old age or widows' protection in old age, but rather the protection of the young widow and children and disability might be a factor." In the end, the Advisory Council came to the principled conclusion that "it is desirable that everyone be included" as soon as practicable without offering a recommendation that everyone be included immediately.[118]

When the issue reached Congress, however, both Brown and Altmeyer ducked. Pushed to accept the decision of the House Ways and Means Committee that "further study is the wise course to take at this time," Altmeyer conceded that, while he believed that administrative problems were not insuperable, "as a matter of public policy" he would agree with the committee's recommendation for further study.[119] Over the Social Security Board's objections, the House Ways and Means Committee voted to revise the agricultural labor provision of the 1939 amendments to exclude even more workers involved in food processing.[120] It also voted to exclude more, not fewer, domestic employees, adding those employed in college clubs, fraternities, and sororities to the ineligible groups. The provision imposed special hardship on workers who had already paid into the system for several years and would now have to forfeit their contributions.[121]

Providing benefits for domestics would offer tangible benefits to poorly paid workers, enhance the appearance of fairness, and solve some of the program's financial problems as well. Yet, for many years, pleas to extend coverage to domestic workers, including the recommendation of the Social Security Board, fell on deaf ears. What had made it possible to ignore domestics, argued a piece in the AFL's journal, *American Federationist*, in the fall of 1939, is that they were thought of as different. Ninety percent female, 45 percent African American, with greater proportions married, widowed, deserted, or divorced, and still working in their older years, they simply did not fit the profile of the stable industrial worker for whom social legislation was constructed.[122] Nor did they conform to the restricted images of womanhood within which the 1939 Advisory Council constructed its system of benefits. So they had been left out partly because they were different and mostly because "we have gotten into the habit of excluding them."

It was not until domestic workers, and their advocates in and out of Congress, put the issue of equity on the agenda in a new way that this changed. This happened during the Second World War and in the immediate postwar period, when women's employment expanded rapidly and issues of race became more visible as a result of the agitation of African-American civil rights leaders like A. Philip Randolph. These changes underscored a new rhetoric about what was fair and to whom, and they drew strength from shifting attitudes toward government subsidies.

The tempting promises of noncontributory assistance gathered steam during the war years. With the door to generous charitable provision wide open, memories of the prewar Townsend plan still haunted members of Congress, as did the continuing pressure of a successful assistance program. A general tax (paid for by the poor as well as the rich and equally shared by states and the federal government) supported the means-tested assistance programs. By the end of 1942, only about three hundred thousand aged beneficiaries (including wives and widows) were drawing benefits under the old age insurance program. These numbers compared unfavorably with the two million needy aged who received means-tested assistance. Recipients of the noncontributory means-tested assistance programs got more generous subsidies as well, an average of forty dollars per month as compared to twenty dollars per month for those with insurance. And wives and widows in the assistance scheme received benefits equal to their living or deceased husbands'; in contrast, beneficiaries of husbands' contributions to the insurance scheme received sharply reduced benefits.[123]

With these differences in mind, California representative Jerry Voorhis enthusiastically offered the House Ways and Means Committee a range of proposals to turn the Social Security system into "an economic stabilization and security act for the whole country." His plan included vastly increased assistance programs to children as well as the aged, a health insurance program, benefits for the disabled, a lower retirement age for both men and women, and, of course, "making every one eligible to a basic old-age annuity."[124] All of this would be paid for by general revenues and increased payroll contributions. Using general revenue could solve a variety of problems, but most especially it could permit early retirement for people in hazardous occupations, like mining, whose own contributions remained insufficient. In a neat twist, using general revenues instead of "contributions" to enhance payments to the poorest individuals would spread the burden of their support, which was now carried by the heaviest contributors. Those who had contributed most to the OASI fund could expect a greater return on their individual investment, shifting the balance for contributors back toward equity. Finally, Voorhis claimed, liberal use of general revenues in the insurance program would dramatically reduce the magnitude of the means-tested assistance program.[125]

Such promises drew immediate resistance from everyone with a stake in the legitimacy of contributory programs, including conservative southern congressmen. Advocates of extending coverage moved into the breach, condemning programs based on general revenue as "simply charity relief," which provided "no incentive for an individual to be thrifty during his working career."[126] The conflict prodded champions of universal coverage within OASI to demonstrate that even the poorest workers could successfully contribute to their own support. Advocates for domestic workers led the charge. Margaret Plunkett, Women's Bureau legislative director, made the point: with access to Social Security, domestic workers could be completely self-supporting; without it, workers who supported families on low incomes, with no possibility of saving and with little hope of eligibility through their husbands, would be forced on the charity of communities.[127]

Domestic workers and their advocates aligned themselves with the spirit of thrift and self-help. They wanted security without charity, argued Helen Hostetter of the American Home Economics Association. "Our members are rugged individualists," she claimed, echoing the AFL's stance for male workers, "and are suspicious of anything savoring of charity or even of paternalism but they certainly would like to have more security in their old age." She was joined by others. Ruth Ligren, who told the House Ways and Means Committee she had been a domestic worker for seventeen years, would "do away with pensions or charity or dole for the aged."[128] Mrs. Sidney Hollander Jr. identified herself as "a housewife and an employer of domestic servants." She told a congressional committee that she supported Social Security not only because it was "more self-respecting for an employee ... to make provision for her old age than to resort to public assistance" but also because "enforced contribution to such a plan is valuable participation in citizenship."[129] By 1949, the notion of something gained by participation had been transformed into nostalgia for something lost that echoed through the testimony of witnesses pleading for inclusion of domestic workers. It was palpable in its urgency, as in the testimony of one witness who remarked, "It is embarrassing to most people to receive something that they have not had a chance to contribute to; and also they feel that they have lost citizenship."[130]

The war raised another issue of justice too: it revealed domestics to be among the largest groups of the intermittently covered. They were among the millions who left uncovered jobs to work for the war effort. When they returned to the excluded sector, they forfeited their contributions. In 1949, Arthur Altmeyer could not provide an accurate estimate of the proportion of workers who had shifted from covered to uncovered occupations since the war, but he insisted that "many have shifted to a non-covered occupation such as self-employment."[131] In an effort to create a more seamless system of insurance, he had advocated including veterans more fully in the program by offering them wage credits for the years they had spent in the armed services.

That still left some four hundred thousand domestic workers (about a fifth of the total) who took advantage of the emergency to work in covered jobs only to be pushed back into housework at war's end. Margaret Plunkett, legislative director of the Women's Bureau, issued a ringing appeal on their behalf, recalling the patriotism of women who had contributed to the war effort, and incidentally to the old age insurance fund: "Not only can they not expect any future benefit from these contributions, but the amount of the contributions itself will be lost to them unless they can again move into covered employment or unless the Congress sees fit to place them on an equal footing with workers in presently covered industry." This was an "issue of equity," she argued. It might "well be raised by many thousands of persons who learn that while in household employment they are losing their insured status and that their contributions under the social-security program have been in vain."[132]

This, thought many advocates of domestic workers, was the most unfair cut. Household workers had a right to protection, just like other workers.[133] To have earned it, and then to be deprived of it, seemed a double burden. Vivian Carter Mason, director of the National Council of Negro Women, was most forceful on this score: the war had introduced many poor workers to insurance protection, she attested, but discrimination and lack of economic opportunity had resurfaced, eroding a benefit once achieved. Under these circumstances, workers had a "right to protection against the hazards of unemployment and seasonal work."[134]

Rectifying the financial sacrifices forced on household workers became the project of wider circles when it became evident that the costs of exclusion resonated widely. Restrictive coverage, as economist Eveline Burns pointed out, tended to hamper the mobility of labor between employments and "to discourage women's entry into such occupations as domestic service." In turn, that disadvantaged the "normal" American family, which relied on paid services from women. A former head of the Women's Bureau, Frieda Miller, concurred that the absence of coverage by all facets of Social Security discouraged women from entering or remaining in domestic service. Covering them would serve a labor market with many attractive options for young women well, helping to "stem the tide of desertion from that field."[135] Gertraud Bakonyi, a domestic worker, testified in 1946 that if domestic workers were included, "this particular type of occupation would become more of a career than just work to support one's body."[136] Absence of protection forced workers to continue to work into old age; "that is harmful not only to the worker herself, but to the American family life; and it tends to degrade the whole occupation of household employment."[137]

These powerful arguments for the value of extending citizenship to all overwhelmed the increasingly vulnerable account of how difficult it would be to persuade housewives to cooperate. "More money put into the hands of elderly persons," argued Thomasina W. Johnson of the National Non-Partisan Council on Public Affairs, "would by the same amount increase the purchasing power and raise the national income since all of this money would go into consumer goods rather than into savings."[138] It was "illogical and unjust," argued a representative of the American Home Economics Association, "to give protection to only part of American workers and their families. We believe that in a democracy all who do socially useful work should have a minimum of security. . . . We believe also in the principle of insurance—in having people pay into a fund themselves . . . and then get their money back as their right when they are old or sick or out of work."[139] A 1947 bulletin of the Women's Bureau, originally appended to the testimony of Plunkett, summed up all these arguments for including household workers in the Social Security Act: removing social "stigma" while providing neither relief nor charity would simply "make the field more attractive."[140]

Still, the task proved difficult. While women's groups offered pictures of domestic workers as mature supporters of families, members of the House Ways and Means Committee persisted in painting them as "girls." Even in the 1949 hearings, when the committee finally recommended including domestic workers, legislators described "girls" who worked for "women," and one congressman spoke of a worker's friend as "some other girl she runs around with." They imagined domestic workers flitting casually in and out of jobs and queried their capacity to "be careful and thrifty and make an effort to see that their taxes were paid."[141] They continued to conflate domestic and farm workers, as if to defuse arguments rooted primarily in an effort to legitimize women's provider roles. For example, the 1946 testimony of attorney Claude A. Williams, representing the Texas Trade Association Executives, took a position excluding domestics and farm workers and explained why with reference to the administrative difficulties of assessing the income of a farm laborer who had been given a "house, a cow, garden, room and board."[142]

Despite the active efforts of women's groups, organizations of housewives, and especially the Women's Bureau to campaign for change, as well as testimony from many representatives, neither legislators nor the Social Security Board acknowledged pressure from women themselves.[143] As far as they were concerned, this was not a women's issue. Senator Milliken challenged one witness to identify domestic and farm workers who favored coverage, avowing that "we have had remarkably few requests from [them] to be covered by the system."[144] Eveline Burns argued that this was only to be expected. Agricultural and domestic workers were, after all, "among the lowest paid and the least organized in our community, and it is those people who are least likely to be sending deputations or representations because of their economic position."[145] In one astonishing example of what can only be described as willful ignorance, Arthur Altmeyer ducked questions from Representative Herman P. Eberharter of Pennsylvania as to whether he knew of "opinions expressed to you or to the Federal Security Agency by women's organizations as to how they look upon a proposal for coverage of domestic servants[.] Have the women's organizations generally taken a stand on that matter?" Altmeyer responded vaguely, "My impression is that they have, but I do not recall any specific women's organizations having done so." Eberharter responded by pushing: "I thought perhaps some of the women's organizations had taken a stand." But Altmeyer would not be persuaded. "I think that some have," he replied, "but I do not recall any specific ones at the present time who have come out in favor of this extension."[146] Following his appearance, Altmeyer's agency had no difficulty assembling a list of women's organizations that had requested coverage for domestics.[147]

Altmeyer's memory lapse mirrors his own preconceptions about who deserved fair treatment. "It would be quite unfair to the uncovered portion of the population," he thought, "to increase the benefits and not enable the rest of the population to have the advantage of those increased benefits." On the other hand, it would be equally unfair to delay increased benefits to covered workers merely because there remained many who were not covered: "It is very difficult to say which is more important; the two go so closely together." Given a choice, however, he would extend benefits to the disabled rather than enhance them for aged widows.[148]

In 1950, legislators once again demonstrated how much easier it was to revalue a gendered concept of fairness than to violate preconceptions about race. The amendments that year extended coverage to about a million household employees who worked at least two days a week for the same employer.[149] Nonprofessional self-employed persons and employees of private educational and charitable organizations and of state and local governments, at their option, also became eligible for old age insurance. Altogether ten million additional workers entered the program. Many of them were women for whom the war and new experiences in the labor force fostered a new sense of justice based on their own working records. Their collective victory lay in extending coverage to a million or so of the least advantaged women workers, for whom one path to economic citizenship had just opened. But the 1950 amendments still excluded hotel and laundry workers and agricultural workers (except for half a million regularly employed, nonseasonal farm workers). These groups finally entered the system in 1954, along with self-employed farmers and professionals and many state and local government employees. With almost all wage earners covered, Barbara Armstrong's dream of an all-inclusive system had achieved fruition.[150]

## It Would Be a Great Comfort to Him

Between 1950 and the early 1970s, the conversations around old age insurance slipped from debates over which occupational groups to cover to how to ensure more adequate coverage. Complicated issues of financing, the level of benefits, and disability and health insurance occupied political attention. With it all came a quiet transformation of a family-based program that featured marital status as the contingency around which equity would be constructed into one that more fully ackowledged the individual contributions and rights of male and female economic citizens. The shift accompanied rising female workforce participation in the 1950s; it accelerated in the 1960s when debates around women's workplace rights entered the public agenda; and it reached its apogee in the mid-1970s when the courts insisted that gender no longer figure in determining the benefits that accrued to the married. The changes reflected a transition in the relationship of women to paid work and heralded new expectations of gender and families.

They are prefigured by debates in the 1939 Advisory Council, which had acted on a particular set of gendered assumptions, many of which shifted in the postwar years. Adopting a family principle for extending adequate benefits had led the 1939 council to imagine the family that would get benefits. It also required members to weigh adequacy for the "normal" family against the expectations of individuals for a fair return on their contributions. In the 1930s, the popular mind imagined (not entirely inaccurately) families that consisted of men and their somewhat younger wives, who only occasionally earned wages. To take account of the needs of these families, the council wrestled with the possibility of allowing retired husbands to collect benefits on behalf of wives who had not yet turned sixty-five, but that produced a conundrum around relative equity. If husbands got benefits on behalf of wives who were younger than sixty-five, shouldn't younger widows be able to collect benefits too? And what of working women who were drawing their own benefits? If working women got benefits at an early age, then why not working men—or everyone? Lowering the age at which wives got benefits threatened to topple the fragile structure of equity.

This was perhaps the most hotly contested issue in the 1939 Advisory Council deliberations. Was it possible to sustain the well-being of husbands by providing secondary benefits on behalf of their younger wives, even if the wife had not yet turned sixty-five? Albert Linton's original proposal had in fact contemplated benefits for wives when they reached age sixty, five years earlier than men. The Advisory Council at first sympathized, not out of concern for women's needs but out of respect for the expectations of their spouses. "It is the normal situation where the wife is younger than the husband," declared one council member, particularly "since the male annuitant at age 65 usually has a wife about five years his junior."[151] More than normal, thought Arthur Altmeyer, articulating his own sense of how the world worked: "With the passing of time, men do marry younger women as they get older." Like other council members, he believed it would be unfortunate if they "have to wait two or three years to get the additional 50% if they have a young wife."[152]

Only the most marginal comments addressed questions of women's physiology or their capacity to work as long as men. The explicit concern was for "the strange situation where the man of 65 who quits is going to get his pension and who has a wife two or three years under 60, where she has to keep on working for a couple of years."[153] "What we are saying here," noted Douglas Brown, "is not whether women should retire at 55 or 60 but whether the play allowed as between the husband and the wife should be not more than five years." Brown carefully voiced his own outraged sense of justice: "If a married man reaches 65 and his wife is 61, let's say, and you don't give him the wife's allowance until the wife becomes 65, you have virtually reduced his benefit during the years when he is 65 to 69."[154]

But the proposal for a sixty-five-year-old husband to claim a benefit on behalf of his sixty-year-old wife quickly ran into trouble as it became clear that expanding benefits to sixty- or sixty-two-year-old wives and widows created a privilege of marriage unavailable to women workers of the same age. If women were thought of as wives, early benefits for them seemed eminently fair; if conceived as workers, early retirement for women evoked invidious comparisons with men. When he was called on a few years later to defend the distinction, AFL president William Green commented that he would lower the age for working women "on the same principle that was recognized when we prohibited women from working in the coal mines and in certain other lines of work and attempted to protect women employed in factories and mills."[155]

Try as it might, the 1939 Advisory Council could not find a way to compensate men who had younger wives without giving the benefit of early retirement to independent wage-earning women. The problem, as Brown posed it, was simply that of "giving the married women an allowance at a certain age but... requiring the single women to continue to age 65." Such a policy would create an "essential discrimination between the fact that women earning their own benefits entirely would have to wait until they were 65 to get benefits, while their sisters, who are married, were getting the wives' allowance as of age 60." The council briefly explored reducing the retirement age for wage-earning women to age sixty, too, and even dropping it to fifty-five. But it abandoned the idea when Brown cavalierly remarked that a husband, after all, "can keep her at work until she is 65."[156] Still, in its final report, it took a moment to regret that the wives' allowances payable to aged men whose wives were several years younger than themselves "will be delayed some time after possible retirement of the husband."[157] Though many in the 1939 Congress concurred in feeling that married men were being unfairly treated, no one came up with a viable resolution.[158]

Through the 1940s, strong sentiment persisted for a lower age for wives' benefits, even if it meant reducing the retirement age for all women.[159] The idea so fully affirmed prevailing notions of equity for male breadwinners that few considered its potential for shaping the horizons of women. Far from it. Women's Bureau director Frieda Miller and her legislative director, Margaret Plunkett, greeted the idea sympathetically. The Women's Bureau, as we have seen, had traditionally supported a male-breadwinner ideal and staunchly defended special protective laws for women workers. Late in the 1940s, Miller, who was herself an unmarried mother, argued for earlier eligibility for wives out of sympathy for husbands. Only 20 percent of husbands who reached sixty-five, she argued, had living wives older than sixty-five, to whom they had been married for more than five years. Lowering the wife's age to sixty would render 60 percent of sixty-five-year-old husbands eligible to draw benefits for them, and the wife would then not be "forced, of necessity, to herself seek employment in order to help maintain the family income."[160]

Plunkett imagined the extra benefit that would accrue to the workforce. "Voluntary retirement of employed women at age 60" would have several advantages: it would induce industry to retire women even younger; it would prevent wives from seeking jobs in order to meet family expenses, and it would prevent widows from competing with younger workers. These rationalizations, which echoed the assumptions of protective labor legislation, captured still unchanged notions of women's places. As Plunkett told a congressional committee, women who had "carried the additional burdens of home responsibilities . . . would welcome the opportunity to ease up a bit from the strong competitive pace of industrial occupations or the burdens of manual toil in households or on farms." They could be replaced by "younger and stronger workers." Retirement at age sixty would also solve the difficulties of middle-aged women, especially widows, who often had "difficulty in supporting themselves" until they reached sixty-five. Older women, she noted, "are at a greater disadvantage in these respects than older men."[161]

The AFL leadership concurred in this position. Evoking similar images of normalcy, and straddling the line between old age insurance as employment policy and as adequate provision for families, its leaders echoed the arguments of 1939. "It is sound policy," argued President Green, "to recognize that retirement age for women is normally earlier than for men and that a wife is younger than her husband in a normal family unit."[162] Nelson H. Cruikshank, the AFL's director of social insurance activities, agreed that women should be eligible at age sixty, first because it was harder for them to find jobs, and then because retiring them at sixty-five worked a hardship on husbands: "In actual practice, the retirement age for the husband is in most cases determined by the age at which his wife becomes eligible for a wife's benefit. In order actually to provide for voluntary retirement of the wage-earning husband at 65, it is therefore necessary to lower the eligibility age for women."[163] While accepting differential retirement ages for men and women, however, the AFL insisted on similar treatment for all women, married and wage-earning. It supported giving benefits, whether "primary, wife's, widow's, parents," to all women at age sixty. The most compelling reason, Cruikshank averred, "is that wives in many cases are younger than their husbands."[164]

Not all women agreed. The divisions among them tacitly acknowledged that women could be treated either as workers or as wives, but not as both. The National Consumers' League, for example, supported a plan to reduce "to 60 the age at which the wives of retired workers would qualify for benefits," while opposing "the corresponding reduction in the retirement age of employed women" on the grounds that women were likely to remain in the labor force as long as men.[165] In contrast, more daring women's groups took the position that all women and all workers should be treated alike. The National Federation of Business and Professional Women's Clubs (NFBPWC) vigorously opposed any reduction in age for women only, on the principle of equal treatment for men and women. Like the American Association of University Women (AAUW), it appealed to the increasing longevity of women to justify its position and declared it "manifestly unfair and inequitable" and not "a satisfactory solution at all" to lower the age for wives to sixty. Both the NFBPWC and the AAUW argued that a lower age for working women in the absence of a lower retirement age for men would "establish the dangerous precedent of arbitrarily forcing women to retire at that age."[166] Their solution was to lower the retirement age for all workers or none; for all women or none.

A range of businessmen's voices proved to be equally inconsistent. For practical reasons, many departed from the traditional historical consensus that honored women's difference. From the business perspective, lowering the retirement age for women could have negative consequences. In the early 1950s, as the country coped with the postwar baby boom and faced the military buildups of the cold war and the Korean War, a shortage of labor loomed. In office work, education, and social and consumer services, the economy demanded labor. Business hopes for expanded labor force commitments from older women led the U.S. Chamber of Commerce to object to the pitfalls of instituting differential legislation for wives and female workers.[167] But smaller businessmen, as represented by the National Association of Manufacturers, chose to sustain the notion that women should be treated alike as women, not as workers. Along with most of the public representatives on the Senate Finance Committee's Advisory Council, they chose to support lowering the retirement age for all women.[168]

Congressional representatives seemed a little taken aback when the conversation shifted from benefits for husbands to equity among women. "One of the reasons for reducing the age," complained New Jersey's Robert Kean, "was the thought that . . . it was a great comfort to him to be able to get the extra retirement for the woman, the extra 50% at an earlier age than if, maybe, he had to wait until he was practically 70." While Kean acknowledged that perhaps the age could be sixty-two or sixty-three, still, he asked, puzzled, "what about . . . really being kind to people by having the husband and wife able to get a little more together and retire together?" Kindness was not, however, what women believed the system was about. It wasn't that she didn't want to be kind, said Olive Huston, executive director of the NFBPWC, "but we are making legislation for all folks, and I think it brings in the entire question of just what is social security; ... is it a plan of insurance, or kindness to people?"[169] Kean riposted by wondering if Huston would rather see a man dead than allow him to collect a benefit for a younger wife. "A man who retires at 65 probably has a life expectancy of only about 5 years," he told her, "and if he cannot get the benefit of the additional retirement of his wife, he may never get any of that benefit." Committed to a maritally neutral stance, Huston never budged from her position that since no questions were asked about "a person's status or sex" in collecting the Social Security tax, "the benefits should be paid in the same way." She was not always alone. When Nebraska's Carl Curtis offered the proposition that "a person who is a wage earner, or self-employed, or whatever the source of his earning is should be treated as a citizen and as a taxpayer and not treated as men or women," Huston uttered a heartfelt "Yes, sir."[170]

Most commentators say that Congress took no action on lowering the age for women in 1949 because it feared the costs involved. When it finally acted in 1956, it conceded the continuing salience of both gender difference and marital status by permitting all women (and disabled men over fifty) to collect benefits at age sixty-two. In a chivalric move, it allowed sixty-two-year-old widows to collect full benefits with no penalty. But it salvaged the cost of this generosity by actuarily reducing benefits to wives who chose to collect them at sixty-two by 25 percent. It treated wage-earning women who chose to collect their own benefits at sixty-two with a putative equity that produced practical inequality. By actuarily reducing their benefits by 20 percent, the new law effectively barred early retirement for most single working women while offering a tangible asset to the married or those with additional means of support.[171] Six years later, in a seeming break with the past and an acknowledgment of the growing centrality of female wage earning in some families, financially *dependent* husbands, widowers, and children were added to the list of beneficiaries by the Senate. They received full benefits even if their covered wives chose to retire early. Men who could not prove dependency still collected nothing on their wives' accounts. For the short term at least, Congress validated the presumption that within OASDI marital status shaped the prerogatives of citizenship for men and women. And gender, far more than any abstract notion of citizenship or response to work experience, carefully calibrated the value of the return.

As long as a general consensus about what constituted the "normal family" persisted, legislators and policy makers happily used it as the grounds for their decisions, slowly bending the system toward greater adequacy and enhancing the legitimacy of what had by the mid-1950s become America's most revered welfare program. When the meaning of what was normal became problematic, the effort to correct gender inequities produced unprecedented tensions. A shift in family structure and wage-earning patterns for women heralded the changes. The 1950s witnessed an unprecedented rise in the numbers of married women in the workforce, and particularly of mothers with small children. By the early 1960s, it seemed clear that rising rates of divorce, of unsanctioned marriages, and of children born out of wedlock would dramatically increase the number of female-headed households. As coverage expanded and as more married women became eligible on their own records (the number of women entitled to primary insurance benefits quadrupled between 1955 and 1967),[172] the built-in advantages to male-headed married couples no longer seemed fair to many.

The 1939 Advisory Council had purposefully built in these advantages. Its final plan contemplated paying for allowances for wives, widows, and children by slightly reducing benefits to single people whose accumulated taxed income exceeded fifteen thousand dollars over a lifetime's work. The proposal had raised questions as to whether the system would unfairly disadvantage the single man in comparison with his married peer and thus threaten the equity principle so carefully built into old age insurance.[173] To maintain equity, one Advisory Council member suggested that the tax rate for single men be cut to compensate for their reduced benefits.[174] Skeptics feared that the cut in rates might encourage more highly paid workers to try to exclude themselves from Social Security, though, so the council had finally settled on capping benefits for all highly paid single retirees.[175]

Members achieved consensus by a series of rationalizations. In the early years, even a single man, like all beneficiaries, would get far more than his money's worth, and certainly much more than he would have got in private insurance protection.[176] Of course, his contributions would insure his dependents if he ever did marry. As the actuary Williamson argued, a single man "doesn't know what he will be in the future, and if . . . each man has his right to marriage and the money that goes with it, it will be all right."[177] Reassuring as this argument was, even in the 1930s it did not compensate those with same-sex partners, nor did it apply to many of the single women, whose benefits were also capped. The latter would be entitled to no additional compensation even if they eventually acquired aged spouses, and their survivors were unlikely to benefit from compensatory family insurance. Still, given the system's bias in distributing benefits toward those with lower incomes, in 1939 men with high incomes (unlike poor women who were taxed on sporadic incomes and got no benefits) complained very little when they found some of their contributions captured for the good of others. The "scaling down somewhat of the single man" did not seem unfair to most people. As Representative John W. McCormack put it, "When a single man dies before retirement that money can be utilized for the general welfare. . . . A married man, of course, gets benefits."[178] The single man's financial needs deemed less, he found himself at the bottom end of the equity scale, as measured by returns on investment.

All of this made sense in the 1930s, when the idea of marriage remained relatively unchallenged. Yet just when marriage itself became less popular in the 1960s, and the numbers of wage-earning women started to climb, legislators increased the advantages of the married state.[179] The 1956 law (passed when the majority of wives still did not earn wages) assumed that the wives and widows of men were dependent and allowed them to collect benefits at age sixty-two without question. The 1965 amendments reduced to sixty the age at which widows could collect. They also added to the list of eligible dependents divorced wives and widows who had been married over twenty years.[180] But the husbands and widowers of even the most faithful female contributors had to prove dependency to collect anything. Adding salt to the wound, the benefits derived from marital status steadily increased. Initially entitled to 75 percent of the combined couple's benefit, widows got 82.5 percent in 1963, then 100 percent in 1972. No one doubted that these increases were justified from the perspective of adequacy, but what had happened to the principle of equity?

Even social commentators who agreed that family need should be a factor in determining Social Security benefits had difficulty justifying the large differentials between the earnings of the Social Security contributions of married men with nonworking spouses and those of single people. "The present formula," noted one pair of experts in 1968, "is incorrectly corrupted in principle and provides a benefit for couples that is much too large," providing a differential in replacement income between married couples and single persons that could not be rationalized by a couple's need for more income.[181]

The issue of equity between families at the same income level was exacerbated by the growing numbers of employed married women who began to raise questions about whether they were not entitled to dual benefits as both wives and workers. In part this was a problem of the system's own making, for its stretch toward adequacy created lower eligibility standards for all workers and recalculated benefits based on average earnings. By 1960, even relatively minimal involvement in the wage labor force, at low incomes, entitled people to benefits. The "bent formula," which proportionally increased benefits for low-earning workers, could inadvertently encourage working wives and low-earning women to remain in the labor force until they achieved their own primary benefits—still small, but larger in proportion to their contributions than the benefits of upper-income workers.[182] By the early part of the 1970s, employed married women often earned benefits that exceeded their 50 percent wives' allowance. And a family that could add together the benefits of both husband and wife raised a complicated set of questions about the justice of adding an extra benefit to the pension of a husband with a nonworking wife. Why should wives who had never had more than a marginal attachment to the workforce receive benefits that sometimes exceeded those of low-income workers?

In the context of women's increasing wage labor, a dual status as wife and wage earner seemed to entitle increasing numbers of women to both sets of benefits. After all, they had sacrificed first when their husbands paid the regressive payroll tax, and then when they paid it on their own earnings. Not only should each spouse get whatever primary benefit that individual had earned, Olive Huston argued, but the lower earner of the two should receive 50 percent of the other's benefit as well.[183] The 1961 President's Commission on the Status of Women debated the issue intensively. Its Social Security Committee forcefully recommended that a wife who had qualified for Social Security on her own account get both her benefit as worker and her benefit as wife, but the commission as a whole rejected the recommendation, "believing it was too narrow a conception of the social security program." Social Security, the commission thought, "is principally a social program, and therefore individual equity must be given secondary consideration."[184] Douglas Brown breathed a hearty sight of relief. Predictably, he had little patience for arguments promoting the justice of dual benefits.

Even widows' benefits came under scrutiny in this period of flux around gender roles. A future commissioner of Social Security, Robert Ball, acknowledged that survivorship protection constituted the big cost to the system. Like almost everyone, he agreed that spending money to improve survivors' benefits "would go to improve the system generally for everyone under it."[185] At the same time, a renegotiation of the boundaries of marriage raised the question of whether a widow's benefits belonged to her as of right or should be rescinded on her remarriage. Here, the same presidential commission that could not agree on dual benefits found the policy of rescinding benefits to those who remarried unnecessarily harsh. It approved a recommendation to restore them to widows who divorced within a year. This mild corrective never earned approval.

This man collects social security.

*This 1970 poster points to the family coverage promised to men of all ages by Social Security.* COURTESY, LARRY DEWITT, SSA HISTORIAN, SOCIAL SECURITY ADMINISTRATION HISTORY ARCHIVES.

Efforts to equalize the situation across gender lines threatened to disrupt a tenuous balance. For example, when, in 1961, Congress debated a proposal to reduce the age of optional retirement for employed men to sixty-two, it raised a series of questions about the meaning of old age benefits. Because it was intended that benefits for those who retired early would be actuarily reduced, their cost was not at issue, but their meaning was. Men required benefits at sixty-two, proponents argued, because if they became unemployed at that age, the chances of finding other jobs were slim; their health often wavered, and there were many jobs they could not do. This, responded opponents, was merely a thinly disguised effort to regulate the labor market: "an effort to get rid of the older ones to make room for the younger ones."[186] Some, seeing a conspiracy to advance the labor movement's "real philosophy . . . to get these people out of the labor market," accused proponents of supporting the "social philosophy" of Walter Reuther. Secretary of Labor Abraham Ribicoff shook off the accusation angrily. "Do not marry me to Walter Reuther," he ordered, announcing that his personal wish was to get more elderly citizens gainfully employed.[187]

Yet Ribicoff's denials could not fend off the labor market purposes of earlier retirement for men. He wanted, he said, to take care of situations where "after the age of 62 there is a certain group of people who for one reason or another cannot get a job, they are unemployable, and this is a good alternative to give them at their own free choice."[188] This opened the door to an attack based on whether men had not falsely won early retirement privileges for their wives. Relying heavily on the rationale that aging men needed their wives at home, Congress had dropped women's age of retirement to sixty-two just five years earlier. "I always thought," said Victor A. Knox of Michigan, that "the concept of it was the fact that the average differential of age between married man and woman throughout the United States was 3 years." Ball conceded the point. Now some congressmen asked whether they would be asked to drop women's ages yet again. "Are you not," New York's Eugene J. Keogh asked Ball, "in effect, destroying the basis for having given the women the right to take reduced benefits at age 62?"[189] Ball's response suggested that he, and perhaps therefore members of his staff, imagined that wives and working women constituted two separate and nonoverlapping categories. In practice, he argued, it was largely women not actively employed who claimed the reduced benefit. On that basis, he did not expect that reducing the age for men would press the Social Security Administration into asking for another reduction for women: "It does not apply to women workers, ... except insofar as they compare themselves with the wife and say, 'Don't pay a wife any earlier than you pay me.' "[190]

But, of course, women did compare themselves with each other, and the debate illuminates some of the singular ways that old age insurance participated in defining gender relations. Curtis raised the issue of whether the earlier legislation, rationalized as a favor to husbands, had not forced women into early retirement. New longevity expectations, he and others argued, should create the opposite effect: the government would be better off spending money to retrain women for jobs for which they were well suited. They could become practical nurses, babysitters, and the like.[191]

Reducing the optional retirement age to sixty-two for both men and women would, some thought, demonstrate admirable consistency in the treatment of the sexes. Others—like business representatives—actively sought the inconsistencies it sustained. The small business owners represented by the National Association of Manufacturers preferred not to see the system expanded at all, certainly not at the risk of increased costs. It endorsed instead "useful employment for vigorous men of 62." A firm conviction as to the value of the sex-based distinctions in the system underlined this position. These small businessmen accepted "the fact that typically a wife and children are dependent upon the father as breadwinner." Their representatives agreed that "man is the breadwinner to whom women and children have traditionally looked for support. This is in the very nature of things and may it always be so. It is not the function of a social welfare system to relegate the male worker to the role and status of the female. OASDI, like the armed forces, should continue to recognize the difference between the sexes in pursuing its basic objectives."[192] The reduced retirement age for men that finally passed speaks to the continuing labor regulation function of OASDI and foreshadows shifting sensibilities about the sexual division of labor in the family.

Still, for most purposes, most members of Congress and officials of the Social Security Administration continued to support programs that radically distinguished between men and women as contributors. From the perspective of contributors, women's taxes continued to buy far less insurance protection than those of men. Until 1961, a woman's contributions, unlike those of men, bought benefits for her surviving children and parents only if they had been financially dependent on her. From that of beneficiaries, men lacked the protections that their wives had. In 1961, Congress changed the law so that a wife's contributions covered aged husbands and widowers as well. Once again Congress insisted that they demonstrate financial dependency. Aged wives, widows, and fatherless children, in contrast, collected benefits regardless of who had provided support. In 1961, these differentials perfectly matched the expectations of most beneficiaries, for whom equity for men remained their biggest problem. Abraham Ribicoff, proposing to increase the widow's benefit, reassured men that their widows and children would be cared for. "Younger men," he thought, would not mind paying more for the benefit because they would know "that through the payment of their Social Security contribution they are building much more adequate protection for their families."[193] It did not seem to matter if younger women, who would also pay an increased tax, minded at all. The debate rendered voiceless a significant minority of women who believed that if they contributed at the same level as men, their contributions ought to buy their spouses and their children the same protection.

In the 1970s, these women found their voices. The rapidly rising numbers of wage-earning women and of women who did not marry, and the emergence of a dynamic and angry women's movement, soon rendered the discrepancies questionable and led some men and women to wonder if they were discriminatory. "The income security programs of this nation were designed for a land of male and female stereotypes," wrote Representative Martha Griffiths in 1973.[194] A series of court decisions confronted the issue, peaking on March 19, 1975, in the landmark decision of *Weinberger v. Wiesenfeld*. Eight justices of the U.S. Supreme Court (the ninth abstaining) agreed that Stephen Wiesenfeld, a widower and lone parent of an infant child, was entitled to Social Security benefits. Wiesenfeld claimed the benefits on the basis of contributions made by his wife, Paula, who had been a schoolteacher before she died in childbirth. But the Social Security Administration had turned him down: widows' benefits were available only to women. Now the Supreme Court demurred. "A father no less than a mother," said the Court, "has a constitutionally protected right to the companionship, care, custody, and management of children he has sired and raised."[195] On this basis, the Court struck down forty years of "archaic and overbroad generalizations," accepting the argument put forth in Wiesenfeld's defense that such generalizations unfairly discriminated against women because their contributions to Social Security did not buy as much as the contributions of men. Wiesenfeld's lawyer, Ruth Bader Ginsburg, had done her part to draw a new image of gender to the Court's attention.

The Court's majority decision, written by Justice William J. Brennan, explicitly challenged assumptions about men's and women's wage-earning that underlay the Social Security Act and anchored its old age insurance provisions. As late as 1971, an Advisory Council on Social Security had insisted that men rarely became homemakers after the death of a spouse and that, given their attachment to the workforce, widowed fathers did not require benefits to enable them to provide a home for their children. Acknowledging the truth of the generalization that men had been, and were more likely to be, the principal supporters of their families, Brennan nevertheless argued that this assumption did not "suffice to justify the denigration of efforts of women who do work and whose earnings contribute significantly to families' support." Dismissing the government's claim that benefits were unrelated to contributions, the Court held that statutory rights to benefits were directly "related to years worked and amount earned by a covered employee, and not to the need of the beneficiaries directly." Benefits had to be related to some reasonable classification; they could not be based solely on sex. Wiesenfeld's wife had not only been deprived of the security "a similarly situated male" would have received, she had been "deprived of a portion of her own earnings in order to contribute to the fund out of which benefits would be paid to others." As Justice Lewis Powell put it in a concurring opinion, the statute "discriminates against one particular category of family—that in which the female spouse is a wage-earner covered by social security."[196]

The decision in *Wiesenfeld* was followed by others. An aged widower was entitled to benefits on his wife's earnings whether or not he had been dependent on her, just as a widow was entitled to benefits earned by her husband, the Court declared two years later.[197] It justified the decision by arguing that "women are given the benefit of a broad, vague definition of dependents, while men are held to a harsh arithmetic standard." It was legal, said the justices, for the Social Security system to attempt to remedy some of the discrimination of low earnings for women by excluding their lowest-paid quarters from benefit calculations.[198] With the Department of Health, Education, and Welfare and the Social Security Administration fighting every step, the Court methodically overturned a carefully structured set of images about women's roles in the family. Henceforth, the Court concluded, classifications by gender "must serve important governmental objectives."[199] Imagining women as nonworkers no longer met that test.

CHAPTER 4

# A Principle of Law but Not of Justice

I n 1937, the state of Georgia levied a poll tax that applied, generally, to all persons in the state. It exempted the aged, the young, the blind, and women who did not register to vote. To ensure that the tax was collected and presumably to provide some controls over who might vote, the state instructed tax collectors not to register as a voter any male who had not paid his current tax as well as all back taxes. Women who chose not to register remained untaxed, and those who did register paid only the current year's tax. The effect was to discriminate against African-American men, most of whom found it impossible to pay large sums for back taxes. But precedent setting legal opposition did not come from that source. Rather, the law was challenged by a man who claimed that his right to equal protection, as specified by the Fourteenth Amendment, had been violated because women did not have to pay the tax on the same basis as men. When the U.S. Supreme Court got the case, it upheld the law. Evoking traditional, and therefore seemingly natural, gender perspectives, it declared in *Breedlove v. Suttles* that "the tax being on persons, women may be exempted on the basis of special considerations to which they are naturally entitled." In support, the Court cited a wide range of equal protection cases, including *Muller v. Oregon*, and then added, "The laws of Georgia declare the husband to be the head of the family and the wife to be subject to him. To subject her to the levy would be to add to his burden."[1]

A little more than forty years later, in 1973-74, the Supreme Court considered a similar case. At issue was a long-standing Florida law that granted widows, the blind, and the permanently disabled a five-hundred-dollar tax exemption from the value of their assessed property. Multiplied by the prevailing tax rate, the exemption was worth about fifteen dollars a year. Mel Kahn, a widower, applied for the exemption and was turned down as ineligible. He appealed. Ruth Bader Ginsburg and Melvin Wulf, who took Kahn's case to the

Supreme Court, argued forcefully that it was no longer plausible "to classify *persons* solely on the basis of an immutable birth trait that bears no necessary relationship to need or ability." Citing several recent Court rejections of sex classifications on Fourteenth Amendment grounds, they tried to persuade the Court that the Florida law perpetuated old myths and stereotypes about women, treated all widows as if they were financially alike, and had no legitimate relationship to state interest. The Court demurred.[2]

This would not have surprised anyone before 1971. Between 1894, when the U.S. Supreme Court sustained the state of Virginia's right not to admit Belva Lockwood to the bar, and 1971, when it agreed that a man had no more right to execute an estate than a woman, special considerations of all kinds could prevent women from being persons under the law.[3] Belva Lockwood had already been admitted to the bar in several states and to practice before the Supreme Court when Virginia's courts decided that only male persons could practice law in that state. And the Supreme Court, in *In re Lockwood*, affirmed a developing sense that nothing in the Fourteenth Amendment's equal protection clause entitled a woman to a license to practice law, or to participate in any other occupation, for that matter. Until 1971, when it declared an Idaho law that automatically preferred men over women to be unreasonable and arbitrary, the Court did not budge.[4] In between, each of the states and the territories could, if it wished, restrict the definition of persons so as to ensure that women were not included within it for a varied array of purposes that changed over time. These included jury service, job eligibility, voting, and taxes. Lacking explicit injunctions to the contrary, the courts maintained that state customs and precedents governed the circumstances under which personhood might or might not encompass women. And unless legislators specifically identified their intent to include women, persons were generally taken to be men.

But the decision in *Kahn v. Shevin* came in 1974—after the Supreme Court had twice explicitly rejected sex classification. Written by Justice William O. Douglas, it resonated with sympathy for "the lone woman" whose difficulties "exceed those facing the man." Douglas remarked on women's persistently low earnings, still only 57.9 percent of a man's wages, and the difficulties a woman faced in "a job market with which she is unfamiliar." Commenting on the reasonableness of the state's policy of "cushioning the financial impact of spousal loss upon the sex for which that loss imposes a disproportionately heavy burden," he concluded by arguing that "the states have large leeway in making classifications and drawing lines which in their judgment produce reasonable systems of taxation."[5] The Court's growing discomfort with gender-specific state laws that regulated working hours and conditions or provided particular benefits to one sex or another did not apply to taxes. Douglas had voted with the majority in the earlier cases and would argue that sex should be a suspect classification in two more discrimination cases the following year. There was something different about taxes—something that called on Justice Douglas to repeat the sex stereotypes invoked by *Muller v. Oregon* and to recall a history of leniency toward state tax classification.[6]

Perhaps that is because over the years gender had not only been a reasonable criterion by which to distribute taxes; it had been central.[7] Fairness in tax codes demanded differential treatment for different income groups—some rational assessment of "ability to pay." To make this assessment, states, and later the federal government, relied on sometimes arbitrary codings of status that conformed to already existing gendered habits of mind. Florida gave a tax exemption to all widows, including "widows of substantial economic means," heedless of dissenting Justice William J. Brennan's request for "rigorous judicial scrutiny" of "a legislative classification that distinguished potential beneficiaries solely by reference to their gender-based status."[8] Georgia exempted the young and the aged on the basis of stereotypes about their ability to pay. It exempted women because it assumed their fees would simply be passed on to husbands and did not wish to burden them doubly. And when the federal government adopted an income tax in 1913, its agents relied on prevailing images of the family and of men's and women's roles in it to produce what they fully believed would be a fair system. Trouble began when several states tried to circumvent the new tax code by using their community property laws to offer an alternative vision of gender. It took a generation for the Treasury to resolve what became known euphemistically as a problem of "geographical equity." This chapter traces the conflict over who should pay the federal income tax and suggests how particular gendered imagery became the measure of fairness in the tax code.

## Apportioning the Income Tax

When the Sixteenth Amendment to the Constitution passed in 1913, it gave the federal government the right to tax individuals for the first time. Ratified only after a four-year struggle, the amendment gave Congress the power to "lay and collect taxes on incomes from whatever source derived, without apportionment among the several states, and without regard to any census or enumeration." The amendment did not define income, nor did it indicate the persons who were to pay taxes. Congress immediately provided, by statute, that the tax be imposed on "the entire net income" of "every citizen of the United States, and of every person residing in the United States, though not a citizen thereof."[9] The silences raised two questions, both of them the subject of long and bitter prior struggle: whether married women were taxpaying persons under this amendment, and whether the states or the federal government had the power to decide who owned and controlled income. The complex interplay of meaning in these issues, brought together by the wording of the amendment, caught many unaware.

Faced with the problem of constructing a tax code that could survive skepticism, hostility, and negativity and appear to be equitable, the Treasury relied on what it believed to be fundamental principles of fairness. In the first instance, its officials argued, the level of the tax should be based on the taxpayer's ability to pay. But was the taxpayer an individual, as most discussions of citizenship imagined, or a family unit with shared income, as the economic viewpoint dictated? Though the tax was technically on individuals, Treasury officials took the second position. They believed that families with equal incomes should pay equal taxes, regardless of how the income was derived. In the view of Treasury officials, the only fair tax was a progressive tax based on the aggregate income of husband and wife. A single-breadwinner family earning the very good wage of five thousand dollars a year in 1913 should in their judgment pay the same as a family in which it took the combined efforts of both husband and wife to make that sum. The principle of family taxation was meant to legitimize an income tax that had little popular support.[10]

The idea that the family constituted the appropriate unit of taxation derived from a vision of normative masculinity: a worldview centered in male perception and in which a particular kind of male standard (that of the male as family provider) measured fairness. In this perspective, the traditional family—in the 1920s, about 85 percent of families included male breadwinners and nonearning wives—served as the standard for "ability to pay." At the time the tax code was enacted, only about 10 percent of married women with husbands present were in the labor force at any one time—a figure that rose to almost 15 percent by the end of the 1930s. Most families with wage-earning wives were, in any event, too poor to worry about taxes. To accommodate the normative, male-headed family, the Treasury adopted a system by which a married man could, if he and his wife agreed, file a single return on behalf of both of them. He would then be entitled to an agreed-upon exemption for her support.

The enabling legislation that Congress immediately considered and soon passed provided for a three-thousand-dollar exemption for an individual filing taxes and, on the assumption that "ability to pay" set the terms of tax levies, allowed an additional thousand dollars to married taxpayers. No specific deduction was allowed for children. The amount of the basic exemption varied over the following decade, as did the size of the extra deduction for the married. Until 1917, married couples got less than twice the exemption of a single person. That changed during World War I when the personal exemption fell to a thousand dollars for a single person and exactly doubled (to two thousand dollars) for a married couple. The married couple also got additional small deductions for children. After 1921, the exemption for a married couple increased to more than twice as much as a single person's—the difference acknowledging the value of marriage to the community and providing an incentive for the married couple to subsume the wife's taxpaying identity into the husband's.[11] The policy allowed a male breadwinner whose exemptions included a wife to avoid taxes until he earned more than double the wage of his single brother. The generosity did not extend to the nonmarried wage-earning woman or man who supported aged relatives or dependent children.

For the vast majority of families, the joint return provided an efficient and apparently fair mechanism for the taxpayer and government alike. If they were affected at all, most ordinary married couples benefited from an interpretation that accorded with normative patterns of family life and seemed merely natural. And, to most people, none of this mattered. The high level of exemptions in those early years created a threshold for individuals and married persons steep enough to exempt all but a small minority of wage earners from any tax at all. In 1913, only 1 percent of the population generated enough income to pay any federal tax. While the figure rose to nearly 8 percent during World War I, it dropped again after the war. Throughout the 1920s and 1930s it never exceeded 5 percent.[12]

But the Treasury's strategy provoked questions about fairness among privileged groups. To enhance progressivity, Congress frequently imposed a small surcharge for those with incomes significantly beyond the taxable minimums. Adding a substantial wife's income (earned or from investments) to that of the husband could make the combined income eligible for tax; or, at progressive tax rates, it could place the family in a higher tax bracket and subject it to a higher payment. Where both spouses generated or earned significant income, a couple could save substantial sums if they each paid taxes on their separate totals. In fact, in the first three decades, married taxpayers tended to file separate returns if each had a substantial income. Conversely, a wealthy husband who could shift some of his own income to his wife might find himself with a sharply reduced tax bill or none at all. Women who were well off in their own right found the Treasury's assumptions ideologically distressing as well. Small comfort as it was, and few as were the women who earned or inherited enough to pay any taxes at all, still the ability to claim their own income seemed like a major victory to those affected. Many women who had fought for property rights within marriage, struggled for suffrage, and believed vigorously in economic independence added their voices to disaffected men's. They wished to maintain symbolic as well as actual control of their own incomes, whether earned or inherited. Out of economic self-interest, affluent men and men whose wives had incomes of their own joined married women with significant earnings or property in questioning the fairness of taxing aggregate rather than individual income.

All through the 1920s, affluent married taxpayers tried to take advantage of legal loopholes to pass some of their incomes over to their spouses in order to reduce their tax burdens. They engaged in a variety of evasive maneuvers to turn economically dependent wives into income-generating taxpayers. Some men gave their wives gifts of income-producing property. Others signed contracts in which they agreed to share their incomes with their wives in perpetuity. Some settled trusts on them—passing over the income but retaining rights of control and management—or created "partnerships" in which the wife was said to have invested time and energy in lieu of money.[13] Treasury officials quickly stamped these separate returns as a form of tax evasion. To them, the family was the appropriate unit of taxation. They did not question that women and their income should be subsumed into it. Indeed, they discussed possibilities of taxing stay-at-home wives on the grounds that they produced imputed income that benefited male breadwinners, and they tried to deny women with incomes of their own the benefits of exemptions derived from filing separately. Short of that, they resisted efforts of affluent men to reduce their taxes by claiming that some portion of their incomes really belonged to their wives. They had to prove that the income was actually generated by the partner filing the return. No partner could slough off onto another (even a spouse) earned or investment income.[14] Either of these circumstances, the Treasury believed, jeopardized the fairness of the tax system.

The courts balked at the Treasury's efforts to impose family ownership on income generated by separate individuals, even if they were married. In deference to principles of property ownership, they declared that federal tax policy could not override claims to property whose legitimacy was rooted in the laws of the several states.[15] The Supreme Court briefly flirted with the argument that since property was everywhere controlled by husbands, it ought to be taxed to them.[16] In the end, though, it agreed that the federal government must tax income to owners, as they were defined by the states.[17] In the best-known of these cases, *Hoeper v. Tax Commission*, the Court declared a Wisconsin law unconstitutional because, despite the fact that the state had granted married women the right to "convey, devise or bequeath her property, real and personal, as if she were unmarried," it had nevertheless tried to tax "as a joint income that which under its law is owned separately and thus to secure a higher tax than would be the sum of the taxes on the separate incomes." This, the Court concluded, was an inequity. "Any attempt by a State to measure the tax on one person's property or income by reference to the property or income of another is contrary to due process of law as guaranteed by the Fourteenth Amendment."[18] Consistent with this decision and with the principle of property rights it upheld, the Court ruled that all the income earned by husbands was taxable only to them.[19] They could not reduce their taxes by claiming that half belonged to their wives even if a couple had contracted to share the income. These decisions, with their seemingly gender-neutral effects on husbands and wives, were taken in the name of due process to protect the property rights of men and women. By the early 1930s, the law was settled "for better or for worse in favor of a legal separate existence for tax purposes of husband and wife who may, in every other vital economic basis and social respect, act on a consolidated basis."[20] The federal government was stymied in its efforts to impose equal taxes on families with equal incomes. Women, married or single, remained persons under the law, the income they had earned, inherited, or created subject to tax only on their own account.

The Treasury might have been able to live with this had there not been eight states in which community property laws prevailed. These states—Arizona, California, Idaho, Louisiana, New Mexico, Nevada, Texas, and Washington— had long ago adopted the Spanish civil law as the basis of their domestic law. Women legally acquired property by virtue of being wives, and the property and earnings acquired by either partner after marriage belonged equally to both. Since the system conceived of property ownership (including earned income) as immediately being divided up between the marital partners, married couples in community property states filed separate tax returns in which each declared half the family earnings and all other income (no matter who brought it in) to belong to each spouse. In deference to state laws, the Supreme Court agreed that in these eight community property states half the income could be attributed to the nonearning spouse; each would then fall into a lower tax bracket, and their taxes fall accordingly.[21] Its decisions treated women as persons for tax purposes: an economic victory for all wealthy residents of community property states, and a practical one for women in the other states who possessed property or who earned substantial wages. As legal expert Edward McCaffery eloquently documents, husbands who could split their incomes with their wives paid significantly lower taxes than they would have been required to pay, at progressive tax rates, on all their earnings.[22] At the same time, the Treasury lamented the loss of what it estimated was approximately three hundred million dollars in taxes—a sum that constituted a burden community property laws placed on the men and women of the remaining forty states who lived in families with a single, generally male, provider.

For the Treasury, this posed less a practical than a moral dilemma. If ability to pay were the major criterion for the progressive tax, then the family seemed like the logical unit of taxation. The only fair solution, Treasury officials insisted, was to deprive male householders of every opportunity to divide their incomes with their wives by taxing the family everywhere as a unit: to demand a mandatory joint income tax return for married people. Discouraged by the courts, they sought legislative relief. In the early 1930s, eager to claim the monies they would get if community property residents paid taxes on aggregate family income, they mounted a full-fledged battle for a mandatory joint income tax return to be filed by all married couples who lived together. They certainly hoped to enhance revenue, but even more, they believed the credibility of progressive taxation was at stake. For them, rational tax collection and equity lay in acknowledging the traditional male-breadwinner family. Filing separate tax returns was, in the Treasury's eyes, an abuse that threatened equity. As its chief tax officer explained, separate returns threatened to "defeat the progressive rate schedule, particularly in the case of the larger taxpayers."[23] Yet a consistent system required commitment to common perceptions of gendered fairness. The price would not be cheap: it would require asserting the rights of the federal government over even the most ancient prerogatives of the separate states.

These efforts to impose rationality evoked three kinds of protests: on behalf of states' rights, on behalf of women's equality, and against the denial of due process under the Fourteenth Amendment. Protests did not come from the community property states alone, though their representatives certainly led the legislative charge, but also from an array of women's organizations, affluent husbands, churchmen, and labor unionists. Each had a different agenda, even if their goals frequently overlapped. Though their definitions of equity differed, all perceived themselves to be acting in its name.

The ongoing debate and its resolution tell us something not merely about winners and losers in the game of social policy but about how appeals to a gendered meaning system participated in the formulation of issues affecting the fiscal health of the state and the most intimate decisions of ordinary people. Deeply gendered conceptions participated in a painful dialogue that tested some of the most crucial issues in the American legal and ideological canon. The debate over relations between husbands and wives and the rights of men and women became a staging ground for exploring the rights of individuals, states' rights versus federal power, fairness and equity between classes, the scope of the Fourteenth Amendment, and the meaning of the family. Women, as citizens, participated in the debate, though by no means as leading players. Yet, in its course, women moved perilously close to personhood. Though the issues they raised led otherwise cautious politicians to declare their fealty to the rights of women, stirring the anxieties of husbands, bachelors, and the business community, women did not succeed. In the end, the principle of "normative masculinity" prevailed. Let us look at what was at issue and at the role played by gender in it.

## More Than Money Is Involved

In the fall of 1933, the Treasury formally proposed that Congress pass a law taxing married couples living together on their joint incomes. Testifying before Congress at the beginning of the debate over the proposal Roswell Magill, a noted tax expert and then a Treasury official, captured the essence of the government's position. Magill explained that income was in fact rarely attributable to both marriage partners, yet, he complained, "if each has an income of any considerable size, each will ordinarily make a separate return in order to reduce the normal tax, and more particularly, the surtaxes which would otherwise be payable." This was, he thought, irrational because, as everyone knew, "the family income is in fact frequently expended and otherwise treated as a unit." Nevertheless, he continued, "if the husband and wife can so arrange their affairs that the wife is in receipt of a portion of the family income, income taxes can be considerably reduced. In other words, the present privilege of filing separate returns operates to that extent to defeat the progressive rate schedule, particularly in the case of the larger taxpayers."[24]

The language of Magill's attack serves as a text for the Treasury's game plan for the following years. Embedded in it was the conviction that since the family unit constituted the unit of consumption, anything other than a tax based on a narrowly defined family was merely evasion. What Magill called the "normal" tax was for most, and ought to be for everyone, he thought, based on family income.[25] It was, he argued, a "privilege" to file separate returns. Dismissing the wife's income as illusory, Magill described it as merely a product of husbands and wives "arranging their affairs." His language underlines the Treasury's fear of critical challenges to the legitimacy of progressive taxation. It posits a deeply rooted system of beliefs and offers them as justification for attacking a powerful political cohort of community property states. Magill grounded his tax program in the moral rectitude of his view of the family—a view that so thoroughly imbued the Treasury that its officials and their congressional allies could see no room for compromise, even when their need for revenues was largest.

This stubborn insistence on a particular view of the family in which married women constituted citizens with an obligation to pay taxes, but disappeared as individuals and as persons with rights to pay them on their own property and income, festered and grew stronger as the debate proceeded into the 1940s. It escalated into a lengthy confrontation between the Treasury and the eight community property states, in which the rights of women were held hostage to the ideal of a male breadwinner. The key to the conflict was the settled belief among many Treasury officials, members of Congress, and, increasingly, the public that any alternative view of the family was a mere subterfuge for tax evasion. Representative David Lewis of Maryland, reporting to Congress for the House Ways and Means Committee, which throughout the period strongly championed the Treasury's view of the family, caught the spirit of attack. The "legal fiction" set up in community property states, he proclaimed, "that the income of the husband is one half the income of the wife should not be allowed to defeat the Federal income tax law and discriminate against citizens in the other 40 states."[26]

In response, the community property states, whose main object was to avoid higher taxes, invoked the long-standing rights of states to define the personhood of women and insisted on their judicially sustained authority to continue to do so. They objected to the Treasury's construction of the marital relationship on the grounds that under their laws the wife owned half her husband's earnings—that she had earned them in her capacity as wife, that she fully owned them, and moreover that the husbands who gave up half of their hard-earned income took on burdens that husbands who lived in common law states never assumed. Their representatives protested the eagerness of the federal government to tax husbands on what their laws declared to be the wife's property and appealed to the due process clause of the Fourteenth Amendment in justification. Such a tax, in their eyes, threatened the principle of states' rights, and specifically the rights of states to define women as persons who could own property.

To defend states' rights and the rights of property, spokesmen for the community property states articulated an astonishingly modern (and perhaps merely instrumental) view of marriage and women's rights, yielding a series of battles on the floor of Congress and in its hearing rooms around the roles of husbands and wives. A 1934 exchange before the House Ways and Means Committee suggests the flavor of the debate. Questioning Senator Tom Connally of Texas (who, as spokesman for the community property states, had volunteered his testimony), Representative Frank Crowther of New York posited that "8 of the 48 states ... have been held to permit each spouse to report one half of the community income, although it was all earned by and was expended under the control of the husband." Connally replied: "That is not true. I don't care whether the Treasurer says it or who said it, it is not true, and as to that under our law it is not all earned by the husband; it is joint earnings of the wife who stays at home, raises the children and helps economize in the kitchen; she is contributing just as much to the success of the husband as the husband is." Connally could not resist a personal jab. He concluded his statement by reiterating, "It is not true that the husband earns it all and I am sure Dr. Crowther will not go home tonight and contend that to Mrs. Crowther."[27]

At another moment, committee chair Robert Doughton of North Carolina tried to break down Connally's conviction that community property was really individually held. To his pugnacious question "If you have a salary does the wife get half of that salary?" Connally responded, "She does." Doughton persisted: "Do you think it is a fair proposition to tax my wife twice as much as under the same circumstances they would tax your wife?" And Connally riposted: "It is the fault of your law. If the law of North Carolina denies to the woman the property rights which other States accord them, that is the fault of the North Carolina law." Finally, Connally articulated a view of wages that a modern feminist would applaud. Responding to a question as to whether husbands in community property states were not merely giving gifts to their wives, Connally opined, "You can't give something you don't own, and you don't own it in my State." Representative Crowther quickly asked, "Even if he earned it all himself?" and Connally came back with "He doesn't earn it all himself."[28]

Though the conversation was about the rights of wives, a taut thread of concern for justice to male breadwinners ran through the legislators' appeal on behalf of the husbands of forty states. As one lawmaker put it, fairness, or justice, resided in "equality, especially in the levying of Federal taxes, upon all the people in similar situations. I do not think anybody can object to that."[29] We understand that "all the people" meant "all the male breadwinners" when we watch the community property states fending off these charges by invoking the "burdens" assumed by husbands in their jurisdictions. Claiming the separate vested interest of wives, they drew lurid pictures of immoral women over whose behavior husbands had little control. Faced with women's cupidity, husbands lamented their powerlessness over their wives' share of the property. They deplored a wife's right to dispose of her half at her death—"even to a lover," or to her illegitimate children. They protested that when she died, a husband could be forced to liquidate his business in order to give his wife's heirs their shares. They claimed that men could be compelled to pay taxes on what they inherited from wives.[30]

Failing to break down the community property defense of the wife's income as separate, the Treasury fell back upon the generally acknowledged notion that, in any event, most husbands controlled and managed their wives' incomes and therefore could and should be liable for paying the appropriate taxes. The House Ways and Means Committee produced a bill to tax the managers and controllers as if the income belonged to them. This move raised starkly the issue of whether one person could be taxed on property actually belonging to another—even if in fact he managed and controlled it—and reveals something of the desperation of Treasury officials to create "geographical equity" by resolving issues of "marital equity." But the courts had already ruled the Treasury's position a denial of due process. Frequently cited by representatives in the debates in Congress and inserted into the record, every Supreme Court decision held that husbands, controlling agents though they might be, could not be taxed on the property and income of spouses.[31]

To sustain their arguments the community property states raised the evocative and undoubtedly racist flag of states' rights, challenging the federal government's capacity to make the states alter their property tax laws. As Connally put it, "It is not a question of what one state may do or another state may do, but the question is whether under the law of one State certain property belongs to one person and other property belongs to another person."[32] These sorts of arguments infuriated some legislators. "The Government of the United States . . . recognizes the breadwinner," sputtered David Lewis of Maryland,

> the lawyer who makes his $10,000 a year of income, which is a fact, and
> he is the cause of causes of that income, and it is the State legislature
> that comes along and insists to the wife one half of that income that is
> violating the constitution, and not the Government of the United
> States.

Lewis's conviction that a breadwinner's income could be construed as his alone led him to conclude that "the Fourteenth Amendment of the Constitution of the United States ought to be read in reference to the loss of taxes and to the primal necessities of the Government.... To deny the government of the United States ... the right to define income in a bona fide and factual way," argued Lewis, "is to largely impair, if not destroy, the power to levy income taxes for its support and for its necessary administration."[33]

Finally, then, the issue turned on whether states had the exclusive right to determine by statute the laws of property or whether the federal government could override them. "Were the interests of one state to prevail over those of another?" asked one representative.[34] For opponents of the joint income tax return, private property, as defined by the states, remained sacrosanct. As Representative Morgan Sanders of Texas put it, "Under our dual form of government each State has the right and the authority to fix its own laws and its own property rights, and these laws and these property rights will not be disturbed by the Supreme Court of the United States provided they do not conflict with the Constitution. These decisions may go over the heads of some folk who do not have proper reverence for our Constitution and our laws." To Sanders, this was the key issue: "I plant my feet squarely on the issue of states' rights," he declared on the House floor.[35] In the end, the community property states had sufficient clout to carry the day. When the Treasury retreated, observers believed the personhood of women, as it was reflected in each state's capacity to make its own laws and to defend its definition of property rights, had prevailed over justice to male breadwinners.

The Treasury's commitment to an idea of justice rooted in fairness to particular family units did not abate. Nor did the behavior it viewed as tax evasion. In 1937, Secretary of the Treasury Henry Morgenthau, who had observed a dramatic extension of what he called "subterfuge" during the depression years, wrote to the president decrying several kinds of tax evasion, including "the device of domestic personal holding companies, husband and wife or father and child partnerships, and the device of splitting income between husbands and wives in the community property states."[36] Only the unwelcome idea of raising taxes during a continuing depression prevented Congress from once again confronting the issue. The discussion emerged once again as the demands of a European war heightened the need for revenue and challenged the patriotism of those who did not pay fairly. Beginning in 1940, and at a rapidly escalating rate after the United States entered the war in 1941, married women took jobs, family incomes rose rapidly, and the secondary costs of women earning wages (including transportation, lunches, special clothing, child care, and replacing household services) became apparent. The Treasury was now in a strong position to plead its case for closing the loophole of inequity and capturing the extra $350 million that it estimated would be brought in by jointly taxing married couples.

In 1941, the Treasury hoped to reduce opposition by proposing a different kind of mandatory joint tax calculated by aggregating the income of a married couple and then assessing each partner a proportional share of the tax.[37] It did not offer to increase the level of the exemption for couples, nor to widen the tax bracket, but it hoped that, by assigning the tax bill to partners in proportion to their contributions, it could circumvent judicial opposition to taxing community property taxpayers jointly. It still had not budged on its principle of taxing families with equal incomes equally. The family where the husband earned all the income and supported his family should, in its view, pay the same tax as the family with two income earners. So two married individuals who together earned the very nice total of five thousand dollars in 1940 would owe the same seven hundred dollars in taxes as a single male breadwinner. The Treasury remained blind to the increased costs paid by the dual-earning couple.

Reported out of committee without hearings and as part of a larger tax bill, the provision met what one commentator described as "a storm of opposition." Not even appeals to patriotic agendas could save it from defeat in the House, and the president withdrew the provision lest the entire bill go down to defeat.[38] A year later, desperate for revenue to fund the war, the administration reintroduced the bill. This time, to give an extra break to those families where the joint income came from the earnings of wives rather than from investments and to take some of the cost of earning into account, it grudgingly attached an earned income credit. The concession spoke to the need for women's labor during the war.[39] The bill was defeated a second time. During the successive campaigns, hard-pressed opponents of mandatory joint tax returns searched for enhanced justifications for their continuing claim to states' rights in the face of the demonstrable need for revenue. To fend off the new tax scheme, opponents joined forces with groups with whom they otherwise had little in common, including those who feared the loss of individual rights and critics of the Treasury's putative defense of the family. Their ammunition increasingly consisted of three issues, all of them marginal to the core issue of raising revenue: the nature of the family, its relationship to patriotism, and women's rights.

The debate recalled challenges that had been raised in the 1930s to assumptions about what constituted a family. These challenges now dramatically escalated. While the Treasury continued to hold that joint taxation of the husband and wife was a "natural" arrangement, others demurred.[40] In 1934,

Representative Fred Vinson of Kentucky had raised the question tentatively. Why, he asked, was the family so arbitrarily defined? "That is the point, to my mind, just why ... you could take the income of a husband and wife together. It occurs to me if you could do that you could go into the entire family and make the return a family affair, sons and daughters and your in-laws; and it occurs to me that when the word 'income' is used in the sixteenth amendment that is referring to particular income of an individual or corporate body."[41] This theme re-emerged in the 1940s, leading one congressman to ask: "Is the tax arbitrary in constituting an economic unit without so classifying other family relationships, such as parents and children or brother and sister?"[42]

In 1941 and 1942, these challenges to the idea of the family and the fairness of including only husbands and wives in the economic unit to be taxed took on a larger shape. In a letter to the *New York Times*, Princeton economist Harley Lutz used the principle of mandatory taxation only of married couples to ridicule the Treasury's cherished defense of a tax levied on "ability to pay." Why stop there, he asked: "In many families there are grown sons and daughters with good incomes. Why not require the father to report all of this income together with his own?"[43] A married couple, argued Judge Dorothy Kenyon (representing the American Association of University Women in congressional hearings), "is not a natural unit for tax purposes." Rather, it was only one of many family types: "Widowed mothers, for instance, are heads of households," their incomes often augmented by sons and daughters.[44]

The Treasury nourished these questions by acknowledging that under a mandatory joint return, two single people who both earned incomes would pay a higher tax if they married than if they remained single. This was fair, in the Treasury's view, because living as a unit would enhance the couple's ability to pay. Of course, that assumed that single people lived apart. The mandatory joint return was quickly labeled an attack on marriage itself because it placed what some called a "penalty" on marriage, providing community property states with a range of allies that they could hardly have anticipated. Representatives of church groups wondered if the Treasury were not misguided in its efforts to identify the family as a taxable unit. A prominent Episcopalian bishop coined the language that became a frequently repeated mantra on the floors of Congress and in the press. He opposed the Treasury's bill, he said, because "it would penalize marriage, place a premium on divorce and upon celibacy—practiced for selfish and unworthy motives—and promote immorality."[45] Another wondered whether the church's maxim that "the wages of sin are death" ought not to be replaced by another suggesting that "the wages of sin are greatly reduced income tax payments."[46] They were joined by the leaders of the chambers of commerce, who estimated that the proposal "could decrease the rate of marriage 10 per cent and increase the rate of divorce by as much as 20 per cent."[47] The popular columnist Arthur Krock offered a pithy summary of the debate: "It is a fact," he wrote in an often-cited piece, "that though the committee was not moved by such objectives, the joint return mandate tends to encourage divorce, celibacy, a mercenary attitude toward intended marriage and, in general, a lower birth rate."[48]

The Treasury ran into more difficulty when it revealed that, in deference to the principle of "ability to pay," it would permit married couples living apart to continue to file separately. The proposal seemed to open a can of worms, providing a vehicle for all kinds of groups to raise questions. "If there is no intent to penalize marriage," wrote one activist, "why is this proposal designed to apply only to those married couples living together? If living under the same roof is used as an excuse to join their incomes for tax purposes why should it not also apply to brothers and sisters who live together, or to any group of relatives who jointly occupy the same household and benefit by the joint income of all who live under the same roof?"[49] Some raised questions about how marital status would be policed. A *New York Times* reporter asked humorously whether "couples living apart shall periodically report their marriage status in order to entitle them to file separate returns." And what, he continued, if a husband joined the army "in order to save income taxes?"[50] The implication of immorality led some commentators to refer to the joint income tax proposal as shocking, wicked, un-American. Ingeniously combining these arguments, a respected congressman wove them together into a formidable barrier: "It is the dignity and stability of Christian civilization we are raising these taxes to protect and defend," declared James Domengeaux of Louisiana. "Defending democracy, we should not attempt to tear down its very foundation, we should rather seek means to uphold it. It is chiefly from married people that this country receives its taxes."[51] The equity of taxing some families more than they were now paying had now been turned on its head. If "dignity and Christian civilization" lay in the hands of married people, as the Treasury itself conceded, then why tax them more than a pair of equivalently affluent single people?

The Treasury responded to these challenges by once again invoking the injustice to the traditional male-breadwinner family of failing to tax all families equally. To its officials, it appeared simply unfair that a husband who earned all the family income pay more taxes than a husband lucky enough to be able to split his income either because he lived in a community property state or because his wife produced some of the family's aggregate income. At

least some congressmen accepted this logic, rejecting even the Treasury's meager effort to persuade Congress to adopt an earned income credit. Led by its
chair, Robert Doughton, the House Ways and Means Committee, which badly
wanted the mandatory joint return and which was cognizant of the rapidly
increasing numbers of wives in the labor force, could not stomach the idea of
providing a break for wage-earning wives. Doughton protested that an earned
income credit would undermine the prerogatives of the traditional male-
breadwinner family. "After careful consideration of the Treasury qualification," he reported, "the committee was unable to see any logic in favoring a
family in which both spouses earned the income as against a family where one
spouse earned the entire amount for the support of the family. . . . I would be
surprised if anyone would be in favor of penalizing the family in which the
husband is the sole breadwinner in favor of the family where the wife also
draws a salary."[52] Inverting the existing situation (in which the first dollar of
income of the working wife was taxed at her husband's marginal tax rate),
Doughton remained unshakably committed to justice for the family unit
rather than for the individuals in it. Fearful that acknowledging the rights of
individuals would open the door to the arguments of the community property
states, he preferred to stake his claim to justice on the already fading idea of
the male-breadwinner family.

Yet this argument, too, was turned on its head as the war provided representatives of women's organizations with alternative constructions of fairness. The most powerful of these revolved around the new need for women in
the labor force. Before the war, something like 80 to 90 percent of tax returns
had been filed by men, and defenders of separate returns had been accused of
representing an affluent minority.[53] A mandatory joint tax, in which the second income was taxed on top of the first at progressively high rates, threatened only the wealthy—about 5 percent of taxpayers with the highest
incomes. During the war, as wives and mothers increasingly entered paid
work and family incomes rose while the level of exempt income declined,
greater numbers of family units hovered on the threshold of taxation, and a
mandatory joint tax threatened increasing numbers of middle-income families. When the war ended, nearly three quarters of all families were paying
taxes, and a quarter of them had two income earners.[54]

To defend the traditional family, and to distinguish male heads of such
families from their counterparts in community property states, supporters of
the mandatory joint income tax conjured up images of manly and patriotic citizens who paid their proper taxes. They juxtaposed these against pictures of
infantile, pitiful tax avoiders. Were the "elite favored 5 percent of the Federal

taxpayers," asked Frank Boehne of Indiana, to continue to ease their consciences by "peering out from behind women's petticoats?" Were they to continue to suck "from the nursing bottle of special privilege?" Should other taxpayers "continue to be the wet nurse for this group"?[55] Appeals to wartime patriotism buttressed these efforts to infantilize elite tax evaders and to depict as mere babies those who refused to acknowledge the justice of family taxation. Boehne continued his peroration with an appeal to those willing to bear adult responsibilities:

> There are many who believe that now of all times when the sons of American mothers and fathers are being drafted and sent to the four corners of the earth to sail the submarine-infested seven seas, to fight and shed their blood, and sacrifice their lives if need be, to preserve our form of government, to preserve our way of life, to maintain the blessings of liberty and freedom, which we enjoy today that it is not too much to ask this elite 5 percent group of taxpayers to do no less than to bear their fair share of taxations: to pay not more but the same amount, as their neighbors with like status and income are paying to give our boys the modern weapons necessary for the protection of their lives in achieving such victory.[56]

Opponents of the mandatory joint tax, some perhaps with tongue in cheek, wondered if a married woman who could file a separate tax return were not more likely to seek work in hungry defense industries since she could retain a greater portion of her income. "One effect of the joint tax would be virtually to force many wives to give up their jobs," a letter writer to the *New York Times* suggested. "This would be particularly undesirable in principle in a period of labor shortage when the country needs maximum production for defense and civil needs."[57] The *New Republic* concurred, editorializing, "Though much sentimental tosh is talked about 'preserving the home,' such a provision might easily retard marriages or discourage women from working."[58] Taking that position encouraged a vigorous defense of the contribution of working wives. During the depression, married women appeared to be parasites on the job market, illegitimate invaders who took jobs from needy family providers.[59] Public perceptions had begun to shift in the early years of armaments buildup. The income tax debate reinforced the change. Arthur Krock neatly encapsulated the new position of working wives. Noting the rise of female "wedded persons with separate incomes," he commented on the positive effects of their work, which had "added to employment, family purchasing power, home investments and most of the components of an economy of high living standards and other culture."[60] At just the moment when the nation needed womanpower, he and others feared, the mandatory joint tax return would discourage women from working. Representatives of the National Women's Trade Union League (NWTUL) told congressmen that the tax would be "a real obstacle to the maximum war effort that we are all anxious to have."[61] In the 1942 debate, Congresswoman Martha Bolton approvingly cited a *New York Times* report that described England's joint return as "a serious deterrent to [women's] entry into full time employment and hence . . . retarding maximum war production."[62]

If the joint income tax without an earned income credit threatened to deprive married women of material incentives to work, it would also, women's groups argued, pose an even larger symbolic and moral barrier. To "consider the man and wife as one person," the NWTUL's legislative representative, Margaret Stone, insisted, would be to "adopt with one hand one of the principles of the very Nazi-ism that we are trying to destroy with the other."[63] Everywhere women equated the freedom of women with the freedoms for which the United States was fighting, alluding pejoratively to Hitler's restrictions and equating them with the return of women to primitive conditions. One articulate correspondent viewed the mandatory joint income tax return as "the defeat of a major principle of our way of life on the home ground. It challenges us to remember what has happened to women in the Axis countries."[64] Republican presidential candidate Wendell Willkie repeated this argument, declaring at one point that "the emancipation of women and the cause of freedom have advanced side by side." The passage of the joint income tax measure, he continued, would be destructive to "the very things for which we fight."[65]

To deflect the attack, the Treasury tried to describe joint taxation as an effort to redistribute the burden of defense more fairly and depicted the women's organizations as representing merely the rich, not speaking for women at large. But an appeal to class differences that might have worked before the war did not work during it. For one thing, women's groups were more united on this issue than they had been since the divisive issue of the ERA had emerged; the NWTUL, for example, represented unionized women. For another, income taxes now touched ten times as many people as they had before the war. "Anyone subject to surtaxes would be affected," warned the *New Republic*, "and surtaxes now extend far down the income scale and will extend further." A joint income tax threatened, in its view, to bring "into the range of the income tax itself many wage-working couples now exempt."[66] A congressman from California, one of the community property states, leaped on this bandwagon: "Is a tax which is unfair and unjust less so merely because it is limited to the families whose income is over $333 per month?" he asked. "What about the unfairness to those families whose income is less than $333 per month, who are bound to be included in subsequent tax legislation and who are not even aware that their interests are being affected?"[67] Far from being a class issue, Judge Dorothy Kenyon argued to Congress, the joint tax was "a fundamental issue of freedom." It could not "be disposed of by saying that the proposal applies only to a limited group of women, and those the richer members of society, and that since it is the intention largely to exempt unearned as distinguished from earned income, working and professional women need not be alarmed."[68]

If the Treasury rallied around patriotism and the traditional family, opponents of the joint income tax found an equally appealing banner: liberty. A range of women's organizations, silenced by the absence of public hearings in the 1941 debate, demanded to be heard in 1942.[69] Now their testimony, as well as the coverage it got in the press, was plentiful, and the arguments consistent. Allying themselves with the position that the joint return would discriminate against all married persons and that it would discourage marriage, these groups also claimed, in the words of Mary Donlon, testifying in 1942 on behalf of the Federation of Business and Professional Women's Clubs, that it "would turn the calendar back for women to those hard years before women came legally of age as citizens entitled to hold and manage their own affairs and property, without discrimination because of marital status."[70] The mandatory joint return, argued several women's rights organizations, constituted a step backward in the struggle for women's freedom. A ringing cry that women would not be returned to the state of chattel resonated broadly. Joint returns could not be disposed of by calling them merely a tax question, maintained Dorothy Kenyon, because "by ending a fiscal problem a greater inequity would be created in the field of women's rights."[71]

As the rhetoric escalated, the Treasury persuaded Eleanor Roosevelt, with her long-standing credentials among women's groups, to intervene. The *New York Times* reported that "Mrs. Roosevelt pooh-poohed today the idea that the proposal requiring married couples to file a joint income tax return would undermine a working wife's independence.... She explained that the government would gain more money because the family tax often is forced into a higher bracket by addition of the husband's and wife's incomes." Arthur Krock mocked what he called "Mrs. Roosevelt's conversion." It demonstrated, he avowed, how firmly fixed was the idea of a particular family structure—so firmly that the rights of individual women who happened to be married became invisible.[72]

Liberty became the unifying cry around which women's organizations that otherwise disagreed with each other came together. It also became a political vehicle for coercing reluctant support from influential legislators from community property states for such dramatic gestures as the languishing equal rights amendment. In support of women's personhood, committees of both the House and Senate for the first time passed the ERA, submitting it to legislators for an approval that never materialized.[73] National Woman's Party activists had anticipated the connection between subsuming women into families and the battle for the ERA. As the NWP's executive secretary, Caroline Babcock, noted, "Of course, the reason why the Ways and Means Committee can legally advance a proposal of this kind is that the Constitution of the United States does not afford women the same protection as it does men."[74] Leading women activists understood that they could take advantage of the moment, and the NWP, whose major interest was passage of the ERA, eagerly took advantage of congressional reconsideration of the mandatory joint income tax to flex its muscles.[75] Babcock wrote to her friend and ally Anita Pollitzer, "This is the opportune time to push hard with the Judiciary committee, for the reason that Senator Connally must be feeling pretty good and must be melting a little toward us when he considers that the General Federation of Women's Clubs have gone on record for opposing the mandatory joint income tax return because of the work of Mrs. Wiley. If that tax bill is proposed and carried, we will lose our hold on Senator Connally."[76] For many women the joint income tax return was not simply a blow at the sanctity of marriage and a discrimination against women of wealth. It was, as the chair of the National Woman's Party wrote to the chair of the House Ways and Means Committee, a "reaffirmation of the position of inferiority and inequality."[77] When the General Federation of Women's Clubs voted to oppose the measure, a member of its board of directors asked bluntly, "What is $389,000,000 compared to the rights of women?"[78]

Angry that the mandatory joint return had been put into the 1941 bill without hearings and despite the expressed wishes of women to be heard, several of the female representatives in Congress welcomed the chance to take up the issue again in 1942. "What," asked Ohio congresswoman Frances Bolton,

> are some of the basic principles for which we stand as a nation? ... Surely the most fundamental is the right of all to be considered persons under the law. ... It is a strange psychology that seizes upon this moment when

increasing demands are being made upon women's energies to attempt time after time to take from them their rights under the law. It is strange, also, to pick out of the great mass of women those who are married, who carry the heaviest responsibilities to the future.[79]

Edith Nourse Rogers of Massachusetts, introducing into the *Congressional Record* a letter from one group denied permission to testify, commented: "Women for years struggled and fought for many rights and privileges which were finally granted them. I do not believe that this Congress will set the clock of progress back."[80]

As the community property states recognized, women's rights could be effectively used for many purposes. Indeed, they turned out to be the trump cards held by opponents of mandatory joint returns. Whether or not its advocates believed it, the notion that the joint return would produce a giant step back in women's status became in the 1940s the iron petticoat that shielded its opponents. It was the key integrating issue that allowed legislators and an influential segment of the public to object to a bill that would have taxed the wealthy somewhat more equitably. As one thoughtful editorial puzzled, "It is true that a husband with a large income from investments may, by transferring part of his holding to his wife, reduce his surtax. But why, on this account, should couples, both of whom earn money or have legitimately independent incomes, be forced to pay higher taxes than if they had remained single?"[81] The question suggested an alternative vision of fairness capable of competing with the normative masculinity that incited demands for a family tax.

On the floor of Congress, the women's lobbying campaigns produced an opportunistic response as the mingled voices of community and realty and common law states noisily defended women's rights. The rafters fairly rang with adulation for the advantages of maintaining women's separate identity, and legislators eagerly sought to identify themselves with what they perceived to be a winning issue. "The requirement of mandatory joint returns, by merging the identity of the wife with that of her husband for tax purposes, is a long step backward in social progress," announced one California legislator.[82] "More than money... is involved...," a midwesterner chimed in. "In essence it involves a return to the old common law idea that a wife's property comes under the control of the husband."[83] Another midwesterner declared:

I believe that it tends to destroy the equality between men and women and the independence of married women from the domination of their

The women in Congress in 1941 included Jeannette Rankin (Montana), Frances Bolton (Ohio), Mary Norton (New Jersey), Margaret Chase Smith (Maine), and Edith Nourse Rogers (Massachusetts). COURTESY, ARCHIBALD S. ALEXANDER LIBRARY, RUTGERS, THE STATE UNIVERSITY OF NEW JERSEY.

husbands. . . . Under the common law a wife had no effective property rights apart from her husband. She was placed in a state of subjugation under the domination and control of her husband. . . . It is obvious that the enactment of a law requiring compulsory joint returns is a backward step toward the old and discredited view of women as chattels.[84]

And a community property advocate inserted similar sentiments into the record. "If the wife's right to make a separate return is denied," noted New Mexico's Clinton Anderson, "then her right to half the property and income is also denied and the law declares her equality is voided."[85]

The rhetoric escalated to the level where the highest constitutional issues and the fate of Christianity itself rested on the defense of women's personhood. At stake was "the principle of the independent status of American citizens, men and women."[86] Nothing less than the dignity of Christian civilization and equality for mankind would be achieved by the defeat of a mandatory joint income tax. Legislators willing to vote for it were accused of selling liberty for a mess of pottage. In the end, its defeat was assured. The mandatory joint income tax had become nothing less than an attack on a "fundamental issue of freedom."

Tail between its legs, the Treasury returned to Congress a year later with a proposal to lower the tax exemption for individuals from one thousand to five hundred dollars. In a twist that conceded defeat, it agreed to deny the five hundred dollars to nonworking spouses. In practice, that meant that husbands with nonworking wives would pay fifteen dollars a year more in income taxes, and it provided subtle encouragement to women who joined the war effort. It was a small concession to the need for revenue and stayed in effect only for the two remaining years of the war, but it foreshadowed the ways in which policy makers could embed particular gendered social messages in the tax code.

## To Confer a Special Benefit on the Marital Relationship

The controversy led several common law states to adopt community property laws, generally halfheartedly and as the lesser of two evils. By 1944, six had passed such statutes, though not all of them escaped challenges from the courts.[87] Many feared that all states would ultimately be pushed into the same position.[88] They bitterly blamed what some labeled a "forced redistribution" on what one congressional witness called "hosts of gold-plated suffragettes" who "descended upon Congress to reenact their epic drama regarding married women's rights, and claim that all will be lost if ever a wife must file a joint return with her husband and thereby again be 'relegated to economic slavery.' "[89] The male residents of common law states did not want, as a California representative put it, to "give up everything to the wife in respect to property; they want to retain everything for themselves to do with it as they please, the wife's viewpoint and the wife's decision notwithstanding."[90] Forced, as they believed, to resort to altering state laws in order to produce equality in taxes, residents of common law states became increasingly discontented with a tax system that fostered unwanted changes.[91]

At last the Treasury agreed to compromise. Blessed with the possibility of reducing taxes at the end of the war and pressured by the legislators of states still flirting with converting to community property status, it accepted a proposal to equalize the positions of common law and community property taxpayers.[92] The new "split-income" proposal went to Congress in 1947. It relied on dividing the aggregate income of a married couple in two, computing the tax at the lower rate applicable to half the combined income, and then doubling that figure. The Treasury estimated that under this method upper-income families in the common law states would get a 20 percent tax cut (those in the lowest brackets would get no benefit, or none to speak of) and all the privileges of splitting income previously enjoyed only by the residents of community property states. The cut would go to married taxpaying residents of all states who filed jointly, providing an enormous financial incentive to joint returns without a mandatory provision. It balanced this largesse to the wealthy with a 20 percent rate cut for low-income taxpayers.

The Treasury could have chosen a variety of ways to reduce taxes, including increasing the level of exempt income and widening tax brackets for individuals while continuing to tax them separately. Those techniques would not have solved the inequities generated by state laws that treated marital property differently; nor would they have created justice for the male-breadwinner families so firmly embedded in the Treasury's conception of normalcy. Just a few months before it received the split-income proposal, Congress had passed a tax reduction measure. President Truman vetoed it for many reasons—one of them because it failed to create geographic equality.[93] Anticipating that defeat, Congress asked Roswell Magill, who had resigned as undersecretary in the Treasury Department to enter private practice, to chair a special commission to make recommendations that would solve the divisions among the states. Magill's futile 1933 effort to persuade Congress to adopt the mandatory joint income tax return now stood him in good stead. Working with Stanley Surrey, the Treasury Department's tax legislative counsel, who had already developed the idea for income splitting and earned the approval of several states, his commission formally recommended it (among a wide variety of other tax programs) to Congress in 1947. Princeton's Harley Lutz called the proposal "a phase of the Treasury's long struggle to change the basis of individual income taxation over to the family income."[94]

The press received the idea as a matter of simple justice, a program that by permitting "husbands and wives to split the family income equally for tax purposes" would "eliminate inequites under present tax laws applying to family incomes." Journalists described the huge tax benefits that would accrue to five million middle-and upper-income people as "a privilege now enjoyed only by residents of community property states."[95] Presented as a way of bringing equity to family taxation by lowering taxes for breadwinner husbands who paid an "unfair" share, the plan avoided the issues of women's rights that had plagued the mandatory joint tax return. When Senator Tom Connally tried to tell a 1934 congressional committee that stay-at-home wives earned half the income their husbands brought home, his congressional colleagues vigorously challenged the idea. But in 1947, when it served the purposes of providing tax relief to many more husbands, they no longer scoffed. "I can't see any justification" for splitting the tax on inherited property, one congressman admitted before he added that he had no difficulty seeing the justification for splitting a husband's earnings, "which are certainly added to by the work of the wife."[96] If some legislators continued to wonder at the sleight-of-hand that defined income as belonging to a wife "even though the husband may have gone down to the office and earned the salary," they could be persuaded that drawing an analogy between a marriage and a partnership made sense.[97] As one conceded, "It is not a radical step to say that the Federal Government will, as between husband and wife, imply a partnership in all states."[98] The step appeared even less radical in light of the sympathy expressed in the popular press for couples who resorted to phony divorces in order to get tax benefits already available to residents of community property states.[99]

The opportunity to reduce taxes enabled the Treasury to enact its assumptions about the family as an appropriate tax unit by turning marriage into a tax partnership and avoiding the onus of a mandatory joint return. Lacking the implication of women's subordination contained in the mandatory lower tax, the new proposal evaded issues of women's rights.[100] But the practical results differed only a little from those that would have accompanied a mandatory joint income tax. Embedded in the split-income provision was a vision of marriage in which two partners had unequal incomes, which they pooled. This was the group that stood to benefit from the new tax law. It was intended to provide no benefit to people who lived together without benefit of marriage, and it assumed that only married couples pooled their income. That assumption as effectively subsumed the identities of married partners into one as a mandatory tax would have done. Perhaps reflecting the difference between a depression mentality and postwar images of suburban prosperity, images of different families vanished, as did concern for the separate identities of married women.

General enthusiasm for the new provision exposes the opportunism of earlier congressional concern for women's rights and separate identities. Legislators who welcomed the combination of tax reduction and geographical equity no longer commented on the negative consequences for women that had bothered them during the labor-hungry war years: a married woman's generally much lower, secondary, wage would be taxed at a far higher rate in a joint return than if she had been single. By amalgamating incomes and using a tax rate based on half the couple's total income, the split-income schedule ensured that a couple with unequal wages paid less total tax than the two together would have paid if taxed on each income. For the partner with the higher income, the lower tax rate meant significant savings. The low-income spouse would continue to pay on all her income at the couple's generally higher marginal tax rate. Thus, a single woman who earned $3,000 a year—a reasonable wage for a schoolteacher or a skilled secretary in 1948—might pay 16 percent of her wage in federal taxes after her personal exemption ($600) and her 10 percent standard deduction. If she married a man making $8,000 a year, she paid taxes at a rate appropriate to someone making $5,500, and a third of her income could be gobbled up by federal taxes, even as the amount he paid declined significantly. To most people this discrepancy seemed moot. Only about 20 percent of all married women earned any income in 1948, most of them in part-time or low-wage jobs. In an environment that discouraged women's wage work, legislators who observed that a wife's generally lower income got taxed at a rate far higher than it would have been had she been single willingly admitted the incentive it provided married women to remain at home with their children. At any rate, the bill made no effort to acknowledge the individual rights of wage-earning wives, nor did it provide preferential tax treatment in light of either the costs of earning or the injustice of taxing their incomes more highly than those of their husbands.

This time, the responses of women's groups drew little support; their negative opinions remained marginal. Women once again rallied by writing letters. The General Federation of Women's Clubs protested its exclusion from the hearings on the bill before reiterating its opposition to any form of mandatory joint income tax.[101] Community property states that had rallied around women's rights when they believed that doing so would fend off a joint income tax quickly dropped the issue. As Caroline Babcock feared, Tom Connally withdrew his support for the ERA. And legislators readily acknowledged their respect for the particular family unit the bill meant to protect. California's Representative Bertrand W. Gearhart bluntly noted, "The wife's position in that joint income tax return . . . is in there for the purpose of reducing taxes of the husband. And on the theory that she, in some way or other, has some interest and should pay something on that return." Not necessarily, replied Albert Reeves of Missouri, one of the bill's sponsors. The provision was meant to function just as the original benefit had: "When you gave a greater tax exemption years ago to a married man than you would have given to the husband and wife had they made separate returns unmarried, you conferred a special benefit . . . upon the marital relationship."[102] That was all, he said, that he was proposing.

But that was not all that the bill did. Though it certainly embedded marital status into tax law, the law became an instrument as well for endorsing certain kinds of gender roles, influencing personal behavior, and encouraging particular forms of activity. The tax code and its many modifications after 1948 revealed as much about notions of gendered fairness as about the need for revenue. The original bill, for example, included no provisions for unmarried heads of households. The committee turned a deaf ear to witnesses who imagined that unmarried people might care for others, rejecting efforts to remedy the bill's neglect of the "many thousands of cases where the father of minor

children would after his wife's death, be deprived of her aid and companionship at the very time that his Federal taxes would be increased up to 40 percent because he no longer is in the favored group." But members also ignored
pleas on behalf of the "million and a third" women who "are still rearing
minor children and who would have all the burdens of any husband and
more."[103] The final provision did not acknowledge the pooled incomes of
unmarried partners, whether of the same or different sexes; it neglected workers who supported parents or other relatives. And it identified the particular
families it wanted to help: unless their aggregate incomes exceeded the first
tax bracket, even intact low-income families with a single male breadwinner
did not benefit from the split-income provision.

At the same time, the bill sent a positive message to married women and
men in traditional families, for whom splitting incomes provided significant
material advantages. At a joint income of twelve thousand dollars a year, each
member of a married couple paid 20 percent less than a single person with the
same income. At progressive rates, these savings grew as incomes rose. Since
the split-income schedule reduced the taxes paid by affluent single-earner
families to the levels of those paid by residents of community property states
and dramatically decreased the taxes of primary income earners (generally
husbands) in two-earner families, it provided persuasive economic incentives
for most married women to file jointly with their husbands and even to stay
out of the labor force. To most middle-class male breadwinners and their non-
income-earning wives (in 1948 only 22 percent of married women with husbands engaged in paid labor), the savings far outweighed symbolic statements
about women's rights to separate taxation. The income-splitting provision
thus reaffirmed the status of male breadwinners, giving the Treasury and the
common law states what in practice they had wanted all along—the same
rights as community property states without the burdens of sharing property.
Best of all, in the Treasury's view, by promising "normal" families dramatic tax
reductions unavailable to other forms of family, the Treasury finally managed
to establish the husband-and-wife family as the unit of taxation. Without
raising the ire of community property states, which also received a sweetener
in terms of more generous estate taxation, the Treasury at last achieved
"equality among married couples at the same income level."[104]

Because the plan was, as Stanley Surrey notes, in a legal sense, voluntary, it
did not challenge the power of the community property states to define the
personhood of women with respect to taxes—but it did remove the financial
incentives to define women as their own persons. By eliminating a husband's
advantage in declaring his wife her own person, and disadvantaging wives

who were their own providers, the new tax code made the principle of women's personhood very costly.[105] Still, women had gained something from the long years of dialogue. The debate clarified the position of wives, encouraging some legislators to defend women's individual rights in radical language that the community property states probably never endorsed and whose substance most legislators certainly never supported. Credible or not, the rhetoric made room in the halls of legislatures for continuing attention to women's claims to be treated as persons under the law. In encouraging common law as well as community property states to exaggerate the equality of women within marriage, the debate paved the way for claims to women's economic rights. Ultimately, the way in which the debate over joint returns framed the discourse—allowing the federal government to define what constituted a proper family, legitimizing federal intervention in the marriage relation, and not incidentally exposing the conviction of many that class differences among the married deserved the attention of tax code writers—signaled a shift in the federal government's willingness to intervene in the most intimate arenas of life.

But neither Congress nor what soon became known as the Internal Revenue Service (IRS) had much time to take satisfaction in their achievement, for in creating marital equity among families of the same kind, Congress and the Treasury produced a hodgepodge of inequities among different kinds of families. In 1948, almost 80 percent of taxpayers (and 85 percent of white families) still lived in families headed by a sole wage earner, generally male. A tax code that created equity among such families resonated with a certain kind of fairness. By 1970, the proportion of single-earner married-couple households had dropped to 60 percent; by 1980, more than 50 percent of all married couples boasted two wage earners. This figure increased to 60 percent by 1990, then began to fall off. At the same time, rising divorce rates and out-of-wedlock births increased the number of households headed by only one adult, generally a woman, to more than 12 percent of all family households in 1990. Unmarried persons increasingly set up homes of their own, with or without partners, their numbers climbing slowly to reach more than 25 percent of all households by 1990. These dramatic changes raised questions about "normal" household configurations scarcely imagined in 1948 and tempted legislators to utilize a tax code already committed to affirming certain kinds of gendered social values to reward and punish different sorts of families.[106]

After 1948, fairness in the tax code would come to rely more explicitly not only on a taxpaying family's income but on its demographic profile and on the changing social value attributed to various kinds of household activity. The conversation turned first to what one expert has called a "quixotic attempt to achieve equity among different kinds of families." Protests against the unfairness of a tax law that granted benefits only to particular types of family units came from unmarried persons, including the widowed and divorced, who immediately recognized that they would pay taxes at the highest possible rates even if they supported others. Congress tried to resolve this issue in 1951 by creating a "head of household" category and providing its beneficiaries with a tax rate that partially closed the gap in rates between married partners on the one hand and single people with dependents on the other. Three years later the House of Representatives passed a bill offering heads of households the full benefits of split incomes, but only if they supported children, siblings, or parents.[107] Faced with complaints that it would create a "divorce" bonus—a benefit to marital partners who separated, took one child each, and then each claimed the split-income advantage—the Senate backed off this provision and returned to the 1951 law.

The same year, the House passed an expanded deduction for divorced and widowed parents of either sex who cared for their children. The deduction, limited to those with children under ten (or sixteen if the child was disabled), was specifically meant to enable a parent to "earn a livelihood." Cautiously, it extended the provision to "a working mother whose husband is incapacitated," specifically omitting the huge numbers of mothers then entering the labor market who had working husbands with low incomes.[108] This time the Senate took a different tack. Arguing that "in many low-income families, the earnings of the mother are essential for the maintenance of minimum living standards even where the father is also employed," it extended the credit to working mothers whose family incomes did not exceed $4,500 a year. That provision made it into the law.[109] President John F. Kennedy's high-powered Commission on the Status of Women approved the idea of tax credits to low-income wage-earning mothers but remained uncomfortable about not giving an equivalent tax break to mothers who chose not to work. It toyed with, and in the end fell short of proposing, a $2,500 tax exemption for women who stayed at home to take care of children.[110]

Arguments over these issues fueled agitation among growing numbers of single people with no dependents (or none that the IRS acknowledged), who now carried heavier burdens of taxation than their married peers. Congress did not correct this inequity until 1969, when it created a separate tax table for them that acknowledged the extra expenses of living alone. The new tax law produced an effective tax roughly equivalent to the split-income provision; it also created what became known as the "marriage penalty." Congress forbade married couples who wished to file separately to use the new table and designed another with less favorable rates for them. In the new formulation, families with a single breadwinner and dual-earning couples in which one spouse earned substantially more than the other benefited from a "marriage bonus." Those with approximately equal incomes paid a "penalty" that increased as their incomes rose; their taxes were higher than had they remained single. In 1969, only about 20 percent of married couples paid this penalty. By 1980, 40 percent did.[111]

By 1969, the Internal Revenue Service boasted four separate tax tables, each of them based on a different marital status. The United States, one scholarly assessment discovered, might be the only country in the world that distinguished "among marital status in providing standard deductions."[112] But this was only the beginning. Given the continuing differences between the opportunities and possibilities available to women and men, the gendered nature of the family profile mattered, even when, after 1969, the laws began to be written in gender-neutral ways. The level of taxation depended on, among other things, the number of wage earners in a household unit, their relationship to each other, whether they had equal or unequal incomes and where the incomes came from (pensions, investments, wages, or government transfers). These factors could affect not only the amount of income tax but what untaxed benefits (including child care, medical care, and home relief) a family might expect. Women were expected to care for some family members without tax relief; for others they might receive a tax credit. Providing financial support for some family members could earn tax deductions depending on who the "others" were and how much was provided. Thus widows whose children got OASDI payments from their deceased fathers might or might not be able to claim "head of household" status depending on whether they provided half the cost of rearing a child. And at various times they could claim the extra deduction on behalf of children aged sixteen, eighteen, or twenty-two, depending on whether the child chose to continue in school or not. Employed and unemployed wives who lived with blind persons, retired persons, or employed workers got different benefits and were taxed at different rates.

By the 1970s, inequities among families, even those with similar incomes, raised stormy questions about whether the tax system ought to strive for marriage neutrality—a situation in which neither marriage nor divorce altered an individual's taxes—rather than marriage equity.[113] In 1972, 158 members of the House cosponsored a bill calling for a "uniform tax rate schedule for all taxpayers, whether they be married, widowed, divorced or single." The same year, the House held hearings on the tax treatment of dual-income couples.[114] And the following summer, a new set of hearings posed the issue of whether "the structure of the federal income tax also encourages married women not to work outside the home."[115] It did not take long before the issue reached the courts. In 1969, John Mapes sued the government for discriminating against single people by providing married couples with the opportunity to split incomes.[116] By the 1980s, with more than 60 percent of married women in the labor market, legal experts and legal scholars joined the outcry against the wisdom of using the family as a unit of taxation and of employing the tax system to influence women's choice of home or wage work. Following the intuitive sense of inequity already articulated by the public, they, too, rejected the assumption that had guided the Treasury since the inception of the income tax. Married couples, they suggested, no longer necessarily pooled their income; the family as a unit of consumption was therefore hardly a fair measure of ability to pay; and a tax that shifted with marital status treated all kinds of individuals unfairly.[117] The protest proved futile.

As community property states had so persuasively recognized in the early part of the twentieth century, the gendered dimensions of the tax code could effectively rationalize tax benefits for upper-income families. Congress, fearful that disturbing an important benefit of the male-headed single-earner family would trigger an even larger political outcry, failed to respond to the growing demand of men and women in newer family formations for a fairer tax code. As late as 1980, when 60 percent of all families had two wage earners, it rejected a proposal to allow married people to file separate returns under the individual tax schedule. To address some of the grievances, it (briefly) provided an earned income credit to the second income earner in a family, increased and expanded child care deductions, making them available to middle-income families after 1980, and raised individual exemptions. Still, women (who earned less than their partners in four fifths of all households) continued to pay higher tax rates as individuals within marriages and to benefit if they chose traditional life-styles.

These issues resurfaced in the presidential election campaign in 2000, when the nation once again debated the use of the family as its tax base. Hoping to pass a preelection tax cut, members of both parties suggested eliminating the marriage penalty—the higher tax paid by about twenty-one million dual-income working couples. They wanted not only to lower this tax to the level paid by unmarried people living together but simultaneously to reduce taxes on all married couples. By increasing the deduction available to a couple filing jointly and expanding the tax brackets for all married couples, Congress could ensure that dual-income couples would pay the same taxes whether they were legally married or lived as partners. In the spring of 2000, it passed a new tax code that included marriage penalty relief. After this fell victim to a presidential veto, the issue of family taxation reemerged. As in the 1930s, some thought that the marriage penalty was immoral. "Our tax code," representative Jerry Weller of Illinois told a CNN interviewer, was not only unfair, it punished "society's most basic institution, marriage." It encouraged unmarried partnerships, unfairly taxed second earners, and discouraged women from earning wages. But the same system that exacted extra taxes from high-income couples paid a bonus to twenty-four million lower-income and single-breadwinner families, perhaps leading wives to stay at home. The only way to correct the inequity, tax expert June O'Neill testified to a congressional committee, was to move to an individually based system.[118] Hooked on the ease with which tax relief could be provided to high-income dual earners by offering lower rates to every married couple, legislators insisted on perpetuating the principle of the traditional married-couple family as the appropriate unit for taxation. In so doing, they left unasked and unanswered questions of how the code could be refigured to ensure equality and full citizenship for women.

# CHAPTER 5

# What Discriminates?

For his book on electrical workers, the historian Ronald Schatz interviewed a number of women who had sacrificed lucrative jobs after World War II. When he asked one of them how she felt about giving up her job, she offered an acerbic reply: "How're you going to feel? You gotta give him a *chance*, right? The fellow that you took his job and [he] went to the service to protect you and your country, the least you can do is give him back his job or there's going to be a war." Other women concurred with the tenor of that comment: "There are some jobs—I don't care how good you are!—you can't begin to have the muscle that a man has," a militant woman organizer for the United Electrical Workers argued. "We felt that there were certain jobs that couldn't be done by women because of the nature of the work," said another.[1]

We catch our breaths as we read these words. Gender differences seem so palpable, so transparent to these women, clearly an acceptable rationale for distributing jobs and the benefits attached to them, and the source of appropriate politics and behavior. The lens of a particular kind of womanhood shapes the way they conceive their obligations as workers, trade unionists, family members, and citizens. Yet their perception of gender seems awkwardly dated: they are on the cusp of an enormous transformation that will sharply differentiate their attitudes toward earning wages from those of their daughters and sons. Less than twenty-five years later, congressional representatives, learned witnesses, and ordinary housewives would testify to the penalties paid by women because all of society had "clung to the comfortable belief that a woman's exclusive and rightful place is in the home."[2]

African-American contemporaries of these electrical workers would not have mirrored that commitment to gender differences with regard to race; they would certainly have denied the relevance of racial distinctions in employment decisions. By 1945, the advantages and disadvantages of race, black and white, no longer appeared as the product of innate biological differences but as the consequence of human behavior. Most African Americans and many other people of goodwill hoped that efforts to pass laws mandating fair treatment would enforce a change in behavior that might, over the long haul, equalize the economic prospects of the races and ultimately yield an end to the vicious prejudice that underlay discriminatory acts. In the 1950s and 1960s, a burgeoning civil rights movement perceived discrimination as a violation of individual rights under the Fourteenth Amendment to the Constitution; it claimed shared human rights to justify an escalating fight for antidiscriminatory legislation.

What was transparent with respect to race remained contested with regard to gender. While the idea, if not the practice, of political equality for women was widely accepted by the postwar period, far less consensus existed about the idea of economic equality along gender lines or about the relationship of women to human rights. In the 1940s, through the 1950s, and into the 1960s, the idea of gender difference remained embedded in marriage patterns and family lives, social tradition and economic possibility. Like the women electrical workers, most people believed that traditional conceptions of family, community, and social order took precedence over demands for women's rights as individuals. In the economic sphere, women were educated, trained, and taught to earn in order to "help" their husbands; to raise their families' standards of living, and to enable their children to stay in school. It did not matter that some women (about 9 percent of adult women, and rising) chose not to marry, nor that others were widowed or divorced early, or had husbands who did not or could not earn sufficient wages.

Widespread beliefs in seemingly natural gender differences limited notions of sex discrimination to a narrower compass than that open to race discrimination. If there was room for debate around how particular jobs would be designated or benefits assigned, few people were disturbed by the idea that gender provided an appropriate rationale for distributing work and providing the benefits attached to it. Most men and women in the early postwar years acknowledged and accepted differential treatment for women in education, the administration of social policies, and the workplace without using the language of discrimination to label their experiences. It was, therefore, the notion of race discrimination that set the standard for what constituted discrimination at all and, for a while, justified continued deprecation of women's rights to economic citizenship. As one astute contemporary commented in 1963, "No one who acknowledges the injustice of racial discrimination could possibly justify differential treatment on the basis of race. However differential legal treatment on the basis of sex in certain instances is considered by many as socially desirable."[3] Such beliefs shaped women's expectations, restricted their educational opportunities, limited their rights to work, and in other ways denied them the individual rights necessary to attain economic citizenship. They mystified the distinctive way women were treated at work, blinding men and women to its disfiguring aspects and obscuring what might otherwise have been called discrimination. In the light of these beliefs, economic equality for women remained a contentious goal and economic opportunity a formidable and elusive barrier.

Yet change was in the air. A relatively narrow set of ideas about what women ought to be did not entirely preclude 1950s women from feeling dissatisfaction with unequal conditions at work, nor from wondering about the restraints that particular ideas of marriage imposed on economic aspiration. Among those who dissented were advocates of the equal rights amendment—the same ERA first introduced into Congress in 1923. Spearheaded by the small but vocal National Woman's Party, this group revealed increasing restlessness with the idea that women's rights could be restrained by family roles or limited and defined by their differences from men. Using aggressive political tactics, members of the NWP persuaded the Republican party to add a weak endorsement of the ERA to its platform in 1940. The Democrats followed suit in 1944 but in 1952 and 1956 offered a stronger commitment. Renewed support for an amendment that would guarantee men and women "equal rights under the law" placed the issue of women's differences on the political agenda, especially threatening the longtime defenders of special protections for women in the workplace because it offered to treat women just like men in the labor force.

The gendered imagination altered more slowly than the political debate following the changing demography of the female labor force. As more women took paid jobs on a more permanent basis, a rising number sought more rights at work in the form of equal pay and access to benefits. During and following World War II, married women moved into the labor force in startlingly high numbers. While the proportion of single women workers remained approximately stable, the proportion of married women doubled between 1940 and 1960, when nearly a third of married women earned wages. By 1970, three times as many married women earned wages as in 1940. Despite virulent attacks on their labor force participation, the proportions of wage-earning mothers increased even more rapidly. In 1960, nearly half of all wage-earning women had children under eighteen living at home. Twenty percent of mothers with children under six worked for a living. These women, older than the eighteen- to twenty-four-year-olds who had dominated the female labor market in 1920, committed themselves to wage work, yet, like their mothers, they worked in sex-segregated jobs and at wages that averaged less than 60 percent of what men earned.[4]

For how long would women tolerate limits on jobs and earnings? The absence of wage work for women had for so long served as the defining characteristic of respectable marriage, for so long been viewed as the measure of male liberty and fairness to women, that women's full participation in the economy required a new mind-set. In this chapter we watch as the gendered imagination grapples with demographic changes until, by the early 1960s, the notion of sex discrimination begins to inflect the vocabulary of ordinary women. Bound by legislative and customary restrictions that continued to limit her economic choices and hedge her expectations, the 1950s white woman, like the female electrical workers who reluctantly gave up their jobs, hesitated when asked whether she was a victim of sex discrimination. Asked the parallel question, her African-American counterpart immediately acknowledged race discrimination. A decade later, astute wage earners could clearly see gendered limits that had earlier passed unnoticed, and they particularly noted how effectively the growing civil rights movement deployed the language of discrimination. Still, discrimination against women remained a contested venue, lacking the powerful cudgel of individual rights to give it force.

## How're You Going to Feel?

None of the conditions that circumscribed gender expectations was without ambiguity. Inspired by the good job opportunities available during World War II and then disillusioned by the occupational sex-stereotyping that followed it, a small core of women felt moved to achieve citizenship in economic as well as political terms. The expanding labor market of the 1950s encouraged their aspirations. As in World War II, a vigorous cold war economy demanded a steady and well-educated supply of labor. A combination of expanding educational opportunities for women and heightened expectations for more comfortable and technologically up-to-date living standards tempted middle-income women into the labor force, where, as more or less permanent workers, they believed themselves entitled to seek its benefits.[5] But this led to discontent. Where some perceived only the logical consequences of a gendered social order, other wage-earning women began to discern invidious distinctions that seemed unjust and unfair. "Can you tell me why," asked one General Motors office worker, "none of the Corporation's Plants have women supervisors?" Nor could she understand why women were ignored in GM training programs. "They say they don't train women because women are not permanent employees. However, about 33 percent of the fellows at GM leave the corporation." Then, too, it seemed to her that her division of GM hired only the very young, with the expectation that they would marry and leave. It was almost impossible, she thought, for "women past thirty who will probably have to work" to get a job with GM.[6]

Prevailing social policies echoed contradictions revealed in the workplace. By 1954, almost all workers, including most women, paid Social Security taxes, yet the contributions of women generally did not secure insurance for their dependents. Young women trained for clerical and office jobs found themselves stymied by the absence of maternity leaves and crèches for young children. Married women often paid proportionately higher income taxes than coworkers who could take advantage of a tax formula that benefited male-headed single-earner families. Significant numbers of trade union women and professional women, black and white, pursued jobs that promised individual satisfaction; in practice most jobs shamelessly limited women's access to upward mobility.

Within trade unions, and in organizations like the National Federation of Business and Professional Women's Clubs and the American Association of University Women, these contradictions produced struggles over the meaning of justice and fairness in relation to equity in the workplace. Equity meant different things to different people. At one end of the class spectrum, it opened the doors to opportunity; at the other, it offered protection against difficult working conditions. Among well-educated white workers, it meant simply lowering barriers to good education and good jobs; among poorly educated African-American and Latino workers, it required active job training. Identifying with union rules was a two-way street. On the one hand, union membership permitted women (in 1950, about 12 percent of the twenty-four million union members) to see that they had job-related rights; on the other, it subordinated those rights to union seniority rules that often disadvantaged them.

Unsurprisingly, many ordinary women, black and white, responded to the apparent contradictions in their lives by testing the boundaries between individual rights and family commitments.

Still, their efforts bent not so much toward capturing new jobs as toward acquiring rights on the job. Rumblings of discontent in the debates over veterans' rights and union seniority conflicts that followed World War II suggest the tension between these two issues. For example, more than 75 percent of war-working women told pollsters that they wanted to continue in their jobs after the war ended. Most gave them up without much of a struggle. A strong sense of the importance of the family and of the principles of justice involved seemed to overwhelm individual desire. Our women electrical workers, who understood they would have to give up their jobs, had successfully fought for equal pay and seniority during the war. After it, torn between their hard-won seniority rights and the job rights of veterans, they did not have much difficulty in deciding for the veterans. Absent any sense of permanent change in the roles of men and women, women's individual desires remained secondary to a shared commitment to families.

In the postwar period, women in the United Automobile Workers of America (UAW) learned about the interdependence of these issues. They used their claims to seniority, sociologist Ruth Milkman tells us, to teach men a lesson about unionism. Incensed when, in 1945, local managers dismissed women with seniority, the women appealed to union officials, who refused at first even to meet with them. "The inference we got from the board, and strongly," reported Mildred Jeffreys, later to become a vice president, "was just who do you women think you are." The sense of aggrieved justice among women resonant in that statement was clearly not shared by the men. Male members did, however, acquiesce when UAW president R. J. Thomas insisted that if management could get away with "disregarding seniority rights of women workers now, they will be in a stronger position to disregard seniority rights of other workers later on."[7] Women's arguments in this period remained tenuous: if men supported their seniority rights at all, they did so out of concern for unionism, not from a sense of fairness to women, and women who claimed those rights more often justified them by pleading family need (widowhood and orphaned children to support) than as a matter of individual rights. Still, the principle of seniority affirmed that all workers, including those who were female, shared some rights, creating an apparently gender-neutral ground on which women could make claims.

If rights *to* work remained an ambiguous concept, bounded by responsibility to family and claimed largely when work was measured either as a necessity for continuing family life or for self-support and hedged by allegiance to union principles, women's work experience fueled demands for rights *at* work. Such demands formed the core of a rising protest among unionized women in the 1950s. Historians Dorothy Sue Cobble, Nancy Gabin, Lisa Kannenberg, and Dennis Deslippes have all demonstrated a persistently high level of consciousness around issues such as equal pay and seniority rights among women within unions and in union jobs.[8] Yet job-related consciousness did not yet encourage women to seek the kinds of social benefits that would enable equal citizenship with men. It involved nothing like the Swedish notion of *jämställdhet* to justify sharing the costs of social benefits. There was no public debate in the United States, as there was in Sweden, for example, and in other Scandinavian countries, over the idea of leveling the playing field for men and women or of promoting conditions that would make it possible to develop equal relations between women and men.[9] In Sweden, in the 1960s, debate around *jämställdhet* created public support for social policies meant to lead to gender equality. The debate shifted the discussion from women's "rights" to the contexts within which men and women functioned. Ultimately *jämställdhet* altered the perquisites of social citizenship for men and women. By creating a series of high-quality universal entitlements (including child care, paid childbirthing and parental leaves, and elder care) and adopting policies (like the individual income tax, individualized medical coverage, pensions, and unemployment insurance) that required each individual to maximize his or her contributions to family life through paid work, gender equality policies deeply influenced Swedish economic and social commitments. The new policies not only accommodated women's wage work but provided tangible help to enable men and women to construct more satisfying family lives as well.[10]

In their absence, in the United States, the idea of gender equality had less purchase. Its limits are most effectively captured by an abortive struggle for maternity leave for working mothers that occupied one group of feminists in the years from 1945 to the mid-1950s. As we have seen, maternity leave for wage-earning women had been a contentious issue since the turn of the century, dealt with largely as a function of women's health rather than as a part of their right to work. Even as the Second World War drew to a close it attracted only marginal attention. Despite a good deal of support from women in the federal Children's Bureau and the Women's Bureau, most Americans dismissed it. Providing even unpaid leaves to women who gave birth violated the notion that men could and should support their families without the help of wives. Offering insurance protection against lost earnings during pregnancy seemed even more threatening. In 1950, only Rhode Island came close to requiring such a program, by including pregnancy under statewide mandates for disability insurance. In an environment in which fewer than 8 percent of babies were born outside marriage, no one acknowledged that women without male partners might need job protections or have any rights. More palatable were sickness insurance programs that subsidized medical care during pregnancy and maternity such as those offered to about a third of unionized women workers. To the American mind, though, even these suggested incentives for men to send their wives out to work. Besides, they were costly, not only in terms of insurance premiums but for the employer's wage bill. Typically, employers simply dismissed women when their pregnancies became known, then hired entry-level replacements. Some, like many municipalities and boards of education, required women to agree to resign in the fourth or fifth month of pregnancy.

The wartime need for women workers raised questions about some of these harsh approaches and promoted a postwar discussion within the United Nations' International Labor Organization (ILO) aimed at establishing standards not only for protecting the health of working women during pregnancy but for preserving their job rights as well. As head of the Women's Bureau of the Department of Labor, and herself the unmarried mother of an adopted daughter, Frieda Miller spearheaded the conversation in the United States. Abetted by Children's Bureau associate chief Martha Eliot, a distinguished advocate for maternal health programs worldwide and, like Miller, a veteran of the 1930s struggle for social legislation, she worked on two fronts: to promote a federal law that would mandate time off for wage-earning women before and after childbirth, and to encourage U.S. participation in the ILO effort to develop a broad range of job protections for wage-earning women. Both women were painfully aware that the United States lagged far behind other industrial countries—worldwide some seventy already offered women medical care and some mixture of paid and unpaid leaves—and each encouraged her bureau to support the ILO's efforts to recommend a wide range of health benefits, paid leaves, and especially job security for pregnant women and new mothers.

Their efforts bore fruit in the ILO but had little impact within the United States. In 1952, the ILO recommended a twelve-week leave period, half of it to be taken after childbirth; it supported job security for women, cash benefits to replace lost wages, and medical care.[11] But the United States never approved the provisions, and there was little public debate about them. There did not appear, according to one high-powered study, to be "any significant body of opinion which looks to legislation as a means of establishing maternity leave programs which provide both income and job security."[12] A few years later, members of Kennedy's Commission on the Status of Women expressed outrage at the paucity of protections for pregnant working mothers, reiterating the need for medical benefits and deploring the absence of reemployment and seniority rights following maternity leaves. Still, Rhode Island remained the only state that treated normal pregnancy as a fully compensable disability, though by then New York, California, and New Jersey offered disability protection to women with medically complicated pregnancies. Several states carried insurance for their own pregnant employees, and some employers and unions did the same. Discussants explained resistance to change in language that echoed efforts to limit women's workforce expectations: as impermanent workers, women threatened to abuse benefits by entering the workforce in expectation of pregnancy; subsidizing the medical costs of childbirth passed on to employers, costs that should be borne by husbands; offering women job security before and after childbirth would unduly burden employers entitled to competitive labor.[13]

Stasis on maternity leaves and insurance reflects the profound ambivalence that filled public commitments to women's wage earning even as the 1960s dawned. The most powerful statement of that ambivalence came in the late 1950s when the Eisenhower administration funded a distinguished commission to explore and recommend ways to develop the country's labor resources. Located at Columbia University and headed by the sociologist Eli Ginzburg and his colleague Henry David, the Manpower Commission published six volumes. Only one of them, the sixth, paid any attention to women. Suggesting its intent to "grasp the distinctive nature of the country's resources of womanpower," it emphatically affirmed what it took to be a shared assumption: "Both men and women generally take it for granted that the male is the family breadwinner and that he has a superior claim to available work, particularly over the woman who does not have to support herself." The claim was justified by opinion surveys that supported the idea that men deserved jobs. *Womanpower*, as the volume was called, cited a 1946 survey that concluded that three quarters of employed men and women, and 70 percent of employed women, said they "believed that an employer should discharge an efficient woman whose husband could support her, in preference to an inefficient man who had a family to maintain."[14]

The commission sharply distinguished between what it called "attitudes and practices prejudicial to the woman worker" and "overt" or "outright" discrimination. It dismissively characterized the former as the target of ERA advocates, who believed that "discrimination against women exists whenever women are treated differently from men." And, in conformity with the felt experiences of most white (but not black) women with marginal labor force attachment, it espoused a teleological vision of expanding possibility for all women: "Decade by decade," it averred, "outright discrimination against women in all phases of American life, including work, has diminished to a point where today most of the objectives of the early feminists have been secured."[15]

Even a restrictive conception of discrimination that excluded "attitudes and practices" did not entirely blind the Manpower Commission to the disadvantages women faced in the job market. It simply did not know when to label prejudicial behavior discriminatory. So, for example, it cited approvingly another government report that suggested that "even where there is no discrimination, the ways in which girls are brought up and educated, together with the continuing responsibilities of women in the home, make it difficult for women to achieve a high order of self-development and fulfillment in work." Then, quoting the report, it asked, "How can current restrictive attitudes and concepts about women workers in general be so changed that women who wish careers will have unfettered opportunities to pursue them solely on the basis of their own abilities?"[16] Identifying employers, the labor market, and even "women who wish careers" as innocent victims of legitimate, natural, sexual distinctions rendered policies enforcing equal employment opportunity for women implausible at best. Unsurprisingly, the wartime and postwar debate around fair employment practices rotated around race, ignoring women entirely. Despite their protests, African-American as well as white women found themselves poorly served.[17] With the exception of New York, no state included women within its fair employment practices laws, and even New York freely excluded women who sought jobs outside their customary spheres.

That attitude explains how President Kennedy's March 1961 Executive Order 10925 excluded sex. Amidst great public fanfare and with the moral authority of the president behind it, the executive order mandated that employers with federal contracts take affirmative action to ensure that "applicants were employed, and that employees are treated during employment without regard to their race, creed, color, or national origin."[18] The President's Committee on Equal Employment Opportunity, chaired by a recalcitrant Vice President Lyndon Baines Johnson, would monitor and enforce the order. Briefly, and in response to Johnson's anxiety about chairing a committee bound to offend many of his southern friends as well as members of the business and labor community, the president's aides considered including sex and age among the categories to be monitored, but the proposal was dismissed as a delaying tactic. Historian Hugh Davis Graham quotes one aide's request to Johnson that he drop the request lest he "throw the committee into complete chaos" and be charged with sabotaging it.[19]

## The President's Commission on the Status of Women

Within a week after Kennedy's exclusionary executive order, Esther Peterson received a note from her boss, Secretary of Labor Arthur Goldberg, forwarding a letter from the National Woman's Party. The letter suggested that Kennedy convene a committee to consider the status of women. Peterson, who disliked the NWP's single-minded advocacy of an equal rights amendment, replied that she was already at work on such an idea and would get back to him.

By all accounts the idea for a high-level commission to explore women's status had floated around for many years. Peterson attributed it to a 1947 notion of Congressman Emmanuel Celler to establish a national study on the status of women. She wanted, she said, "to use the approach that President Truman used in his pioneering study on the status of American blacks, which produced an Executive Order, 'To Secure These Rights,' that ended many discriminatory Federal race practices."[20] And she was annoyed that Kennedy had excluded women from early discussions with black civil rights leaders. Katherine (Kitty) Ellickson, who later became the commission's executive secretary, claimed that it was the brainchild of trade union women. Ellickson, who had been assistant secretary of the Social Security Department of the AFL-CIO, recalled that she suggested "a Commission to Esther in her office" around the third week of February and that her suggestion produced a meeting of trade union women on February 28, 1961.[21] It was here that the idea of what constituted discrimination for women seems to have begun its public career.

No doubt the melding of trade union sensibilities about workers' rights, especially for black women, and civil rights for individuals of every race and sex played a crucial role. Peterson was herself a product of the labor movement. A dedicated trade union activist, she had worked for many years for the Amalgamated Clothing Workers of America, most recently as a highly respected legislative representative, or lobbyist. She had gone out on a limb to support Kennedy's presidential aspirations in 1960. Horrified that the Republican platform endorsed an equal rights amendment with its threat to extinguish a painstakingly accrued body of state-based special protective laws for women wage earners, and fearing that some of the Democratic Party's key women would encourage Kennedy to follow suit, Peterson led her female colleagues in the labor movement into his campaign. To reward her, Kennedy offered her a post in the administration. She chose to be director of the Women's Bureau and became the highest-ranking woman in the administration when she accepted an invitation to extend the job to include the duties of an assistant secretary of labor as well.

Whatever its origins, Peterson immediately seized on the idea of a commission to explore the status of women as a way to undermine the specter of a constitutional amendment mandating equal rights. To develop the idea, she worked closely with Katherine Ellickson and with Evelyn Harrison, a high-ranking official in the Civil Service Commission, as well as with Arthur Goldberg (who had been general counsel to the AFL-CIO) and a very supportive Vice President Johnson. As they drafted the call for a commission, the needs of wage-earning women and the model of the civil rights movement were both very much on their minds. Like most of her trade union colleagues, Peterson believed that under her predecessor, Alice Leopold, the Women's Bureau had neglected the needs of working-class women. From the first days of her appointment, she counted on little support from the civil servants in the Women's Bureau, believing that these holdovers from the Eisenhower era resented her concern with "factory workers and fruit pickers."[22] To overcome this bias, she recalled some nineteen years later, "I made a decision—Arthur and I decided this together—to use the civil rights executive order format." Peterson clarified what she had in mind: "I recall discussing that with Arthur," she told an interviewer, "and our saying, 'Now look, what we're trying to do really is give to women the kind of citizenship we're trying to give to blacks through the civil rights.' "[23]

Through the spring, as members of Peterson's team sweated over the several drafts required to produce a document the president could sign, the threat of an ERA hovered over them. The civil rights model and the language of citizenship seemed reasonable alternatives to a constitutional amendment that, in their view, threatened as many rights as it might protect. At first, drafts asked only "to examine critically the status of women under the law as citizens, workers, and family members." Later drafts called for an examination of "what action can be immediately taken under existing law . . . to assure to women their fundamental rights as citizens without placing protections afforded by necessary and desirable legislation in jeopardy."[24] Soon, drafters transformed "fundamental rights" into "the fundamental human rights of all citizens," asserting their importance to "our future as a free and democratic nation" and acknowledging that they were "inherent in our Constitution." Later, Peterson penciled in sharper language, linked to economic choice: "Questions continue to be raised about the status of women both under law and under economic practice. Some question laws which limit women as citizens—in jury service, in ownership of property, in inheritance. Some question practices which restrict women's opportunities for employment, education, or training." Always there was a caveat to ensure that women had full access to the rights of citizens "without jeopardizing the protections afforded by necessary and desirable legislation."

The final draft, and the one that Kennedy signed on December 14, 1961, as Executive Order 10980, omitted the word *citizenship*. Fostering "women's basic rights," it declared, formed part of "our nation's commitment to human dignity, freedom, and democracy." Women, it acknowledged, had been treated "as a marginal group whose skills had been inadequately utilized." They "should be assured the opportunity to develop their capacities and fulfill their aspirations." And yet a qualification had crept in: while recommending that a commission be created to ensure women's basic rights, the president's statement assured the public that "measures that contribute to family security and strengthen home life will advance the general welfare." The executive order duly called for "developing recommendations for overcoming discriminations in government and private employment on the basis of sex *and* [my emphasis] for developing recommendations for services which will enable women to continue their role as wives and mothers while making a maximum contribution to the world around them."[25] Unlike the forceful and immediate mandate of the 1961 executive order on race, which authorized the Equal Employment Opportunity Commission to take affirmative action for minorities, the minimal investigatory powers conferred on the President's Commission on the Status of Women (PCSW) seem sparse indeed. They fell far short of the outright prohibition of other forms of discrimination and carried not even the admittedly weak sanctions proposed for them. The contrasts suggest a continuing perception of minorities and women as quite differently situated at least with regard to economic opportunity, the significant degree of overlap held to be of little account. They imply that solutions to issues of racial discrimination seemed as necessary as the conception of sex discrimination remained troubling.

If the executive order toyed with the relationship between opportunity and discrimination, the press release that accompanied it exacerbated the ambiguity. It began by deploring "those economic conditions which require women to work unless they desire to do so," promised to improve family income so that more women could choose not to work, and then, in a somewhat contradictory and more assertive mode, declared that nevertheless "women should not be considered a marginal group to be employed periodically only to be denied opportunity to satisfy their needs and aspirations when unemployment rises or a war ends."[26] Secretary of Labor Arthur Goldberg picked up this theme and affirmed Peterson's vision of a government that could defend women's rights as individuals when, a few months later, he welcomed representatives of women's organizations to Washington. Acknowledging that some people in his department still believed "that women are in the labor force because they think it is a kind of a *nice* thing to pursue careers," he declared his own commitment to two concepts with respect to women's employment: "One is that women are vitally *necessary* in the labor force .... But there is a second more fundamental thing. Women have a *right* to be in the labor force, just as men do." Lest he leave any doubt in his listeners' minds, he went on: "If a woman is married and wants to work, she has a right to work. If she is divorced or widowed, she may have a duty to work and a right to work, too, and a necessity for work .... There ought not to be an argument about the right of anybody in the country who wants to work, man or woman."[27]

These brave words notwithstanding, the visions of women that danced in the heads of PCSW members, and many of the 250 or so men and women who served on its committees or consulted with it, mitigated the commission's unqualifying support for the kinds of rights Goldberg described. There had, wrote PCSW member and historian Carolyn Ware in an influential background paper, once been an important feminist image in which women were "seen as individuals with varied capacities, interests and talents" who filled family roles among other social functions and for whom "the biological function of child-bearing is seen as incidental to the broader role of woman as a human being and a member of a democratic society." But Ware thought this view unfortunately discredited. Unrealistic as they were in her judgment, traditional images of white middle-class family lives continued "to dominate not only the attitude of many adults but the self-image and aspirations of many girls."[28] This second image pervaded PCSW discussions. They repeatedly affirmed that expectations of marriage, motherhood, and national need appropriately conditioned opportunity for women and necessarily limited women's citizenship. Lodged in the customs, preferences, attitudes, and habits of mind of a generation, traditional ideas produced the ambiguity that still surrounded notions of discrimination on the basis of sex. Less contentious around issues of political and legal status than around economic ones, ambiguity was to haunt the commission's deliberations. It challenged the best efforts of PCSW members to create a civil rights model and would emerge most starkly when sex and race were both at issue.

Given the composition of the commission, this was all but inevitable.[29] The PCSW was chaired by Eleanor Roosevelt, whose participation provided Kennedy with valuable legitimacy on the human rights front and who had been selected as perhaps the only woman of stature who could reconcile the competing interests of commission members; its guiding light and, by her own account, its architect was Executive Vice Chair Esther Peterson. Peterson, along with Roosevelt and with input from Daniel Patrick Moynihan, representing the Department of Labor, selected the twenty-six Commission members. She wanted high-powered representatives from government departments concerned with women's issues—people with status, men and women. "I very definitely wanted industry, labor, women, all people who were concerned, and I did not want a women's commission," Peterson explained in justification of her appointment of a man, Princeton University economist Richard Lester, as vice chair. Lester's long government experience, she thought, would be a useful political asset.[30] In the end, the PCSW included five cabinet members, four members of Congress, and a range of labor, business, and civic leaders. The group divided into seven committees (Civil and Political Rights; Education; Federal Employment; Home and Community; Private Employment; Protective Labor Legislation; and Social Insurance and Taxes), each of which invited twelve to fourteen knowledgeable and interested people to participate and to make recommendations to the full PCSW.

In selecting comission and committee members, Peterson tried to avoid people whose stance on the ERA differed from hers. She acknowledged this frankly: "It was very necessary to be sure that we had enough people there who would vote along the lines that I thought the commission should go."[31] As a result, with the considered exception of Marguerite Rawalt, president of the National Federation of Business and Professional Women's Clubs, she chose members likely to reflect her perspective. No other known member of the NWP was deliberately invited to serve on the PCSW, though several crept into some of the seven committees and a few appeared at the consultations called over its two-year life span. One participant unknown to Peterson, Macon Boddy of Texas, was added at the request of Lyndon Johnson—the only "political" appointment to which Peterson succumbed and one that she later grew to appreciate.[32]

Despite the PCSW's declared aim of seeking alternatives to the ERA, members had difficulty finding alternative strategies for assuring women's access to full opportunity. Peterson and many other members of the commission and its committees objected less to the ERA's demand that "equality of rights under the law shall not be denied or abridged by the United States or by any state on account of sex" than they did to its rigid refusal to provide exceptions for what most men and women still believed to be legitimate gender differences that courts should acknowledge.[33] While they conceded the desirability of eliminating gender differences for most civil and political purposes, they had a hard time imagining a world in which some of the functions women regularly performed, particularly motherhood, would not require special protection in the economic marketplace. The most important conflicts within the commission, and the most significant debates, therefore rehearsed issues that had dominated women's search for citizenship since the turn of the century.

Not even Peterson's "civil rights model" could entirely defuse the tension. For if Peterson and her allies shared a commitment to maintaining women's capacities to perform their traditional family roles without sacrificing either legal standing or potential economic opportunities, none of them could point the way to accommodating difference without sacrificing equality. Requested to comment on the potential use of the Fourteenth Amendment to protect women, one sympathetic consultant asserted pithily that the biggest roadblock was "the sharp difference of opinion as to what constitutes a discrimination."[34] The PCSW's deliberations and those of its subcommittees confirmed this observation. Their debates over what constituted discrimination rotated around two poles. Participants who imagined that women's major stake lay in their family functions could not imagine that job-related restrictions meant to protect their health and safety could have other than benign effects on women. Those who foregrounded the civil and political rights of women tended to emphasize the individual claims sustained by liberal theory.[35]

Perhaps because they had been deliberately chosen by Peterson and the Department of Labor (though they very likely mirrored common attitudes as well), most commission members assumed that women wanted and preferred home roles. Senator Maurine Neuberger, who chaired the Committee on Social Insurance and Taxes, reported to the PCSW that her committee had resolved the issue by assuming that "women given the choice, as a rule, other than that professional group, would prefer to stay home to rear their children, to entertain the husband's boss, to have a nice home and to work in some volunteer committee activity."[36] Daniel Patrick Moynihan, then an assistant secretary of labor, assigned by the department as liaison to the commission, affirmed her decision. He objected to the tone of one of its early draft reports declaring what he called his "R[oman] C[atholic] objection to the widespread notion that women can and *ought* to work." He "would like to see a country and an economy in which men made enough money that their women can stay home and raise their families."[37] Still, there was space for dispute between the desire of many to see some groups of women stay home and the perceived rights of women to engage in paid work. When Wilbur Cohen, an assistant secretary of health, education, and welfare, repeated the discredited notion that mothers who worked produced delinquent children, Peterson took him immediately to task.[38] Yet limiting women's rights to equal employment opportunity out of consideration for their work at home (and in the conviction that all women had homes in which they worked) did not always appear to constitute discrimination. To the Protective Labor Legislation Committee, concessions to home roles appeared more benign than otherwise. In a discussion that might have echoed one of fifty years earlier, it asked for an absolute maximum forty-eight-hour weekly limit on the hours that women could work. The committee acknowledged that such limits could "have adverse consequences on employment opportunities of women," yet it was convinced that the advantages "far outweigh[ed] the disadvantages."[39]

The thinking of the PCSW demonstrates how difficult rights were to assert in the face of conceded differences. Whether traditional family roles were thought of as natural, as some argued, or as socially developed and culturally desirable, as others suggested, mattered little. Advocates of both positions assumed women's primary commitment to families; their arguments contained unspoken expectations about the limits of women's wage work that echoed the arguments of the early 1900s and justified continued differential treatment by sex in the workplace. As one PCSW committee member—a businessman—understood it, women paid a price for performing their "natural duties ... God-given duties." When a woman left the labor force to bring her family up, she would return to the workforce "selling a weak product .... She can't help it, she brought a family up. She can't help it. This is because she is a woman."[40]

At their best, toned down and not essentialized, such perceptions limited the commission's sense of the meaning of discrimination, modifying it to incorporate a sense that what was natural could legitimately be treated differently and not labeled bias. At the same time, recognition of women's increasing needs for income as well as of the nation's growing demand for labor encouraged committee and commission members to think about affirmative steps to induce women into the labor market. Margaret Ackroyd, chief of the Women and Children section in the Rhode Island Department of Labor and a member of the Committee on Protective Labor Legislation, thought that because their weaknesses in the labor market stemmed from their primary obligation to family, women deserved to be treated "in a positive manner." After all, she concluded, their services benefited "the whole nation" and the community.[41] In this context it is not surprising that committee and commission members advocated constructive services to women who wished to work, as well as jobs that complemented their vision of women as family members who could participate differentially in the workforce at different life stages.

The Home and Community Committee (sometimes called the Committee on New and Expanded Services) took just such a position, advocating education, counseling, and training programs for a select group of women: mothers with grown children. It saw these and other services as maximizing opportunities to "help women carry out their responsibilities in the home, in the community, and in gainful employment."[42] Moynihan proposed targeting efforts at "the college educated mothers of grown families," suggesting that "the use of such women as teachers, government executives, community workers, etc., surely provide the prospect of getting a large vocational return for the money we invest in women's education and household appliances."[43]

Tension between advocates of enhanced employment opportunities for women and those who sought to link economic opportunity to their ideal models of women's lives pervaded the PCSW's deliberations. At one extreme, an irritated and bored member of the Committee on Protective Labor Legislation offered to resign because he objected to "the social wisdom of ranking the role of employee first." He feared the committee was concentrating its "attention on the less important of women's two roles—mother and homemaker on the one hand and employee on the other." There did not, in his view, "remain in this country such serious conditions of exploitation that we should risk the stultifying effect of further restriction on business." Besides, women belonged at home: "Whatever tends to divert her from her role in the home represents a negative force which we must reckon with."[44] Senator George Aiken agreed that the commission as a whole had placed too much emphasis on women as workers: "Recognizing the fact that there is no good substitute for women as mothers and homemakers, I would put a little more emphasis on and give a little more credit to the homemaker and mother."[45] Willard Wirtz, who succeeded Goldberg as secretary of labor in 1962, concurred with these viewpoints. Addressing a PCSW-sponsored conference to explore employment opportunities for women, he told his distinguished audience that he hoped there did not emerge from the conference "an over-emphasis on the employment of women, if you see what I mean. We are not here, as I understand it, urging more work for women or urging that more women move from the home to the economy; that isn't the point."[46]

Inevitably such attitudes restrained the range of possible solutions and invited a balance between policies that expanded women's opportunities for good jobs and those that encouraged them to stay at home. Along with training opportunities for women workers and vocational counseling for women, for example, members of the PCSW advocated equal opportunity in private and federal employment, as well as equal pay, expanded tax deductions for child care, and the right to organize collectively. Yet it intended these shifts for women who "preferred employment" while trying not to rock the boat with regard to women's family and home lives. Members of its many committees debated, without recommending changes in, some of the restrictive social policies that limited the free exercise of individual rights for women—especially for married women, who now constituted the majority of female workers—but not for men.[47] They considered whether a wife who earned might receive old age insurance benefits based on her husband's record, as well as those she had accrued on her own account. They argued the paradox of denying unemployment insurance benefits to women who would not agree to make themselves available for new jobs distant from their families while custom and some state laws insisted that marriage required a woman to share her husband's domicile. And they explored how to limit the income tax obligations of women (whose incomes were taxed at marginal rates that reflected their husbands' generally higher salaries) while the split-income provisions of the federal income tax codes provided seductive financial incentives to treat families as indivisible units. Yet despite sometimes heady debate, the PCSW took no position on any of these issues, preferring instead a paradoxical affirmation of women's traditional family roles along with unrestricted opportunity for those who chose employment.

While the PCSW's various committees could at least debate the ways that marriage limited rights, they had a more difficult time acknowledging that women's maternal roles might generate a range of social citizenship rights—as they did in many European countries. For example, many people around the PCSW believed the time had come to support cash maternity benefits that treated childbirth like a temporary disability. Others, however, feared that such benefits could attract pregnant women into the workforce. "When a woman has been working," Mary Keyserling, who supported cash benefits through unemployment insurance, asked Loyola economics professor Doris Boyle, who opposed them, "and leaves because of pregnancy and receives compensation for those weeks before and after, does that in itself encourage her to return to employment?" Boyle replied ambivalently that she had "no objection to that part," but she wondered if "this committee should advocate policies which will contribute to married women remaining in the labor force during child-bearing years."[48]

The lengthy discussion that followed makes it clear that issues of family policy weighed heavily against the rights of women as individuals and that class (or low income) was the most effective mediator. Women with their own resources who could afford child care, everyone agreed, had the right to choose to work or not. But as a matter of policy, members of at least one committee rejected the idea that mothers of young children should be encouraged to return to work. To discourage them, one committee member wanted the group to support "a statement of recognition that the employed woman does have very strong social obligations and family obligations." That abstract position obscured the potential rights of new mothers not only to job security but to medical care and cash benefits during maternity leave and child care allowances when they returned to work. Maternity benefits remained, as they had long been, a sticking point. One lone voice vehemently protested this discrimination against women. Men who were alcoholics, she complained, could be committed for six months and still have reemployment rights. "But just the fact you have a baby you automatically are taken away from the labor market and all rights and privileges." Most members pleaded custom and tradition, arguing that women's obligations to the family exceeded their rights as working mothers and appropriately subjected them to more stringent eligibility standards than applied to men. Women should not, declared Rhode Island Department of Welfare official Margaret Ackroyd, participate in these benefits unless they intended to return to the labor market. In practice, the absence of benefits most negatively affected needy mothers, who tended to return to the workforce as soon as they could after childbirth, generally without benefit of paid leaves and unable to afford appropriate child care. In light of these disadvantages, the PCSW did, in the end, adopt a lukewarm position in favor of maternity benefits.

Providing wage-earning women with income tax credits or deductions for child care posed a comparable dilemma. When it came up tentatively in the Committee on Civil and Political Rights, the witness who introduced it suggested it as a matter of policy.[49] Many of the nurses she represented, who were badly needed in the labor force, would gladly return to work if the cost of household help and babysitters were defrayed. As in the maternity insurance debate, class mediated the solution. Everyone recognized that well-off and professional women had no difficulty hiring household help. At issue, then, were the messages that government wanted to send to less well-off working women. Committee members divided sharply. New York City lawyer Harriet Pilpel responded with an appeal for a strong committee resolution for "an additional tax deduction for women who have to spend money to replace themselves in the home in order to do socially desirable and useful jobs." Judge Florence Murray pleaded for the political value of supporting tax benefits for working mothers, at least in principle, on the grounds that it would earn the attention and gratitude of a younger generation of women.

But the committee split over questions of equity as between a deduction for the household expenses of women who earned wages and its denial to those who hired household workers and stayed home. They also divided over whether a tax deduction would enhance women's capacity to exercise their civil and political rights. And they argued over whether a resolution should encompass only working mothers or all those with responsibility for children. With one member abstaining, they agreed, finally, on a motion to support, in principle, additional tax deductions to enable all those who cared for young children to work. The abstention came from Frank Sander, professor of law at Harvard and a staunch opponent of tax credits to working wives and mothers. His parting shot captured the threat that many felt tax credits embodied. "Does this mean," he asked acerbically, "that this committee expresses itself in favor of encouraging mothers with children to go out and work and get people to take care of their children?"[50]

Sander might have felt more comfortable in the Committee on Social Insurance and Taxes, where the two sides were more evenly represented. Committee chair Senator Maurine Neuberger supported the idea of tax credits for mothers who found that, when they went back to work, "they couldn't make any money at it because when the family hired a housekeeper and suitable governess for the children they were just not very well off."[51] Other members wondered if "it would be a good idea to have provisions to assist the young married women with small children, at that stage to stay out of the labor market."[52] Since policies that benefited women who needed to work while their children were small could be construed as encouraging women to return to work regardless of family need, the PCSW focused on the line between two men's needs and their desires. Its members imagine that opportunities should not be so attractive as to pull women out of the home while at the same time they encouraged policies that sustained certain kinds of families. Senator Neuberger saw this as a critical divide. Futilely, she begged for clarification of the PCSW's position. Was it the policy, she asked simply, "to encourage or discourage wives from working?"[53] Moynihan had an easy answer to this question. He wanted to be sure that the final report did not "indicate any desire to arrange the tax laws so that wives are encouraged to get jobs."[54]

In line with this view, members of the various committees located women's rights within the penumbra of their national service as homemakers as well as workers, rather than within the framework of liberal individualism. Commitment to nation had always been part of the commission's mandate. As vice president, Lyndon Johnson had opened the 1962 Conference on Employment Opportunities for Women by reminding the assembled company that the "adjustments and changes" they would recommend "must be made because they will enhance our prosperity and because they will protect the security of our country."[55] In this respect, they held the struggle for economic rights hostage. As Hyman Bookbinder, one of its most active members, liked to remind the group whenever they were heading off in the direction of "what the woman needs and not what society needs," this was not part of their mission.[56]

Like President Kennedy and many other government officials, Johnson echoed a compromise position. He decried the loss of labor market resources embodied in women's neglected skills, calling it "a waste we can no longer afford."[57] Yet he called for women's participation in ways respectful to the needs of the home. Opportunity and discrimination operated within this context. "Isn't it true," asked one commission member, "that we need women in the labor market? While we are not trying to force women into the labor market, we certainly would like to see ... opportunities that would make it possible for them to meet this manpower need that we are told they are needed for."[58] For women, the argument for ending discrimination as a matter of human dignity was offered up only incidentally as a matter of individual liberties or civil rights; more often it was an artifact of the country's ideological and economic needs during the cold war. A classic example of this occurred during one of the many debates on maternity insurance when a frustrated Kitty Ellickson tried to persuade other members of her committee that the PCSW needed to take a position on the issue because it was an object of great curiosity among foreigners that "there are no maternity benefits in this country in a government program." People from other countries, she added, "the people who are concerned about demonstrating the value of the American system as compared with communism ... find this a really serious problem."[59]

Contention around the meaning of discrimination permeated the deliberations of many of the PCSW committees, resulting ultimately in an agreement to define it as simply the absence of opportunity. This happened because the commission could not agree on the language of a clause it hoped to recommend that advocated access to employment for women "without discrimination and under suitable working conditions."[60] When Bookbinder objected to the use of the word *discrimination*, he sparked a telling exchange that ultimately concluded that it was not "discrimination" they were talking about at all. Rather, it was "opportunity" that the commission wanted. Even Marguerite Rawalt, the most active ERA supporter on the PCSW, agreed that this was not "the place to put the *d* word," and the conversation moved on.[61] Still, the commission was convinced that it was far ahead of most women, both

*Esther Peterson in a 1966 photograph with President Lyndon Baines Johnson.* COURTESY, SCHLESINGER LIBRARY, RADCLIFFE INSTITUTE FOR ADVANCED STUDIES, HARVARD UNIVERSITY.

complaining that women were content "to keep at lower levels, to act as though we weren't in the labor market permanently," and blaming women's poor labor market positions on the "widespread belief around the country that women are the marginal earners."[62]

If the PCSW could not reconcile the contradiction between prevailing assumptions about women's home roles and women's growing expectations for rewards in the labor force, it reflected an understandable confusion. Certainly no widespread sense of entitlement to work yet existed among women. Popular conceptions of work for women remained constrained by notions of fairness and justice rooted in the home. As such they could not fuel a sense of grievance sufficient to enable most married women to label restraints on their work as discrimination. "Women, at least in my opinion, don't know that there are discriminations," commented one committee member. They had not, said a second, "in large numbers exercised themselves on behalf of their own rights."[63] At the same time, by the early 1960s, the PCSW accurately discerned that significant numbers of women in the labor force faced formidable obstacles, especially with regard to fair pay and promotion, and that these seemed to them to be increasingly unfair. This growing sense of injustice strengthened ERA supporters and jolted even those PCSW members who claimed to have heard little discontent from women.

## Calling into Question the Entire Doctrine of Sex

Among the increasingly restless women were women of color, and especially African-American women. The fact that black women appeared at the bottom of the wage charts, that 30 percent of those who earned still worked as domestic servants in private households, and that the vast majority (even in 1960) remained excluded from the provisions of the Fair Labor Standards Act appeared to the PCSW as an artifact fact primarily of race rather than of sex discrimination. Roosevelt and Peterson had originally hoped to thread issues of minority women throughout the discussions of the various committees, but "White House and Department interest in this matter" apparently convinced Peterson to adopt a more visible strategy.[64] Late in the day, when the committees were drafting their final reports, Peterson urgently assigned Ellickson to consult with various groups and prepare a paper on the issue. Ellickson organized a consultation for April 19, 1963, with a group of eleven African-American leaders, men and women, and some PCSW members and staff. The group, chaired by Dorothy Height, president of the National Council of Negro Women and the only black woman on the PCSW, placed the limits of opportunity for black women firmly within the context of racial discrimination. Discrimination against African-American men, it concluded, forced women of that race to take a much more active role in the economic support of families than white women. At the same time, discrimination against African-American women confined most to the poorest jobs while encouraging the few who could take advantage of education and professional training to play leadership roles in families. The consultants viewed the results as a problem, leading to what they described as the "more matriarchal" structure of the Negro family.

The language of matriarchy, widely used by the consultants, and understood by them to refer to the prevalence of female-headed or female-dominated households within the African-American population, encompassed what consultants referred to as "the problems of Negro women." These problems existed at both ends of the economic scale. Black women who traditionally worked long hours at the lowest-paying jobs could not adequately mother their children; those who earned professional degrees had difficulty finding appropriate partners, thus distorting what one consultant called "the family unit" and creating what another described as "the ego aspect" among black men.[65] Both groups of women were victims of racism against black men, which led not only to neglect of families but to neglect of their communities as well. Among educated women, discrimination created a double bind because emphasis on work allowed a woman far less time for "emphasis on cultural enrichment than her role among the culturally deprived demands of her."[66] Moynihan had already reached these conclusions. Just two weeks earlier, he had written a forceful letter to Peterson before rejecting her initial effort to equate the relationships of black and white women to family life. "To my limited understanding," he had commented, "Negro society in America is still substantially a matriarchy. This ... may in fact be one of the principal keys to understanding and resolving the Negro problem."[67]

The word *matriarchy* might have been conceived in a positive light, an effective resolution to problems of racial discrimination beyond the control of most families. In practice, it connoted disadvantage and rapidly became a code for what was wrong with the Negro family. At best, it set the stage for a discussion of Negro women that described them not at all as rights-bearing individuals but rather as the innocent victims and unwitting progenitors of racialized economic structures. "What can be done," Moynihan had asked Peterson, "to establish the responsible male head of a family?"[68] After their daylong discussion, the consultants posed the same issue: "The progress of the Negro woman—her personal advancement and that of the whole family—is inextricably bound to the improvement of opportunities for the Negro male." Underlying the conclusion was a consensus that many black families were not integrated into "what we would consider the normal values and standards of American life." Cernoria Johnson, representing the National Urban League, articulated the issue eloquently: "We agree that what we consider to be the acceptable average family is that there is a mother and a father in the home.... We are trying to strengthen family life, which means we are not going to be able to deal with the Negro female, but deal with the male, in order to bring the picture together."[69]

The consultants' recommendations did not entirely subsume black women into family life. Like several of the PCSW committees, they wanted policies that would enhance job opportunities for black women, including vocational guidance, job training, and expanded employment options. They called in addition for such creative initiatives as unionizing household workers to ensure better wages and benefits for them, more extensive child care, better public services in poor neighborhoods, and support for black women's voluntary activities in their communities. But they believed ultimate solutions to economic deprivation lay in reinforcing the economic positions of black men rather than by opening economic opportunities to black women. They proposed an end to the "man in the house" rule, which even in 1961 permitted two thirds of the states to cut off Aid to Dependent Children payments if a male lived in the home. They also insisted on training opportunities for black men, including an expansion of college admissions. "If the Negro woman has a major underlying concern," concluded consultancy chair Dorothy Height, "it is the status of the Negro and his position in the community and his need for feeling himself an important person, free and able to make his contribution in the whole society in order that he may strengthen his home."[70]

The PCSW's eagerness to ensure respect for family roles even at the cost of individual rights framed its views of black women. On the whole, the commission imagined that equal opportunity in the workforce could open blocked pathways and provide white women with freedom to choose whether to stay at home or go out to work. Yet they understood that access to full civil and political participation would be required if white women were to successfully compete for jobs that would contribute to the security of their families.[71] With regard to black women (who were imagined as universally poor), they had a somewhat different perspective. Protecting the civil and political rights of black women, like offering them economic opportunity, would not alone suffice to improve family life. Only enhancing economic opportunity for black males would do that. In the PCSW's view, ending sex discrimination without attending to race discrimination was at best a partial solution, complicated by its threat to further distort the black family. And even the narrower economic interests of black women demanded attention to race. Several committee members (black and white) argued that an attack on race discrimination would be necessary if black women were to benefit from policies against sex discrimination.

The PCSW did not try to resolve the tensions inherent in seeking to break down barriers between black and white women, nor did it fully discuss them. Instead, it marked racial differences as of a different, and perhaps more important, order than sex differences. Struggling with the issue, economics professor Doris Boyle suggested that "many more women will be deprived of employment opportunities due to the fact of race and color than would be due to weight lifting or something."[72] The clarity of vision with regard to racial discrimination contrasted sharply with the murkiness surrounding sex discrimination. One member speculated out loud, "I may be going too far ... but it is easier for all of us to discuss equal employment opportunity as it pertains to color. I find it easier to talk about this subject.... You find you are dealing with a reality of feelings that most people will get with you." But when it came to sex, he asked, "Aren't we faced with a more mixed emotion?" The commission's vice chair, Richard Lester, had to agree that "it is a less clearcut problem."[73]

The consensus reflected deeply rooted sensibilities about the relationship of race and sex to the labor market and may account for the willingness of many women to defer to race in the struggle for civil rights. Consistent with it, members of the commission did not respond negatively when President Kennedy prohibited federal contractors from engaging in racial and other forms of discrimination, yet omitted to mention sex. Peterson herself commented that she had not been distressed when Kennedy's 1961 executive order prohibiting discrimination in employment by federal contractors omitted sex, because excluding all women would "open up job opportunities for Negro women," who would still be eligible for racial preferences.[74] Nor would the commission approve a recommendation to study adding sex to fair employment practices legislation, because it preferred not to "link discrimination because of sex with discrimination because of race."[75] "Discrimination based on sex," explained the PCSW, "involves problems sufficiently different from discrimination based on the other factors listed to make separate treatment preferable."[76]

In the midst of these disagreements about the meaning of sex discrimination, one forceful voice offered an alternative. Pauli Murray, a member of the Committee on Civil and Political Rights, proposed that an ERA could be most effectively avoided if women were brought within the protective umbrella of the Fourteenth Amendment. Her vision explicitly equated race and sex. Murray, one of a handful of black female attorneys with a long record of activity in the civil rights movement, was completing a doctoral dissertation at Yale Law School when Peterson invited her first to join the committee and then to write a brief that would rationalize the use of the Fourteenth Amendment.[77] Like other members of that committee, she was mostly concerned with issues around the legal status of women such as maintaining the rights of those who married, eligibility for jury service, and child custody than with economic issues. But like many other women of her generation, she feared that a "blanket amendment" would deprive many poor and wage-earning women of necessary labor protections.

Seeking advice as to how to avoid what historian Cynthia Harrison calls the "minefield" of the ERA, Murray wrote to some of the leading civil rights lawyers: "What I am after, of course, is a clear cut decision from the Supreme Court of the United States that the Fourteenth Amendment is applicable to discrimination because of sex."[78] She wanted, she said, to reexamine the "applicability of the Fourteenth Amendment to state laws and practices which discriminate arbitrarily because of sex."[79] Bringing women under the umbrella of that amendment, would, she thought, call into question "the entire doctrine of 'sex as a basis for legal classification'" and ensure that women were covered by the "equal protections of the law." Murray believed

*Pauli Murray, about 1964, around the time when her ideas about gender and racial equality came together.* COURTESY, SCHLESINGER LIBRARY, RADCLIFFE INSTITUTE FOR ADVANCED STUDIES, HARVARD UNIVERSITY.

that such a strategy required political action as well as state-based efforts to repeal laws that validated differential treatment of married women. And, she argued, if the strategy failed, if she did not succeed in modernizing "the rights of women in keeping with the supreme value of individuality in a democratic society," she would be prepared to turn to the equal rights amendment.

She knew that such arguments had failed before. For many years, and with little success, feminists had sought the inclusion of women under the protective mantle of the Fourteenth Amendment. Despite their efforts, the judiciary had historically insisted on the rights of the separate states to make reasonable classifications of who constituted a "person" and for what purposes.[80] While the courts had held that most classifications by race were unreasonable, they had failed to provide the same protection to women. But in 1962, "against the backdrop of mid-twentieth century notions of democracy," Murray believed that by creating a parallel between sex and race she could convince the Court that most classifications by sex were not "reasonable" within the meaning of the Fourteenth Amendment.[81] If the strategy worked—if the states were stripped of the power to classify women as different sorts of persons—there would, she thought, be no need of an ERA. Murray later wrote a piece with PCSW staff member Mary Eastwood in which the two identified the nub of the problem as "the failure of the courts to isolate and analyze the discriminatory aspect of differential treatment based on sex."[82] Was it, they asked, simply respectful of tradition to treat women differently from men, or did judicial failure to perceive the analogy of sex to race reflect the Supreme Court's own blindness to the idea that distinctions and perquisites conditioned on the sex of the recipient could constitute discrimination?

There were moments, Murray argued in her proposal, when a legal classification based on sex might be considered reasonable. Those occurred when placing women in separate categories protected their maternal and family functions. Murray in 1962, and Murray and Eastwood in 1965, proposed to substitute for a generic classification what they called "functional criteria" in order "to redelineate the boundaries of social policies which are genuinely protective of the family and maternal functions and those which are unjustly discriminatory against women as individuals."[83] Treating all women alike, Murray argued, was like treating all the members of a race alike. It would be more equitable to legislate for those functions of women (childbearing, child rearing, and the administration of the home) in which society had a genuine stake. Laws that made distinctions based on motherhood and actually existing sex differences, Murray and Eastwood thought, would protect appropriate women without jeopardizing the rights of the significant numbers of others who could and should be treated as individuals.

Could such a strategy succeed? Murray was optimistic. She pointed to two factors on her side. The first was a growing social science literature that equated sex and race discrimination. Second, she noted great changes in women's roles, their increasing independence from men, and even the increasing democratization of society as manifested in the 1948 U.N. Human Rights Convention. But there was a pessimistic scenario as well: the courts seemed quite unready to view discrimination against women in the same light as discrimination against African Americans. Many judges, Murray wrote, "appear to recoil from the concept that discrimination because of sex is the equivalent of discrimination because of race."

Despite the evidence generated by the PCSW, Murray believed that "women who suffer the effects" of differential treatment had little difficulty in recognizing the parallel. So when she circulated a draft of her proposal to good friends and lawyers, she was surprised to discover that it provoked skepticism even among them. True, some, like the American Civil Liberties Union's Dorothy Kenyon, applauded, noting that Murray's position affirmed the ACLU's sense that the Fourteenth Amendment offered "the most hopeful constitutional approach" to avoiding the ambiguity of an ERA. "I couldn't agree with you more that the Amendment is ideally fitted to deal with discriminations against women if only judges could be made to see it," she wrote to Murray.[84]

Others were disturbed by what they called the Jane Crow/Jim Crow analogy and urged her to modify it. A representative of the National Council of Jewish Women called it the document's "one general weakness." Phoebe Morrison reported that "some of the conservatives" found it especially hard to take. "I think you may get into some trouble carrying it very far," wrote one of her friends. "The comparison with the desegration litigation, of course, cannot be pressed too far," agreed Harvard law professor Paul Freund. "There are so many people who would deny there is any problem currently with respect to the status of women or discrimination against them," wrote Murray's friend Thacher Clark Anderson, counsel for the New York State Division of Human Rights. He complained that the scope of Murray's argument, which ignored the "psychological and emotional" dimensions of sex discrimination, was too narrow. And, crucially, he urged her to pay more attention to the most difficult issue of all, the arena of employment. Murray's response acknowledged that she had raised only the "piddling" tip of an iceberg and regretted that she had not pursued employment issues further. That was the province, she wrote back, of another committee. She begged Anderson to write directly to Katherine Ellickson to inquire about how the PCSW was treating employment problems. The issue plagued her, and a couple of months later she herself followed up with a letter to Ellickson expressing her concern at the neglect of private employment in the PCSW's deliberations and asking for it to be placed on her committee's agenda. Ellickson peremptorily refused.[85]

It comes as no surprise, then, to discover that, bold as the commission's final recommendations were, they reflect the tensions inherent in its continuing adherence to traditional assumptions about women and family life and its unwillingness to see sex and race as equally the targets of invidious discrimination. Though it issued a powerful call for improving women's status under the law through a Supreme Court validation of the Fourteenth Amendment's applicability to women, the PCSW did not use the touchstone of discrimination—the analogy with race—to make its point. It did urge the United States to become a party to the U.N. Human Rights Convention, which its honorary chair, Eleanor Roosevelt, had helped to draft. But it accompanied these sweeping desires with a narrower agenda that promoted what it called "women's freedom of choice" rather than women's rights.[86] It recommended education, counseling, and training for women, job security after a maternity leave, child care benefits scaled to income, and community and volunteer services to support families. It proposed an executive order mandating equal opportunity for women in private employment to parallel the one that already existed in federal employment and urged the extension of the Fair Labor Standards Act to additional groups of women. It targeted recommendations for enhanced part-time employment opportunities to the federal government, which it hoped would serve as a model for private employers. It asked for increased benefits for widows under old age insurance and an expansion of unemployment insurance to cover more women, including household workers. It proclaimed continuing allegiance to protective labor legislation by endorsing a maximum forty-hour week for women until such time as men and women both benefited from reduced hours.

Yet there were curious gaps in the commission's recommendations. At a moment in time when a civil rights bill was high on the congressional agenda, the PSCW shied away from the implications of the sex/race analogy Murray proposed. With respect to employment, its recommendations were decidedly limp. It advocated "equal opportunity for women in hiring, training, and promotion" as "the governing principle in private employment" yet urged only an executive order that would state the principle and "advance its application to work done under federal contracts." It endorsed preservation of reemployment and seniority rights for women workers on maternity leave but committed itself only to urging governments, employers, and unions to "explore the best means of accomplishing" ways of paying for leaves. It asked that a widow's pension under Social Security equal that of the deceased husband but suggested more modest changes in unemployment insurance.

It is hard to read the PCSW's final recommendations without seeing in them as much restraint as encouragement for freedom of choice. They affirm the vision of Margaret Hickey, who had announced, "I would like to encourage the building up of social legislation which would make it important for women to make a choice to stay in the home."[87] They also fully justify the conclusions drawn by the renowned anthropologist Margaret Mead, who summed up the PCSW's achievements in one published version of its report. Gently, she chided the commission for assuming that "our style of early marriage and family life will contine more or less unchanged." And, she commented, "women who are not fitted for or who do not like marriage and motherhood will continue to marry and to try to be wives and mothers. But they will try to get through this phase quickly." Still, she noted, ultimately "women's right to work" would have to be "underwritten with all necessary public help and facilitation."[88] That, the PCSW had not done.

Yet the PCSW did have a crucial impact. It fostered the political effort that became the 1963 Equal Pay Act. It started a dialogue about discrimination that would ultimately help to tie women's rights to a broader conception of civil rights, moving away from gender justice to individual self-reliance. And, through a series of state-based commissions on the status of women created

*Pauli Murray and Esther Peterson in November 1963, just as the work of the President's Commission on the Status of Women drew to a close.* BY PERMISSION, THE PROVIDENCE JOURNAL COMPANY, PROVIDENCE, RHODE ISLAND.

to follow through, it helped to develop a network of women who provided the political muscle for continuing activity. Pauli Murray described this step warmly: "Like-minded women found one another, bonds developed through working together, and an informal feminist network emerged to act as leaven in the broader movement that followed."[89]

## Equal Pay for Equal Work

While she drafted the PCSW's final report, Peterson already had her eyes on the new equal pay bill, just then before Congress. This bill, which followed on one that had been passed by both houses of Congress but never reconciled in conference just the previous year, was heir to a long campaign by the Women's Bureau and its allies to ensure that women working in jobs comparable to those of men got paid equally. Unlike earlier efforts, this one would succeed. The compromise that paved its road to triumph transformed "comparable" work to "equal" work. Congressional satisfaction with this change suggests something of the force embedded in dominant conceptions of discrimination as well as something of its constraints. Above all it tells us how gender could and could not be deployed in the moment of transformation in the early 1960s.[90]

Ever since the war, feminists had been fighting for legislation to equalize the pay of men and women who performed substantially similar jobs. Their efforts were fueled by the National War Labor Board's General Order 16 (1942), which allowed wage equalization of rates paid to women who worked with men "for comparable quality and quantity of work on the same or similar operations."[91] That language had encouraged others to think in the same terms: equal pay commissions, activists in women's groups and unions, and professionals in the Women's Bureau all proposed legislation that called for "equal pay for comparable work." When Secretary of Labor Louis Schwellenbach testified on behalf of a 1948 equal pay bill, for example, he had insisted that "if a woman does the same job or a job requiring comparable skill she ought to be paid the same rate as a man."[92] But in 1963, the bill that passed Congress called for equal pay for equal, rather than comparable, work.

The language of the final bill dramatically narrowed the venue within which women could claim a grievance. Given the sex segregation of occupations that sharply defined men's and women's jobs, and the tendency of entire job categories to become the province of one sex or the other, demanding equal pay only if men and women did exactly the same work offered greater symbolic consolation than practical benefit.[93] Nor did it speak to issues of sex discrimination, for if putting women in the same jobs as men would require employers to pay them equally, their tendency would be to maintain sex barriers rather than reduce them, to protect women in jobs they already filled, not to open new categories of work for them. This, as the rhetoric surrounding the bill's passage reveals, was exactly the point. As one scholar notes, all the discussions of equal pay that occurred throughout the postwar period and came to fruition in the 1963 Equal Pay Act "never prompted anyone, even women testifying about sex discrimination, to propose including sex discrimination in the EEO [equal employment opportunity] bill."[94]

Equal pay was, in that sense, a perfect compromise. As we have seen, it could be and often was construed as protecting men's jobs by ensuring that women would not undermine male wages. Schwellenbach himself had acknowledged his desire to eliminate a "dual wage system" because it could produce disruptive consequences among workers.[95] Even more important was the sense that a rigidly limited equal pay act held less potential for disturbing existing sex roles. Supporters acknowledged that some twenty-four million women (about a third of the labor force) worked for wages in 1960 and that 60 percent of these were married, yet they told opponents that the legislation, "while fair and effective, would not be excessive nor excessively wide-ranging."[96] New Jersey representative Frank Thompson made clear just what this meant to him: because the legislation applied only to discriminations based on sex, it would not "affect the wage of women vis-à-vis women or men vis-à-vis men." It would therefore leave untouched the wages of the vast majority of women, who worked in predominately female occupations. Because it was part of the FLSA, it would not apply to many women who were not already covered by the act, including those who worked in establishments with fewer than twenty-five workers. Enforcement and administration would be through the courts.

On the House floor, however, provisions deplored by long-standing supporters of the ERA became strengths. As Peter J. Frelinghuysen of New Jersey pointed out when he rose to defend the bill, its big attraction was its restrictiveness: "In hotels, which would be exempt, the work which women do in those establishments is almost exclusively women's work . . . and therefore, even if they were covered under the act, very, very few of them, and then only in larger establishments employing more than 25 persons, would be able to benefit in any way." Like Frelinghuysen, who had repeatedly pointed out that the bill ensured only that "men and women . . . doing the same job under the same working conditions . . . will receive the same pay," Thompson seemed eager to distance himself from any potentially radical consequences. Representative Charles Goodell of New York, who had conceived many of the key compromises, echoed this line. When "the House changed the word 'comparable' to 'equal,'" he told the assembled lawmakers, "the clear intention was to narrow the whole concept." Its specificity allowed lawmakers to rise in defense of "justice, fairplay, and equity" for women, even as they supported continuing occupational segregation.

A handful of women in Congress and a few men on the floor made no secret of their discontent with the rewritten act's limited value. She had wished, said Representative Edna Kelly, for wider coverage, especially of hotel maids and laundry workers. Like her, Goodell, who had been instrumental in narrowing coverage in the bill by proposing that it become an amendment to the FLSA, wanted "comparable" rather than "same" work inserted into the act. Others, like New York's Katherine St. George, a proponent of the "same work" compromise, claimed that the bill was only a start or hoped that it would be a prelude to a comprehensive bill to eliminate employment discrimination. Later there would be public anger and distress at how readily women in Congress had given up the demand for "comparable work." Peterson vented her rage against St. George ("this woman who was supposedly really in our corner") for proposing the floor amendment that changed the language.[97] Still, it is difficult to read the floor debate without acknowledging that the limits in the act, rather than the opportunities to which it might lead, provided the rationale for congressmen to accede to what they repeatedly referred to as simple justice.

In the minds of most legislators—male and female—justice in the end lay in affirming rather than rejecting natural differences: in providing equal pay despite the differences, not in full acknowledgment of them. Edith Green produced a chuckle when she reminded her colleagues that the committee report supported the bill because its aims were consistent with the notion that women were more prone to homemaking and motherhood.[98] No one disputed the offending words, and they were repeated later by others as items that the bill would not disturb. A few legislators continued to cling to the idea of some form of equal pay based on comparable jobs, and even to the notion that jobs should be distributed without regard to sex.[99] Most, however, agreed with Jeffrey Cohelan of California, who argued, "It is obvious and true that there are certain types of work which can be best performed by men. It is equally true that there are other types of work in which women excel." Only "in the middle ground," in the jobs that men and women could perform with equal ability, should there "be no distinction in pay based on sex."[100]

The debate reveals a subtle distinction in the minds of even the most supportive legislators. Women remained different from men. To sustain their differences, to perpetuate family life, they were forced to work for wages. Therefore they deserved to be supported by equal pay. Even New York's William F. Ryan, an ardent supporter of more comprehensive legislation, invoked nostalgic images of an earlier generation when "a girl left school, worked for a few years, married, and left the labor force for good" to explain why the tradition of paying women less now had to be abandoned.[101] By 1961, when married women constituted 60 percent of working women, women's legitimate needs for pay that could contribute to educating children and sustaining families, justified an end to wage differentials. The Equal Pay Act decreed that women should not be paid less just because they were different but only if they occupied different jobs or performed differently in the same jobs. It therefore incorporated women into notions of individual merit without disturbing the notion that gender differences still mattered when it came to the workplace.

Opponents of equal pay claimed that enacting a statute would promote an even greater form of discrimination by giving employers an incentive to give jobs to men rather than women. "Its enactment would worsen rather than improve job opportunities for women," said Paul Findley of Illinois, who believed an equal pay statute might "cause employers to quit hiring women for some jobs," and thus serve as a "subtle but effective way to get some women out of the labor force." The bill's supporters, thought Findley, were no friends of women at all: "Although this bill may have motives in the finest tradition of gallantry, it actually is about as ungallant as a kick in the shins."[102]

If few people in 1963 disagreed about the existence of gender differences that employers and public policy might take into account, discussions of fairness and justice took place within the range of available perspectives. The discussion over equal pay addressed the widespread conviction that women wage earners suffered differential treatment, without going so far as to remedy the sources of their disadvantaged status. Keeping discrimination within this narrow framework, equal pay for equal work effectively distinguished rights at work from any effort to end discrimination in jobs and occupations. And yet it had an important effect in opening up a dialogue about justice for women and revealing to an increasingly impatient network of political activists and women workers how the boundaries of justice remained gendered. It also helped to bring the word *discrimination* into more general usage with respect to sex. A year later, when Title VII entered the public vocabulary, it built on this stilted discussion to alter forever perceptions of sex discrimination and provide the basis of a full-scale legal assault on that notion.

# CHAPTER 6

# What's Fair?

American political mythology boasts a fairly well known story about the inclusion of sex as a protected category in the 1964 Civil Rights Act. Title VII of that act forbids discrimination in employment on the grounds of race, creed, color, or national origin as well as sex. It is the only provision of the original act to incorporate the word *sex*. Popular lore holds that *sex* was added to this title of the bill as something of a joke.[1] And in fact there is significant evidence that Howard Smith, chair of the powerful House Rules Committee, a Virginia Democrat, and an ardent segregationist, believed that adding sex would discourage some members of the Congress from voting for civil rights for African Americans. Smith "really wanted to kill the civil rights bill," recalled Assistant Secretary of Labor Esther Peterson.[2] Adding sex would focus attention on what he believed was a ridiculous effort to alter long-standing habits of mind with regard to racial beliefs.

Smith had good reason for derision. No fair employment practices bill had become law since 1941. Only once—in 1951—had such a bill made it through even one of the two houses of Congress. When it came to the floor, opponents attempted to subvert it by tossing in clauses to forbid discrimination on the basis of political affiliation, physical disability, and sex. Though the bill passed in the House, the Senate had turned it down flat.

Smith knew his history. Perhaps he hoped to repeat it. In December 1963, the National Woman's Party, which for forty years had fiercely advocated an equal rights amendment to the Constitution, sent messages to several members of Congress asking them to add the word *sex* to the new civil rights bill. This had been its practice for many years. Whenever the opportunity offered, the NWP had suggested that sex be included along with every other category against which discrimination was enjoined. Generally, its pleas were disregarded. But this time when the group broadcast its appeal to add the word *sex*,

Smith latched on to the idea. "I am very serious about this amendment," he declared as he introduced it into a House chamber sharply divided over whether and how to achieve racial justice. "I do not think it can do any harm … maybe it can do some good."[3]

We may never know whether Smith was a serious defender of sexual equality or whether he smelled a way to defeat a bill he disliked without appearing to oppose the civil rights of African Americans. He could add sex, he must have thought, safely, because relatively few Americans were convinced in 1964 that denying jobs to women constituted an unfair practice. Like the bill's major sponsor, Brooklyn congressman Emmanuel Celler, they found the idea that women might seek equality in the workforce unnatural, even funny. "Why not put sex in?" Smith had asked Celler in the opening round of what was meant to be merely a routine session of the Rules Committee that, after sitting on the bill for many months, would finally send it to the floor. But Celler clearly thought this was mixing apples and oranges. "This is a civil rights bill," he had sputtered as though women simply did not fit into that category. And when Smith responded mildly, "Don't women have civil rights?" Celler replied, "They have lots of them. They are supermen."[4]

In 1964, Celler's position did not seem preposterous. Respected advocates of women's causes in the Women's Bureau of the Department of Labor echoed his skepticism, as did members of the newly founded state commissions on the status of women. To be sure, everyone knew that women faced limited opportunities in the labor force. The word *sex* had occasionally appeared in such federal laws as the 1938 Fair Labor Standards Act, where it protected women from differential wages. More often, though still infrequently, it had shown up in state-based fair employment practices laws, where it was largely ignored.[5] We have seen how the 1961 presidential commission created by John Fitzgerald Kennedy to investigate the status of women agreed that women's commitments to families perpetuated their relatively weak positions in the labor force. The relatively more cautious feminists meeting under the auspices of the PCSW advocated stretching the protections of the Fourteenth Amendment (which the courts had decreed applied to race) to "persons" of both sexes while explicitly rejecting the more aggressive option of binding sex to race discrimination. And, like many women's organizations at the time, they balked at designating as invidious all sex discrimination. On these grounds Congress had, just the year before, crafted a narrow mandate for equal pay for equal work for men and women.

The evidence suggests that on the eve of the Civil Rights Act of 1964, and for some months after, well-intentioned people could disagree as to how far women's disadvantaged labor force positions were fair and how far unfair. Even active advocates of women still assigned to men the primary obligation to support wives and children. It required a leap of the imagination to argue that the labor market ought not to take account of these obligations. And most people still believed in women's complementary responsibility to maintain and sustain family life. Many continued to view women's marginal places in the workforce as natural, even positive, corollaries to prevailing family roles rather than as products of prejudice, bias, or discrimination. Part-time, contingent, and temporary work could be construed as generous concessions to women's special needs. As labor lawyer Carrie Donald recalled the 1964 moment, "the concept that women . . . had equal rights, let alone the idea of providing preferential treatment to secure those job rights, had not gained public acceptance."[6]

By 1970, all that had changed. In the aftermath of the Civil Rights Act of 1964, the civil rights movement became a model, and the equal opportunity slogan a political strategy to create a new meaning for sex discrimination. The new usage foregrounded the desire of many women to locate themselves in the polity as individuals rather than as family members. It competed with a continuing popular belief in gender difference to produce unanticipated consequences for class and racial equality. Identifying sex with race as the subject of oppression and the target of invidious prejudice might have been expected to yield justice across the board. It did foster new ways of seeing that quickly refigured the meaning of discrimination as it applied to women. Yet as the vortex of individual rights powerfully reshaped conceptions of gender in the workplace, it left unspoken and imminent the issue of gender equality with relation to family roles and social relationships. In the backwash, burgeoning claims to sex discrimination left poor women and women of color vulnerable to racial and class biases, turning the promise of equal opportunity for some into equal jeopardy for others. This chapter illuminates how the sometimes ironic and always complicated effects of these powerful shifts in imagination intersected with policies that affected race and class to set the stage for the dramatic changes that would come in the 1970s.

## Constructing an Equal Opportunity Framework

Ripples of laughter accompanied Howard Smith's introduction of the "sex" amendment to Title VII of the 1964 Civil Rights Act. The echoes persisted as Michigan's Martha Griffiths rose in its support, allying herself with a growing number of women whose minds were slowly changing. Griffiths later claimed that she had, all along, wanted to introduce sex into Title VII, deferring to Smith only because she believed that his imprimatur, ill intentioned as it might be, would increase the bill's chances of passage.[7] Like Pauli Murray and Mary Eastwood, Griffiths had begun to believe women were unfairly constrained by society's "legitimate interest in the protection of women's maternal and familial functions."[8] None of these women doubted that society, whatever that was, still had a stake in women's reproductive and family lives, but they believed it was time for a reexamination of the line between social investment in women and women's own civil rights. That profoundly unsettling notion accounts for the amusement that greeted Smith's efforts to justify the additional word.

No one laughed when Griffiths outlined her defense: if the rights of black women were to be protected because of their color, she argued, then those of white women would suffer because of their sex. Griffiths was neither the first nor the last to try to remove the blinders on discrimination toward women by drawing a racial analogy. Less than a year before, in the debate over the 1963 Equal Pay Act, Oregon's Representative Edith Green had invoked the moral authority of the growing rejection of race discrimination. "As we make progress in working against the Jim Crow laws of the nation," she argued, "it is high time that we also work against the Jane Crow laws."[9] No one else then pursued the analogy. Nor was sex discrimination, as political scientist Donald Robinson has discovered, mentioned in the thousands of pages of hearings that preceded the passage of the Civil Rights Act.[10]

On this occasion, Griffiths, already in her fifth term and known as an advocate for women, hammered the point home. She defended her sharp racial juxtaposition as an effort to advance the fortunes of black as well as white women. Omitting sex, she suggested, would exclude half of African Americans from coverage. Echoing the early nineteenth-century abolitionists, she insisted that women of all races, like African-American men, required protection of their individual rights. This bill, she argued, was not meant to promote equal rights so much as to promote equal employment. And it was in employment that women would suffer. "If you do not add sex to this bill . . . you are going to have white men in one bracket, you are going to try to take colored men and colored women and give them equal employment rights, and down at the bottom of the list is going to be a white woman with no rights at all." Insisting that she wanted "colored" women to have equality, Griffiths proclaimed her incredulity "that white men would be willing to place white women at such a disadvantage except that white men have done this before."[11]

*Representative Martha Griffiths of Michigan in a 1956 photograph.* COURTESY, LIBRARY OF CONGRESS.

The argument stirred ambivalent feelings among feminist women. To some it recalled the debates within the PCSW, where a clear consensus had rejected the idea that sex and race discrimination sufficiently resembled each other to combine them legislatively. Esther Peterson's response typified the negatives. Absent any grassroots support for adding sex to the bill, she later recalled, "I just felt, that as an American woman I didn't want to ride the coattails of an issue that I thought was more important at that time."[12] Edith Green agreed. Almost immediately she took the floor to object to including sex. As impeccably credentialed an advocate of women's causes as Griffiths, Green located herself in a different political vein. She had entered Congress in 1955, the same year as Griffiths. For years, she and Griffiths had agreed on most subjects except on those of how to account for female difference. Green had been a member of the PCSW, an architect of the successful equal pay strategy, and a close friend and ally of Peterson. Now, she chose to disagree with Griffiths. She had experienced discrimination, she asserted, and she fully agreed that it prevailed everywhere. But adding sex to this title would place solutions to a more cruel discrimination in jeopardy: "For every discrimination that has been made against a woman in this country, there has been 10 times as much discrimination against the Negro of this country. There has been 10 times, maybe 100 times, as much humiliation for the Negro woman, for the Negro man and for the Negro child."[13]

But Griffiths had started a refrain that none of her other women colleagues (of either party) rejected and that was perversely adopted by southern Democrats, all of them male. New York's two female representatives, Katherine St.

George, a Republican, and Edna Kelly, a Democrat, rose to defend equal opportunities and civil rights for all. "I do not want any person to secure more rights than any other. All I want is the same opportunities and rights," said Kelly.[14] Catherine May, a Republican congresswoman from Washington, exacerbated the racial divide, reading into the record a letter from the chair of the National Woman's Party that objected to statutes that excluded sex because they could be interpreted "in a way that has discriminated against the white, native born American woman of Christian religion." With the exception of Kelly, the women in Congress had all been long-standing ERA supporters, a fact that may account for their unanimity and their eager participation in the debate.[15] And St. George had apparently already agreed to support Smith before Griffiths's intervention.[16]

Some of the bill's advocates echoed May's fears that certain kinds of white women would be excluded. She was followed by a long line of southern Democrats who gleefully pitted black and white women against each other. "Unless this amendment is adopted," declared Glenn Andrews of Alabama, "the white women of this country would be drastically discriminated against in favor of a Negro woman."[17] He was followed by the senior congressman from South Carolina, who summed up the prevailing sentiment. "It is incredible to me," said Lucius Mendel Rivers, "that the authors of this monstrosity . . . would deprive the white woman of mostly Anglo-Saxon or Christian heritage equal opportunity before the employer." "There can be no plausible reason," said Tom Gathings of Arkansas, "that a white woman should be deprived of an equal opportunity to get a job simply because of her sex and a colored woman obtain that position because of her preferential rights." The speeches confirm the conclusions of political scientist Carl Brauer that if Griffiths's appeal to chivalry attracted anyone, it spoke most effectively to racist southern congressmen who feared that white women would lack the protections that the bill would afford to people of color, including women of color. Brauer counted nine southern men, including Smith, who rose in support of the amendment declaring that they "could not support legislation that would discriminate against women" and vowing that it was beyond comprehension that "a southern gentleman would vote for such legislation." Despite the inclusion of sex, all voted against the final bill.[18]

Other refrains punctuated the debate. Briefly, it prefigured two interrelated issues that would later trouble the Equal Employment Opportunity Commission created by Title VII: who could decide the circumstances under which women would be considered persons, and how far marriage (existing and expected) subsumed women's individual rights. Opponents raised questions about whether banning discrimination against sex threatened the dearly held state prerogative of defining women as persons for purposes that the states thought relevant. This practice, thoroughly tested and approved by the Supreme Court of the United States, continued to sustain legislation and policy that validated social commitment to women's family roles even where it conflicted with women's rights as individuals to serve on juries, for example, or pay equitable taxes, or obtain education and jobs of their choice. During the fleeting Senate debate on the issue, Republican Everett Dirksen, who opposed the amendment, assured his listeners that it could in any event have no real impact. Widely approved patterns of sexual discrimination would not diminish under the impact of the new law, he contended, "because we [in the United States] do not believe that women should do heavy manual labor of the sort which falls to the lot of some men."[19] Notions of ideal marriage underlined these remarks. As in previous discussions of the applicability of the Fourteenth Amendment, deference to the needs of the family and the state's interest in female reproduction constrained arguments for women's rights. Implementing a more inclusive Title VII, speakers feared—it turned out, presciently—would require renegotiating the relationship of women's individual rights to their traditional roles in the family.

Pauli Murray had little doubt about where she stood on the issue. From her home in New Haven, she responded joyously to news that the House had included sex in Title VII, "particularly because as a Negro woman, I knew that in many instances it was difficult to determine whether I was being discriminated against because of race or sex and felt that the sex provision would close a gap in the employment rights of all Negro women."[20] She describes her "cohorts" in Washington as "equally pleased." When the bill arrived in the Senate, this group of women, connected by their work for the PCSW, was fully prepared. Faced with stiff opposition from Dirksen, among others, Murray joined a successful campaign to ensure the viability of the word *sex*.

The provision's final passage sent a quiver of excitement down the spines of some women, generating an unprecedented optimism. In defining behavior that restricted employment access on the grounds of sex as discrimination, the new act created a constituency and pinpointed a target of change. It drew those who still shied away from an equal rights amendment, like Murray and Eastwood, and provided a strategy for women who believed the Fourteenth Amendment could serve as their umbrella. If sex and race were treated as comparable classifications before the law, women might finally achieve full economic citizenship. More broadly, including sex in Title VII of the Civil Rights Act of 1964 introduced the language of sex discrimination onto the national stage, casting a new light on seemingly natural patterns of accommodating sex differences such as assigning women to sex-segregated jobs or providing differential Social Security benefits to working men and women. By connecting the agendas of race and sex, even as the meaning of discrimination, which constituted the link between them remained vague and undefined, the Civil Rights Act helped to create a self-conscious women's movement. This not only placed gender at the center of an impassioned national conversation around equality but reconfigured the debate around the meaning of equality itself. Thus the Civil Rights Act fostered a discussion about the nature of public expectations of women that revealed the limits of economic citizenship for privileged women and welfare mothers alike. That painful process would powerfully shape policies that affected men and women across the lines of race and class.

## Standing with Lot's Wife

The alliance of race and sex formed by the Civil Rights Act of 1964 could never be called comfortable, but over a period of several years it became imaginable. Its viability rested on a conceptual transformation that relocated disparate treatment because of sex from the venue of tradition to that of discrimination. The transformation occurred everywhere, but nowhere more visibly than in the actions of the Equal Employment Opportunity Commission (EEOC), the agency created to implement Title VII's job discrimination provisions. Historian Hugh Davis Graham has effectively documented how the EEOC fumbled and stalled on its way to achieving a kind of parity in the treatment of sex and race. It took until 1969, he argues, for the EEOC to conclude that sex could be treated like race for administrative purposes.[21] In the five-year interim, as the EEOC responded both to the latent discontent of wage-earning women and to the impatient expectations of an emerging feminism that it helped to spawn, the commissioners assimilated the notion that denying women economic opportunity was unfair. Their actions encapsulate, in the most concrete way, the shift in their imaginations.

When it started work in July of 1965, the EEOC was immediately overwhelmed. In its first hundred days, it received nearly 1,400 complaints. They kept coming, numbering nearly five thousand within the first eight months of its operation. With some surprise, the New York Times reported that nine of the first forty-eight complaints charged discrimination on the grounds of sex.[22] That was only the beginning. At the end of the year, the commission calculated that 37 percent of complainants protested sex discrimination.[23] A year earlier, the Labor Department had asked for, and received, assurances from Mary Dublin Keyserling, head of the Women's Bureau, that adding forty people to the 150 already on its staff would be sufficient to deal with the additional complaints induced by "the sex provision."[24] But now the unprepared EEOC discovered that, despite the NAACP's active efforts to encourage complaints on the grounds of race, it could not cope with the rising crescendo of claims of sex discrimination. These complaints reveal the latent anger of women against the constraints on their working lives and voice concerns that certainly existed before the sixties.[25]

About a third of the complainants charged differentials in their employee benefits, some of them written into union contracts.[26] Women generally got lower life insurance and accident protection; they received less generous health insurance than men, and their pension and retirement plans differed dramatically. Some employers paid for the entire cost of family medical coverage for male employees and asked women to pay part of the price. Some plans paid women lower pensions but allowed them to retire earlier than men. Another quarter complained that jobs were unavailable to them because of separate seniority lists, or that men got called back first after layoffs, regardless of seniority. More than 10 percent of the complainants protested that state labor laws prohibited them from taking advantage of overtime to earn extra pay; and almost equal numbers argued that job classifications arbitrarily assigned some jobs to one sex or the other. Several other concerns involved smaller numbers of complainants but large matters of justice: women objected to losing their jobs when they married, became pregnant or gave birth, or reached a certain age and to being denied jobs if they had children. While women filed most of the protests, men also complained, particularly about differential retirement benefits, about not getting the rest periods or long lunch breaks that some states mandated for women; and about women's access to seniority (which they deemed unfair). Taken together, the complaints demonstrate a sense of injustice around gender that probably preceded the creation of the EEOC and was held in check by long-standing institutional custom and practice. The creation of the commission released latent discontent that ultimately pushed it into reimagining the kinds of liberties to which women were entitled.

Staff members, most of whom had come from the now defunct President's Commission on Equal Employment Opportunity and whose mandate there had been racial equality, at first responded resentfully to the flood of complaints. They puzzled about having "to deal with sex discrimination when more pressing matters [of race] needed their attention."[27] The atmosphere could not have been pleasant. Aileen C. Hernandez, the only woman and one of two persons of color among the original five commissioners, recalled later that she had "found no humor in the frequently repeated statement that 'sex' had found its way into Title VII as a 'fluke'—that it was a 'joke'—that it did not need to be enforced—that the 'real' discrimination in society was on the basis of race and ethnic origin and that's where the emphasis of the commission should be directed."[28]

Even the best intentioned and most skilled EEOC might have been confused and lacking in direction. This one was neither particularly sensitive with regard to the meaning of sex discrimination nor particularly well intentioned. The appointment of Hernandez, a black former member of the California Human Relations Commission, whose Spanish surname came from a former husband, had led Mexican Americans to complain of neglect. Angry about the commission's lack of attention to sex, and under pressure because some staff members believed she paid too little attention to "national origin," Hernandez resigned in October of 1966, eventually to become the second president of the new National Organization for Women (NOW). The only other sympathetic advocate of women's rights, Republican Richard Graham, served a one-year term that expired in June 1966, despite last-minute expressions of concern from women's groups. Graham, a Wisconsin native, had earned the enmity of the EEOC's vice-chair, Luther Holcomb, who strenuously opposed putting sex on a par with race. A charter member of NOW, he became a vice president a few months later. Commission chair Franklin Delano Roosevelt Jr., inattentive for most of his short term, resigned in May 1966. Like Samuel Jackson, an African American and Kansas native who had come out of the civil rights movement, he could at best be described as benignly indifferent to the issue of sex. Holcomb hailed from Texas and was the longest-serving member of the original commission. He actively opposed policies that threatened to disrupt traditional family arrangements. Not all of the blame for the EEOC's ineffectiveness in its early years falls on these individuals. Its operations were severely hampered by a Senate-engineered compromise that denuded it of direct enforcement power and by unceasing public pressure and commentary.

The level of skepticism over the sex provision of the law can be gauged by some of the public commentary surrounding the EEOC as it took shape and began to meet in the summer of 1965. Commission chair Roosevelt opened with a press conference at which he ducked the issue of whether the commission would enforce the sex provision. Then he went off on an extended fishing trip. After his return, he held a news conference in which he declared, "The whole issue of sex discrimination is terribly complicated."[29] In August, the

White House called a two-day conference on equal employment opportunity to highlight the commission's mission. Only nine of its seventy-five speakers were women, and six of them appeared on one panel organized by Hernandez. Ignoring most of the issues raised at the conference, a *New York Times* report devoted much of its space to covering a short discussion of what might happen if a male applied for a job as "bunny" in one of the Playboy clubs. The *Times* promptly ridiculed efforts to eliminate sex discrimination as the "bunny problem," assuring readers in an editorial that "it would have been better if Congress had just abolished sex itself."[30] The *New Republic* saw no humor in the situation. It angrily attacked the commission for wasting time, asking, "Why should a mischievous joke perpetrated on the floor of the House of Representatives be treated by a responsible administrative body with this kind of seriousness?"[31]

In the meantime, the House convened hearings to guide the EEOC in its deliberations. Its chambers rang with commentary about the "sex amendment" that suggests that the idea of sex discrimination had barely begun to penetrate public consciousness. James B. O'Shaughnessy, representing the Illinois State Chamber of Commerce, weighed in with a strong protest against "the strange, incredible inclusion of the word 'sex' in Title VII" and a strong request to delete the offending word. In written and oral testimony, he argued that deletion "would be welcomed by all those covered by the act—and probably those in charge of enforcement of the act's provisions." Difference in his eyes did not yield discrimination, but efforts to legislate sameness led to chaos and confusion: "If ever difference were manifested, it is between the sexes, and I believe this is a desirable difference and I believe that women should be put in a different category." Roosevelt remained perplexed. Appearing at the hearings, he asked Congress to give "additional consideration . . . to the matter of employment discrimination based on sex" because there was little legislative history as to "the general principle of non-discrimination on account of sex."[32]

While these words may have harbored as much hostility as confusion, the record suggests that even men like George H. Fowler, chair of New York State's Commission for Human Rights, who projected a more thoughtful attitude toward the issue, could hardly conceive of transcending the cultural and institutional barriers that defined a sex-segregated labor market. New York had included sex in its fair employment practices law for two decades, so the problem of enforcement did not disturb veterans like Fowler, and he was unconcerned about women wanting what one congressman called "male-type" jobs. "I think," he averred with utter misapprehension, "that the cultural factors are such that we won't be confronted with lines of women bringing complaints because they are not allowed to become coal miners. . . . The kind of complaints that exist in the minds of women are those that have to do primarily with promotional opportunities in various areas." In practice, male congressional representatives and many congressional witnesses shared that viewpoint. Women would feel discriminated against, they thought, not when they were denied jobs that had typically been held by men but when they were denied promotions or "the employer refused to rehire the women who had been here doing the job before."[33]

A casual exchange between two congressional committee members, both sympathetic to the concept of sex discrimination, sums up popular conceptions of the boundaries of women's imaginations. James Roosevelt, a California Democrat, raised the possibility that the woman who had formerly been offered a job as a telephone operator because "this was the limit to which that employee probably would go" might now be given the "opportunity to move on up through the system." He was interrupted by his colleague Roman C. Pucinski of Illinois, who commented that "the more surprising thing would be when we see the woman climbing up the telephone pole to make the repairs," an innovation of which Roosevelt apparently could not conceive and so simply ignored.[34] Eight short years later the EEOC settled its first big class action suit against the giant telephone company AT&T with an agreement that allowed women access to all kinds of jobs, including those that required them to climb telephone poles.[35] In the meantime, however, the EEOC painfully rejected the popular notion that "sex, unlike race, creed or national origin, has generally been regarded as a reasonable and occasionally necessary basis for personnel decisions." Instead the commission offered the modest proposition that there was no such thing as "reasonable" sex-stereotyping.[36] It took until 1969 for the EEOC to conclude unequivocally that "the principle of non-discrimination requires that individuals be considered on the basis of individual capacities and not on the basis of any characteristics generally attributed to the group."[37]

But in 1965, the language of resistance still prevailed in the commission. Some historians have suggested that the absence of an active women's pressure group allowed the EEOC to dally or that the lack of a legislative record left the new EEOC without guidance. These surely mattered. More persuasive is the evidence that many men and women, influential and not so, believed in the salience of sex differences for economic decision making of all kinds, lacked a clear idea of what constituted discrimination, and remained reluctant to overturn lives they had known. Most of the staff and members of the EEOC were no exception. In public, they deflected questions about whether they would move as quickly on sex discrimination as they had on race with what the press called "common sense." In private, common sense seemed to emerge as evasion, if not contempt for the law. "We're not going out on our charger to overturn patterns," commented one commissioner.[38] The EEOC's executive director told a *Washington Post* reporter that "there are people on this Commission who think that no man should be required to have a male secretary—and I am one of them."[39]

Like the explicit language of resistance to the idea of sex discrimination, the most restrictive cultural blinders disintegrated in the face of daily assaults mounted under cover of the new law. We can watch them fall apart in the daily efforts of the EEOC to grapple with particular issues. There was, for example, the issue of what effect a woman's marriage had on her economic rights and obligations. Most state laws contained the common assumption that married women would be domiciled with and dependent on their husbands. The assumption constrained women's economic opportunities, limiting access to credit, penalizing them with respect to income taxes, depriving them of some old age insurance and unemployment benefits, and, especially, diminishing their employment options. Before the passage of Title VII, employers routinely considered marital status in selecting and promoting female employees. As we have seen, the PCSW, which certainly disapproved of firing married women, encouraged their employment only under certain circumstances and stopped short of suggesting that wage work for married women was a right. Seeking sanction for a long-standing policy, one large employer explained to the EEOC, "The practice of terminating employment of married women has been in effect ... for the past 20 years and has been included in all labor agreements since 1946."[40] Yet in light of Title VII's "positive mandate of equal opportunity for the sexes" and what the EEOC described as "the increasing importance of the woman worker in our economy," the commission attacked the practice. "Traditional ideas of what is or is not appropriate work for women must be drastically revised," it announced.[41] And in a 1966 directive, it declared that "absent a similar rule for men (and none was discovered)" hiring, firing, and promoting workers on the basis of marital status violated the law.[42]

The flat prohibition contained in the directive obscured a complicated set of prejudices about how marriage could affect women's attitudes toward work. Within the EEOC and outside, influential policy makers continued to see the problem of marriage as far more complex and to sympathize with employers who refused to hire "young single girls for jobs that require extensive training, for fear they will become married in the near future and leave."[43] Young women refused jobs for this reason might never know why. Nor would they necessarily be deemed victims of discrimination if they did discover the source of their rejection. The EEOC decided to deal with such cases on an individual basis by investigating a woman's "background and ambitions and so forth." Under those circumstances, as one expert advised the commission, a woman who acted out "her role that woman should—that womanhood would demand" need not be designated the victim of discrimination.[44]

That left a difficult vacuum around the issue of whether an employer could choose to apply these standards arbitrarily to women who married, and especially to those with children. Much of the airline industry, for example, claimed that marriage disqualified a woman from the job of cabin attendant. Because "our society places the responsibility for home-making and childrearing on women," one airline argued, "married women's absences from home would be more likely to put a strain on family harmony than similar absences by married men."[45] Women immediately challenged the argument and their dismissals—leading to a controversy so fierce that it provoked the EEOC to hold hearings on the subject and, finally, to agree with the women that marriage ought not disqualify them from their jobs. Yet in refusing airlines the right to "make assumptions about married women as a class," the EEOC left open the possibility that airlines could fire married women for "individual dereliction" that resulted from their marital status.[46]

What rights did the class of married women have? Here the EEOC was less certain. Just before Title VII became law, Mary P.'s employer, a public utility, altered a long-standing policy of refusing to promote married women. Mary P., a married woman who had worked at the company for twenty-four years, was happy with the change, but she wanted "compensatory seniority"—credit for the years between 1951, when the company had first hired and retained married women, and 1964, when it agreed to promote them.[47] Such a remedy, the equivalent of back pay, was routine in race-based cases.[48] It would protect her from layoffs, make her eligible for faster promotions, and, not incidentally, enable her to bump more junior men with jobs for which she might otherwise have been eligible had those years counted. The EEOC could not see it her way. Because the effect of the policy had been merely "to freeze each woman upon marriage, in the job classification she had attained," the damage had not been "sufficiently extensive" to merit a remedy. In a similar case of racial discrimination, surely the damage would have been judged significant. In this case, it was measured against women's then existing opportunities, and "the failure of the seniority scheme to make special provision for those married female employees who were frozen in their job classifications" appeared to the EEOC "not discrimination on account of sex."

The commissioners took a different tack with regard to the negative attitudes of many employers toward "married females with children of pre-school age." Unless they refused jobs to men in the same position, employers could no longer require that women be childless to hold jobs.[49] But, perhaps ironically, on what may be the only occasion where the EEOC addressed the issue of discrimination against *un*married women with small children, the commission concluded that the discrimination involved was based on race, not sex. On July 8, 1966, two qualified black women applied for jobs at a local company. The company later admitted that, though it did not have a written policy to that effect, it had denied both women jobs because "they were mothers of illegitimate children." Since, the EEOC decided, the company could not show that the status of these children would adversely affect job performance, the company's purpose must have been to exclude "otherwise qualified Negro applicants." It recommended Justice Department prosecution.[50] The disturbing conclusion locates the prevailing negativity toward unmarried mothers as an artifact of race alone and reveals a continuing tendency to dichotomize racial and sexual issues.

Marriage also figured as an assumption in calculating benefits for employed women. Typically employers provided more niggardly benefits for women, and sometimes none at all, on the patently false grounds that all women were or would be married and that married women were secondary wage earners. In the mid-1960s, two of every five women workers were single, widowed, or divorced; more than half of them supported other family members, and especially children.[51] Despite these figures, the EEOC continued to balk at equalizing men's and women's benefits. Because the proportion of female breadwinners among women of color far exceeded the proportion among white women, assumptions about marriage and family support particularly disadvantaged the former. Early on, the EEOC held that differences in health benefits and insurance policies violated Title VII, but at the same time it permitted imputed sexual differences to participate in calculating the amounts of insurance contributions and benefits and the assignment of accident insurance. It also refused to reconsider the fairness of differential retirement ages for men and women because it feared to disturb current contractual arrangements.[52]

Like marital status, the possibility of pregnancy indelibly barred a melding of racial and sexual discrimination in the minds of EEOC commissioners. In its early days, the EEOC ducked problems posed by employees who became pregnant, assuming, as the PCSW had before it, that pregnant women would not wish to work. Encouraged by its general counsel to face the issue in May 1966, the commission agreed that it was "unreasonable" to terminate employment for pregnancy, labeling it an "unlawful employment practice."[53] But not at all times. Sometimes, and at a certain point in the process of producing a child, it was "reasonable to imagine that employment might be terminated." The question was, under what circumstances and when? To resolve it, the EEOC adopted a standard so fuzzy at the edges that it revealed yet more confusion in the minds of the commissioners. The EEOC thought this decision could not be left to women, whose self-interest would inhibit their reason. Nor could it be left entirely to employers: after all, as Commissioner Jackson asked, if an employer "could use his own judgment as to what is reasonable, what is to prevent him from saying that all pregnant employees must resign immediately?"[54] At the same time, commissioners could not agree on a useful model for thinking about how pregnant women might continue to work or be reinstated in their jobs. Drawn at first to the practice of the federal civil service, which allocated sick leave, vacation days, and unpaid leave to those giving birth and included an "automatic right to come back even though the job is filled," the commissioners quickly realized that this would be unworkable for small employers. When they turned their attention to whether and how jobs could be held, their imaginations failed. Though they could conceive of women wanting leaves up to three months, they rejected the notion that longer leaves might be desirable and necessary to ensure equal employment opportunity. Nor could they imagine that women (especially needy women) might not benefit from leaves at all in the absence of salary replacement. Unlike the PCSW, however, the EEOC never considered the issue of lost wages in evaluating the rights of women. In the end it settled for a vague policy prohibiting employers from terminating pregnant women without first offering a leave of absence (which could be compensated for by a combination of deferred vacation and sick pay) with reemployment after the birth.

Its vague provisions grew out of uninformed notions of what was reasonable. Drawing on anecdote and personal experience, and over the objections of Aileen Hernandez, who sought repeatedly to investigate alternative models, EEOC general counsel Charles Duncan proposed a case-by-case response that rested on a blanket statement of policy. He wanted the blanket policy to declare the EEOC unwilling

> to compare an employer's treatment of illness or injury with his treatment of maternity, since maternity is a temporary disability unique to

the female sex and more or less to be anticipated during the working life of most women employees. Accordingly ... to provide substantial equality of employment opportunity for both sexes, there must be special recognition of absence due to pregnancy.[55]

After some dispute, the commission agreed to communicate its own measure of reasonableness, adding to the boilerplate the phrase "it is not uncommon for women to work through the sixth or seventh month of pregnancy." They had changed this from the "fifth or sixth month" that Duncan originally proposed. What followed after the boilerplate was a response to particular situations. In one instance, Duncan's office informed a pregnant clerical worker that it was not unreasonable for her employer to require her to take a three-month unpaid leave before the anticipated birth. Within some culturally accepted definition of reasonableness, the option was clearly the employer's. "We do not as yet have a complete policy statement," Duncan wrote to a West Coast savings bank, "but we incline to the view that an employer . . . may require a pregnant employee to cease work at a reasonable point in her pregnancy and, furthermore, that he may do so by rule rather than on a case-by-case basis."[56] Additional exemptions permitted employers whose businesses might suffer to evade the bounds of reasonableness altogether by firing pregnant women. In such cases, provisos encouraged (but did not require) employers to offer them preferential treatment in rehiring.[57]

The same commissioners who ruthlessly attempted to wipe out every form of racial discrimination remained blind to many forms of sexual discrimination. If some of these were sanctioned by marriage and the putative needs of pregnancy, others derived authority from the admission within the text of Title VII that some circumstances rendered choices made on the grounds of sex appropriate, or fair. Title VII includes a well-known clause that excludes men or women from jobs for which their sex is a "bona fide occupational qualification," commonly known as a BFOQ. The clause became a wall behind which employers could easily hide by declaring that particular jobs required skills (like lifting heavy weights, operating heavy equipment, or working with intricate detail) that were characteristically male or female. To its credit, the EEOC tried to define the BFOQ narrowly, immediately challenging the gender ideology that allowed employers and coworkers to make assumptions "as to the employment characteristics of women in general." In principle, it also refused to acknowledge "stereotyped characterizations of the sexes," such as, for example, "more aggressive salesmanship on the part of men."[58] Over the years, however, many of these stereotypes had become institutionalized in law and policy (as in protective labor legislation) as well as in custom and tradition (such as separate seniority lists for men and women). Originally developed to legitimize and rationalize traditional sex differences and to shore up the boundaries between home and wage work, they now seemed to encapsulate belief systems about gender. And since, unlike the ideas that had sustained racial inequality, neither the EEOC nor the courts nor popular opinion was ready to declare every acknowledgment of gender difference unreasonable, the EEOC repeatedly drew fine distinctions between respecting tradition and deflating stereotypes. Its plodding and ineffective efforts to deal with these issues earned it a richly deserved, and perhaps unavoidable, reputation for stalling.

The seniority lists constructed over a generation by trade unions and employers to prevent arbitrary firings had commonly been kept separately by sex and race because black and white men and women generally did different jobs. Most unions, however disgruntled, could agree to dismantle formal racial barriers by merging the racially divided lists. When Title VII provided women with an opportunity to challenge the occupational divisions embedded in seniority systems, they proved less amenable. A fifth of the first year's complaints of discrimination were filed against trade unions; nearly a quarter of all sex discrimination charges came from women protesting their unions' failure to integrate seniority lists.[59] These complaints pitted two notions of fairness against each other: the idea that longevity earned a worker (generally thought of as a married man with responsibilities) an interest in his job versus the idea that women (thought of as primarily committed to their homes) had rights in the workplace. The conflict left employers and trade unions wondering whether to abandon time-honored practices in the interests of a principle they did not yet fully understand. Hearings with trade union and employer representatives did little to resolve the issue. Fairness seemed to reside on both sides of the issue. Finally, relying on the "bona fide occupational qualification" of the law, commissioners determined that only an employer who could demonstrate that a particular job absolutely required a male or female employee would be exempt from integrating seniority lists and in other ways ensuring that women as well as men had an equal chance at jobs.[60]

In that instance, as in so many of the positions taken by the EEOC, the language and sensibilities of fairness seemed to have moved the commission to take positions that contravened accepted practice. Yet their decisions ultimately stretched the boundaries of acceptable behavior. A series of cases brought by present and potential airline cabin attendants illustrates the point. In the most famous of these, several men charged airlines with denying them access to the traditionally female job of cabin attendant. Sex, they claimed, was not a bona fide occupational qualification for that job, which could be done just as readily by men as by women. At the same time, female cabin attendants charged that airlines forced women, but not men, to retire at age thirty-two or thirty-three, to routinely submit to being measured and weighed, and in other ways to embody sexual desirability. The commission held hearings in September 1967 and readily decided that sex was not a bona fide occupational qualification: men could have those jobs. But it refused to rule that airlines could not terminate women for age, marriage, or excessive weight, leaving the burden of charging discrimination to individuals.[61] Where was the logic here? Stewardesses represented the youth and vitality of the industry, the airlines argued. To women, it appeared that this job rested on particular conceptions of womanhood.

Issues of fairness took a more controversial turn when it came to job advertisements. In August of 1965, EEOC chair Roosevelt announced that newspaper columns segregating jobs by race would no longer be permitted. Unsure as to whether segregating advertisements by sex fell within the bounds of reasonableness, he appointed Richard Graham to chair a task force to study the issue of sex in help-wanted columns. Graham's report commented on the strong opposition of newspaper publishers and the absence of any public pressure for gender integration of help-wanted advertisements in proposing a compromise that would allow newspapers to list jobs under "male" and "female" columns. Pressed by Aileen Hernandez, the commissioners considered asking each employer to disclaim a preference for one sex over another. Finally, in its first comprehensive guidelines on sex discrimination, the EEOC simply forbade employers to write copy that suggested a preference for men or women unless the job met BFOQ guidelines. "For the convenience of readers" newspaper publishers might, however, list jobs in "male" and "female" help-wanted columns as an acknowledgment of the likely preference of job seekers. Under these rules, the EEOC construed separate job listings for men and women not as "an expression of preference for sex, but their desire to reach the greatest number of interested readers."[62] This finesse enraged activist women who correctly understood it to reflect the commission staff's own refusal to believe that sexual discrimination in hiring ultimately constituted an unfair act. Yet newspaper publishers successfully persuaded the EEOC that even these guidelines were too rigid, leading the commissioners to adopt even less restrictive rules. On April 20, 1966, a deeply divided EEOC announced that jobs open to both sexes could be listed in columns marked "male" and "female" in order "to indicate that some occupations are considered more attractive to one sex than another."[63]

The commission had crossed an invisible line. In a rage, Martha Griffiths took to the floor of the House to charge that EEOC officials had "displayed a wholly negative attitude toward the sex provisions of Title VII" and to accuse them of "casting disrespect and ridicule on the law": "By emphasizing the difficulties of applying the law in these odd cases, the impression is created that compliance with the law is unnecessary and that its enforcement can and will be delayed indefinitely or wholly overlooked." How was it, she asked, that an individual could "be genuinely concerned about the rights of 'some' others but not 'all' others"? The EEOC, she declared, had "reached the peak of contempt for women's rights."[64] Sex discrimination had suddenly become an issue, moving within a few short years from being something close to an oxymoron to occupying a central place in the vocabulary of workplace issues.

More than any other single incident, the EEOC's inconsistent policies on help-wanted advertising galvanized a rising impatience among some women for attention to the language of sex discrimination. To many, it seemed as if the EEOC's persistent confusion about appropriate meanings of gender and its continued vacillation, embodied in announcing weak policies and then backtracking even on them, added up to flouting a policy with which it disagreed. Frustrated by their failure to move the commission to act more forcefully on their behalf, especially when compared with its attention to race, women of many persuasions began to protest. In late May, shortly after the EEOC released its unfortunate new formulation on job advertising, female members of the United Automobile Workers union persuaded the national convention to adopt a resolution that urged full compliance with Title VII.[65] A month later, following on Griffiths's bellicose attack, representatives of the state commissions on the status of women met. An angry caucus conceived the National Organization for Women, scheduling a first, organizational meeting for the following November. Finally, women had a broad-based lobbying group.

NOW quickly gathered support from Washington insiders and women all over the country and rapidly became effective at lobbying both Congress and the EEOC. Presided over by Betty Friedan, the best-selling author of *The Feminine Mystique*, its founding members included a range of feminist opinion, black women as well as white, supporters of the ERA and advocates of the Fourteenth Amendment strategy. Aileen Hernandez resigned from the EEOC to become an executive vice president; Richard Graham joined the board, as did Edith Green, Pauli Murray, Mary Eastwood, and others who had been active in the old PCSW. Kathryn Clarenbach, chair of the Wisconsin Commission on the Status of Women, signed on and soon became a powerful influence. Five trade union officers, including the UAW's Dorothy Haener, served on the first board. Ellickson and Peterson, still government employees, expressed solidarity.[66]

In the spring of 1967, NOW launched a major campaign aimed at convincing the EEOC to alter its rules on help-wanted advertising. To break down resistance to the idea of sex discrimination, it entwined racial and gender justice into a single braid. "The excuses used by employers practicing sex-based discrimination are not substantially different from excuses regarding racial bias," wrote officers Kathryn Clarenbach and Betty Friedan to Secretary of Labor Willard Wirtz.[67] Then they presented the EEOC with a petition to change its policy on help-wanted advertising. Edith Green, who had originally opposed the addition of sex to Title VII on the grounds that it might interfere with attaining civil rights for African Americans, seemed to have changed her mind. Had the commission, she asked Stephen Shulman, then chair of the EEOC, adopted an equivalently lenient rule with regard to race, allowing advertisers to "place advertisements for jobs open to all races in columns classified by publishers under negro or white headings?"[68] The commission decided to conduct hearings. Two years later, somewhat chastened, it altered the 1966 policy, declaring, finally, "the listing of jobs in columns segregated by sex" to be an expression of preference by sex and therefore against the law.[69] Acknowledging the psychological dimensions of discrimination, the EEOC noted that "few women, however qualified, will pursue opportunities appearing only in the 'Help wanted, Male' column."[70] There would be offsetting benefits: employers would now have a larger pool of qualified candidates from which to choose. In the same session in which it declared sex-segregated advertising to be off limits, the commission tacitly noted the contribution of NOW by indicating that it would inform the organization of "the disposition of the actions raised by their petition."[71] And just a year later, the EEOC publicly claimed that "in most instances, the same principles applicable to race and national origin discrimination are also applicable to sex discrimination."[72]

If activist women almost immediately agreed that sex-segregated help-wanted advertising constituted an unfair barrier, they were less sure about state-based protective labor legislation for women. Even before the EEOC's operations began, officials in the Department of Labor worried about a potential conflict between the antidiscrimination provision of Title VII and state-based labor laws. Most states still had labor laws that restricted women's rights to work more than a specified number of hours a day (usually eight) even at overtime pay. Some states still legislated how much weight a woman could lift on the job, prescribed hours of rest, and denied them access to jobs perceived as dangerous. These state laws required all women to be treated differently from men in deference to their "special responsibilities as mothers and home-makers" and their unique "physical qualities." Title VII required all employees to be treated the same way. These protections had become increasingly valuable for less skilled women in poor jobs, whom the Fair Labor Standards Act still did not cover. Fearing that women could plead discrimination if they were denied jobs, promotions, or access to "male" seniority lines because state laws prevented them from lifting heavy weights or from working overtime, Labor Department officials sought legal advice as to whether state or federal law prevailed.

They felt enormous pressure. Letters kept coming from women like Mrs. Martin J. Walters, a Beloit, Wisconsin, auto worker who challenged her state's special labor laws for women. "I am writing about civil rights," she wrote to her union president in the autumn of 1964.

> You say that a man and woman should have equal rights. You also said that if woman did a man job she should get man pay. This should go the same in how many hours a woman can work. Why should some states say that woman can only work eight hours a day and another state say woman can work nine hours or more a day? I think a woman should work as many hours a day as the man as long as she is capable.[73]

Her local's president, John Renny, did not demur when he forwarded the letter to Esther Peterson. He had supported the newly passed and not yet implemented sex provisions of Title VII. But he wondered if the state laws of Wisconsin might make it difficult for Mrs. Walters to work those extra hours.

Within a year, reconciling the conflict between state laws regulating women's work and the antidiscrimination provisions of Title VII of the Civil Rights Act of 1964 became a hotly debated topic. Because the Civil Rights Act forbade sexual discrimination only with respect to employment, differential labor standards for men and women immediately took on an ambiguous status. Officials in several states urged the EEOC not to interfere with their rights to legislate for women; officials in others thought the laws might be anachronistic and asked if federal law superseded state law.[74] They noted the large number of complaints from women protesting that state-based laws prevented them from earning lucrative overtime wages and wondering why they had fewer "rights" at work than men. Virginia's commissioner of labor strongly suspected that weight limits disadvantaged women, and he was convinced, on the basis of the number of complaints his department had received from female employees, that maximum hours "do discriminate against women." When Labor Department officials advised him just to be reasonable, he protested vehemently. The issue, he thought, was not reasonable application. His state had been more than reasonable. Yet what might be quite "reasonable to one person may be perfectly ridiculous in the eyes of another."[75] Delaware simply repealed all its laws, the first state to do so. Pennsylvania was rumored to have done the same, but, the director of Pennsylvania's Bureau of Women and Children wrote to the commission to correct the impression. Noting that her bureau had received many letters "from women protesting that their opportunities for increased earnings from premium overtime pay and for promotion to higher paying jobs are curtailed because they may not work the same number of hours as men," Marjorie Tibbs described the compromises the state had made: Pennsylvania had relaxed restrictions on overtime work, eliminated requirements for rest periods when they imposed hardships on women, and removed the forty-eight-hour cap on women's working hours. These changes, she thought, had already allowed women to bid on jobs to which seniority entitled them but that had been proscribed as a result of state law.[76]

The EEOC's first annual report described women's complaints around state labor laws as "numerous" and counted them, after benefits, the most frequent source of women's protests. This was, said a spokesperson, "probably the most difficult area" it had considered.[77] The issue was a major item on the agenda of the cabinet-level Interdepartmental Committee on the Status of Women (set up to continue the work of the PCSW) and a source of extensive debate within the newly formed EEOC. From the White House, Charles Horsky forwarded a letter to Esther Peterson wondering how a woman could function as an executive if the state limited her to working eight hours a day. He begged Peterson to "give me some idea as to how we might go forward."[78]

What appeared to some women as "going forward" seemed to others to be stepping backward. For years, protective labor laws had been the subject of contentious debate among women, radical feminists having declared that special labor laws for women limited their opportunities and prevented them from competing with men. The National Woman's Party and such feminist groups as the National Federation of Business and Professional Women's Clubs sought to use Title VII to challenge notions of social protection. Since the 1920s, their arguments for women's individual rights had constituted the continuing intellectual rationale and powerful emotional appeal fueling the campaign for an equal rights amendment to the Constitution. In contrast, feminists like those in the PCSW considered special laws for women among their great achievements. They continued to believe that women's secondary labor market positions, and particularly the poor bargaining power of less skilled women, made their protection essential. For four decades, theirs had been the most popular position. Until 1964, many advocates of women's equality, including large numbers of wage-earning women and representatives of the Women's Bureau, resisted the idea of individual rights for women embodied in an ERA, fearing it would undermine the collective responsibility of society to protect vulnerable women. The Civil Rights Act of 1964 provoked a dramatic change. To be sure, some of the more cautious feminists (like Edith Green, Esther Peterson, and some of the women attached to the Women's Bureau) tried for a while to hitch the wagon of sexual equality to that of racial equality without renouncing women's special legislative protections. But "civil rights" belonged to individuals, and to take advantage of the association between race and sex, they found themselves severing the tenuous links of women to the family that had guided perceptions of social policy since long before the achievement of suffrage.

The conflict put Esther Peterson in an uncomfortable position. Even before the EEOC formally convened, at the request of the secretary of labor she asked Mary Dublin Keyserling, head of the Women's Bureau, along with a small working group including Mary Eastwood and Evelyn Harrison (both of whom had worked with the PCSW), to prepare a report on "the problems arising out of the anti-sex-discrimination provision of Title VII," and especially to report on "the issue of protective labor legislation and whether such legislation is in violation of Title VII." The group worked well together until it came to the question of how to handle restrictions on hours. Keyserling reported to Peterson that "we might find it necessary in this connection to state alternative views, which we hope the Secretary's Committee will itself want to reconcile." Peterson forwarded the report, which contained Keyserling's strong recommendation for continuing state labor laws, to Willard Wirtz in the spring of 1965. She added a covering memo permeated with ambivalence: "The interpretation which should be suggested as most reasonable at the present time," she wrote, "is that State labor laws generally continue to apply in employment situations subject to [Title VII's] provisions."[79]

But Peterson was already beginning to have doubts. The department had a long stake in the issue, she acknowledged: "In opposing the Equal Rights Amendment we have repeatedly made the argument that one of its harmful effects would be to sweep aside State protective labor legislation." Still, she added, "I do not think that the Department should stay in dead center on the desirability of State protective labor legislation. We may well be standing with Lot's wife. I am ready to look ahead and see if we can move forward but I think we must have a map to give us some idea of where we will go." And she urged Wirtz to authorize "a comprehensive study" to find out whether "State labor laws do in fact, protect—not discriminate."[80] Abetted by Ellickson and Alice Morrison, her old allies from the PCSW, and under the auspices of the high-powered Interdepartmental Committee on the Status of Women, she set up a technical committee to investigate the issue and to begin a long and painful discussion within the Department of Labor as to the merits of state labor legislation as against the benefits of women's seeking full advantage under Title VII.

Peterson's confusion spoke to that of many thoughtful women. Determined to see Title VII enforced, she did not want its injunction against sex discrimination defused by state laws. At the same time, like many of her peers, she had worked long and hard to achieve the very laws that were now being dismantled. Had times changed enough to make that possible, even desirable? As recently as the 1963 report of the PCSW, she had not thought so. Nor did many other women. Mary Keyserling's Women's Bureau remained strongly committed to protective laws for women, as did many of the old women's groups. Among these, the National Consumers' League, the Young Women's Christian Association, the National Councils of Negro Women, of Jewish Women, and of Catholic Women, and the American Association of University Women expressed support as the EEOC affirmed the validity of state laws, and then dismay as it backtracked. The National Consumers' League pressed its campaign to maintain state protective labor laws by urging that they be extended to men and, at the same time, that new groups of workers be included under the umbrella of the Fair Labor Standards Act. Echoing the arguments of the 1920s that subordinated the rights of individual women to the greater good, the league declared, "The value of laws protecting those with the least skill and bargaining power should not be sacrificed because a much smaller number of highly skilled or favorably situated women and men may find them restrictive."[81]

Many powerful labor unions joined the refrain. In 1965, and for several years thereafter, the AFL-CIO convention unanimously endorsed continuing state labor laws, asserting that "such laws are not inconsistent with equality of employment opportunities for women."[82] Within the organization, however, some unions and many female members and officials departed from the line.[83] Working women, as one member of the Communications Workers of

America put it, "are destroying the laws themselves by going to court and filing sex discrimination charges."[84] In fact, the EEOC repeatedly commented on the number of cases brought by members who believed that their own unions had colluded with employers to enforce moribund state laws. The Women's Committee of the United Auto Workers persuaded its parent body to oppose protective laws for women only and to support an equal rights amendment. Its chair, Dorothy Haener, joined NOW, along with four other union officials. In response, the AFL-CIO pulled back a bit. A new policy asked states to enact minimum wage laws with time and a half for overtime after eight hours for both men and women, agreed that states that already enforced FLSA standards could exempt women from special laws, and urged replacement of rigid weight-lifting prohibitions with "reasonable statutory requirements related to the capacity of the individual."[85] Yet in principle the AFL-CIO remained convinced both of the efficacy of protective labor laws and of the need to oppose the ERA. Andrew Biemiller insisted that this position had the strong support of "the unions with the largest membership of women" including the original women-dominated unions, like the International Ladies Garment Workers, the Amalgamated Clothing Workers, the Hotel Employees and Restaurant Employees International, the Communications Workers of America, and the Retail Clerks International Association.[86]

For women's organizations, this was a period of flux and dissension. The federal government's Interdepartmental Committee on the Status of Women and the Citizens' Advisory Councils, which had grown out of the state commissions on the status of women, championed state protective labor laws until 1967. Then their language altered to incorporate a primary concern for the rights of women to make their own decisions about earning overtime pay or working long hours. In light of efforts "to achieve the goal for women of equality with men in economic, political and legal rights," the committee called for "modernization of much of our State legislation which now applies to women only" and wondered whether such laws, rigidly applied, might not result in the "denial of the rights of a particular group." Echoing Murray, it questioned the "continued justification for special labor laws that are based on sex as a classification" and proposed instead to take account of all those "who have special needs."[87] Several members of the state commissions reenacted the debates inside NOW, which could not at first decide what position to take; its commitment to treating sex and race discrimination alike eventually put the board on the side of the working women who actively sought relief from restrictive legislation. Like NOW, these groups came around first to dismantling protective labor laws and then to supporting the ERA as they began to see the value of the sex/race liaison for judicial action. Others helped to found the Women's Equity Action League, to bring judicial cases. NOW joined the older National Federation of Business and Professional Women's Clubs in supporting an equal rights amendment that would eliminate such laws forever.[88]

The EEOC, like the Labor Department, at first took the position that it did not believe that Congress intended to disturb "laws and regulations which are intended to, and have the effect of protecting women against exploitation and hazard."[89] Accordingly, it considered such state laws benign, covered by the clause permitting bona fide occupational qualifications. It encouraged individuals who believed the restrictions "unreasonable" simply to seek exemptions. At the same time, it insisted that to refuse a woman a job that offered extra benefits like overtime work or extra pay would probably violate Title VII. The confusing division allowed a peaceful legal coexistence with state laws that treated women as different sorts of persons as long as differential treatment did not disadvantage them. If states demonstrated flexibility in allowing appeals and exceptions, the EEOC argued, women's rights as individuals would be protected. But rigid application of state laws would be frowned upon as evidence that "the clear effect of a law ... is not to protect women but to subject them to discrimination."

In June, still tormented, EEOC commissioners met with officials of twelve states and four representatives of the Labor Department to address the question "When does protection become discrimination?" The group was sharply divided, some of them believing that the EEOC should take the lead in setting policy that would encourage state legislators to abandon outmoded laws, others insisting that the protective laws still served an important function.[90] Finally, on August 19, 1966, the EEOC gave the states even more leeway by ruling that it would no longer "decide cases involving such a conflict and instead direct the aggrieved party to seek a judicial remedy."[91] This decision, which seemed to some "a considerable withdrawal from its earlier position," set off alarm bells.[92] Ultimately it led to hearings on May 2 and 3, 1967, on the relationship between Title VII and state legislation. There the EEOC encountered the diversity of opinion among women's groups and began to rethink its own position. On February 13, 1968, the EEOC moved a step closer to defining sex discrimination, like race discrimination, as an incursion on women's individual rights, even when women's efforts to exercise those rights seemed to violate social norms.[93] Backing off its year-and-a-half-old effort at neutrality, it agreed to decide whether state laws conflicted with Title VII and to seek congressional approval to prosecute some cases of sex discrimination against employers and unions whose policies conformed to state law but treated men and women differently.

By now the courts had begun to make themselves heard. With regard to minorities, they had more or less consistently applied a simple notion of discrimination, defining it as hostile or prejudicial behavior based on assumptions about group characteristics rather than on individual merit. This had not been the case with women. On the several occasions in 1966 and 1967 when the EEOC found cause for action because employers refused to hire women into jobs that required lifting heavy weights, the courts acknowledged the sex-stereotyping involved and yet concurred with state lawmakers that "generally recognized physical capabilities and physical limitations of the sexes may be made the basis for occupational qualification in generic terms."[94] By the end of 1967, an EEOC just short of accepting a common definition of discrimination for sex and race summed up the difference between it and the courts on this issue, noting the courts' penchant for finding that "there is a social interest that justifies this otherwise prohibited practice."[95]

A change of heart loomed. Lena Rosenfeld, a fifty-nine-year-old California railroad telegrapher and mother of twelve, sued for a job denied her because California law prohibited women from working overtime. In a decision with nationwide reverberations, a U.S. district court abruptly rejected the argument that the general characteristics of a sex were sufficient justification for treating men and women differently and overturned state limits on hours.[96] Rosenfeld got the job she wanted. So did Lorena Weeks when she asked for a job that involved occasionally lifting moderately heavy weights. In March of 1966, Weeks bid for the job of switchman at Georgia's Southern Bell Telephone and Telegraph Company. The company told her it could not assign women to that job, so she went first to the EEOC and then, with EEOC sanction, to court. She argued, appealing to the Fourteenth Amendment's equal protection clause as well as to Title VII, that the company had placed a male with less seniority in a position for which she was fully qualified. Southern Bell replied that "a bona fide occupational qualification was created whenever reasonable state protective legislation prevented women from occupying certain positions." The court disagreed. Concurring with, and citing the positions of, the PCSW and the Citizens' Advisory Council on the Status of Women, it decried the sex-stereotyping that led to assumptions about how much weight a particular woman could lift. That the average woman might not want to lift the thirty pounds allowed under Georgia law did not mean that some women could not or would not choose to do so, declared a federal district court in giving Weeks the switchman's job she wanted.[97] Claudine

Cheatwood had something of the same experience. Her boss refused to promote her to a job as a commercial representative in a rural area because the job might require her to change a tire on a rural road and to collect money in sleazy and perhaps hazardous places. A particular job might be "somewhat unromantic," said the court, but Title VII "vests individual women with the power to decide whether or not to take on unromantic tasks."[98]

Faced with court decisions that unambiguously supported women's individual rights, its tenuous view of special legislation for women eroded by the fading influence of the Women's Bureau and the National Consumers' League, and encouraged by increasing pressure from newer women's organizations, the EEOC once again changed its mind. In the summer of 1969, it announced that state laws and regulations, "although originally promulgated for the purpose of protecting females, have ceased to be relevant to our technology or to the expanding role of the female worker in our economy[,] ... do not take into account the capacities, preferences and abilities of individual females and tend to discriminate rather than protect."[99] On August 19, 1969, it issued a new and stronger set of guidelines on sex discrimination. Laws that "prohibit or limit" the employment of women were in conflict with Title VII, it declared unequivocally. An employer who refused to employ women, even in jobs barred to them under state law, would be in violation of Title VII; men and women were entitled to equivalent economic benefits, including overtime pay; employers could no longer plead inadequate physical facilities as an excuse for failing to hire or promote either men or women.[100] Within five short years, the capacity of the law to treat women primarily as family members, valuable for their reproductive roles, had been transformed. Formally, at least, women of all races had become individuals under employment law.

## Divided Women

In some respects piggybacking sex onto race had proven a more politically effective strategy than anyone could have imagined. By providing women with an evocative conception of individual rights—a conception that substituted a new idea of fairness and justice for the old notion that fairness to women resided in the family—legislators unwittingly allowed challenges not only to rights denied but to the attitudes and behaviors on which historic labor force patterns rested. Women who began by attacking sex-segregated seniority lists and limited access to jobs soon became aware that they lacked equal pension benefits and pregnancy leaves; and then of the educational, cultural, and instititutional forces like men's clubs and pervasive sexual harassment that perpetuated limits on women's opportunity.[101] As wage-earning women continued to barrage the EEOC with complaints, the newly created Women's Equity Action League began a campaign of legal challenges that supported and sustained NOW's lobbying activities. Suddenly, it looked as if Pauli Murray's strategy—to fulfill the promise of the Fourteenth Amendment—might be achieved. The officers of NOW hesitated to support an ERA because, they believed, the Constitution already provided the basis for giving women equal protection under the law. Many women thought they would quickly join African-American men and other minority groups in pushing the Constitution to new limits.

For some women, this was what happened. But not for others. Severing women's rights from the family and releasing women to pursue individual or civil rights had an enormously positive impact on the freedom of many women; it also had unforeseen consequences for poor women and women of color, especially those who depended on government support. For one thing, a notion of discrimination entirely denuded of its benign, or protective, potential encouraged law- and policy makers to ignore social and cultural factors peculiar to women, even when paying attention might have served the broad principle of equality better. While attacks on racial discrimination could and did address the "starting gate," making at least a bow to the impoverished economic and educational circumstances that inhibited African Americans and increasing numbers of Latinos from taking full advantage of economic opportunity, attacks on sexual discrimination rarely did so. Only the most far-sighted feminists in the early 1970s dared to talk about transforming language, or the family, or early education programs. Icons of the early second wave of the feminist movement like Shulamith Firestone or Kate Millet might suggest that only sweeping changes in women's socialization, education, and culture would ensure their economic independence. Like many more ordinary women who dared to propose alterations in their families and workplaces, they incurred rabid attacks for undermining traditional families or ignoring the biological value of sex differences. As a result, the largely white and middle-class women whose education, job training, race, or class positions already placed them at the starting gate benefited far more, and more immediately, than others. NOW had begun with inclusionary promise, even, as Betty Friedan's biographer Daniel Horowitz argues, a larger vision of social justice.[102] In following the model of a civil rights movement that advocated individual rights, however, it chose an effective politics that did not, perhaps could not, equalize social conditions among women. In so doing, NOW and the political wings of the newly formed women's movement may have helped to exacerbate divisions among them and to earn the new feminism of the late 1960s the opprobrium of being white and middle class.

Martha Griffiths's June 1966 attack on the EEOC illuminates why. On the one hand, Representative Griffiths deplored the EEOC's failure to enforce the natural rights of women and demanded equal protection under the Fifth and Fourteenth Amendments for all women. On the other, by offering statistical data on the disadvantaged employment status of all women, and particularly of black women, she hoped to foster what she called a "practical equality."[103] Women who worked in increasing numbers and who supported families, Griffiths argued, deserved to be treated equally. But Griffiths's desire for "practical equality" could easily be interpreted as sustaining the restrictive apparatus of protective labor legislation and therefore of resurrecting detested concepts of benign discrimination. While she fully understood that equality for poor women (whom a large public imagined as disproportionately black) required more than removing discriminatory barriers to jobs, neither she nor her allies could fully imagine the political process providing the kinds of social services required to undermine a class-mediated and racially tinged perception of individual rights. Women would never be equal competitors as long as poverty denied them safe neighborhoods, adequate health care, decent housing, good child care, and efficient transportation. Yet this was precisely what was unachievable in the American political context. Lacking such services, intrinsic in the social democratic regimes out of which the Swedish policy of *jämställhedt* emerged, women divided along lines of class and race.

Under the circumstances, treating women as individuals in the job market or with respect to job-related benefits disadvantaged poor women, closing access routes to economic citizenship for many of them. The historical context tells us something about why. The civil rights bill passed into law in 1964 followed on a decade of struggle among African Americans (who then constituted more than 90 percent of people of color in the United States) for voting and job rights. By the mid-1960s, an increasingly militant civil rights movement fostered a climate of unrest and discontent that led to urban riots in every large American city. As Washington moved to handle the "Negro problem," policy makers imagined solutions in male terms. In March of 1965, Daniel Patrick Moynihan, then a special assistant to the president for labor, completed a report entitled *The Negro Family: The Case for National Action*. Because its contents were thought to be explosive, the administration refused to release the report at first, and when it finally emerged six months later, its powerful analysis met a skeptical audience. Moynihan drew a portrait of "tangled pathology" sustained by economic prejudice that denied black men access to jobs and positioned black women as heads of a virtual matriarchy. Though they held poorer jobs than white women, black women nevertheless tended to be more highly educated and economically productive than black men. For the health of the black family, this imbalance needed to be remedied. "Ours is a society which presumes male leadership in private and public affairs," intoned Moynihan. "A subculture, such as that of the Negro American, in which this is not the pattern, is placed at a distinct disadvantage."[104] Though Moynihan refused to offer suggestions for action, his solution was clearly to reposition black men as more effective breadwinners.

Liberals and feminists alike later vilified Moynihan for failing to look at the social sources of poverty and for his blindness to the leadership qualities of women.[105] At the time, his analysis reflected the thinking of leading African-American and white labor and civil rights leaders, women as well as men. Initially floated within the councils of the PCSW, it had drawn approbation from the African-American women consulted there. But no one anticipated that emphasizing male opportunity in a context of limited resources meant neglecting women. After 1965, the Moynihan Report provided fuel for many black organizations increasingly convinced that training for men, not women, would remedy the race discrimination that had emasculated black men. Beginning tentatively with equal opportunity legislation in 1964, and with increasing intensity as Moynihan's analysis took hold, policy makers everywhere created education, training and job incentives that were apparently gender-neutral. In practice they privileged male African Americans, enacting a racial agenda meant to salvage black families at the cost of individual rights for black women. Despite repeated protests by female legislators, almost all of the job programs excluded or discriminated against women.[106] This included the Manpower Training and Development Act, first passed in 1962 and repeatedly renewed through 1969, and the 1964 Job Corps, created as a first response to urban distress and unemployment. The proportion of women in both remained small, and as late as 1970 more than 70 percent of Job Corps beneficiaries were male.[107]

Poor black women found themselves doubly disadvantaged: once by the equal opportunity policies and second by official acknowledgment of the needs of black males. The first attempted to place women in positions where they could compete with men in the job market and ignored ways of enabling women to cope with home and family while they worked. The second led mainstream civil rights and radical black power groups to support and sustain the competitive economic position of black men while ignoring or underplaying the difficulties faced by black women. Pauli Murray described the results of these policies in bitter language: "The tragedy of black women today is that they are brainwashed by the notion that priority must be given to the assertion of black male manhood and that they must now stand back and push their men forward."[108]

While racial politics excluded black women from potentially valuable training, the politics of a racialized gender suggested taking advantage of women's new assertiveness in the job market to push into it mothers whose preferences might otherwise have led them to stay out. In 1967, Congress debated and then amended the Social Security Act to require mothers receiving welfare to engage in paid labor. The mandate dramatically reversed the policies adopted in the original Social Security Act of 1935. That welfare legislation, like the protective labor legislation that created boundaries for women's paid work, affirmed a social interest in every woman's capacity to fulfill the role of homemaking and motherhood, as well as to keep her family intact. As Dorothy Ferebee, a member of the National Board of the YWCA, told a senatorial committee considering the idea: "The original premise of AFDC . . . regards this assistance as part of a basic right of protection for needy women and children . . . including the option open to the mother to choose to work or to remain in the family, so that she can maintain the family structure." Mothers should be offered employment, testified George K. Wyman, commissioner of New York State's Department of Social Services, except when "the best interests of their children would not be served in so doing."[109]

But the politics of equality caught the unwary in their grip. In vain did women now plead the privileges of their traditional roles. In vain did congressional witnesses try to persuade legislators that "it is bad social policy to pursue a goal of regularly removing mothers from their normal duties of caring for their young children in their own homes where fathers are absent."[110] In the antagonistic climate of job-related individual rights of the late 1960s, claims to public support for full-time mothering floundered.[111] Ignoring the tensions implicit in requiring some women to work while encouraging others to stay at home, the House voted to require women on welfare to be available for paid labor. When the bill came to the Senate, representatives of organized labor as well as other advocates of women loudly objected. The debate turned on whether mothers had the "right" to expect public support if they refused to participate in wage work. The politics of the moment, and particularly a heightened racial context in which welfare was viewed (incorrectly) as the province of black women, pitted arguments for women's individual rights or freedom of choice against the social value of work. It created an awkward tension between the desire of many women (perceived as white) to defend their rights to work and opportunities at work and congressional demands that some women (poor women) be required to work. Ferebee defined the tension for a Senate committee: "Many women are eager to work, and would benefit from training programs, especially if they lead to meaningful and productive work with a future. But to make this a condition of assistance is to deny them the privilege which other women have of deciding whether to remain in the home. It is putting a higher value on work outside the home than within it."[112]

The problem, of course, was that the policies generated by Moynihan's analysis disproportionately disadvantaged poor women. While skilled female wage earners and professionals stood to benefit from expanded job opportunities, women on welfare lacked the social support systems or the economic resources to command the training they needed. For those who viewed themselves primarily as mothers, serving their families was doing good work, worthy of support, yet a larger public perceived them as deriving benefits of citizenship without having earned them. If mothering young children no longer provided sufficient justification for middle-class women to stay at home, why should it be a necessary cause for the public to support poor women? "I am frank to say that I am not impressed with the idea that those welfare mothers are doing something constructive sitting around those homes," declared Russell Long of Louisiana, who chaired the Senate committee considering the issue.[113]

For half a century, Congress and the states had asked women to relegate their individual rights to the background in the service of a changing array of social needs. In return for a dependent status, women received a putative constitutional protection for their capacity to mother. As various agencies of government moved toward granting women individual rights, Congress backed off the promise of social protection. Yet the interests of different women were at stake. "Would you mind telling me," Long asked a beleaguered welfare official who had stammered that he didn't think "all mothers, you know, willy nilly, so to speak, should be expected to take employment without considering the impact of being absent from the home or the children," why "a welfare client who has never done a day's work in his life ought to be put above a man who works for a living and pays to support those people?" After all, he asked, if a recipient of unemployment insurance could not turn down an appropriate job, why should a welfare client have that privilege? Labeling mothers on welfare "female broodmares" and "riffraff," he offered neither sympathy nor understanding for the problems that poverty posed for safety, transportation, or child care, asserting simply that "other mothers are supporting their families and it seems to me those welfare mothers could strive to do the same thing."

A vivid image of welfare mothers participated in many of Long's harsh interchanges with witnesses before his committee. Repeatedly, he emphasized their laziness—raging, for example, at a group of New York women who had noisily picketed the committee's proceedings on a hot September day: "Yesterday this whole room was filled with mothers who sat around this committee room all day and refused to go home. Why can't those people be told that if they can find time to impede the work of the Congress they can find time to pick up some beer cans in front of their house?" And again, he intoned, "If they are able to work, have work right in front of them, but can't find time to so much as catch the rats in their own house, I don't see why we ought to have them on the public payroll." Nor should women whose partners failed to work benefit. Long wanted the federal government to chase after the men he called "runaway daddies." Confronted with issues of due process and fairness, he asked rhetorically, "Does it seem fair to you for those mothers who work in my office ... to pay taxes to suport welfare mothers who don't feel like working? ... I don't see why we ought to pay them when there is work, honorable, good, decent work available to them, but they won't take it." Such favoritism, he contended, would make "superclass citizens" of women who can draw government money and decline to work while others worked "by the sweat of their brow to make an honest living."

To counter these arguments, representatives of poor women sought to articulate the constitutional issues involved. Elizabeth Wickenden, technical consultant on public social policy at the National Social Welfare Assembly and a veteran social worker, consultant to the Citizens' Advisory Councils, and part of the friendship network that surrounded the Women's Bureau, tried to explain why justice and fairness demanded free choices for poor women. A policy that required work, she told Long's Senate committee, reverted back to the assumptions of a century before, which thought poverty the consequence of individual failing. The Social Security Act of 1935, in contrast, assumed child rearing to be socially useful work; the enforced absence of their mothers would thus doubly deprive children who had already lost their fathers. Any mother, she argued, "should have some choice in deciding whether she could safely manage the double burdens carried by all working mothers."[114]

But it was exactly this that Congress would no longer concede. In 1961, it had changed the Social Security law to make women who lived with unemployed mates eligible for benefits provided that the mate had actively sought a job and had not refused one when offered. The flip side of this blatant effort to institutionalize female dependency was that women whose partners could not so demonstrate lost their benefits if welfare officials found the pair living together. The 1967 law laid yet another obligation on mothers. Absent a husband or mate willing to provide economic resources, mothers of children over the age of six could no longer choose how to manage their families. Wickenden and others correctly perceived that the issues were not economic but punitive and that the excessive punishment exacted captured the constitutional issue involved: forcing poor women to work was simply a policy unworthy "of a nation whose constitution promises due process, equal treatment under the law, and freedom from involuntary servitude to all its people." UAW official Melvin Glasser concurred: mothers should have "free choice as to whether to work or not: I think all Americans are entitled to that."[115]

If it had not always been clear that work trumped motherhood in the arrogation of citizenship rights, the Senate's decision to join the House in passing a mandatory labor requirement for mothers receiving aid made it so. When the Supreme Court finally reviewed the issue in the spring of 1973, it upheld the position not merely that Congress could limit benefits for women who did not register in supervised federal employment training programs but that states could go beyond federal mandate to refuse benefits to women who refused to work in state-sponsored programs as well. In a scathing dissent Justice Thurgood Marshall attacked the employment requirement for mothers of small children, insisting that it violated the spirit of the original act, which was designed to "release the parent from the wage-earning role," as well as of subsequent amendments covering the needs of relatives with whom the child lived.[116] In sharp contrast to all but one of his colleagues on the Court, Marshall believed that Congress had a broader purpose than to promote work opportunities. But Marshall was in the minority.

While poor black women slowly found their rights to due process eroding as they faced coercive job market choices without compensatory education or training, and without adequate support for their children's safety and wellbeing, the equal opportunity vehicle spawned by the black civil rights movement began to move forward for more educated and professional women, black and white. In part, this was a result of the enormous attention paid to this group of women, whose prior education and training contrasted starkly with their job status. Because admissions quotas to professional schools of law, medicine, architecture, and business, among others, still existed, it was easy to demonstrate that even privileged women had been routinely and unapologetically denied access, channeled into limited jobs, and treated as if home and motherhood were their life's work. The idea of discrimination against women was easy to see for this group. As the barriers dropped, educated women quickly moved into institutions that had excluded them. At the same time, the rhetoric of individual rights that opened the door to opportunity for some pushed uneducated and unskilled women, many of them hampered by family needs, into a job market that exacerbated their problems. The contrast could not have been sharper.

## At First Glance, the Idea May Seem Silly

The EEOC's affirmative action programs emerged in this moment of contested consciousness. Bemoaning the slow pace necessitated by waiting for and acting on individual complaints, the commission sought to take preventive action to speed up the process by identifying employers with few minority employees, warning them that they were likely to have charges leveled against them, and suggesting goals and timetables for correcting imbalances. The documents, which allude frequently to "minority workers" and "minority hiring," are silent on the subject of gender.[117] Clearly the EEOC imagined race as the appropriate target for these programs. In fact, the idea of preferential action for women still seemed rather strange.

In the 1950s, fair employment practices regulations of seventeen states included the authority to order employers with few minority workers "to cease and desist." These orders proved to be largely ineffective—more moral pronouncements than remedies. With the exception of New York State's, they did not apply to women. At the federal level, the executive orders barring discrimination issued by Presidents Roosevelt and Truman did not mention sex, nor were women mentioned in President Kennedy's Executive Order 10925 of 1961.

As it was first introduced by Kennedy's executive order, which created the President's Commission on Equal Employment Opportunity, affirmative action required federal contractors to take positive steps to ensure equitable treatment of workers. Like preceding executive orders, this one spoke only to issues of race and ethnicity. Unwilling to offend the women who were then deliberating in his own Commission on the Status of Women, Kennedy did ban sex discrimination in the civil service and in the executive branch.[118] But his executive orders, like those of Truman and Roosevelt, constituted more a rhetorical gesture than a planned attack. President Johnson's 1965 Executive Order 11246, issued less than a month after the 1964 Civil Rights Act went into effect, was only marginally stronger. The new order prohibited racial discrimination among federal government contractors and, in a new initiative,

mandated that employers take preferential action to correct statistical disparities between the pool of minority workers available for jobs and the numbers
actually employed. Like Kennedy, Johnson omitted women. A year and a half
later he amended the order. Warned by Esther Peterson and the Women's
Bureau that the omission was a problem, and under intense pressure from
women's groups, especially NOW, Johnson issued a second directive in 1967
(Executive Order 11375) that mandated preferential action on behalf of
women as well as minorities.[119]

As the enforcement arm of antidiscrimination legislation and of sequential
executive orders, affirmative action in theory offered to correct an imperfect
labor market by enhancing the job chances of disadvantaged groups through
more aggressive education, training, and mentoring. Affirmative action recognized that most discrimination was less the result of deliberate decisions
taken against individual employees than of "systemic patterns."[120] To find
patterns of underutilization, programs relied on a judgment of what the
appropriate number of women, or blacks or other minorities, should be in a
particular occupation in a particular regional labor market. For African-American males, these figures, no matter how contested, were easily come by. If
people of color constituted a particular percentage of the labor force in a particular area, then they could be expected, over time, and with such affirmative
steps as active recruitment, training, counseling, and antidiscrimination policies in the workplace, to constitute approximately the same percentage of a
particular employer's workforce.

For women, the task was not so simple. Since not all women wanted to be
in the workforce, how did one arrive at a target number for female employment in the first place? Congressional witnesses who documented women's
exclusion from professional schools, their underrepresentation in good jobs,
their poor pay, and their lack of opportunity for advancement still faced ultimately the question of whether these were not the result of "natural" laws, of
differences beyond the control of employers, rather than the product of overt
bias. As late as 1970, Edith Green was still trying to make the point that the
idea of statistical discrimination applied to women as well as minorities.[121]
When the EEOC measured progress against discrimination by employers'
efforts to achieve mandated goals (quickly perceived as quotas), the world
seemed to have turned upside down: assigning jobs by sex validated and
affirmed women's traditional roles, and forcing employers to choose women
over white men seemed to privilege an effort to overturn family life. When it
came to women, goals and timetables seemed to undermine the centrality of
sex "difference," to challenge gender as a system of social order.

Labor force patterns, many argued, simply reflected women's own preferences for raising families, their willingness to place their own careers second to their husbands', and their ambivalent attitudes toward wage work. Others, however, believed these patterns to be the results of generations of discrimination—precisely the reason for affirmative action. An endless debate ensued: Should "availability" for particular jobs take into account behavior occasioned by long-standing cultural biases predicated on women's mothering and nurturing roles? Should it be measured against women's present proclivities in the workforce or against the choices they might have exercised were the world different? Were employers who favored male breadwinners for the most lucrative jobs and training guilty of discrimination? What about those who balked at hiring women with small children? Was sexual harassment a form of discrimination? What about displaying "pin-up" pictures in the workplace?[122] The questions pointed up the difficulties with treating gender bias and racial bias in the same way. Perhaps, said former EEOC counsel Sonia Pressman, commenting on the numbers of blacks and whites who "refuse to see the analogy between discrimination based on race and that based on sex," this was because "the aura of moral opprobrium which today surrounds racial discrimination has not yet attached itself to discrimination based on sex."[123] Lacking moral clout, affirmative action on the grounds of gender was, as one observer noticed, almost immediately "painted as a policy of institutionalized discrimination against white men, rather than as an antidiscrimination program."[124]

Even when the EEOC took relatively strong positions, as it had begun to do by the end of the 1960s, the Justice Department, charged with enforcing its claims, demurred. Until 1970, the Justice Department did not prosecute a single discrimination case against women. In contrast, the department took forty-five claims of racial bias to court, an action defended by Jerris Leonard, the assistant attorney general for the Justice Department's Civil Rights Division, in congressional hearings that year. He sparred a bit with the committee investigating sex discrimination before which he was testifying, then challenged what he called the assumption that "there is equal visibility and in fact equal quantity of the problem." Law enforcement, he maintained, "tends to act on those problems which are more aggravated," and, he continued, "the truth of the matter is there is, at least as far as what is brought to our attention, far greater discrimination on the ground of race than there is on the ground of sex."[125]

Like the Department of Labor, the EEOC, and the Department of Justice, the judiciary continued through the 1960s to query whether discrimination

*Edith Green of Oregon was first elected to Congress in 1954 and served through the crucial years of debate on women's issues.* COURTESY, LIBRARY OF CONGRESS.

existed when employers, schools, and other institutions deferred to traditional cultural norms. Faced with multiplying requests to reconsider the meaning of gender roles, it resisted. After all, including women in compensatory and preferential treatment mandates would negate an image of women as dependent mothers fostered since the famous *Muller v. Oregon* decision in 1908. It would also, and not incidentally, increase the proportion of workers covered to more than three quarters of the workforce. Taken seriously, preferential treatment for a group this size would certainly undermine the idea that getting a job, a promotion, or a bank loan rested on individual merit. Unsurprisingly, the courts refused, year after year, to classify sex in the same way they classified race.[126]

Until the end of the decade, the EEOC continued to apply procedures and remedies for minorities (mostly male) in quite different ways than it did for women. But by 1969, it had begun to try to convince officials in the Department of Labor to adopt a more encompassing definition of sex discrimination, one that did not tolerate differential treatment even when cultural traditions seemed to demand it. In 1970, when the department excluded women from its aggressive "Order 4," it claimed that the same standards could not be applied to women workers as to minority groups. Order 4 required federal contractors and subcontractors to recruit and train members of minority groups. To enforce its decree, the Labor Department asked employers to set goals and timetables for hiring African-American and other protected workers based on an EEOC determination of their availability. Confronted with a delegation of women demanding inclusion, Labor Department officials insisted that they had "no intention of applying literally exactly the same approach to women in Order no. 4, which was designed for racial minorities."[127] They could not, they said, because the procedures established for noncomplying firms to establish goals and timetables by which they expected to hire a reasonable proportion of minorities "are not totally suitable to sex discrimination." The department could not approve goals and timetables for women because its leaders could not imagine them working in the same way. "The work force pattern of women and racial minorities differs in significant respects," argued Women's Bureau director Elizabeth Duncan Koontz. "Many women do not seek employment. Practically all males do."[128]

The comment, and the minimal attention given to sex as a protected "class," or category, during this period of developing civil rights law, suggest the continuing skepticism of almost everyone in power, including black civil rights and labor leaders, about the idea of sex discrimination in employment. It also suggests the relative isolation of the still incipient women's movement, which managed to push the EEOC into accepting women's treatment as individuals before the idea had general currency. Just at the point that women protested their exclusion from the Labor Department's Order 4, Andrew Biemiller, director of the AFL-CIO's Legislative Department, wrote to civil rights leader Bayard Rustin to object to the inclusion of items raised by NOW on the agenda of a coming meeting. "This must have happened when I wasn't looking," he wrote. "I do not regard them as a civil rights organization. They are interested in absolutely nothing but superfeminism."[129]

Such comments set Congresswoman Edith Green afire. What the Department of Labor described as unavailability because of lack of interest, Green understood as evidence of deeply rooted cultural and social discrimination. Faced with the department's unwillingness to concede its blindness, Green flatly opposed its request for authority to enforce Title VII even with investigatory powers in the hands of the Women's Bureau. It was time, she said as she endorsed the EEOC's competing effort to acquire enforcement powers, that women be treated as human beings by the government with all of its machinery at their disposal, not offered "a little part over here for women." Yet the Labor Department clung to its outmoded sense of the meaning of gender difference, insisting that it did not constitute discrimination. Consistently, it supported the continuing exemption of professional and executive women from the Equal Pay Act; it believed the increase in the number of women in the Job Corps (to 29 percent) to be satisfactory, and it could not bring itself to support an ERA.

What the Department of Labor still could not see, others had begun to perceive in all its dimensions. That same year, 1970, the EEOC finally altered its rationale for including women in the admittedly weak plans for preferential treatment it offered to African Americans, adding its voice to the women's groups intent on persuading the Department of Labor to change its mind. A year later, the Court had a change of heart. In the first Title VII sex discrimination case to reach the Supreme Court, *Phillips v. Martin Marietta Corp.*, the Court held that a woman could not be denied a job because she had small children, if similarly situated men were not refused.[130] In December of 1971, the Labor Department yielded to the notion that sex was not an appropriate classification. Henceforth, employers would be required to provide goals and timetables illustrating how they intended to incorporate women into their workforces.[131] Finally, in 1972, Congress passed a revised Equal Employment Act that gave the EEOC power to sue in court and lowered the threshold for compliance to as few as fifteen employees. The same act protected public employees from discrimination and made their employers responsible for taking affirmative action to ensure equal employment opportunities for women. It had taken six tortuous years, but at last women's complaints of sex discrimination would be backed by enforceable regulations.

## History Is Moving in This Direction

For all the effective pressure of women's groups, these milestones could not have been reached without substantial changes in the public understanding and legal meaning of discrimination. There was still no consensus. Nor could there be. While feminist advocates could agree that social and cultural factors sustained the legal and institutional barriers that inhibited equality, they continued to disagree over the extent to which society and culture should be modified. Many men and women continued to believe that any change in women's status would undermine traditional family lives. Yet there was some common ground on which to build a more complex relationship between deeply gendered cultural tradition and governmental actions.

Times had changed. By 1970, the dramatic postwar increase in women's labor force participation had convinced most experts that most women would work for a living for most of their lives—a change that one national magazine headlined as a "Revolution in American Family Life."[132] More than 40 percent of all women earned wages—a proportion double that of the 1920s, and still rising. But it wasn't just the numbers—it was the pattern of labor force participation that mattered. More than 60 percent of young women were in the labor force, and though a third of these would drop out to have babies, they tended to do so for shorter and shorter periods. Their wage-earning lives continued when their children grew up. Rising divorce rates, greater numbers of men and women who chose not to marry, increasing numbers of women who chose to become parents without partners: all these trends confirmed the sense that it would no longer be appropriate to define women largely as family members. A clamorous women's liberation movement demanded individual rights with access to political and social citizenship. As it did so, the barriers to economic citizenship began to erode.

A snippet of one of the reports in a series published by the Citizens' Advisory Councils (CAC) that had grown out of the PCSW illustrates the transition. Like the officers of NOW, many members of these state-based councils became impatient with the limited agenda of the EEOC and sought to expand access routes to economic citizenship for women. In 1968, the CAC issued a series of reports that revisited the recommendations of the PCSW and offered some amendments. Comparing these reports to those of the 1963 PCSW illuminates how quickly the perspective of some leading women had altered. Threaded through the documents is the same sense of women's dual interest as wives and mothers on the one hand and as workers on the other. But while the 1963 recommendations could not shake the idea that work for women would be wrapped around their families, their economic security heavily contingent on their relationships as dependents, the 1968 recommendations perceptibly modified that stance.

The report of the CAC Task Force on Social Insurance and Taxes portrayed women as enmeshed in an intertwined work/family nexus; it recognized the unconventional nature of many families; and it perceived the need for equal treatment of women family heads. Its sweeping recommendations suggested something of the transformation that might be expected if the social policies of the 1930s comprehended a new and fuller citizenship for women. To reduce married women's dependency, it proposed to combine the earnings of a husband and wife for the purpose of calculating credits in the old age insurance program. To enhance the economic power of single women, it suggested paying survivor benefits to any relative dependent on her. It considered fundamental changes in income tax law, which would reduce the inequities on working wives by making child care expenses deductible, and finally recommended an earned income credit for all wage earners.[133]

To eliminate continuing discrepancies in the treatment of male and female workers, the task force urged amendments to unemployment insurance regulations. Like the PCSW, it advocated a uniform set of benefits to pregnant women and new mothers based on a standard that measured, rather than imputed, ability to work. It proposed to use disability insurance to cover lost pay during confinement and postnatal care. This, in the task force's words, constituted "a logical part of a broader program of replacement of wages lost because of short term illness or accident."[134] Like its predecessor, the 1968 task force advocated that states that provided unemployment benefits for dependents cease to measure the eligibility of women by whether there was an employed male in the house. But the 1968 task force also offered a series of sweeping recommendations to alter the requirements of the unemployment insurance program for all workers in ways that would specifically benefit the lowest-paid sectors of the labor force, many of them women. Objecting to the classification of women as secondary workers, to whom unemployment compensation was often denied when a male breadwinner lived in the home, the task force argued that raising the question of "need" before benefits were granted "is to strike at the foundations of the program." It also advocated benefits for the long-term unemployed and reduced waiting periods for benefits (because delays of up to nine months discriminated against new and returning entrants into the labor market). It expressed skepticism about the impact of experience rating and recommended raising the top limit on wages for which the payroll tax would be applied, in order to capture a greater return on behalf of higher-paid workers. It proposed to lift the bar against married women built into legislation like the Manpower and Development Training Act, which made training available to all unemployed male heads of households but only to unemployed women with unemployed husbands or without hubands at all.[135]

A far greater sense of entitlement of women to wage work, along with less privilege for the nonworking wife, and concern for the welfare of poor working women characterized these recommendations. While still treating most individuals as if they were in two-parent families, the report suggested modifying the tax structure to treat working wives as individuals. It acknowledged the existence of families in which women were the primary breadwinners and of single women with complicated arrangements to support dependents. Its recommendations challenged the assumptions underlying "unconscious" discrimination and demanded more equitable arrangements with regard to support for different kinds of wage earners.

The shift signaled by the women who authored this report positioned them on one side of a growing divide between increasing numbers who believed that discrimination existed and those who did not. Their efforts drew support from surprising places. A special task force set up by the newly elected Republican president, Richard Nixon, to explore "women's rights and responsibilities" unexpectedly affirmed the CAC position. Yet many women and men deeply believed that sexual differences, especially the sexual division of labor, were part of the natural order of things. As late as 1971, only 4 percent of the general public believed sex discrimination to be a problem.[136] To fulfill their roles, argued skeptics, males fully deserved the best education, the most lucrative jobs, and unchallenged authority within the family. Policies such as those proposed by the CAC task force or by proponents of affirmative action challenged traditional, seemingly natural, belief systems that affirmed social order. Worse, by disputing the value of individual effort and the capacity of employers to act on the merit of their employees, they threatened to undermine the free labor market itself.

Small wonder, then, that efforts to transform the law called forth a deep skepticism toward the idea of sex discrimination itself. The Nixon administration delayed the report of its own Task Force on Women's Rights and Responsibilities for months before endless leaks persuaded the administration to release it.[137] Nixon's chief economic adviser, Arthur F. Burns, was puzzled when an accomplished group of women reporters told him in 1969 that they had all been victims of discrimination. "If there is discrimination against women," he responded, "it is of the unconscious variety."[138] Shirley Chisholm, the distinguished black congresswoman from Brooklyn, acknowledged the unconscious roots of discrimination against women when she asked rhetorically, "How could it be that women are discriminated against? At first glance the idea may seem silly."[139] NOW's southern regional director, a member of the Louisiana Commission on the Status of Women, recalled the "wave of laughter" that permeated the courtroom during one of the early efforts to bring a sex discrimination suit. "Of course," she commented, "it is better than being spat upon."[140] And *Business Week*, acknowledging the disparities in men's and women's pay and benefits, nevertheless lamented the "incalculable cost" of equality. After all, it commented of the advocates, "their fight is concerned more with salary, position, and promotion inequalities than with citizenship rights."[141]

By the late 1960s, though, it had become apparent to too many people that access to economic equality was a necessary condition of citizenship. Once again, advocates for women made use of racial analogies. Nixon's Task Force on Women's Rights and Responsibilities couched its report in a thinly veiled warning: "We have witnessed a decade of rebellion during which black Americans fought for true equality. . . . Nothing could demonstrate more dramatically the explosive potential of denying fulfillment as human beings to any segment of our society." The report then called for "a national commitment to basic changes that will bring American women into the mainstream of American life."[142] When *Washington Post* columnist Elizabeth Shelton commented that "sex bias takes a greater economic toll than racial bias," her column reappeared in the *Congressional Record.*[143] What accounts for the change of heart?

Edith Green spoke about how her position had changed at congressional hearings on discrimination against women in 1970.[144] She confessed that she had "stayed away from discrimination because some might accuse me of being less than objective—of having a bias." But no one could grow up in America "and not be keenly and very pointedly aware of the innumerable times that discrimination occurs." She had been aware of this all of her life, though she had "remained fairly silent on it." The time for silence was over. The idea of women's commitment to family, which had inhibited the full-fledged analogy to race, had dissolved. She and many other participants in these hearings were ready to make a full-fledged assault on the idea of discrimination, even if it meant finally giving up the tradition of family protection and protective labor legislation as well. For years, explained Green, she had thought that "just reason and commonsense would bring about fair administration of the law," but now she had abandoned that conclusion: "I thought that fairness and persuasion would bring the change. I have also abandoned that position—because the years have not brought about those changes." She was ready to support the equal rights amendment.

Edith Green offered this explanation as she chaired public hearings that attacked discrimination against women. Called to solicit testimony on a bill (H.R. 805) to expand the reach of the federal government with regard to making sex a suspect category, these hearings represented a coming-together of legislative purpose to define the meaning of discrimination. They focused on three areas: removing exemptions in Title VII for educational institutions; authorizing the Civil Service Commission to study discrimination against women; and bringing executive, administrative, and professional employees under the "equal pay for equal work" provision of the FLSA. The narrow concept of discrimination that dominated these hearings—which concerned primarily professional and educated women—could not disguise the broader concerns of committee members and witnesses. Green made no secret of her own stance. She hoped, she said as the proceedings got under way, that the new provisions "would be of some help in eliminating the discrimination against women which still permeates our society."

In Green's view, discrimination on the grounds of sex could no longer trail after racial discrimination. Green had been the lone female member of Congress actively to oppose the addition of sex to Title VII on the grounds that it

*Representative Shirley Chisholm of New York in a 1968 photograph.* COURTESY, LIBRARY OF CONGRESS.

would disadvantage black women. Six short years later, she vociferously insisted that sex could no longer take second place. How was it, she asked, that "in a period when we are more concerned with civil rights and liberties than ever before in our history—when minorities have vigorously asserted themselves—that discrimination against a very important majority— women—has been given little attention?" The insight fueled her rage and turned the hearings into increasingly confrontational debates around the invisibility of sex discrimination, on the one hand, and the differential treatments of sex and race discrimination, on the other. If she had her vote to cast over again, she said, thinking back on her opposition to Title VII, she would vote to add sex.

To our minds a debate over whether sex bias or race bias takes a greater toll seems an exercise in futility. Yet because women believed that race discrimination had come to be the template by which sex discrimination would be measured—because they were convinced there would be no change without abandoning protection—this was precisely the argument that permeated the 1970 hearings and continued through the discussions of the ERA that followed. Green desperately wanted to make this point. Why, she asked repeatedly, was the absence of women from jobs not construed as prima facie evidence of sex discrimination in the same way that the absence of African Americans appeared to be incontestable evidence of race discrimination? "If they are right ... that the absence of a black is the evidence of discrimination," as the EEOC and the Civil Rights Division of the Justice Department had ruled, "then it seems to me you can also say that the continual absence of women is evidence of discrimination."[145] It was not that women were like men, she argued, but that their differences justified their inclusion (on the grounds that they would enrich the workplace) rather than their exclusion.

Nor was it sufficient to assert a likeness between sex and race discrimination. Rather, she encouraged witnesses to declare the first greater than the second, eagerly anticipating the testimony of Shirley Chisholm, who she hoped would do just that. When Chisholm appeared and said that "my sex has been a far greater handicap than my skin pigmentation," Green applauded her description "of the very systematic discrimination that does occur from very early years in a girl's life." The African-American female civil rights commissioner, Frankie M. Freeman, incurred Green's wrath when she took quite a different stance. Freeman argued that while the Civil Rights Commission would theoretically defend members "of any group whose members are oppressed by discriminatory practices and social customs," it could not take on sex discrimination without more resources. Green was enraged. Freeman stuck to her guns. She was a woman and black, she said; "my life has been spent in the constant struggle to overcome the inferior status which both of these categories have imposed upon me." She was "not unmindful of the problems faced by women because of their sex," but she wanted to add a note of caution: "I urge you not to forget that the great issue in this country, the great danger and the great source of despair is the discrimination endured by minority people." She could not, she said, see the commission's work diluted if sex were added to its charges without additional funds. Green persisted: she was in favor of additional funds, but she did not understand how Freeman placed "one discrimination above another." But Freeman would not back down: "Oh yes, I do. I absolutely believe, and I think the factual situation in this country will indicate that racial injustice is more pervasive."[146]

Freeman was by no means Green's only target. She fulminated at the EEOC, which had not been forceful enough in sending cases up to the Justice Department. She lambasted the Justice Department in turn for failing to take a single sex discrimination case to court, insisting that its preference for pursuing race cases over sex cases "can't be interpreted as anything except discrimination on the part of the Justice Department."[147] She railed at the Department of Health, Education, and Welfare (HEW) for a general refusal to recognize the seriousness of sex discrimination, mocking the three officials sent to testify at the hearings. In a remarkably candid assessment of their department's inability to attract more women into the Office of Education despite their best efforts, these three officials told the committee that their failure was one of understanding. "I think I understand the problems relative

to the discrimination of black women much more than I do white women,"
one HEW witness admitted, "and when you say that black women are discriminated against because of race and then discriminated on top of that because
of sex, I am not sure I understand it as well as women do." Green followed
with a barrage of complaints against HEW, which, despite her personal
request to the secretary, had sent "three men to discuss discrimination against
women."[148]

The Labor Department did not escape. Even as the hearings got under way,
Green accused its administrators of clinging stubbornly to outmoded definitions of what constituted women's traditional roles. She wondered if they
would send anyone to testify at her hearings, because "as of yesterday morning, . . . the Labor Department had not thought about it sufficiently, and they
had no position to take." At last, after several weeks of evading invitations to
testify, the Labor Department tapped Elizabeth Duncan Koontz, head of the
Women's Bureau, to do battle with Green. Koontz, a teacher by training, a former official of the National Education Association, an ally in many women's
causes, and an ERA supporter, offered the committee an explanation for why
the Labor Department's June 9, 1970, guidelines on sex discrimination differed from its guidelines on race. She began her statement by reviewing the
distinguished record of her bureau in investigating the condition of women
wage earners and affirming her commitment to ending employment discrimination against women. But when she turned to a program for action, she read
an official statement written by her boss, Secretary of Labor George Shultz.
Green impatiently proclaimed her discouragement with the Labor Department's "intention to act" before she allowed Koontz to continue to explore
the differences. "Occupations sought after by all racial groups may not have
been sought by women in significant numbers," read Koontz. These differences meant employing different criteria "in examining work force patterns to
reveal the deficiencies in employment of women than are used in revealing
racial deficiencies." As Koontz came to an end, Green jumped in. She had the
utmost confidence in Koontz personally, she said, and knew that the statement was not written by her, but, she avowed, "this is the biggest bunch of
gobbledygook I have heard for a long, long time."[149]

Sandwiched between two Senate debates on the ERA, and virtually coin-
ciding with House debate and passage of the amendment, Green's hearings
capture the cries of outrage over a discrimination still only partially acknowledged. By now, almost every major female leader of the 1960s tacitly or openly
recognized what Mary Eastwood labeled "the refusal of the courts to regard
women as fully human 'persons' under the Fifth and Fourteenth Amend-

ments."[150] Pauli Murray had only just moved into the ERA camp. Architect of the compromise around substituting the Fourteenth Amendment for the ERA, she had nevertheless responded joyously to the passage of Title VII and helped to found NOW when the EEOC stalled. By the late 1960s, she had become discouraged with efforts to persuade the Supreme Court that women were "persons" for the purpose of the Fourteenth Amendments's equal protection clause. Then teaching at Brandeis, Murray appeared before the committee as a member of the American Civil Liberties Union's executive board. Once again, she drew a parallel between the position of African Americans of both sexes and that of women of all races, reiterating her position in the PCSW. But whereas earlier she had argued that the great tradition of human rights promised as swift an end to sex discrimination as it seemed to offer for race discrimination, now she believed in the efficacy of political clout. Speaking as "a Negro and a woman," she called for an extension of democratic opportunity to both groups. She did not want, she said, black rights achieved at the expense of women. Rather, she preferred the two groups to move forward hand in hand. Murray had sometimes lamented the absence of political power to enforce women's demands. Now she predicted that a growing women's liberation movement could become "an instrument for potential widespread disruption" if concessions were not made to its "legitimate claims."[151]

Congressional debates over the ERA testify to Murray's wisdom. For ninety-eight years, claimed Martha Griffiths, floor leader of the campaign to pass the amendment, "the Court has held ... that women as a class are not entitled to equal protection of the laws. They are not 'persons' within the meaning of the Constitution."[152] The exclusions might have been well intentioned, as several speakers claimed, a residue of a moment when men "sought to protect our women from the rigors of the business and work-a-day world."[153] But in the modern world, as one legislator after another rose to acknowledge, conceiving of women as primarily family members subjected them, as individuals, to economic discrimination and denied them rights of citizenship. Sympathetic speakers noted that the right to work headed the list of rights to which women deserved access.[154] Sometimes angrily, legislators acknowledged that they had conceded much to arguments for racial equality; sometimes bitterly, they contended that the woman's hour had come. It was past time, as Representative Catherine May of Washington put it, "for action to protect women's rights as citizens, as human beings, as persons."[155]

Esther Peterson did not come around to the ERA until more than a year later, sometime after Elizabeth Koontz and the Women's Bureau had gracefully abandoned the struggle to maintain protective labor legislation and well before the AFL-CIO changed its mind. Then she wrote a fulsome letter to Martha Griffiths. "After much soul-searching," she wrote, "I have come to the conclusion that the time for waiting for court action is past and enactment of an equal rights amendent would be a constructive step."[156] It was, she added, difficult for her to make this statement; she regretted disappointing "many individuals and organizations with whom I have shared the opposite view for many years." But times had changed: recent legislation had improved prospects for women, and "much state protective legislation for women has been, in effect, nullified." With a nod to the past, she urged attention to efforts to enact good labor standards for men and for women. "History is moving in this direction," she said, "and I believe women must move with it."

# Epilogue

As an avid observer and marginal participant in many of the 1970s changes that transformed the lives of men and women, I thought for many years that the transformation merely had to play itself out, that women's economic independence was assured and that with it, the full range of economic citizenship would soon be available to both sexes. I was convinced that words like *liberty, individual rights,* and *freedom* would soon have new meanings, unconstrained by gender. Then, in 1985, I got caught up in a court case that powerfully captured both the effect of the transformation still under way and the depth of resistance to it.

The case began in 1979 when the EEOC sued Sears, Roebuck and Company for discriminating against women. The EEOC charged Sears, among other things, with refusing to hire or promote women into well-paying commission sales jobs in anywhere near the numbers equivalent to their representation in retail sales. Sears admitted that few women held the jobs in question, but it defended itself from charges of discrimination by claiming that women were simply not interested in them. These were jobs, argued the company, that required competitive sales techniques, evening and night work, or recreational and mechanical interests that women did not have. It had tried to find women to work in these areas; indeed it had set up its own affirmative action program. But it had failed. This was not the fault of Sears but the result of women's deeply conditioned socialization. To buttress its contention that no appropriate pool of women workers existed, Sears called in a historian to argue that women had historically placed their home roles ahead of labor force commitments and would indeed be uninterested in the jobs in question.

As the EEOC's rebuttal witness, I argued that throughout the twentieth century, women had worked at a variety of jobs when and as opportunity had become available; that, like men, they worked for income to support themselves and their families; and that given the potentially high rewards of commission sales, it was hard to imagine that sufficient numbers of women could not be found to fill the jobs that Sears claimed to have made available to women. Their failure to appear in these jobs was surely a reflection of Sears's discriminatory hiring patterns rather than of women's choices or desires.

I argued to no avail. Judge John Nordberg, who heard the case without a jury, ruled for Sears. Convinced that some women "feared or disliked the perceived 'dog-eat-dog' competition" while others expressed "fear of being unable to compete, being unsuccessful, and of losing their jobs," he concluded that women were "more interested than men in the social and cooperative aspects of the workplace" and therefore less interested in commission sales jobs.[1] A three-judge appeals panel divided two to one, with the majority concurring in Nordberg's assessment that women simply preferred jobs with "more social contact and friendship, less pressure and less risk." A single judge took strong issue with this perspective, condemning it for repeating "the same stereotypical qualities for which [women] have been assigned low-status positions throughout history." That judge, Howard Cudahy, puzzled at "the willingness of the district court and the majority to accept the 'interest' defense uncritically, and without recognition of its close parallel to the stereotypes that Title VII seeks to eradicate."[2]

Like many who followed the case and its outcome, I interpreted the loss as a setback to the momentum of women's economic independence.[3] For if women's lack of interest, their own choices, were thought to account for their skewed labor market distribution, then few employers could be held responsible for discrimination. Other courts have since come to that conclusion, and the decision in the Sears case has been effectively nullified.[4] Still, the case vividly illuminates the historical process traced in this book. For women, family attachment has vied with individual rights; dependence and protection with autonomy and liberty; and tradition with the market. The case reveals the continuing force and tenacity of the gendered imagination even as it suggests the ways that alternative visions of gendered equity try to write themselves into law and policy.

The EEOC's case against Sears was rooted in the effort to undermine the sex-segregated labor market that had infected the American experience and that still characterized the decade of the 1970s. That effort sometimes took the form of affirmative action. It stemmed from a widespread desire to test the belief that women's commitments to home and family explained their absence from particular sectors of the labor force—a belief that, as we have seen, was supported by several generations of social policy in a variety of arenas. In this view, women's preferences contributed to their choosing jobs that reflected their presumed nurturing qualities and that accommodated attachment to the home. If women were underpaid, according to this perspective, they had no one to blame but themselves for crowding into jobs that responded to market conditions. By 1973, when the EEOC first informed Sears that it was under investigation, many people accepted the possibility that women could be barred from good jobs, while continuing to believe that they were also responsible for their own choices. Sex discrimination could be imagined in two forms: as the overt refusal of employers to train, hire, and promote women; and as the indirect consequence of subtle signals that discouraged women from reaching for certain kinds of work.

In the summer of 1973, Martha Griffiths presided over a set of hearings sponsored by Congress's Joint Economic Committee that revealed both kinds of discrimination. In those hot July days, few of the twenty members of this prestigious committee attended; often Griffiths sat alone, complaining impatiently about witnesses who were late and listening to experts lament the absence of men to hear the testimony. Perhaps the resistance was to be expected. This was the third major set of hearings on issues of female equality in the span of four years. Yet Griffiths persisted. Over seven long days, she gathered the testimony of experts on the economic problems of women: on problems with credit, insurance, taxes, transfer payments, Social Security and private pensions, earnings, and employment. All this, to help Congress formulate "a comprehensive economic policy which includes women as first class citizens."[5]

As she questioned witness after witness, the language written into the social policies of half a century reverberated eerily through the hearing room, and the gendered imagery inscribed into social policy recurred. But what had once seemed fair now took on the shape of oppression. Tax expert Grace Ganz Blumberg complained about inequitable taxes on two-earner families. Aggregating the family income for tax purposes, she argued, constitutes "a substantial work deterrent both in economic and normative terms" to wives. This applied, as she carefully explained, to all secondary family wage earners—but that most often meant women. Taxing each worker individually would cost high-income single earners more, but then, they benefited from the services of imputed income generated by a nonearning spouse. Economist Carolyn Shaw Bell noted the discouragement of married women whose Social Security contributions yielded very little "over what she would have received as her husband's dependent." Robert Ball, a former Social Security commissioner, agreed that this was a major inequity in the system. Griffiths, critical as ever, inveighed against the use of "secondary earner," arguing that it translated "in the Department of Labor into secondary rights and they always inhere to the woman in the family. Over in Social Security, it translates into secondary rights. And so her beneficiaries get no benefits out of her Social Security." Margaret Dahm, the Labor Department's expert on unemployment insurance, protested the system's refusal to provide benefits for women who left work for domestic or marital reasons or pregnancy. It was time, she said, to recognize "women workers as bona fide members of the labor force, entitled to be considered as individuals on the same basis as men."[6]

By now deeply rooted in the interstices of all kinds of social policies, gender had become perhaps their principal operating mechanism, the core rationale for important distributional decisions, and no longer invisible. But not everyone thought anything could or should be done. Economist Joseph Pechman shrugged his shoulders over the irrationalities that income splitting produced for married women with earned income. Income splitting was tolerated, he thought, "because it gives a very substantial tax benefit to families, and therefore seems to be the right thing to do." Nor could Margaret Dahm conceive that simple statutory alterations would solve the problem of differential treatment of unemployed women. Determining whether an individual was available for work was, after all, "a matter of judgment."[7] And the general consensus presumed women to be more eager to take time off than men.

The courts experienced no less difficulty in drawing a line between custom and tradition on the one hand and discrimination on the other. Before the passage of Title VII, they had little trouble concluding that, at the discretion of state legislatures, sex could constitute an appropriate classification. The rapid changes of the next decade left them confused and unclear, utterly failing, in one commentator's words, "to recognize sex discrimination as a pervasive problem deriving from ancient preconceptions about the role of sex in determining a person's social functions."[8] By 1971, they had concluded that, unlike race, sex, while subject to some degree of scrutiny, might continue to be a reasonable classification, if it had some rational relationship to state interests. But what did that mean? Rejecting "stereotyped" images of women, the Supreme Court decided that school boards could not dismiss pregnant teachers in their fifth months.[9] Accepting those images as suitable, the Court agreed that Florida's aged widows appropriately paid a little less tax than widowers; sometime later, it also concurred that young women need not risk the dangers of military conscription.[10] Clearly, the justices had not transcended what Justice Thurgood Marshall later described as powerful assumptions embedding "their unstated points of comparison inside categories that bury their perspective and wrongly imply a natural fit with the world."[11]

Heedless of the confusion in Congress and the judiciary, and often hoping to persuade particular judges to its point of view, the 1973 EEOC took the liberal end of this debate. That was the year that it successfully concluded a major class action case against AT&T, then the monopoly telephone company in many parts of the country. The agreement heralded other victories. It was the year that the Coalition of Labor Union Women met for the first time; the year that the AFL-CIO finally came around to supporting the equal rights amendment. And it was the year the *Economic Report of the President*, which acknowledged women's economic progress, officially regretted their failure to achieve full equality in the labor market. This was, the Council of Economic Advisors wrote, partly a consequence of "direct discrimination" and partly "the result of more subtle and complex factors originating in cultural patterns that have grown up in most societies through the centuries."[12] The only important question remaining, and it was crucial, was whether statutory revision could bring about such a change. The distinguished economist Paul Samuelson thought it might, as did Elizabeth Duncan Koontz, recently resigned as director of the Department of Labor's Women's Bureau.[13]

Good grounds existed for optimism, beginning with the municipal official who cheerfully told a reporter that with all the racial discrimination laws on the books, it would be "a snap" to implement new federal guidelines on sex: "We just take them and add 'and sex.'"[14] At the 1973 hearings, the idea of ending sex discrimination exercised a palpable presence, its parameters more broadly and inclusively defined. Paul Samuelson characterized sex discrimination as "attitude-conditioned" and explained that it functioned in "a self-fulfilling and a self-perpetuating circle." Koontz drew no objections when she referred to "prevailing cultural conditioning" as the source of preferences for men in job training programs. To correct it would require what Margaret Dahm of the Labor Department called a "change in attitude."[15] And if sixteen short years ago the National Manpower Commission's report *Womanpower* had argued that overt discrimination was the only appropriate subject for legislation, rejecting out of hand the idea that "discrimination exists wherever women are treated differently from men," the tide had now decisively turned.[16]

By 1979, when the EEOC, having failed to conciliate, filed suit against Sears, the commission acted from the conviction that social attitudes toward women's traditional roles had altered, even as efforts to achieve individual rights for women persisted and strengthened.

The EEOC relied on this shift as it planned its courtroom strategy for the 1984 trial. It constructed statistical tables as if all women believed and behaved like men when it came to the workforce and passed lightly over the possibility that residual attachments to the home might shrink the pool of available workers. Sears made the opposite assumption. It presented a case that depicted old social attitudes among women as barriers powerful enough to prevent them from applying for its commission sales jobs; at the same time, it assured the court that it had trained its personnel officers to overlook their own negative attitudes and to treat men and women evenhandedly. To Sears's inestimable advantage, Judge Nordberg shared the habits of mind to which the company appealed. In court, he repeatedly placed evidence in the context of his own experience and that of his wife, convinced that his own family experience provided the standard for judging the desires of the wage-earning women who typically sought jobs at Sears. As legal expert Joan Williams concludes, he sided with Sears because their legal arguments reflected a social reality he understood and implicitly believed.[17]

A couple of years later, Supreme Court Justice Antonin Scalia put words into the kind of reasoning that might well have been behind the successful argument in Sears. Diane Joyce applied for a job as a California road construction supervisor; though her scores were slightly lower than those of Paul Johnson, her experience was equivalent, and in light of the fact that no woman had ever been hired for this job, she got it. Johnson sued all the way to the Supreme Court, whose majority affirmed Joyce's claim to the job. Scalia vigorously dissented, arguing that the majority had given its approval to a "rank form of social engineering." Social attitudes, he argued, caused women to choose certain kinds of jobs and avoid others; it was, he thought, absurd to attribute the absence of women on road maintenance crews "to systematic exclusion of women eager to shoulder pick and shovel." The majority had "manipulated the law in order to sanction social attiudes, a direction sanctioned neither by statute nor by the Constitution."[18]

Scalia's comments reveal both the extent to which the tide had turned and the degree to which, even when they become visible, gendered perspectives remain in the sphere of the natural. Scalia could see the social attitudes that encouraged women to make particular job choices; he could even acknowledge that these attitudes had "nefarious" effects. But he could not participate in destroying the social and historical linkages that perpetuated them. His comments suggest the importance of understanding not only the ways in which traditional habits of mind have become embedded in our legislative, judicial, and policy-making apparatus but the difficulties of redefining social policies in the light of persistent gendered tensions surrounding them. They warn us that constraints on the choices women and men make govern the possibilities for securing equity and achieving the goal of full economic independence for women. And they suggest the complicated ways that informal as well as formal rules constrain options in tension with a historical process that has yet to reach its conclusion.

# NOTES

## Introduction

1. Nolan Breedlove v. T. E. Suttles, Tax Collector 302 U.S. 277 (1937).

2. Goesaert et al. v. Cleary et al., 335 U.S. 464 (1948).

3. Gøsta Esping-Andersen, *The Three Worlds of Welfare Capitalism* (Princeton: Princeton University Press, 1990), 11.

4. I am indebted to Eileen Boris for the term *racialized gender*. See her use of it in " 'You Wouldn't Want One of 'Em Dancing with Your Wife': Racialized Bodies on the Job in WWII," *American Quarterly* 50 (March 1998), 77–108.

5. See especially the pathbreaking work of Joan Kelly, whose landmark essay "The Social Relations of the Sexes: Methodological Implications of Women's History," in her *Women, History, and Theory* (Chicago: University of Chicago Press, 1984), 1–18, provided the inspiration for this direction. More recently, the work of Joan Wallach Scott has become a touchstone; see "Gender: A Useful Category of Historical Analysis," in her *Gender and the Politics of History* (New York: Columbia University Press, 1988), 28–50; and see Bonnie Smith, *The Gender of History: Men, Women, and Historical Practice* (Cambridge: Harvard University Press, 1998); Elizabeth Kamarck Minnich, *Transforming Knowledge* (Philadelphia: Temple University Press, 1990).

6. Alice Kessler-Harris, *A Woman's Wage: Historical Meanings and Social Consequences* (Lexington: University Press of Kentucky, 1990).

7. Carol Pateman, *The Sexual Contract* (Stanford: Stanford University Press, 1988), 41.

8. Quoted in John Andrews and W.D.P. Bliss, *A History of Women in Trade Unions*, vol. 10 of *Report on Condition of Woman and Child Earners in the United States*, Senate Doc. 645, 61st Cong., 2d sess. (Washington, D.C.: GPO, 1911), 48.

9. These examples can be found in Alice Kessler-Harris, *Out to Work: A History of Wage-Earning Women in the United States* (New York: Oxford University Press, 1982), 79, 83, 85.

10. Joan Wallach Scott, *Only Paradoxes to Offer: French Feminists and the Rights of Man* (Cambridge: Harvard University Press, 1996), chs. 2 and 3. The international connections are documented in Bonnie Anderson, *Joyous Greetings: The First International Women's Movement, 1830–1860* (New York: Oxford University Press, 2000); and see Ulla Wikander, "Some 'Kept the Flag of Feminist Demands Waving': Debates at International Congresses on Protecting Women Workers," in Wikander, Alice Kessler-Harris, and Jane

Lewis, eds., *Protecting Women: Labor Legislation in Europe, the United States, and Australia, 1880–1920* (Urbana: University of Illinois Press, 1995), 29–62.

11. Deborah Gray White, *Too Heavy a Load* (New York: Norton, 1998); Paula Giddings, *When and Where I Enter: The Impact of Black Women on Race and Sex in America* (New York: Bantam, 1984); on the issue of dual consciousness, see Peggie R. Smith, "Separate Identities: Black Women, Work, and Title VII," *Harvard Women's Law Journal* 14 (Spring 1991), 21–75.

12. Nancy Cott, *The Grounding of Modern Feminism* (New Haven: Yale University Press, 1987), ch. 4; also see Kessler-Harris, *Out to Work*, ch. 7.

13. White, *Too Heavy a Load*; Glenda Elizabeth Gilmore, *Gender and Jim Crow: Women and the Politics of White Supremacy in North Carolina, 1896–1920* (Chapel Hill: University of North Carolina Press, 1996); for a more general discussion of the issues of race in women's history, see Evelyn Brooks Higginbotham, "African-American Women's History and the Metalanguage of Race," *Signs* 17 (Winter 1992), 251–74.

14. I focus on the divide between African Americans and whites up until the 1960s, not to denigrate the racialism that undergirded relations between whites and other groups, including Hispanics and Asian Americans, but because this was then the salient legislative issue. Until 1950, African Americans constituted between 10 and 12 percent of the whole population and 92 percent of the nonwhite population.

15. T. H. Marshall, *Citizenship and Social Class and Other Essays* (Cambridge: Cambridge University Press, 1950), 15, 17. Some theorists have also seen in equal citizenship rights the source of self-respect, making the denial of them to women a source of lagging social and self-expectation. See Kenneth L. Karst, "The Supreme Court: 1976 Term," *Harvard Law Review* 91 (November 1977), 7–9.

16. Jon Elster, "Is There (or Should There Be) a Right to Work?" in Amy Gutmann, ed., *Democracy and the Welfare State* (Princeton: Princeton University Press, 1988), 56.

17. Walter Korpi, "The Institutionalization of Citizenship: Class, Gender, and Citizenship Rights," paper delivered at Conference on State Welfare and Citizenship Rights, Stockholm University, August 1997, p. 17.

18. Marshall, *Citizenship and Social Class*, 18.

19. *Truax v. Raich*, 239 U.S. 33 (1915), 41.

20. Quoting a speech he originally made before Congress on December 30, 1930, *Hearings before a Subcommittee of the Committee on Banking and Currency on Full Employment Act of 1945, S. 380*, 79th Cong., 1st sess., July 30–September 1 (Washington, D.C.: GPO, 1945), 1.

21. In "Treating the Male as Other: Re-defining the Parameters of Labor History," *Labor History* 34 (Spring-Summer 1993), 190–204, I argue that class is a function of the household as much as of work. Here, I invert that argument to suggest that gender is a function of "work" as much as of the household.

22. Carol Pateman, *The Sexual Contract* (Stanford: Stanford University Press, 1988); see also Susan James, "The Good-Enough Citizen: Citizenship and Independence," in Gisela Bock and Susan James, eds., *Beyond Equality and Difference: Citizenship, Feminist Politics, Female Subjectivity* (New York: Routledge, 1992), 52–53, on the restraints imposed by motherhood and wifehood. See Pateman's essay "Equality, Difference, Subordination: The Politics of Motherhood and Women's Citizenship," ibid., 17–31, for her use of Marshall.

23. Helga Hernes, *Welfare State and Woman Power: Essays in State Feminism* (Oslo: Norwegian

University Press, 1987); Diane Sainsbury, *Gender, Equality, and Welfare States* (Cambridge: Cambridge University Press, 1996).

24. Judith Shklar, *American Citizenship: The Quest for Inclusion* (Cambridge: Harvard University Press, 1991), 98–99 and ch. 2. Shklar argues that a presumption of the right to work has existed since Jacksonian times.

25. Hernes, *Welfare State and Woman Power*, ch. 2, esp. 35–37; and see Ann Phillips, *Engendering Democracy* (London: Polity Press, 1991), 83–84, on the relationship between political representation and economic power in the Nordic countries. Susan James also makes use of the notion of economic independence as a vehicle for political participation; see "The Good-Enough Citizen," 54.

26. Reprinted in Stuart Kaufman, ed., *The Samuel Gompers Papers*, vol. 4, *1895–1898* (Urbana: University of Illinois Press, 1991), 498.

27. Quoted in Ronald W. Schatz, *The Electrical Workers: A History of Labor at General Electric and Westinghouse, 1923–60* (Urbana: University of Illinois Press, 1983), 16.

28. Bryan S. Turner, "Citizenship Studies: A General Theory," *Citizenship Studies* 1 (February 1997), 12; for my own previous uses of the term, see esp. Alice Kessler-Harris, "Gender Identity: Rights to Work and the Idea of Economic Citizenship," *Schweizerische Zeitschrift für Geschichte* 46 (1996), 411–26.

29. Frank Parkin, *Class Inequality and Political Order: Social Stratification in Capitalist and Communist Societies* (New York: Praeger, 1971), ch. 3.

30. Anna Shola Orloff and Theda Skocpol, "Why Not Equal Protection? Explaining the Politics of Public Spending in Britain, 1900–1911, and the United States, 1880s to 1920," *American Sociological Review* 49 (December 1984), 726–50; Seth Koven and Sonya Michel, "Womanly Duties: Maternalist Politics and the Origins of Welfare States in France, Germany, Great Britain, and the United States, 1880–1920," *American Historical Review* 95 (October 1990), 1076–108; Pat Thane, *The Foundations of the Welfare State* (New York: Longman, 1982); Jane Lewis, "Gender, the Family, and Women's Agency in the Building of 'Welfare States': The British Case," *Social History* 19 (January 1994), 37–55.

31. Robyn Muncy, *Creating a Female Dominion in American Reform, 1890–1935* (New York: Oxford University Press, 1991); Landon R. Y. Storrs, "Gender and the Development of the Regulatory State: The Controversy over Restricting Women's Night Work in the Depression-Era South," *Journal of Policy History* 10, no. 2 (1998), 181–205. This recent work suggests that women's networks promoted legislation that in the end hindered women's economic citizenship.

32. Kessler-Harris, *Out to Work*, ch. 7, for example, and Eileen Boris, *Home to Work: Motherhood and the Politics of Industrial Homework in the United States* (New York: Cambridge University Press, 1994), argue that protective labor legislation had long-term harmful effects for poor women. Katherine Kish Sklar, "The Historical Foundations of Women's Power in the Creation of the American Welfare State," in Seth Koven and Sonya Michel, eds., *Mothers of a New World* (New York: Routledge, 1991), 43–93, suggests that these effects were benign. Similarly, Joanne L. Goodwin, *Gender and the Politics of Welfare Reform: Mothers' Pensions in Chicago, 1911–1929* (Chicago: University of Chicago Press, 1997), and Molly Ladd Taylor, *Mother-Work: Women, Child Welfare, and the State, 1890–1930* (Urbana: University of Illinois Press, 1994), argue that mothers' pensions effectively discriminated against women of color and those who violated traditional

family norms. Muncy, *Creating a Female Dominion*, focuses on the positive consequences of this legislation. "Mother-citizens": Ruth Lister, *Citizenship: Feminist Perspectives* (New York: New York University Press, 1997).

33. See Nancy Fraser and Linda Gordon, "A Genealogy of 'Dependency': Tracing a Keyword of the U.S. Welfare State," in Nancy Fraser, *Justice Interruptus: Critical Reflections on the 'Postsocialist' Moment* (New York: Routledge, 1997), on dependence and differential male/female citizenship.

34. Stephen Skowronek, *Building a New American State: The Expansion of National Administrative Capacities, 1877–1920* (New York: Cambridge University Press, 1982); Theda Skocpol and Gretchen Ritter, "Gender and the Origins of Modern Social Policies in Britain and the United States," *Studies in American Political Development* 5 (Spring 1991), 36–93; Theda Skocpol, *Protecting Soldiers and Mothers: The Political Origins of Social Policy in the United States* (Cambridge: Harvard University Press, 1992); Anne Shola Orloff, *The Politics of Pensions: A Comparative Analysis of Britain, Canada, and the United States, 1880–1940* (Madison: University of Wisconsin Press, 1993).

35. Edward D. Berkowitz, *America's Welfare State: From Roosevelt to Reagan* (Baltimore: Johns Hopkins University Press, 1991); Colin Gordon, *New Deals: Business, Labor, and Politics in America, 1920–1935* (New York: Cambridge University Press, 1994); Jill Quadagno, *The Transformation of Old Age Security: Class and Politics in the American Welfare State* (Chicago: University of Chicago Press, 1988).

36. Goodwin, *Gender and the Politics of Welfare Reform*; Gwendolyn Mink, *The Wages of Motherhood: Inequality in the Welfare State, 1917–1942* (Ithaca: Cornell University Press, 1995); Linda Gordon, *Pitied but Not Entitled: Single Mothers and the History of Welfare* (New York: Free Press, 1994); see also several of the essays in Koven and Michel, *Mothers of a New World*.

37. Barbara Nelson, "The Origins of the Two-Channel Welfare State: Workmen's Compensation and Mothers' Aid," in Linda Gordon, ed., *Women, the State, and Welfare* (Madison: University of Wisconsin Press, 1990), 123–51.

38. I distinguish here between questions of how welfare states affect women and how women participate in the making of the welfare state; the former is the subject of Mimi Abramovitz, *Regulating the Lives of Women: Social Welfare Policy from Colonial Times to the Present* (Boston: South End Press, 1988). Deliberate efforts to segregate the rewards offered to men and women in the workforce form the subjects of other explorations of the 1930s legislation that established the American version of the welfare state; see esp. Suzanne Mettler, *Dividing Citizens: Gender and Federalism in New Deal Public Policy* (Ithaca: Cornell University Press, 1998), and Landon R. Y. Storrs, *Civilizing Capitalism: The National Consumers' League and the Politics of 'Fair' Labor Standards in the New Deal Era* (Chapel Hill: University of North Carolina Press, 2000).

39. Michael Walzer, *Spheres of Justice: A Defense of Pluralism and Equality* (New York: Basic Books, 1983), 240.

## Chapter 1

1. U.S. Congress, *Hearings before a Subcommittee of the Committee on Banking and Currency on Full Employment Act of 1945*, S. 380, 79th Cong., 1st sess., July 30–September 1 (Washington, D.C.: GPO, 1945), 1–2. Hereafter, Senate, *Full Employment Hearings, 1945*.

2. Ibid., 12. Seemingly gender-neutral support was not limited to Democrats. Thomas

Dewey's 1944 acceptance speech for the Republican presidential nomination had declared unequivocally that "by full employment I mean a real chance for every man and woman to earn a decent living." Russell A. Nixon in Alan Gartner, William Lynch Jr., and Frank Riessman, eds., *A Full Employment Program for the 1970s* (New York: Praeger, 1976), 16.

3. Quoted from the 1945 Murray-Wagner bill's Declaration of Policy, Senate, *Full Employment Hearings, 1945*, p. 6.

4. Ibid., 19. Murdock also objected mildly to the schooling clause as being overly broad.

5. Ibid., 29.

6. Joan Scott, *Only Paradoxes to Offer: French Feminists and the Rights of Man* (Cambridge: Harvard University Press, 1996); Ulla Wikander, "Political and Economic Citizenship in the International Women's Movement at the Turn of the 20th Century," in Birgit Christensen, ed., *Demokratie und Geschlecht* (Zürich: Chronos, 1999), 53–74; Nancy Cott, *The Grounding of Modern Feminism* (New Haven: Yale University Press, 1987).

7. David Montgomery, *Worker's Control in America: Studies in the History of Work, Technology, and Labor Struggles* (New York: Cambridge University Press, 1979), chs. 1 and 2; Ava Baron, "An 'Other' Side of Gender Antagonism at Work: Men, Boys, and the Remasculinization of Printers' Work, 1830–1920," in Baron, ed., *Work Engendered: Toward a New History of American Labor* (Ithaca: Cornell University Press, 1991); Anthony Rotundo, *American Manhood: Transformation in Masculinity from the Revolution to the Modern Era* (New York: Basic Books, 1993), ch. 8.

8. For the racial assumptions of free labor, see David R. Roediger, *The Wages of Whiteness: Race and the Making of the American Working Class* (London: Verso, 1991). Its patriarchal assumptions have yet to be fully explored, but for a start, see Jonathan A. Glickstein, *Concepts of Free Labor in Antebellum America* (New Haven: Yale University Press, 1991), 11–16. See also Eric Foner's now classic *Free Soil, Free Labor, Free Men: The Ideology of the Republican Party before the Civil War* (New York: Oxford University Press, 1970). For the relationship of race and slavery to the idea of women's free labor, see Amy Dru Stanley, *From Bondage to Contract: Wage Labor, Marriage, and the Market in the Age of Slave Emancipation* (New York: Cambridge University Press, 1998). For legal developments in the Gilded Age, see William Forbath, "The Ambiguities of Free Labor: Labor and the Law in the Gilded Age," *Wisconsin Law Review* (1985), 767–817; Mary Ann Clawson, *Constructing Brotherhood: Class, Gender, and Fraternalism* (Princeton: Princeton University Press, 1989).

9. I am indebted to Ulla Wikander for pointing out in conversation that the idea of women's economic freedom was everywhere more threatening than that of political participation. Wikander suggests the possibility of a "trade-off" by which political rights are granted while economic opportunity remains constrained.

10. T. H. Marshall, *Essays in Citizenship and Social Class* (Cambridge: Cambridge University Press, 1950), 33, 24.

11. The most acerbic analysis of this legislation is still Roscoe Pound, "Liberty of Contract," *Yale Law Journal* 18 (May, 1909), 44–87. The relevant cases begin with *The Butchers' Benevolent Association of New Orleans v. The Crescent City Livestock Lending and Slaughter-House Company*, 16 Wall. 36 (1873); this case is one of several known as the *Slaughter-House Cases*, 83 U.S. 394 (1873), which sets precedents that proceed through *Joseph Lochner v. People of State of New York*, 198 U.S. 45 (1905).

12. As in Britain, the state was theoretically responsible only for providing a fair field and

no favors. See Jane Lewis and Sonya O. Rose, "Let England Blush: Protective Labor Legislation, 1820–1914," in Ulla Wikander, Alice Kessler-Harris, and Jane Lewis, eds., *Protecting Women: Labor Legislation in Europe, the United States, and Australia, 1880–1920* (Urbana: University of Illinois Press, 1995), 91–124. For voluntarism, the classic source is Selig Perlman, *A Theory of the Labor Movement* (New York: Macmillan, 1928); and see George Gilmary Higgins, *Voluntarism in Organized Labor in the United States, 1930–1940* (New York: Arno and New York Times, 1969 [1944]), and William Forbath, *Law and the Shaping of the American Labor Movement* (Cambridge: Harvard University Press, 1991).

13. On exclusions from apprenticeships, see Ava Baron, "Questions of Gender: Deskilling and Demasculinization in the U.S. Printing Industry, 1830–1915," *Gender and History* 1 (Summer 1989), 178–99, and "Women and the Making of the American Working Class: A Study of the Proletarianization of Printers," *Review of Radical Political Economics* 14 (Fall 1982), 23–42. On women's entrepreneurship, see esp. Wendy Gamber, *The Female Economy: The Millinery and Dressmaking Trades, 1860–1930* (Urbana: University of Illinois Press, 1997), and April F. Masten, "The Work of Art: American Women Artists and Market Democracy, 1820–1880," Ph.D. diss., Rutgers University, 1998.

14. *Slaughter-House Cases*, 16 Wall. 36, (1873); *Myra Bradwell v. State of Illinois*, 16 Wall. 130 (1873), 141, 143. A discussion of the relationship between the two cases is in Joan Hoff, *Law, Gender, and Injustice: A Legal History of U.S. Women* (New York: New York University Press, 1991), 165–170. The Court reaffirmed Bradley's reasoning twenty years later when it declared that denying women admission to the bar did not violate the privileges and immunities section of the Fourteenth Amendment; *In re Lockwood*, 154 U.S. 116 (1894).

15. For an extensive discussion of women's labor in this period, see Alice Kessler-Harris, *Out to Work: A History of Wage-Earning Women in the United States* (New York: Oxford University Press, 1982).

16. John Stuart Mill, *The Subjection of Women* (Cambridge: MIT Press, 1970 [1869]), 50.

17. These strategies affirmed male-breadwinner roles that later became the locus for many (but not all) welfare states' legislation; see Jane Lewis, ed., *Women's Welfare, Women's Rights* (London: Croom Helm, 1983). But such developments were by no means inevitable, as Lena Sommestad's multiple-breadwinner model suggests for Sweden, Lena Sommestad, "Private or Public Welfare? A Gender-Based Perspective on the History of the Formation of the Welfare State," *Historisk Tidskrift* [Sweden] 4 (1994), 601–29. Nor was the dichotomy between citizenship and work inevitable for women. In France, for example, as Laura Frader and Susan Pedersen separately demonstrate, women adopted a discourse of work and family and argued for social rights of citizenship to sustain both roles; Laura L. Frader, "Engendering Work and Wages: The French Labor Movement and the Family Wage," in Frader and Sonya O. Rose, eds., *Gender and Class in Modern Europe* (Ithaca: Cornell University Press, 1996), 142–64, and Susan Pedersen, *Family, Dependence, and the Origins of the Welfare State: Britain and France, 1914–1945* (Cambridge: Cambridge University Press, 1993).

18. Rev. Anna Garlin Spencer, "Fitness of Women to Become Citizens from the Standpoint of Moral Development," in Mari Jo and Paul Buhle, eds., *The Concise History of Woman Suffrage* (Urbana: University of Illinois Press, 1978), 365.

19. Norma Basch, *In the Eyes of the Law: Women, Marriage, and Property in Nineteenth-Century New York* (Ithaca: Cornell University Press, 1982), esp. ch. 5.

20. Reva Siegel, "The Modernization of Marital Status Law: Adjudicating Wives' Rights to Earnings, 1860–1930," *Georgetown Law Journal* 82 (September 1994), 2164.

21. For a discussion of the emergence of the family wage, see Alice Kessler-Harris, *A Woman's Wage: Historical Meanings and Social Consequences* (Lexington: University Press of Kentucky, 1990) ch. 1. For "provider" ideology, see Anna Rachel Igra, "Other Men's Wives and Children: Anti-Desertion Reform in New York, 1900–1935," Ph.D. diss., Rutgers University, 1996; Lawrence B. Glickman, *A Living Wage: American Workers and the Making of Consumer Society* (Ithaca: Cornell University Press, 1997); and Joanne L. Goodwin, *Gender and the Politics of Welfare Reform: Mothers' Pensions in Chicago, 1911–1929* (Chicago: University of Chicago Press, 1997).

22. Virginia Penny, *Think and Act: A Series of Articles Pertaining to Men and Women, Work and Wages* (Philadelphia: Claxton, Remsen and Haffelfinger, 1869), 28–29; Laura Vapnek, "The Idea of Independence among Wage-Earning Women," Ph.D. diss., Columbia University, 1999.

23. Charlotte Perkins Gilman, *Women and Economics: A Study of the Economic Relation between Men and Women as a Factor in Social Evolution* (New York: Dover, 1998), 167.

24. "The Tragedy of Woman's Emancipation," in *Red Emma Speaks: Selected Writings and Speeches by Emma Goldman*, ed. Alix Kates Shulman (New York: Vintage, 1972), 136, 36.

25. Stephanie J. Shaw, *What a Woman Ought to Be and to Do: Black Professional Women Workers during the Jim Crow Era* (Chicago: University of Chicago Press, 1996). Shaw notes that though African-American women expressed skepticism about the efficacy of marriage for support, they nevertheless found it reduced their capacity to earn, often for reasons not of their own choosing (114–33). Paradoxically, the numbers of women of color in the workforce in low-paying jobs may have helped to affirm racial bias by sharpening racial distinctions among women. See Evelyn Brooks Higginbotham, "African-American Women's History and the Metalanguage of Race," *Signs* 17 (Winter 1992), 251–74, and Tera W. Hunter, *To 'Joy My Freedom: Southern Black Women's Lives and Labors after the Civil War* (Cambridge: Harvard University Press, 1997), ch. 5.

26. In *Bradwell*, the majority opinion ducked the issue by ceding it to the separate states.

27. *William E. Ritchie v. People of the State of Illinois*, 155 Ill. 98 (1895), 98, 113, 111. Related cases are summarized in Felix Frankfurter, "Hours of Labor and Realism in Constitutional Law," *Harvard Law Review* 29 (February 1916), 353–73; contrast this discussion with that in Pound, "Liberty of Contract," esp. 475–76.

28. *Commonwealth v. Beatty*, 15 Pa. Sup. Ct. 5 (1900), 16; John R. Commons and John B. Andrews, *Principles of Labor Legislation* (New York: Harper & Brothers, 1936), 112; and see the discussion in Ronnie Steinberg, *Wages and Hours: Labor and Reform in Twentieth-Century America* (New Brunswick: Rutgers University Press, 1982), 76.

29. Pound, "Liberty of Contract," 463.

30. *People v. Williams*, 189 N.Y. 131 (1907), 131.

31. *Curt Muller v. State of Oregon*, 208 U.S. 412 (1908), 421–24.

32. Frankfurter, "Hours of Labor and Realism in Constitutional Law," 365, 367. On Brandeis, see Sybil Lipschultz, "Hours and Wages: The Gendering of Labor Standards in America," *Journal of Women's History* 8 (Spring 1996), 114–36.

33. Restricting the capacity of working women to make their own contracts became a major political preoccupation of a generation of men and women who often did not labor for

wages and who insisted that the families of wage-earning women deserved protection from the consequences of women's harsh working lives. The National Consumers' League led the effort nationwide, followed after about 1912 by the National Women's Trade Union League, and then by other groups like the General Federation of Women's Clubs and the American Association for Labor Legislation.

34. The question had been raised in *Ritchie v. Illinois* by the majority opinion written by Justice Magruder. Given the Court's insistence that only rights secured in the Constitution need be honored, he asked, is it "not pertinent to inquire whether married women could have made any contract when the Constitution was adopted? If they could not, would it follow that legislation could regulate the labor and wage contracts of married women but not those of unmarried women, or would the faith of the court in its distinction be shaken?"

35. *People v. Charles Schweinler Press*, 214 N.Y. 395 (1915), 401, 409, 407.

36. Sonya Michel, *Children's Interests/Mothers' Rights: The Shaping of America's Child Care Policy* (New Haven: Yale University Press, 1999), ch. 2; for Europe, see Frader, "Engendering Work and Wages," and Pedersen, *Family, Dependence, and the Origins of the Welfare State*.

37. On this point, see esp. Beatrix Rebecca Hoffman, *The Wages of Sickness: The Politics of Health Insurance in Progressive America* (Chapel Hill: University of North Carolina Press, 2001), ch. 6.

38. Elizabeth Rose, *A Mother's Job: The History of Day Care, 1890–1960* (New York: Oxford University Press, 1999), 29–30.

39. Ulla Wikander argues that in the international congresses the big division was over whether to prioritize political or economic citizenship; see "Political and Economic Citizenship," 53–72. For differences among several countries, see Wikander et al., *Protecting Women*; Helmut Gruber and Pamela Graves, *Women and Socialism/Socialism and Women: Europe between the Two World Wars* (New York: Berghahn Books, 1998); Pedersen, *Family Dependence and the Origins of the Welfare State*; Frader, "Dissent over Discourse"; and Alissa Klaus, *Every Child Is a Lion: The Origins of Maternal and Infant Health Policy in the United States and France, 1890–1920* (Ithaca: Cornell University Press, 1993).

40. The best account of the bureau's creation is still Judith Sealander, *As Minority Becomes Majority: Federal Reaction to the Phenomenon of Women in the Workforce, 1920–1963* (Westport: Greenwood Press, 1983).

41. The most nuanced discussion of this legislation is Goodwin, *Gender and the Politics of Welfare Reform*, chs. 3 and 5. See also Molly Ladd-Taylor, *Mother Work: Women, Child Welfare, and the State, 1890–1950* (Urbana: University of Illinois Press, 1994), ch. 6; J. Stanley Lemons, *The Woman Citizen* (Urbana: University of Illinois Press, 1973), ch. 6; and Theda Skocpol, *Protecting Soldiers and Mothers: The Political Origins of Social Policy in the United States* (Cambridge: Harvard University Press, 1992), ch. 9.

42. U.S. Congress, *Hearings before the Joint Committees on Labor on S. 4002, H.R. 1134, H.R. 12679: Women's Bureau*, 66th Cong., 2d sess., March 4–5, 1920 (Washington, D.C.: GPO, 1920); Hereafter, *Women's Bureau Hearings*. Nestor represented the National Legislative Committee of the National Women's Trade Union League. Quotations in this discussion are from 11 (Ruker); 23 (Nestor); 31 (Lathrop); 51 (Senator William Kenyon of Iowa); 48 (Stewart); 70 (Sterling); 10, 75–77 (Raker and MacCrate); 31, 34, 61, 81 (Lathrop and Anderson).

43. Mary Anderson, "Should There Be Labor Laws for Women? Yes," pamphlet reprinted by National Women's Trade Union League from *Good Housekeeping* (September 1925), 6, 7.
44. *Women's Bureau Hearings*, 28.
45. Dolores Hayden, *The Grand Domestic Revolution: A History of Feminist Designs for American Homes, Neighborhoods, and Cities* (Cambridge: MIT Press, 1981); Blanche Wiesen Cook, ed., *Crystal Eastman on Women and Revolution* (New York: Oxford University Press, 1978); George MacAdam, "Henrietta Rodman: An Interview with a Feminist," in June Sochen, ed., *The New Feminism in Twentieth-Century America* (Lexington: D.C. Heath, 1971), 51. Historians Susan Becker and Nancy Cott have persuasively documented the ideas of American feminists who argued in the prewar period that the "right to labor" was fundamental to women's equality and assumed after the war that economic independence was to be the next step; see Susan D. Becker, *The Origins of the Equal Rights Amendment: American Feminism between the Wars* (Westport: Greenwood Press, 1981), ch. 2, and Nancy F. Cott, *The Grounding of Modern Feminism* (New Haven: Yale University Press, 1987), ch. 4.
46. Anderson, "Should There Be Labor Laws for Women? Yes," 4. The most effective response to this piece is Alma Lutz, "Shall Women's Work Be Regulated by Law?" *Atlantic Monthly* 146 (September 1930), 321–27. Lutz took up the "right to work" issue, declaring that "too long have women been told that they must sacrifice their best interest for the good of the race" and insisting that "if man's right to work is inviolate, woman's right to work is just as inviolate" (327, 324). The best overall discussion of these issues is in Cott, *The Grounding of Modern Feminism*, ch. 4.
47. Mary N. Winslow, *Married Women in Industry*, Women's Bureau Bulletin no. 38 (Washington, D.C.: GPO, 1924).
48. Maurine Weiner Greenwald, "Working-Class Feminism and the Family Wage Ideal: The Seattle Debate on Married Women's Right to Work, 1914–1920," *Journal of American History* 76 (June 1989), 118–49; Gerald Zahavi, *Workers, Managers, and Welfare Capitalism: The Shoeworkers and Tanners of Endicott Johnson, 1890–1950* (Urbana: University of Illinois Press, 1988), looking at northeastern workers in the 1930s, argues that while substantial numbers claimed that married women's work was necessary for economic reasons, those who believed married women should not work generally drew on women's separate sphere: "Every woman's place is in the home taking care of her family, and if she has none, taking care of her house work" (75).
49. Shaw, *What a Woman Ought to Be and to Do*, ch. 4.
50. Gordon, "Black and White Visions of Welfare," 586–87; Bonnie Thornton Dill, "The Dialectics of Black Womanhood," *Signs* 4 (Spring 1979), 543–555.
51. Martin Anthony Summers, "Nationalism, Race Consciousness, and the Constructions of Black Middle-Class Masculinity during the New Negro Era, 1915–1930," Ph.D. diss., Rutgers University, 1998.
52. Melinda Chateauvert, *Marching Together: Women of the Brotherhood of Sleeping Car Porters* (Urbana: University of Illinois Press, 1998), 136–137.
53. Linda Gordon, *Pitied but Not Entitled: Single Mothers and the History of Welfare, 1890–1935* (Cambridge: Harvard University Press, 1994), ch. 5.
54. Dorothy Canfield, *The Home-Maker* (New York: Harcourt Brace, 1924). See as well Arthur S. M. Hutchinson, *This Freedom* (Boston: Little, Brown, 1922).

55. Dorothy West, *The Living Is Easy* (New York: Arno Press, reprint 1969).

56. See Cott, *The Grounding of Modern Feminism*, ch. 4, for the best summary of feminist divisions around these issues.

57. Cott, *The Grounding of Modern Feminism*; Susan Lehrer, *Origins of Protective Labor Legislations for Women, 1905–1925* (Albany: State University of New York Press, 1987); Jane J. Mansbridge, *Why We Lost the ERA* (Chicago: University of Chicago Press, 1986).

58. *The Effects of Labor Legislation on the Employment of Women*, Women's Bureau Bulletin no. 68 (Washington, D.C.: GPO, 1928), 27.

59. Frank B. Gilbreth, *Primer of Scientific Management* (New York: D. Van Nostrand, 1912), 62. On scientific management in general, see Frederick Winslow Taylor, *Scientific Management: Comprising Shop Management, the Principles of Scientific Management, Testimony before the Special House Committee* (New York: Harper & Brothers, 1947); Robert Franklin Hoxie, *Scientific Management and Labor* (New York: Augustus M. Kelley, 1966 [1915]); Milton J. Nadworny, *Scientific Management and the Unions: 1900–1932, a Historical Analysis* (Cambridge: Harvard University Press, 1955); and Samuel Haber, *Efficiency and Uplift: Scientific Management in the Progessive Era, 1980–1920* (Chicago: University of Chicago Press, 1964).

60. Harry Braverman, *Labor and Monopoly Capital: The Degradation of Work in the Twentieth Century* (New York: Monthly Review Press, 1974); Margery Davis, *A Woman's Place Is at the Typewriter: Office Work and Office Workers, 1870–1930* (Philadelphia: Temple University Press, 1982); Elyce J. Rotella, *From Home to Office: United States Women at Work, 1870–1930* (Ann Arbor: UMI Research Press, 1981); Lisa M. Fine, *The Souls of the Skyscraper: Female Clerical Workers in Chicago, 1870–1930* (Philadelphia: Temple University Press, 1990).

61. Summaries of these programs can be found in Andrea Tone, *The Business of Benevolence: Industrial Paternalism in Progressive America* (Ithaca: Cornell University Press, 1997); Stuart D. Brandes, *American Welfare Capitalism, 1880–1940* (Chicago: University of Chicago Press, 1976); Sanford M. Jacoby, *Employing Bureaucracy: Managers, Unions, and the Transformation of Work in Amerian Industry, 1900–1945* (New York: Columbia University Press, 1985). Brandes notes that a third of companies with pension programs in the 1920s required thirty years of continuous service; 87 percent required twenty years of service, in addition to an age requirement (108). Such conditions were impossible for most women to meet, even when they were formally eligible. See Daniel Nelson and Stuart Campbell, "Taylorism versus Welfare Work in American Industry: H. L. Gantt and the Bancrofts," *Business History Review* 46 (Spring 1972), 1–16, for a discussion of initial conflicts between the two systems.

62. Ronald W. Schatz, *The Electrical Workers: A History of Labor at General Electric and Westinghouse, 1923–60* (Urbana: University of Illinois Press, 1983), 20–21.

63. Stephen Meyer III, *The Five Dollar Day: Labor Management and Social Control in the Ford Motor Company, 1908–1921* (Albany: State University of New York Press, 1981), 117. The profit-sharing system fell apart in 1920, partly as a result of worker resentment against intrusive investigations into their domestic arrangements, and partly out of the inflationary pressures that increased wages and cut into profits. Wayne A. Lewchuk, "Men and Monotony: Fraternalism as a Managerial Strategy at the Ford Motor Company," *Journal of Economic History* 53 (December 1993), 824–56; Martha May, "The Historical Problem of the Family Wage: The Ford Motor Company and the Five Dollar Day," *Feminist Studies* 8 (Summer 1982), 399–424.

64. Gerard Swope, "Management Cooperation with Workers for Economic Welfare," *Annals of the American Academy of Political and Social Science* 154 (March 1931), 131–132.

65. Ibid., 135.

66. Brandes, *American Welfare Capitalism,* 5, 35.

67. Zahavi, *Workers, Managers, and Welfare Capitalism,* 72–73.

68. The original published source describing and summarizing these experiments is F. J. Roethlisberger and William J. Dickson, *Management and the Worker: An Account of a Research Program Conducted by the Western Electric Company, Hawthorne Works, Chicago* (Cambridge: Harvard University Press, 1964 [1939]). The exciting discovery of reveries came from the Mica Splitting Room—one of the shorter experiments that paralleled the RATR. It is recorded by G. A. Pennock, a Western Electric Company researcher, in "Industrial Research at Hawthorne: An Experimental Investigation of Rest Periods, Working Conditions, and Other Influences," *Personnel Journal* 8 (February 1930), 296–313, and drawn on by Elton Mayo in *The Human Problems of an Industrial Civilization* (New York: Macmillan, 1933), ch. 5; Mayo's interest in the psychopathology of the workers did not mesh with that of many of the company researchers who were encouraged when the more traditional W. Lloyd Warner joined the team in 1930.

69. A sixth woman determined the layout for the variety of switches on which the operators worked and acted in a semisupervisory position. The two of the original women replaced in the RATR were returned to their regular jobs. Managers accused them of not cooperating and of talking too much in the test room, noted that their production was falling, and cited the complaints (never adequately documented) of coworkers. Good friends, both insisted that they were merely following the experimenters' directives to work as they felt. When they were let go, the room adjusted quickly, and one of the two replacements, Julia, became by all acounts its leader. The fullest discussion of the RATR is in Richard Gillespie, *Manufacturing Knowledge: A History of the Hawthorne Experiments* (New York: Cambridge University Press, 1991), ch. 2. I have put this summary together from the Relay Assembly Test Room, "Records of Interviews" and "Operator Comments," Boxes 2 and 3, Western Electric Company, Hawthorne Studies Collection, Baker Library, Harvard Business School; hereafter, RATR.

70. Bank Wiring Test, Record of Interview, March 17, 1932, Box 9, Western Electric Company, Hawthorne Studies Collection, Baker Library, Harvard Business School.

71. Roethlisberger and Dickson, *Management and the Worker,* 560–61.

72. This point is made by Gillespie, *Manufacturing Knowledge,* 81, 94; and see Martha Banta, *Taylored Lives: Narrative Productions in the Age of Taylor, Veblen, and Ford* (Chicago: University of Chicago Press, 1993).

73. Roethlisberger and Dickson, *Management and the Worker,* 560.

74. Ronald Schatz confirms these findings. He concludes that as a result of the social solidarity encouraged in particular jobs, some women workers, "who ordinarily manifested little interest in unions, proved to be the most tenacious fighters in shop-floor disputes and strikes." Schatz also comments that women's sociability and solidarity at work helped to restrict their output. Schatz, *The Electrical Workers,* 33.

75. Roethlisberger and Dickson, *Management and the Worker,* 560–61; see also Henry A. Landsberger, *Hawthorne Revisited:* Management and the Worker, *Its Critics, and Developments in Human Relations Industry* (Ithaca: Cornell University Press, 1958), 74–75.

76. Roethlisberger and Dickson, *Management and the Worker*, 231.
77. Ibid., 245. This contrasts sharply with Sanford M. Jacoby's conclusions about what a male blue-collar worker in the same period might have wanted. To him, "a good job is one that pays well, offers stability and promotion opportunities, and protects against arbitrary discipline and dismissal" (*Employing Bureaucracy*, 2).
78. To support statements that follow, see Roethlisberger and Dickson, *Management and the Worker*, 238–39 and 242–43, figures 22 and 23; see also 232–33, table XXI.
79. This in contrast to the arguments of the Women's Bureau, which insisted that women did not want to work at night. Cf. Anderson, "Should There Be Labor Laws for Women? Yes."
80. Alice Kessler-Harris, "The Double Meaning of Equal Pay," in Kessler-Harris, *A Woman's Wage: Historical Meanings and Social Consequences* (Lexington: University of Kentucky Press, 1990).
81. Banta, *Taylored Lives*, 166; women who have apparently eluded the claims of family or transcended them (widows or overeducated women) are granted some of the status of "real boys," though hardly of men.
82. Meyer, *The Five Dollar Day*, 140.
83. Mary Barnett Gilson, *What's Past Is Prologue: Reflections on My Industrial Experience* (New York: Harper & Brothers, 1940), 99; see also 98, 186, 290, 122–23.
84. Ida M. Tarbell, "The New Place of Women in Industry—V: The Forewomen" *Industrial Management* 61 (February 1, 1921), 135.
85. Gilson, *What's Past Is Prologue*, 32; her thoughts echoed those of the founders of the Boston-based Bureau of Vocational Information who, in the 1920s, tried to encourage women to find paths of advancement in office jobs.
86. Western Electric Company, Hawthorne Studies Collection RATR, Carton 3, Operator Comments 1927–30. August 6, September 11, 1930.
87. Microfiche 163, Operating Branch, Employee interview no. 11, November 22, 1929, Western Electric, Hawthorne Studies Collection, Baker Library, Harvard Business School; Hawthorne microfiche 76, Bank Wiring Test Room Study, Employee Interview no. 96, January 13, 1932; Hawthorne microfiche 186, Technical Branch, Employee Interview no. 300, June 19, 1930.
88. Hawthorne microfiche 167, Operating Branch, Employee Interview no. 142, June 27, 1929, Employee Interview no. 131, May 27, 1929, and Employee Interview no. 133, May 23, 1929.
89. Hawthorne microfiche 184, Technical Branch, Employee Interview no. 287, November 11, 1930.
90. Mrs. C. C. Beach to Frances Perkins, 27 April 1933, Record Group 174 Box 183, File 838 National Archives and Records Administration Alice Kessler-Harris, "Gender Ideology in Historical Reconstruction," *Gender and History* 1 (Spring 1989), 39, has a full discussion of this issue.
91. Zahavi, *Workers, Management and Welfare Capitalism*, 74; the quotation is from the Endicott Johnson newspaper, ibid.
92. Hawthorne microfiche 163, Operating Branch, Employee Interview no. 7, August 27, 1929.
93. Western Electric Company, Hawthorne Studies Collection, RATR, Carton 3, Operator Comments, 1927–1930, April 23, May 8, 1930; Hawthorne microfiche 184, Technical Branch, Employee Interview no. 287, November 11, 1930, 18.

NOTES TO PAGES 58–60

94. Hawthorne microfiche 64, Mica Splitting Test Room Studies, Operator no. 4, March 1, 1931.
95. Hawthorne microfiche 104, Operating Branch, "Résumé of Methods, Practices, Employee Interviewing Program," April 17, 1929.
96. Hawthorne microfiche 164, Operating Branch, Employee Interview no. 52, June 3, 1929.
97. This figure comes from Lois Scharf, *To Work and to Wed: Female Employment, Feminism, and the Great Depression* (Westport: Greenwood Press, 1980), 48. Other estimates of the effects vary in detail but agree in general. The National Women's Trade Union League estimated the number of married women dismissed at 1,200, of whom 82.4 percent earned under two thousand dollars a year. Testimony of Florence Barnes, representing the National Women's Trade Union League of America, U.S. Congress, *Hearings before the House Committee on the Civil Service, on H.R. 5051: To Amend Married Person's Clause*, 74th Cong., 1st sess., April 18–24, 1935 (Washington, D.C.: GPO, 1935), 25–26; hereafter, *Civil Service Hearings, 1935*. The National League of Women Voters suggested that 75 percent of those separated from the civil service were women, 80 percent of whom earned less than two thousand dollars a year. Testimony of Mrs. Harris T. Baldwin, first vice president of the National League of Women Voters, ibid., 13. A 1934 Women's Bureau study estimated that though only 16 percent of the total number of federal government employees were women, 78 percent of those dismissed were female. Cited in testimony of Mrs. Edwin Avery, representing the Government Workers' Council, ibid., 38.
98. Testimony of Rep. Emmanuel Celler of New York, ibid., 4.
99. Ruth Shallcross, "Portrait of the Working Wife," *Independent Woman* 19 (August 1940), 234–35 and Winifred D. Wandersee, *Women's Work and Family Values, 1920–1940* (Cambridge: Harvard University Press, 1981), 100.
100. Elizabeth Faue, *Community of Suffering and Struggle: Women, Men, and the Labor Movement in Minneapolis, 1915–1945* (Chapel Hill: University of North Carolina Press, 1991), 83.
101. Cindy Sondik Aron, *Ladies and Gentlemen of the Civil Service: Middle-Class Workers in Victorian America* (New York: Oxford University Press, 1987).
102. Testimony of Florence Barnes, *Civil Service Hearings, 1935*, 24–26.
103. See testimony of Rep. James W. Taylor of Tennessee, *Congressional Record—House*, July 8, 1937, 6925. His colleague Rep. Joe Starnes of Alabama argued that the clause never barred married women from teaching, only those married women whose husbands were teaching; *Civil Service Hearings, 1935*, 21.
104. Ibid., 32.
105. In Washington, the proportion of married women was slightly higher than the national average, 8.77 percent; testimony of E. Claude Babcock, national president, American Federation of Government Employees, ibid., 56.
106. Ibid., 17.
107. Ibid., 22.
108. Testimony of Florence Barnes, ibid., 25. After an argument about the need of married women to work, Barnes continued: "Moreover as an organization that worked for 30 years that women workers may have equal pay for equal work and equal opportunity at jobs and promotions, in other words that ability not sex shall determine women's opportunities, we are alarmed at the implications in the present law. Are we to come to a time when not a person's worth but the number of his dependents is to determine

whether or not he shall work, and how much he shall be paid? Already the law requiring marital status be considered in reducing the numbers employed has been followed by an Executive Order requiring that the number of positions held by one family is likewise to be considered. What is the next step? Are heads of families to be preferred to single persons in hiring workers of unusual ability and is remuneration to be based on the number of dependents? The organized working women know that women are the first group who suffer from ideas such as these. It places in the hands of unscrupulous employers a way of hiring women cheaply on the plea that their needs are less than men. Organized women are too intelligent not to realize that the 1,200 positions opened by dismissing married women do not mean as much to them as having the Federal Government, by its word and example, stand firmly for the principles of equal opportunity, equal pay for equal work for women" (25–26).

109. Ibid., 19.

110. Included in the testimony of Mrs. Harris T. Baldwin, ibid., 13–14.

111. Kessler-Harris, *Out to Work*, ch. 8; Ruth Milkman, *Gender at Work: The Dynamics of Job Segregation by Sex during World War II* (Urbana: University of Illinois Press, 1987); Karen Anderson, *Wartime Women: Sex Roles, Family Relations, and the Status of Women during World War II* (Westport: Greenwood Press, 1981); and the wonderfully evocative film *The Life and Times of Rosie the Riveter*.

112. Senate, *Full Employment Hearings, 1945*, 17, 9–10. "Floating pool of unemployed" is Senator Murray's phrase.

113. See esp. the testimony of Rep. Wright Patman, (Texas), Senate, *Full Employment Hearings, 1945*, 60; Col. William Menninger, U.S. Army, chief, Psychiatric Division, War Department, and psychiatrist of the Menninger Clinic, Topeka, Kans., ibid., 434–35; Ralph E. Flanders, president, Jones & Lambson Machine Company and Bryant Chucking Grinder Company, chairman of the Boston Federal Reserve Bank, and chairman of the Research Committee of the Committee for Economic Development, ibid., 358; Dr. Harlow Shapley, vice president, Independent Citizens' Committee of the Arts, Sciences, and Professions and director of the Harvard Observatory, Harvard University, ibid., 783–88; Thomas K. Finletter, Washington, D.C., ibid., 795. For the House, see *Hearings before the Committee on Expenditures in the Executive Departments on H.R. 2202: Full Employment Act of 1945*, 79th Cong., 1st sess., September-November 1945 (Washington, D.C.: GPO, 1945): for Hines, 391; for the quoted questions, 182, 400, and 776; see also comments of Rep. Robert F. Rich of Pennsylvania, 54; Rep. George H. Bender of Ohio, 650–51; and James L. Donelly, executive vice president, Illinois Manufacturers' Association, 718.

114. "Report of the Department of Labor on the Full Employment Bill," ibid., 16. Perkins was still secretary of labor when this was written.

115. Ibid., 1101.

116. Ibid., 55.

117. Ibid., 20.

## Chapter 2

1. Steve Fraser, "The 'Labor Question,'" in Steve Fraser and Gary Gerstle, eds., *The Rise and Fall of the New Deal Order, 1930–1980* (Princeton: Princeton University Press, 1989), 77;

and see Howell Harris, "The Snares of Liberalism? Politicians, Bureaucrats, and the Shaping of Federal Labor Relations Policy in the United States, 1915–1947," in Steven Tolliday and Jonathan Zeitlin, eds., *Shop Floor Bargaining and the State: Historical and Comparative Perspectives* (New York: Cambridge University Press, 1985), 148–91. Among the many discussions of the new administrative state, see esp. Alan Brinkley, "The New Deal and the Idea of the State," in Fraser and Gerstle, *The Rise and Fall of the New Deal Order*, 88–92.

2. Colin Gordon put it this way: "In historical memory, of course, the New Deal is virtually synonymous with a transformation of labor relations and labor law"; Gordon, *New Deals: Business, Labor, and Politics in America, 1920–1935* (New York: Cambridge University Press, 1994), 2. See as well Stanley Vittoz, *New Deal Labor Policy and the American Industrial Economy* (Chapel Hill: University of North Carolina Press, 1987), 170, and the large literature on the new administrative state, including Fred Bloch, *Revising State Theory: Essays in Politics and Postindustrialism* (Philadelphia: Temple University Press, 1987); Dietrich Rueschemeyer and Theda Skocpol, eds., *States, Social Knowledge, and the Origins of Modern Social Policies* (Princeton: Princeton University Press, 1996); Margaret Weir, Ann Shola Orloff, and Theda Skocpol, eds., *The Politics of Social Policy in the United States* (Princeton: Princeton University Press, 1988); Peter B. Evans, Dietrich Rueschmeyer, and Theda Skocpol, eds., *Bringing the State Back In* (New York: Cambridge University Press, 1985); Ellis Hawley, *The New Deal and the Problem of Monopoly: A Study in Economic Ambivalence* (New York: Fordham University Press, 1995); and Edward D. Berkowitz, *America's Welfare State: From Roosevelt to Reagan* (Baltimore: Johns Hopkins University Press, 1991).

3. Alice Kessler-Harris, "Gender Ideology in Historical Reconstruction: A Case Study from the 1930s," *Gender and History* 1 (Spring 1989), 31–49; Lois Scharf, *To Work and to Wed: Female Employment, Feminism, and the Great Depression* (Westport: Greenwood Press, 1980); Winifred Wandersee, *Women's Work and Family Values, 1920–1940* (Cambridge: Harvard University Press, 1980).

4. Jill Quadagno, *The Transformation of Old Age Security: Class and Politics in the American Welfare State* (Chicago: University of Chicago Press, 1988); James T. Patterson, *Congressional Conservatism and the New Deal* (Lexington: University of Kentucky Press, 1967); Harvard Sitkoff, *A New Deal for Blacks: The Emergence of Civil Rights as a National Issue* (New York: Oxford University Press, 1978); Mary Poole, "Securing Race and Ensuring Dependence: The Social Security Act of 1935," Ph.D. diss., Rutgers University, 2000.

5. These policies have sometimes been identified as the products of a two-channel state that assigned most women and men of color to means-tested policies. See, for example, Barbara J. Nelson, "The Origins of the Two-Channel Welfare State: Workmen's Compensation and Mothers' Aid," in Linda Gordon, ed., *Women, the State, and Welfare* (Madison: University of Wisconsin Press, 1990), 123–51, and Gwendolyn Mink, *The Wages of Motherhood: Inequality in the Welfare State, 1917–1942* (Ithaca: Cornell University Press, 1995). They were also the product of shared assumptions about wage work, as is argued by Linda Gordon, *Pitied but Not Entitled: Single Mothers and the History of Welfare, 1890–1935* (New York: Free Press, 1994), and Joanne Goodwin, *Gender and the Politics of Welfare Reform: Mothers' Pensions in Chicago, 1911–1929* (Chicago: University of Chicago Press, 1997).

6. Raymond Williams, *Marxism and Literature* (Oxford: Oxford University Press, 1977), 128–35.

7. John Frey, in *Report of the Proceedings of the 52nd Annual Convention of the American Federation of Labor*, Cincinnati, Ohio, 1932, 342; hereafter, *Proceedings of the AFL*.

8. On the history of voluntarism in the 1930s, see George Gilmary Higgins, *Voluntarism in Organized Labor in the United States, 1930–1940* (New York: Arno and New York Times, 1969 [1944]).

9. Samuel Gompers, "Labor vs. Its Barnacles," *American Federationist* 23 (April 1916), 270.

10. Beatrix Hoffman, *The Wages of Sickness: The Politics of Health Insurance in Progressive America* (Chapel Hill: University of North Carolina Press, 2001), ch. 7; Patricia Brito, "Protective Labor Legislation in Ohio: The Interwar Years," *Ohio History* 88 (Spring 1979), 178–97.

11. Paul Scharrenberg, "Labor Legislation," in Spencer Miller, ed., *American Labor and the Nation* (Chicago: University of Chicago Press, 1933), 5.

12. Louis Reed, *The Labor Philosophy of Samuel Gompers* (New York: Columbia University Press, 1930), 126.

13. Gompers, "Labor vs. Its Barnacles," 270–71.

14. The best discussion of this is in Grant Farr, *Origins of Recent Labor Policy* (Boulder: University of Colorado Press, 1959), 45, 63–65.

15. This story is best covered in Benjamin Kline Hunnicutt, *Work without End: Abandoning Shorter Hours for the Right to Work* (Philadelphia: Temple University Press, 1988), chs. 3 and 4. For one successful business-initiated experiment, see Hunnicutt's *Kellog's Six Hour Day* (Philadelphia: Temple University Press, 1996); and see Marion Cotter Cahill, *Shorter Hours: A Study of the Movement Since the Civil War* (New York: Columbia University Press, 1932).

16. See, for example, Thomas Flaherty to William Green, December 2, 1930, File 44, Box 44, RG21–001: Legislation Department, Records, The George Meany Memorial Archives, (GMMA). See also the resolution of the Toledo Central Labor Union, December 4, 1930, which urged the AFL to "use its great power and influence to in an effort to urge upon the President of the United States the wisdom and logic of issuing a proclamation proclaiming the shorter work day and the shorter work week" in government establishments. The aim of both unions was not only to shorten the hours of their own members but to set an example for industry. The resolution and the response from the AFL are in unattributed memos, December 19, 1930, File 46, ibid.

17. *Proceedings of the AFL*, 1932, 342; for more on Green's position, see 292–93.

18. Ibid., 245–46.

19. Ibid., 244–47. The comment of Andrew Furuseth continued: "I cannot see any reason why we should follow some of the mad ideas of Europe when they set out from an entirely different point of view in dealing with governmental and social questions than we do" (246). Donnelly pursued his point by arguing, "Hours and wages fixed by law do not mean anything to the individual worker in the mass if back of it there is not an economic organization."

20. Ibid., 292–93. See also David R. Roediger and Philip S. Foner, *Our Own Time: A History of American Labor and the Working Day* (Westport: Greenwood Publishing, 1989), 246–47.

21. Legislation quote from U.S. Congress, *Hearings before a Subcommittee of the Committee on the Judiciary*, 72d Cong., 2d sess., January 1933, "Thirty-Hour Work Week," 1; hereafter, *Senate Hearings*, "Thirty-Hour Work Week." I found this story in Vittoz, *New Deal Labor Policy and the American Industrial Economy*, 83–85; Farr, *Origins of Recent Labor Policy*, 63–65.

22. *Senate Hearings*, "Thirty-Hour Work Week," 419, 426.

23. Ibid., 286. He continued: "During a depression, who can estimate the number of people who have become reconciled to charity, professional pensioners on the public bounty or professional hobos and criminals?"

24. This sense was fueled by the fact that some of the same people who sought a thirty-hour week to expand employment and maintain citizenship attacked the rights of married women to work. Rank-and-filer Louis Draudt wrote William Green that he thought it would be a "God-send" if the AFL could "get a 30 hour week for all wage-earners." He then urged "a national law passed eliminating all married women working where their husbands are working." Louis Draudt to William Green, October 16, 1933, File 46, Box 44, RG21–001, GMMA.

25. *Proceedings of the AFL*, 1932, 247.

26. *Senate Hearings*, "Thirty-Hour Work Week," 22; for a revealing discussion of the issues around wages see Christopher Tomlins, *The State and the Unions: Labor Relations, Law, and the Organized Labor Movement in America, 1880–1960* (New York: Cambridge University Press, 1985), 128–30.

27. *Proceedings of the AFL*, 1932, 288.

28. *Senate Hearings*, "Thirty-Hour Work Week," 378.

29. Hunnicutt, *Work without End*, 154, and discussion, 153–63. For the following discussion, see Farr, *Origins of Recent Labor Policy*, 63–64, 99–101.

30. "President Limits 30-Hour Week Bill," *New York Times*, April 13, 1933; Hunicutt, *Work without End*, 153.

31. Daniel Levine, *Poverty and Society: The Growth of the American Welfare State in International Comparison* (New Brunswick: Rutgers University Press, 1988), 250; the best general account of unemployment insurance is Daniel Nelson, *Unemployment Insurance: The American Experience, 1915–1935* (Madison: University of Wisconsin Press, 1969).

32. These two groups are frequently conflated under the "social insurance" rubric in order to distinguish their proposals from those of the champions of assistance to the needy. See, for example, Linda Gordon, "Social Insurance and Public Assistance: The Influence of Gender and Welfare Thought in the United States, 1890–1935," *American Historical Review* 97 (February 1992), 19–54. Despite their overlapping concerns, I have sharpened the distinctions for the purposes of examining the sources of the employment legislation.

33. The following material draws on Roy Lubove, *The Struggle for Social Security, 1900–1935* (Cambridge: Harvard University Press, 1968), 18–25; Nelson, *Unemployment Insurance*, 16; and Berkowitz, *America's Welfare State*, ch. 7, 28–38.

34. Louis Leotta, "Abraham Epstein and the Movement for Old Age Security," *Labor History* 16 (Summer 1975), 358–77.

35. "Isaac Max Rubinow," *Dictionary of American Biography*, Supp. 2, 585–87.

36. Abraham Epstein, *Insecurity, a Challenge to America: A Study of Social Insurance in the United States and Abroad* (New York: H. Smith and R. Haas, 1933), 23.

37. Van Kleeck was friend and ally to a wide network of reformers, including Lucy Randolph Mason, head of the NCL, Mary Anderson, director of the Women's Bureau, and John Andrews of the Association for the Advancement of Labor Legislation.

38. U.S. Congress, *Hearings before the Senate Committee on Education and Labor*, 74th Cong., 2d sess., April 14, 1936, 2. The progress of the bill can be traced in Kenneth Casebeer, "The Workers' Unemployment Insurance Bill: American Social Wage, Labor Organization, and Legal Ideology," in Christopher Tomlins and Andrew King, eds., *Labor Law in America: Historical and Critical Essays* (Baltimore: Johns Hopkins University Press, 1992); See also the rationale for the bill and the final text, which can be found in the *Hearings*, cited above, as well as the discussion in Mary van Kleeck, untitled typescript, November 14, 1934, Mary van Kleeck Collection, Sophia Smith Archives, Nielson Library Smith College; hereafter, MVK Collection. This was apparently prepared for the *New Masses* but, as far as I can tell, never published.

39. Casebeer, "The Workers' Unemployment Insurance Bill," 232.

40. John R. Commons, *History of Labor in the United States*, vol. 3 (New York: Macmillan, 1935), xix.

41. John R. Commons, "The Right to Work," *Arena* 21 (February 1899), 134.

42. Commons, *History of Labor in the United States*, xxvii.

43. John R. Commons, *Myself: The Autobiography of John R. Commons* (Madison: University of Wisconsin Press, 1964), 143.

44. Phillippa Strum, *Louis D. Brandeis: Justice for the People* (Cambridge: Harvard University Press, 1984), 373.

45. Louis D. Brandeis, "The Road to Social Efficiency," *Proceedings of the National Conference of Charities and Corrections* (Fort Wayne: Fort Wayne Printing, 1911), 159.

46. See Commons's description in John R. Commons, *Institutional Economics: Its Place in Political Economy* (New York: Macmillan, 1934), 840–75.

47. Eveline M. Burns, interview by Peter Corning, February 10, 1965, 17, Social Security Project, Columbia Oral History Research Collection, Butler Library, Columbia University.

48. Commons, *Myself*, 143; Berkowitz, *America's Welfare State*, 30, puts the distinction this way: "In Commons' view the employers rather than the state should serve as the focal point of social action. The state should regulate employment conditions in a way that prohibited unsocial behavior, but it should not become intimately involved in providing social benefits."

49. Nelson, *Unemployment Insurance*, 182–85.

50. See Lubove, *The Struggle for Social Security*, 172; cf. Nelson, *Unemployment Insurance*, 152ff. Within a year, by January of 1934, the plan had been considered by the legislatures of seventeen states. It would soon be adopted not only by Ohio but, in a modified version, by New York.

51. Quoted in Casebeer, "The Workers' Unemployment Insurance Bill," 232.

52. Employers also objected to a tax based on a percentage of payroll, which would penalize those who paid good wages by requiring a larger net contribution from them. For the comments of some employers and their representatives, see Jacoby, "Employers and the Welfare State," 538; Gerald Zahavi, *Workers, Managers, and Welfare Capitalism: The Shoeworkers and Tanners of Endicott Johnson, 1890–1950* (Urbana: University of Illinois Press, 1988), 141–42; and Nelson, *Unemployment Insurance*, 194.

53. Epstein, *Insecurity*, 23. On this basis, Ohio's State Federation of Labor voted its approval for unemployment insurance in 1932.

54. Ibid., 101.

55. Quoted in Casebeer, "The Workers' Unemployment Insurance Bill," 232. This is, of course, exactly what protective labor legislation did to women. Gompers continued, "The whole of our activity organized to assert and to live our own lives would be subject to every petty or high official . . . according to the government's conception of what is and what is not voluntary employment." See Nelson, *Unemployment Insurance*, 66–68, for a discussion of voluntarism and unemployment insurance in the AFL.

56. *Proceedings of the AFL*, 1931, 397.

57. Ibid., 370, 369.

58. Ibid., 369.

59. Ibid., 369, 394.

60. Ibid., 372–74; Florence Hanson of the Teachers' Union stated: "I believe . . . unemployment insurance will increase the freedom of the worker and his self-respect, and that unemployment insurance will be of great strength to trade unionists"; *Proceedings of the AFL*, 1931, 383.

61. Ibid., 1932, 339.

62. Ibid., 336.

63. Ibid., 40–41.

64. Ibid., 346.

65. Ibid., 39, 43.

66. Ibid., 43.

67. Ibid., 1934, 10.

68. Edwin Witte, "Organized Labor and Social Security," in Milton Derber and Edwin Young, eds., *Labor and the New Deal* (Madison: University of Wisconsin Press, 1961), 252–53.

69. Thomas Eliot, interviewed by Peter Corning, August 9, 1965, 3–4, Columbia Oral History Research Collection, recalls that on a December 1934 visit to Washington to visit Elizabeth's parents, Raushenbush gathered together Perkins, Corcoran, Ben Cohen and Charlie Wyzanski, and some industrialists to develop the Wagner-Lewis bill. He and Raushenbush worked for two weeks in January 1935 to write a bill "on this one subject which later turned out as Title 9 of the Social Security Act."

70. U.S. Congress, *Hearings before a Subcommittee of the House Committee on Ways and Means on H.R. 7659*, 73d Cong., 2d sess., March 24, 1934, 256; hereafter, *Wagner-Lewis Hearings*.

71. This and the first quotation in the paragraph are from the *New Masses* typescript, 7 (see note 38 above); "Security for Americans," *New Republic*, December 12, 1934, 123.

72. The bill was also supported by the National Negro Congress; see Raymond Wolters, *Negroes and the Great Depression: The Problem of Economic Recovery* (Westport: Greenwood Publishing, 1970), 379.

73. U.S. Congress, *Hearings on Unemployment Insurance before the House Committee on Labor on H.R. 7598*, part I, 73d Cong., 2d sess., February 21, 1934, 34 and passim; hereafter, *Unemployment Insurance Hearings*.

74. Witte, "Organized Labor and Social Security," 255.

75. Thomas Eliot interview, 5 and 6. See also Eliot, *Recollections of the New Deal Era: When the People Mattered* (Boston: Northeastern University Press, 1992), 93–95.

76. Nelson, *Unemployment Insurance*, 167.

77. Strum, *Louis Brandeis*, 384, 386. Marion Folsom concurs in this judgment, commenting that "Brandeis behind the scenes was quite effective" and crediting him with inducing Frank Graham to support experience rating. He "went out to Brandeis' home and when he returned had made up his mind to support it." Marion Folsom, interview by Peter Corning, June 19, 1965, 21, 29, Columbia Oral History Research Collection.

78. Barbara Nachtrieb Armstrong, interview by Peter Corning, December 20, 1965, 42, Columbia Oral History Research Collection.

79. Marion Folsom interview, 20–21.

80. Testimony of Mrs. William Kittle, *Wagner-Lewis Hearings*, 160.

81. See testimony of Elizabeth Magee, secretary of the Consumers' League of Ohio, *Wagner-Lewis Hearings*, 223–28; Magee, also supportive of state-based programs, suggests that in Ohio the league had worked for unemployment insurance for several years and describes the legislation "as the greatest ray of hope that we have had" (223). She also suggests that states are better prepared with information. Note that in these hearings the YWCA seems to have constituted something of an exception: though she testified for the bill, Elizabeth Eastman, representing the national YWCA, noted that she did so because it would induce states to enact their own bills, which would counter the "difficulty and pitfalls of interstate competition" (160–62).

82. Grace Abbott is a good example: she testified before the Senate Finance Committee that she would have preferred a bill with national standards in it but believed that, even without them, the unemployment insurance provisions were worth preserving because they would provide a precedent for states to continue. U.S. Congress, *Hearings before the Senate Committee on Finance, on S. 1130, Economic Security Act*, 74th Cong., 1st sess., January 22–February 20, 1935, 1080–91; hereafter, *Economic Security Act Hearings*. No one seemed interested in issues of coverage or eligibility. See also the testimony of Mrs. Beatrice Pitney Lamb of the National League of Women Voters (442–44) and Mrs. Frederic Shelton of the National Board of the YWCA (444–45) and a letter from the National Consumers' League (445).

83. *Wagner-Lewis Hearings*, 276–79. Two things may account for this: the close relationship with the Brandeis group stemming from early protective legislation days and the comfortable reliance by women's groups on their state connections based on many years of influence in state boards and bureaucracies.

84. Edwin Witte, *The Development of the Social Security Act: A Memorandum on the History of the Committee on Economic Security and Drafting and Legislative History of the Social Security Act* (Madison: University of Wisconsin Press, 1962), 58. Grace Abbott, Mary Dewson, Elizabeth Morissey, and Belle Sherwin supported Wagner-Lewis. Helen Hall of the Henry Street Settlement opposed it.

85. For an extended discussion of the silences of social reformers on this issue, see Gordon, *Pitied but Not Entitled*, ch. 8.

86. Minutes of a Special Meeting of the Board of Directors of the National Consumers' League to discuss unemployment insurance, May 8, 1933, Box A3, 1933 Minutes Folder, microfilm edition, NCL Papers, Library of Congress.

87. Minutes of the 56th Meeting of the Board of Directors of the National Consumers' League, November 22, 1934, Box A3, 1934 Minutes Folder, microfilm edition, NCL Papers.

88. Katharine Lenroot, interview by Peter Corning, June 1, 1965, 63, 21 Columbia Oral History Research Collection. Lenroot was quite taken with Altmeyer's promise to provide more funds than she ever imagined.

89. Witte, *The Development of the Social Security Act*, 167; discussion, 165–67.

90. J. Douglas Brown, interview by Peter Corning, February 5, 1965, 21, Columbia Oral History Collection, recalls a conversation during which Green told him, "We'll go along with you on joint contributions for old age insurance, but we will not make contributions to the unemployment insurance."

91. *Economic Security Act Hearings*, 167–73. Green had remained a reluctant supporter until the very end—a reluctance that undermined his influence. For example, in the Wagner-Lewis hearings the year before, he testified that he wished such unemployment insurance were not necessary but that he would support it in order to protect the purchasing power of families. "We have always believed that it would be far better for our social and economic order if employment could be furnished workers so that they could earn their living as decent, upstanding American citizens. We prefer that." The male content of both work and citizenship is apparent as the statement continues: "We believe a man will maintain his independence and his manhood better if he is permitted to earn a living, but we have found from experience that we have not yet mastered our economic forces, so that we can maintain an economic order which will guarantee and grant to the workers of this country even limited opportunities to earn a living" (256–57). On organized labor's silence, see Arthur J. Altmeyer, *The Formative Years of Social Security* (Madison: University of Wisconsin Press, 1966), 32–33.

92. Witte, *Development of the Social Security Act*, 132; see 130–43, for an account of these changes. Witte notes that the Senate Finance Committee tried to return to an earlier proposal for a four-employee/ten-week but that the final compromise was for eight employees over thirteen weeks.

93. For these figures, see Marc Linder, "Farm Workers and the Fair Labor Standards Act: Racial Discrimination in the New Deal," *Texas Law Review* 65 (1987), 1366.

94. *Economic Security Act Hearings*, 640–41.

95. Witte, *Development of the Social Security Act*, 132.

96. Lubove, *The Struggle for Social Security*, 175, says Douglas was not consulted by the CES.

97. Paul Douglas, *Standards of Unemployment Insurance* (Chicago: University of Chicago Press, 1933), 48–50. Douglas estimated that 6 percent of employed workers worked in the agricultural sector. More than two million women and 60 percent of all employed African-American women worked in domestic service in 1930; they constituted about 40 percent of all domestic servants in the United States. Jessie Carney Smith and Carrell Peterson Horton, *Historical Statistics of Black America* (New York: Gale Research, 1995), 1089, 1093, 1103.

98. Diana Pearce, "Toil and Trouble: Women Workers and Unemployment Compensation," *Signs* 10 (Spring 1985), 441. See Eveline Mabel Burns, *Towards Social Security* (New York: Whittlesey House, 1936), 82, on the point that excluding farm and domestic workers was merely gratuitous: "Theoretically," she tells us, some of those excluded, including domes-

tics and employees of state and local governments as well as of nonprofits, "could have been included since no question of making products non-competitive exists. But in fact they are unlikely to be." Migratory workers who worked in more than one state were also not eligible, and the exclusion of farm labor may well have been gratuitous as well.

99. *Proceedings of the AFL*, 1938, 48.

100. Ibid., 141, 145.

101. Douglas, *Standards of Unemployment Insurance*, 57. Douglas cited the example of British women who had purportedly been able to claim benefits because the British required only eight weeks' work over a two-year period.

102. For this and the following two quotations on married women: ibid., 58–59.

103. Ralph Altman, *Availability for Work: A Study in Unemployment Compensation* (Cambridge: Harvard University Press, 1950), 216.

104. Berkowitz, *America's Welfare State*, 53–54.

105. Arthur Larson and Merrill G. Murray, "The Development of Unemployment Insurance in the United States," *Vanderbilt Law Review* 8 (February 1955), 204; Ralph Altman, *Availability for Work: A Study in Unemployment Compensation* (Cambridge: Harvard University Press, 1950), 228–30; and see 215, where Altman comments of women: "No other group has occasioned more special legislation concerning their availability for work. Most state unemployment compensation laws contain special provisons aimed directly at women who seek benefits."

106. Richard A. Lester, *The Economics of Unemployment Compensation* (Princeton: Princeton University Industrial Relations Section, 1962), 51, 53, 126–29; and see the discussion in the most influential textbook on the subject, William Haber and Merrill G. Murray, *Unemployment Insurance in the American Economy: An Historical Review and Analysis* (Homewood: Richard D. Irwin, 1966), 271–79. Note that J. Douglas Brown was one of four faculty associates in the Princeton University Industrial Relations Section.

107. Altman, *Availability for Work*, 235.

108. Larson and Murray, "The Development of Unemployment Insurance in the United States," 201–4, 213. Note also that coverage of smaller firms (under eight employees) expanded slightly to 1946, then not at all to 1954, when the federal government changed the minimum to four employees. Note, too, that benefits as a percentage of wages declined to less than 50 percent—leaving some beneficiaries much worse off and reducing the impact on purchasing power for which labor had hoped.

109. Frances Perkins, *The Roosevelt I Knew* (New York: Viking, 1946), 256–67, provides an account of the origins of the FLSA. As an activist in the broader movement for protective labor legislation for women, Perkins had relied on the police power protections of the Fourteenth Amendment, which, according to the courts, permitted the state to intervene to protect the health of mothers and future mothers, but generally not of men. See as well Suzanne Mettler, *Dividing Citizens: Gender and Federation in New Deal Public Policy* (Ithaca: Cornell University Press, 1998), chs. 7, 8.

110. *West Coast Hotel Co. v. Parrish*, 300 U.S. 379 (1937); see also *Morehead v. Tipaldo*, 298 U.S. 587 (1936). For background, see John W. Chambers, "The Big Switch: Justice Roberts and the Minimum Wage Cases," *Labor History* 10 (Winter 1969), 49–52, and Robert P. Ingalls, "New York and the Minimum-Wage Movement, 1933–37," *Labor History* 15 (Spring 1974), 179–98.

111. The standards were to be determined by a board of five presidentially appointed administrators who would (after consulting with industry committees) collectively set minimum wages and maximum hours for workers in a range of industries. This first draft of what was to become the FLSA specified neither the maximum hours nor the minimum wages to be imposed, leaving these to the discretion of Congress or the board it would create, and subject only to the provision that the board would have no discretion to alter wages over $1,200 a year. The bill allowed the board great flexibility in setting both hours and wages, especially encouraging it to take account of different regional conditions in determining wages.

112. Steve Fraser, *Labor Will Rule: Sidney Hillman and the Rise of American Labor* (New York: Free Press, 1991), 391–94; Elizabeth Brandeis, "Organized Labor and Protective Labor Legislation," in Derber and Young, *Labor and the New Deal*, 218.

113. U.S. Congress, *Joint Hearings before the Senate Committee on Education and Labor, and the House Committee on Labor, on S. 2475 and H.R. 7200*, 75th Cong., 1st sess., June 7–15, 1937, 183–84; hereafter, *FLSA Joint Hearings*. Jackson's testimony, ibid., 4–5.

114. Representatives of the National League of Women Voters, the National Federation of Business and Professional Women's Clubs, and the National Council of Jewish Women all limited their testimony to the child labor provisions.

115. *FLSA Joint Hearings*, Mason, 407–08, and Herrick, 363–71. Lucy Randolph Mason would shortly resign from the NCL to work for the CIO.

116. Ibid., 365. Herrick had been a student of William Leiserson at Antioch. On the role of the NCL in advocating fair labor standards, see Landon R. Y. Storrs, *Civilizing Capitalism: The National Consumers' League, Women's Activism, and Labor Standards in the New Deal Era* (Chapel Hill: University of North Carolina Press, 2000). On the inclusion of industrial homeworkers, see Eileen Boris, "The Regulation of Homework and the Devolution of the Postwar Labor Standards Regime: Beyond Dichotomy," in Christopher L. Tomlins and Andre J. King, eds., *Labor Law in America* (Baltimore: Johns Hopkins University Press, 1992), 260–82.

117. Testimony of John P. Davis, *FLSA Joint Hearings*, 571–76; Sitkoff, *A New Deal for Blacks*, 258–60.

118. *FLSA Joint Hearings*, 274.

119. Mary T. Norton, "Madam Congressman: The Memoirs of Mary T. Norton of New Jersey," unpublished typescript in Mary Norton Papers, Series 5, Box 6, Alexander Library, Rutgers University, 145–46.

120. Frank Friedel, *F.D.R. and the South* (Baton Rouge: Louisiana University Press, 1994), 75.

121. Patterson, *Congressional Conservatism and the New Deal*, 242–43. See also Friedel, *F.D.R. and the South*, 73–75, and Vivien Hart, *Bound by Our Constitution: Women Workers and the Minimum Wage* (Princeton: Princeton University Press, 1994).

122. Clara Beyer to Mary W. Dewson, July 27, 1937, Carton 1, Wages and Hours File, Mary W. Dewson Papers, Franklin Delano Roosevelt Library.

123. Paul Douglas and Joseph Hackman, "The Fair Labor Standards Act of 1938," *Political Science Quarterly* 53 no. 4 (1938), 491–515; John S. Forsythe, "Legislative History of the Fair Labor Standards Act," *Law and Contemporary Problems* 6 (Summer 1939), 464–90.

124. Brandeis, "Organized Labor and Protective Labor Legislation," 223.

125. Norton, "Madam Congressman," 153–54; in this crucial spring, the National Con-

sumers' League, still eager to see a wages and hours bill emerge from Congress, agreed that "the league should not commit itself to specific recommendations until the board has had an opportunity to study the redrafted bill as it emerges from the labor committee." Minutes of the 74th Meeting of the Board of Directors, National Consumers' League, March 29, 1938, Box A3, 1938 Minutes Folder, microfilm edition, NCL Papers.

126. On the child labor provisions, see Hart, *Bound by Our Constitution*; on homework, see Eileen Boris, *Home to Work: Motherhood and the Politics of Industrial Homework in the United States* (New York: Cambridge University Press, 1994).

127. Mettler, *Divided Citizens*, 198–205, offers a more positive assessment of the impact of the FLSA, including an argument that the bill covered fifteen million workers rather than the eleven million (or 39 percent of wage-earning men) that the Labor Department computed. For the purposes of hours, 31 percent of men and 23 percent of women were included. Ronnie Steinberg, *Wages and Hours: Labor and Reform in Twentieth-Century America* (New Brunswick: Rutgers University Press, 1982), 109–14, has the most detailed figures. The most scathing indictment is Marc Linder, "Farm Workers and the Fair Labor Standards Act: Racial Discrimination and the New Deal," *Texas Law Review* 65 (1987), 1335–93. For figures on domestic servants excluded from the bill, see Phyllis M. Palmer, *Domesticity and Dirt: Housewives and Domestic Servants in the United States, 1920–1945* (Philadelphia: Temple University Press, 1989). For additional information on the bill's disproportionate exclusion of women workers, see Hart, *Bound by Our Constitution*; Mimi Abramovitz, *Regulating the Lives of Women: Social Welfare Policy from Colonial Times to the Present* (Boston: South End Press, 1988); and Mink, *The Wages of Motherhood*.

128. Samuel Herman, "The Administration and Enforcement of the Fair Labor Standards Act," *Law and Contemporary Problems* 4 (Summer 1939), 369.

129. Carroll R. Daugherty, "The Economic Coverage of the Fair Labor Standards Act: A Statistical Study," *Law and Contemporary Problems* 6 (Summer 1939), 407–9.

130. Palmer, *Domesticity and Dirt*, 122.

131. Storrs, *Civilizing Capitalism*, 62.

132. Brandeis, "Organized Labor and Protective Labor Legislation," 229.

133. Theda Skocpol, *Protecting Soldiers and Mothers: The Political Origins of Social Policy in the United States* (Cambridge: Harvard University Press, 1992); Ann Shola Orloff, *The Politics of Pensions: A Comparative Analysis of Britain, Canada, and the United States, 1880–1940* (Madison: University of Wisconsin Press, 1993); Margaret Weir, *Politics and Jobs: The Boundaries of Employment Policy in the United States* (Princeton: Princeton University Press, 1993); Quadagno, *The Transformation of Old Age Security*.

134. Gordon, *Pitied but Not Entitled*; Mink, *The Wages of Motherhood*.

135. Hillman testimony, *FLSA Joint Hearings*, 948.

136. Brito, "Protective Legislation in Ohio," 173–97.

137. Ulla Wikander, Alice Kessler-Harris, and Jane Lewis, eds., *Protecting Women: Labor Legislation in Europe, the United States, and Australia, 1880–1920* (Urbana: University of Illinois Press, 1995), introduction.

138. Skocpol, *Protecting Soldiers and Mothers*, 235–36, notes that state labor federations often disagreed with the AFL on issues of social policy. But on minimum wages they tended, like the AFL, to sanction minimum wage laws for women while opposing such laws for men.

139. The quote comes from Brito, "Protective Legislation in Ohio," 191. I have relied on Brito's interpretation of the events here; see 190–92.

140. Ibid., 191.

141. *Proceedings of the AFL*, 1937, 166.

142. Ibid., 501, 500.

143. Ibid., 501. Cf. ibid., 1938, 153.

144. Once again, Green resorted to the explicit language of voluntarism: "We want to be free American laboring men, we demand that we be free—free to work out our own problems. We resent governmental control and governmental dictation." Ibid., 12.

145. Alice Kessler-Harris, *Out to Work: A History of Wage-Earning Women in the United States* (New York: Oxford University Press, 1982), ch. 7. The data suggest the limits of the argument that constitutional constraints inhibited men from benefiting from state legislation.

146. *Congressional Record—House*, December 13, 1937, 1397.

147. Ibid., December 14, 1937, 1465. Kent E. Keller of Illinois described the bill that same day as "the baby she said she found on her doorstep, the poor little foundling which has no birth record, which has no mamma and no papa, and which in all fairness to the child as well as to its parents and to the public at large, ought to be sent to a foundlings' home until it is old enough to show whether it has a sound body and sane mind before asking anybody to adopt it. In the meantime, we ought to seek its parentage, try to find out who is responsible for bringing it into the world" (1493).

148. Ibid., May 23, 1938, 7287.

149. Bert Lord of New York, ibid., December 13, 1937, 1406. Cf. Arthur B. Jenks of New Hampshire, ibid., December 14, 1937, 1470, arguing for the bill because "the purchasing power must be put into the pockets of the rank and file of the consuming public if the products of industry and agriculture are to be absorbed"—in other words, to solve the unemployment problem; and Gerald J. Boileau of Wisconsin, ibid., 1471–72, argued in favor because he could not conceive of any man, "living in any section of the country being able to support a family in decency on the so called American standard of living at a weekly wage of less than $16."

150. *FLSA Joint Hearings*, 618. For another negative assessment, see Walter E. Boles Jr., "Some Aspects of the Fair Labor Standards Act," *Southern Economic Journal* 6 (April 1940), 499, who comments: "The one motive which has long been recognized as a sound justification for wage and hour legislation, that of protecting the health and morals of workers seems not to have played a dominant part in the enactment of the FLSA."

151. Testimony of Earl Constantine, National Association of Hosiery Manufacturers, *FLSA Joint Hearings*, 595: "Most of them are girls, and their earnings are merely contributory earnings, and frequently there are two or more girls in the same family working in the plant."

152. Testimony of John E. Edgerton, ibid., 782; asked by Representative Wood whether "these old women you talk about . . . just came down there to keep themselves occupied," he replied that the "old women" were given "easy and comfortable jobs that they could do and make some contribution to the family expense."

153. Ibid., 846, 597. Many opponents placed southern black workers in the same categories as women.

154. Fred C. Gilchrist of Iowa, *Congressional Record*, December 17, 1937, 1777.

155. Ibid., 1810.

156. *FLSA Joint Hearings*: testimony of William Green, 233; statement of John L. Lewis, 273.

157. Ibid.: Perkins, 193; Hillman, 949.

158. See the discussion at the League of Women Voters, Twelfth National Convention, Cincinnati, Ohio, April 27–May 1, 1936, microfilm, Part 2, Series A, Reel 16, 1936, 283–86; and Clara Mortenson Beyer interview by Vivien Hart, Washington, D.C., November 14, 1983, 15–18, Schlesinger Library.

159. Testimony of Elinore Herrick, *FLSA Joint Hearings*, 365; Mary Dublin to Lucy Mason, April 28, 1938, National Consumers' League Papers, Reel 63, Microfilm Corporation of America. Landon Storrs suggests the NCL was primarily responsible for saving the bill; see Storrs, *Civilizing Capitalism*, 198–200. See also Elizabeth Brandeis, "Organized Labor and Protective Labor Legislation," 219–20; and Douglas and Hackman, "The Fair Labor Standards Act of 1938," 491.

160. Testimony of Elinore Herrick, *FLSA Joint Hearings*, 364.

161. Storrs, *Civilizing Capitalism*, 369–71, recounts a story about Mary Dublin calling Roscoe Pound and urging him to pressure his students to vote for the final bill.

162. *Proceedings of the AFL*, 1938, 154. From the Frey Resolutions Committee, ibid., 1937: "These experiences make us reluctant to approve the creation of any additional boards or commissions having to do with industrial relations" (501).

163. Charles A. Eaton of New Jersey, *Congressional Record*, December 13, 1937, 1402. Wilcox, ibid., continued: "It proposes a bureaucratic control of business and industry and a dictatorship over labor which if enacted, must ultimately result in a destruction of the right of collective bargaining and which may easily reduce labor to a state of economic slavery."

164. Kent E. Keller of Illinois, ibid., December 14, 1937, 1495. See also Sam D. McReynolds of Tennessee, ibid., 1465: "They are undertaking to create a dictator in this new bill, who will have more authority than the President of the United States."

165. Ibid., December 13, 1937, 1404.

166. Brandeis, "Organized Labor and Protective Labor Legislation," 218.

167. Recall that in *Breedlove v. Suttles*, 302 U.S. 277 (1937), a tax case, the Court had ruled that a state could exempt women but not men from certain taxes on the grounds that a "tax being on persons, women may be exempted on the basis of special considerations to which they are naturally entitled."

168. Steinberg, *Wages and Hours*, 98, notes that until 1970, two to three times as many women were covered by state laws as by federal laws. In 1938, when 14 percent of adult female workers were covered by federal wages and hours legislation, 43 percent were covered by state laws.

169. Hunnicutt, *Work without End*, 248; and Hunnicutt, "The New Deal: The Salvation of Work and the End of the Shorter-Hour Movement," in Gary Cross, ed., *Worktime and Industrialization* (Philadelphia: Temple University Press, 1988), 224.

## Chapter 3

1. Peter Kilborn and Leslie Wayne, "End to Social Security Penalty Welcomed by Companies and Their Workers," *New York Times*, March 5, 2000.

2. Richard Stevenson, "House Backs End to Earnings Limit on Social Security," *New York Times*, March 2, 2000.

3. The average unemployment rate from 1930 to 1933 was 25.8 percent according to estimates prepared for the Committee on Economic Security, *Social Security in America* (Washington, D.C.: GPO, 1937), chart, 58–59. This average disguised wide swings from year to year and substantial variations among the states, some of which may be attributable to imprecise and idiosyncratic counting methods. Georgia seems to have had the lowest average rate (17.0 percent); Rhode Island, the highest (29.7 percent).

4. Barbara Nachtrieb Armstrong, interview by Peter A. Corning, December 20, 1965, 255, (emphasis in original), Columbia Oral History Research Collection, Butler Library, Columbia University. The best summary of these provisions and of the entire Social Security Act is still to be found in CES, *Social Security in America*; part 2 deals with the old age provisions. For the development of old age insurance up to 1935 and after, see Edward D. Berkowitz and Kim McQuaid, *Creating the Welfare State: the Political Economy of Twentieth-Century Reform*, rev. ed. (Lawrence: University Press of Kansas, 1992); W. Andrew Achenbaum, *Social Security Visions and Revisions: A Twentieth Century Fund Study* (Cambridge: Cambridge University Press, 1986); Richard V. Burkhauser and Karen C. Holden, *A Challenge to Social Security: The Changing Roles of Women and Men in American Society* (New York: Academic Press, 1992); and Jerry R. Cates, *Insuring Inequality: Administrative Leadership in Social Security, 1935–1954* (Ann Arbor: University of Michigan Press, 1983).

5. J. Joseph Huthmacher, *Senator Robert F. Wagner and the Rise of Urban Liberalism* (New York: Atheneum, 1968), 177.

6. Edwin E. Witte, *The Development of the Social Security Act: A Memorandum on the History of the Committee on Economic Security and Drafting and Legislative History of the Social Security Act* (Madison: University of Wisconsin Press, 1962), 160.

7. William Graebner, "From Pensions to Social Security: Social Insurance and the Rise of Dependency," in John N. Schacht, ed., *The Quest for Social Security: Papers on the Origins and the Future of the American Social Insurance System* (Iowa City: Center for the Study of the Recent History of the United States, 1982), 19–33. See also William Graebner, *A History of Retirement: The Meaning and Function of an American Institution, 1885–1978* (New Haven: Yale University Press, 1980), ch. 7. Jill Quadagno, *The Transformation of Old Age Security: Class and Politics in the American Welfare State* (Chicago: University of Chicago Press, 1988), 19, concurs, arguing that removing older workers from the labor force "was a primary justification among policy makers for legislating social security." With less justification, Benjamin Kline Hunnicutt, *Work without End: Abandoning Shorter Hours for the Right to Work* (Philadelphia: Temple University Press, 1988), 211, argues that debate was over how leisure should be distributed—whether during a person's work life, by shorter days and weeks, or at the end of it, by retirement with a pension.

8. Barbara Nachtrieb Armstrong, *Insuring the Essentials: Minimum Wage Plus Social Insurance—A Living Wage Program* (New York: Macmillan, 1932), 394.

9. Typescript, "Preliminary Report of the Staff of the Committee on Economic Security, Presented to the Committee on Economic Security and the Technical Board on Economic Security," September 1934, in Papers of Harry Hopkins, Group 24: Federal Emergency Relief Adminstration, Container 48, "Relief Plans and Programs, 1933–38: Memoranda and Reports," 3381, Franklin Delano Roosevelt Library, Hyde Park, New York. I am indebted to Mary Poole for calling my attention to this report. CES, *Social Security in America*, 170–74.

10. I have relied for this material on CES, *Social Security in America*, part 2, as well as Armstrong, *Insuring the Essentials*, 389–93. See also Graebner, *A History of Retirement*, ch. 7.

11. Armstrong, *Insuring the Essentials*, xiii and ff.

12. Armstrong interview, December 19, 1965, 38.

13. Theron F. Schlabach, *Edwin E. Witte: Cautious Reformer* (Madison: State Historical Society of Wisconsin, 1969), ch. 6.

14. Barbara Nachtrieb Armstrong, Appendix C, 1, "Preliminary Report of the Staff of the Committee on Economic Security."

15. "Getting out of hand," from J. Douglas Brown, interview by Peter Corning, March 16, 1965, 27, Columbia Oral History Research Collection. As Brown recalled, "What Barbara Armstrong and I fought for was a constructive device that would keep old-age assistance from getting bigger and bigger and bigger" (ibid., February 22, 1965, 12). Remaining quotes, Armstrong, Appendix C, 2, "Preliminary Report of the Staff of the Committee on Economic Security."

16. The plan also included a lump sum death benefit equal to contributions made by those who had not yet begun to collect benefits. The details of this proposal can be found in Armstrong, Appendix C, 1–10, "Preliminary Report of the Staff of the Committee on Economic Security"

17. Ten years after old age insurance began paying benefits in 1941, more people were still getting old age assistance than insurance (2.8 versus 2.1 million); cf. Martha Derthick, *Policymaking for Social Security* (Washington, D.C.: Brookings Institution, 1979), 272–73. From then on, the balance began to shift. By 1973, only 56 people per 1,000 population aged sixty-five and over were getting both OASDI and old age assistance benefits, suggesting that OASDI benefits were sufficiently high to keep most aged persons off the welfare rolls. George E. Rejda, *Social Insurance and Economic Security* (Englewood Cliffs: Prentice-Hall, 1976), 115.

18. Arthur J. Altmeyer and Edwin E. Witte were both veterans of Wisconsin's unemployment insurance campaigns. See Arthur J. Altmeyer, *The Formative Years of Social Security* (Madison: University of Wisconsin Press, 1966), ix, where Altmeyer states that before he moved to Washington in 1933 he had been director of the Labor Compliance Division of the National Industrial Recovery Administration. In 1934, Witte was serving as director of unemployment compensation in Wisconsin; Schlabach, *Cautious Reformer*, 97. See Armstrong on Witte's position: Witte initially changed an early proposal of hers for insurance, deleting insurance entirely and leaving only assistance; Armstrong interview, December 19, 1965, 67–68.

19. Altmeyer, *The Formative Years of Social Security*, 13.

20. The CES consulted influential individuals on their priorities early in the process. Witte noted that Frankfurter told him that if unemployment insurance, aid to dependent mothers and children, and old age annuities were "too much to carry at once he would leave old age annuities out of the picture for the present": Typescript, "Memorandum on the Views Relating to the Work of the Committee on Economic Security Expressed by Various Individuals Consulted," August 19–21, 1934, Box 21, Entry 9, PI 183, RG47: Records of the Social Security Administration/Social Security Board, National Archives and Records Administration (NARA).

21. She commented: "In any case, they didn't want to interfere with the unemployment insurance." Armstrong interview, December 19, 1965, 31.

22. Brown interview, June 1, 1965, 106. And see Thomas Eliot, *Recollections of the New Deal Era: When the People Mattered* (Boston: Northeastern University Press, 1992), ch. 5.

23. Edith Abbott, "Social Insurance and/or Social Security," Notes and Comment, *Social Service Review* 6 (September 1934), 537–40. See also Mary Poole, "Securing Race and Ensuring Dependence: The Social Security Act of 1935," Ph.D. diss., Rutgers University, 2000, ch. 5; and Lela B. Costin, *Two Sisters for Social Justice: A Biography of Grace and Edith Abbott* (Urbana: University of Illinois Press, 1983), ch. 9.

24. Schlabach, *Cautious Reformer*, 106, cites Edith Abbott on this point; Brown interview, June 16, 1965, 111–12.

25. Armstrong interview, December 19, 1965, 83.

26. These included the National Consumers' League and the National Women's Trade Union League as well as the General Federation of Women's Clubs.

27. File: Joseph P. Harris to Dr. Frank P. Graham, March 14, 1935, Box 13, Entry 4, PI 183, RG47, NARA; and see Harris to Jane Perry Clark, "The southern Democrats in particular are very anxious not to give any Federal Administrator the power to tell the sovereign State of Arkansas how it shall administer old-age pensions or any other phase of social legislation, or how much of a pension shall be granted" (April 2, 1935, ibid.).

28. Witte, *The Development of the Social Security Act*, 28. Epstein believed that the only sympathetic member on the Technical Board was William Leiserson, whose appointment Epstein welcomed; Abraham Epstein to William Leiserson, September 21, 1934, William M. Leiserson Papers, State Historical Society of Wisconsin, Madison. Theda Skocpol and G. John Ikenberry suggest that all advocates of a more radical redistributionary social welfare policy were excluded from the CES planning committees in order to ensure that a contributory plan would emerge. While it is certainly the case that the composition of the staff and committees remained in the hands of Wisconsin players, old age insurance itself seems not to have been seriously on the agenda until Armstrong insisted that it was the only way to go. Theda Skocpol, *Social Policy in the United States: Future Possibilities in Historical Perspective* (Princeton: Princeton University Press, 1995), 154.

29. "Preliminary Report of the Staff of the Committee on Economic Security," 48.

30. Later Brown added, "We also felt that benefit as a matter of right was far more to be preferred than one for which there would be a needs test." Brown interview, February 5, 1965, 12, 27.

31. Armstrong interview, December 20, 1965, 275–76.

32. Brown interview, June 16, 1965, 133–35. "The graduated benefits," he recalled, "was an adequacy concept and also the wives and the widow's benefits. Those are all adequacy concepts."

33. Armstrong interview, December 19, 1965, 125.

34. U.S. Congress, Senate, *Hearings before the Committee on Finance on Social Security Act Amendments of 1939*, 76th Cong., 1st sess. (Washington, D.C.: GPO, 1939), 283; hereafter, Senate, *Finance Committee Hearings on Social Security Act Amendments of 1939*.

35. These quotes come from Armstrong interview, December 20, 1965, 255, 258–59.

36. Marion Folsom, interview by Peter Corning, June 9, 1965, 53, Columbia Oral History Research Collection.

37. Brown interview, February, 22, 1965, 22.

38. In 1935, three thousand dollars a year constituted the upper limit of taxed income.

Brown recalls that the limit was chosen partly for its "aesthetic logic" and because 97 percent of income earners earned less than that sum. The Technical Board Committee on Unemployment Insurance did not exempt people who earned more because they felt that in a democratic country, where there were a lot of people who had vertical mobility, coverage for everyone was important. "I'm dead sure we were right in covering everyone up to a certain level and not excluding anyone for the very simple reason that people who have a higher income for a period, especially just over a break point, don't necessarily always have it." Brown interview, June 1, 1965, 61, 66.

39. Altmeyer, *The Formative Years of Social Security*, 5–6, vii.

40. Armstrong interview, December 19, 1965, 31. Thirty years later, Armstrong still felt angry about this slight and about Perkins's lack of cooperation and enthusiasm for OAI. On Witte, see Schlabach, *Cautious Reformer*, 108.

41. Armstrong interview, December 19, 1965, 75–76; Brown interview, February 22, 1965, 23, and June 16, 1965, 109.

42. Louis Stark, "Roosevelt Bars Plans Now for Broad Social Program; Seeks Job Insurance Only," *New York Times*, November 15, 1934; "President Asks Job Insurance; . . . Old Age Pensions Held in Abeyance," *Washington Post*, November 15, 1934; "Pension Speech Clarified," *New York Times*, November 23, 1934. See also Armstrong interview, December 20, 1965, 158–63; Brown interview, February 22, 1965, COHRC, 13, and June 16, 1965, 116–21.

43. See, for example, Witte, *The Development of the Social Security Act*, 122; only one reference to Armstrong appears in Wilbur J. Cohen, *Retirement Policies under Social Security* (Berkeley: University of California Press, 1957).

44. Armstrong interview, December 19, 1965, 46; and see additional acerbic comments, ibid., December 22, 1965, 275–76.

45. See Brown interview, February 22, 1965, 14, and June 16, 1965, 113, for his assessment of the congressional response. Edwin Witte continued his attack on Townsend even after the Social Security amendments had been signed into law; "Are Old Age Pensions Worth Their Cost?" *American Labor Legislation Review* 26 (March 1936), 10–11.

46. Paul H. Douglas, *Social Security in the United States: An Analysis and Appraisal of the Federal Social Security Act* (New York: McGraw-Hill, 1936), estimates that 47 percent of those working would not come under the old age insurance features and thus would require old age assistance.

47. Federal Advisory Council Minutes, February 18, 1938, 33, File 025, Box 12, Chairman's Files RG47, NARA, indicates that 40 percent of employed *women* worked in covered industries at the start; hereafter, Advisory Council Minutes. Ewan Clague, then assistant director of research for the Social Security Board, claimed that though more than twenty-one million workers were excluded—twelve million self-employed and nine million in uncovered occupations—many of these would ultimately be included in the system because they would occasionally work in covered jobs. But the assertion directly contradicts the assumptions of Williamson and others that the costs of the system would be reduced by the contributions of those who were not eligible for benefits. See "The Problem of Extending Old Age Insurance to Cover Classes Now Excluded," typescript, File: December 1937, Social Security Box 20, J. Douglas Brown Papers, Seeley G. Mudd Manuscript Library, Princeton University Library, published with permission of

the Princeton University Library. The most careful analysis of the data concludes that 86.69 percent of black female workers and 53.6 percent of black male workers were excluded; F. Davis, "The Effects of the Social Security Act upon the Status of the Negro," Ph.D. diss., University of Iowa, 1939, 99, n. 211, and 102, tables 21, 23.

48. Quadagno, *The Transformation of Old Age Security*, 72, notes that state-based old age assistance programs permitted payments of up to $30 per month to individuals, male or female, compared to the $17.50 per month that an average worker might expect under Social Security's old age insurance program; by 1941, twenty-two states offered means-tested pensions more generous than old age insurance benefits. U.S. Congress, Senate, *Preliminary Report of the Special Committee to Investigate the Old-Age Pension System, Senate Resolution No. 129*, August 28, 1941, 77th Cong., 1st sess. (Washington, D.C.: GPO, 1941), 11; hereafter, *Senate Resolution Preliminary Report, 1941*.

49. Witte, "Are Old Age Pensions Worth Their Cost?" 7–14; "The New Pension Scale," *New York Times*, April 1, 1939, 18. Quadagno, *The Transformation of Old Age Security*, 108–9, 119–21, notes the pressures of various protest groups on the initial Social Security Act. See also Linda Gordon, *Pitied but Not Entitled: Single Mothers and the History of Welfare, 1890–1935* (New York: Free Press, 1994).

50. *Senate Resolution Preliminary Report, 1941*, 4.

51. Witte, "Are Old Age Pensions Worth Their Cost?" 11.

52. Some observers have argued that adequacy governs women's programs and equity those of men; for example, Barbara J. Nelson, "The Origins of the Two-Channel Welfare State: Workmen's Compensation and Mother's Aid," in Linda Gordon, ed., *Women, the State, and Welfare* (Madison: University of Wisconsin Press, 1990), 123–51. A fully gendered perspective demonstrates the need for a more complicated interpretation.

53. The CIO representatives were Harvey Fremming, president, Oil Field, Gas Well, and Refinery Workers International Union; Sidney Hillman, president, Amalgamated Clothing Workers of America; and Philip Murray, vice president, United Mine Workers of America. The AFL representatives were G. M. Bugniazet, secretary, International Brotherhood of Electrical Workers; John Frey, vice president, Metal Trades Department of the AFL; and Mathew Woll, president, International Photo Engravers' Union of North America. Brown frequently expressed concern at the lack of labor participation. For example, when Brown surveyed the council members in February 1938, not a single labor representative responded. See Untitled Chart, Folder 1, Box 19, Brown Papers.

54. Brown interview, June 16, 1965, 136–37.

55. Linda Gordon, "Social Insurance and Public Assistance: The Influence of Gender in Welfare Thought in the United States, 1890–1935," *American Historical Review* 97 (1992), 19–54.

56. "Social Security Advisory Council is Appointed," typescript of press release, May 10, 1937, File 025: Advisory Council 1937, Box 10, Chairman's Files, RG47, NA2.

57. Typescript, I. S. Falk to the Advisory Council, November 5, 1937, "Benefits for Disabled Persons and Survivors, and Supplemental Allowances for Dependents," ibid., passim.

58. U. S. Congress, House, *Hearings before the Committee on Ways and Means, House of Representatives, Relative to the Social Security Act Amendments of 1939*, March 3, 1939, 76th Cong., 1st sess. (Washington, D.C.: GPO, 1939), 1217; hereafter, House, *Hearings on the Social Security Act Amendments of 1939*.

59. See, for example, Abraham Epstein, *Insecurity: A Challenge to America, a Study of Social Insurance in the United States and Abroad* (New York: Random House, 1938[1933]), part 9; Joanne L. Goodwin, *Gender and the Politics of Welfare Reform: Mothers' Pensions in Chicago, 1911–1929* (Chicago: University of Chicago Press, 1997); Theda Skocpol, *Protecting Soldiers and Mothers: The Political Origins of Social Policy in the United States* (Cambridge: Harvard University Press, 1992), ch. 8.

60. Arthur J. Altmeyer estimated that 43 percent of the children then being helped by ADC had deceased fathers and another 25 percent disabled fathers. These would be removed from that system to OASI, leaving 32 percent on ADC. House, *Hearings on Social Security Act Amendments of 1939*, 2263.

61. Advisory Council on Social Security, *Final Report*, Senate Document no. 4, 76th Cong., 1st sess., December 10, 1938 (Washington, D.C.: GPO, 1939), 17–18; hereafter, Advisory Council, *Final Report*.

62. Ibid., 18. At least early on, Brown seems to have been ambivalent about this idea. On February 25, 1938, he wrote to Gerald Morgan suggesting that it might be better to include aged widows first and then slowly phase in younger widows. File: February 1938, Box 22, Brown Papers.

63. Advisory Council Minutes, April 29, 1938, morning session, 8–10 and ff. That it was the role and not the woman being rewarded emerged clearly in the discussion on February 18 (morning session, 51), around the question of whether the "wife's" allowance should be given to "a single person who has a sister or mother who is acting in lieu of spouse and taking care of the household for that person." The Advisory Council provided a rather elaborate defense of this decision to the House Ways and Means Committee, arguing that middle-aged widows were less likely to be in need, that any other age selected would seem arbitrary, and finally that the retirement age for women in general could not be lowered without discriminating against men. See House, *Hearings on Social Security Act Amendments of 1939*, 6.

64. Advisory Council, *Final Report*, 17.

65. House, *Hearings on Social Security Act Amendments of 1939*, 6.

66. Advisory Council Minutes, April 29, 1938, second half of morning session, 9, A. L. Mowbray of the University of California, Berkeley, speaking.

67. Ibid., 3, 40. The following discussion suggests that on the one hand the Advisory Council distrusted widows, who, they thought, were likely to spend their death benefits all at once, and that on the other they acknowledged the real need of widows with children. My sense is that this ambivalence led to their consensus that widows' benefits be based on need, thus justifying their removal if a recipient remarried. Falk pointed out the discrepancy when he acquiesced in the council's decision: "I think we should recognize that there are two quite separate provisions written there, one following from a banking principle and the other from a social insurance principle, and then to give some income to persons who need it" (40ff.).

68. Ibid., October 21, 1938, morning session, 57.

69. Typescript, "Discussion of Revisions Made in Plan AC-12," July 1, 1938, 1, File 025, Advisory Council, 1938, Box 10, Chairman's Files, RG47, NARA.

70. Advisory Council Minutes, February 19, 1938, afternoon session, 18. The actuary was William Williamson.

71. Ibid., April 29, 1938, first half of morning session, 41.

72. Advisory Council Minutes, April 29, 1938, second half of morning session, 5–6. Mary Dewson followed up Brown's comment, not by questioning the explicit stereotypes in his statement but by reaffirming that the "single woman who has earned enough can get just as high an annuity as a single man." No one else on the Advisory Council challenged the image of the aged woman.

73. Ibid., first half of morning session, 37–38. This restriction seemed lacking in rigor to Research Director Falk, who protested that the council had opened the door to "deathbed marriages" that would entitle a woman to a widow's pension when she reached age sixty-five (3).

74. Wilbur J. Cohen, untitled memo, October 4, 1937, p. 1; and see Falk, "Benefits for Disabled Persons and Survivors and Supplemental Allowances for Dependents," typescript, November 5, 1937, File: November 1937, Box 20, Brown Papers. Falk included widowers and husbands in his recommendations, the only time I have seen them mentioned as possible beneficiaries.

75. Advisory Council Minutes, December 11, 1937, morning session, 37. All the quotes in the following discussion come from 37–39.

76. Ibid., February 18, 1938, morning session, 66; and see Brown's summary of the discussion on February 19, 1938, morning session, 2: "After some discussion, the alternatives of course being the enhancement of the individual benefit or the adding of an arrangement for wives, the statement worked out was that the enhancement of early benefits be attained by the method of paying allowances to aged wives."

77. Advisory Council Minutes, October 22, 1938, morning session, 5.

78. Typescript headed "Strictly Confidential," October 22, 1938, File 025, Box 138, Executive Director's Files, Advisory Council on Social Security, RG47, NARA.

79. J. Douglas Brown, *An American Philosophy of Social Security: Evolution and Issues* (Princeton: Princeton University Press, 1972), 135, italics in original.

80. Dewson indicated her desire to resign on June 10, 1938, but her formal resignation is dated six months later, on December 10, 1938. She was replaced by Ellen Woodward, director of the Works Progress Administration, on December 21, 1938. MWD to Arthur Altmeyer, June 10, 1938, Carton 8, Mary W. Dewson papers, Franklin Delano Roosevelt Library. Susan Ware, *Partner and I: Molly Dewson, Feminism, and New Deal Politics* (New Haven: Yale University Press, 1987), 238, comments that Dewson used the excuse of her health "to extricate herself from a job that no longer offered satisfaction." The evidence here raises questions about maternalist interpretations of the development of the welfare state such as are found in Skocpol, *Protecting Soldiers and Mothers*, and Seth Koven and Sonya Michel, *Mothers of a New World: Maternalist Politics and the Origins of Welfare States* (New York: Routledge, 1993).

81. Dewson began an October 1937 speech entitled "What the Social Security Act Means to Women" by proclaiming her lack of enthusiasm about the subject which had been assigned to her; Carton 9, 1937, Speeches and Addresses, Dewson Papers. In the course of the council debate, she published several speeches and an article, none of which mentioned the issue embroiling the council; see esp. Mary W. Dewson, "Next Steps in Social Security Legislation," *Social Service Review* 12 (March 1938), 21–33. Other women reformers do not seem to have been particularly concerned with the issue. For example,

wives, farmers, and domestics are not mentioned by Sophonisba Breckinridge in her October 24, 1937, lecture entitled "Social Security and Public Welfare: A Comprehensive Program," pamphlet in Carton 8, Dewson Papers.

82. Gordon, "Social Insurance and Public Assistance," 47–50.

83. For example, Grace Abbott to Mary Dewson, February 3, 1938, Carton 1, Dewson Papers, where Abbott urges on Dewson the importance of paying special attention to men over forty-five as well as to integrating unemployment compensation and "invalidity" assistance with grants for relief. In the same period, Dewson also seems to be profoundly interested in what she calls an "integrated system" for men; Dewson to Ed Dewson, April 25, 1938, Carton 8, Dewson Papers. There is some evidence that these concerns survived the depression. On August 24, 1946, Clara Beyer (according to Eileen Boris, an early supporter of gender-neutral labor legislation) wrote to Mary Dewson (Carton 1, Dewson Papers) with regard to the Women's Bureau's continuing efforts to promote special legislation for women, "My feelings on the subject rather correspond with yours. I can't get excited any more about separate legislation for women and believe we are losing a lot of the push for real improvement of conditions by the emphasis on sex."

84. Quadagno, *The Transformation of Old Age Security*, 39, and see ch. 6 on the influence of southern politicians on the old age assistance portion of the Social Security Act.

85. Brown, *An American Philosophy of Social Security*, 138.

86. These amendments also included altering the fiscal plan to a pay-as-you-go system, paying benefits on the basis of a wage-averaging device rather than on the basis of accumulated benefits, and expanding the categories of agricultural and domestic workers excluded from coverage. See Edward D. Berkowitz, "The First Social Security Crisis," *Prologue* 15, no. 3 (1983), 133–49, for a summary of their full contents.

87. These figures come from the testimony of Sumner Slichter, *Hearings on the Social Security Act Amendments of 1939*, 1512. Slichter estimated that eleven million self-employed farmers and others, and about a million employees of nonprofit corporations, also remained uncovered.

88. Advisory Council Minutes, February 19, 1938, afternoon session, 20.

89. Gwendolyn Mink, *The Wages of Motherhood: Inequality in the Welfare State, 1917–1942* (Ithaca: Cornell University Press, 1995), 175.

90. The best discussion of this issue is in ibid., chs. 6–7.

91. Edward J. McCaffery, *Taxing Women* (Chicago: University of Chicago Press, 1997), ch. 4.

92. Brown, Advisory Council Minutes, February 18, 1938, morning session, 14.

93. House, *Hearings on the Social Security Act Amendments of 1939*, 1218.

94. Ibid., 2176; California's Sen. Sheridan Downey described this provision as "one of the most extraordinary platitudes of asininity that has ever been published in the Congressional Record." *Congressional Record—Senate*, July 13, 1939, 9012.

95. The debate on this issue occurred within the Advisory Council on February 18 and February 19, 1938; the following quotes come from the minutes of February 18, morning session, 15, 33, and February 19, afternoon session, 19.

96. Testimony of Sen. Sheridan Downey of California, *Congressional Record—Senate*, July 13, 1939, 9012.

97. Arthur J. Altmeyer to Sen. Vic Donahey of Ohio, April 27, 1940, File 721.4, Box 240, Entry 20, PI 183, Central File, RG47, NARA. And see Nan S. Ransone to Hon. Vic Dona-

hey, April 22, 1940, and Donahey to Mr. Walter J. Cohen (this is probably Wilbur J. Cohen), April 25, 1940 ibid.

98. Downey, *Congressional Record—Senate*, July 13, 1939, 9012.

99. *Senate Resolution Preliminary Report, 1941*, 8. This seemed no small issue to many. On March 31, 1942, the New York State Assembly transmitted to FDR a resolution protesting the exclusion from Social Security of formerly covered workers "when through no action or choice on their part, they became employees of uncovered employers." File 720, Box 239, Entry 20, PI 183, Central Files, RG47, NARA.

100. Thus, though African Americans made up about 10 percent of the labor force, they constituted nearly half of the women in domestic service. Cf. Testimony of Margaret Plunkett, chief, Division of Legislation, Women's Bureau, Department of Labor, U.S. Congress, House, *Hearings before the Committee on Ways and Means, House of Representatives on Social Security Legislation, Amendments to the Social Security Act of 1946*, 79th Cong., 2nd sess. (Washington, D.C.: GPO, 1946), 542; hereafter, House, *Hearings on Amendments to the Social Security Act of 1946*. Plunkett also says that 6 percent of agricultural workers were women (545).

101. Figures from Albion Hartwell, "The Need of Social and Unemployment Insurance for Negroes," *Journal of Negro Education* 5 (January 1936), 79–87; testimony of Elmer W. Henderson, director, American Council on Human Rights, Washington, D.C., House, *Hearings before the Committee on Ways and Means on HR 2893 on the Social Security Act Amendments: Old-Age, Survivors, and Disability Insurance*, 81st Cong., 1st sess. (Washington, D.C.: GPO, 1949), 1505–6; hereafter, House, *Hearings on the Social Security Act Amendments of 1949*.

102. This argument appears in the testimony of Edgar G. Brown, director, National Negro Council, Washington, D.C., at U.S. Congress, House, *Hearings on Social Security Act Amendments of 1949*, 1878.

103. Brown interview, March 16, 1965, 30.

104. See the account of this incident in Witte, *The Development of Social Security*, 152–53. According to Witte, Treasury Secretary Morgenthau persuaded the House Ways and Means Committee that exclusion would be prudent; Perkins, anxious to get the bill through, did not fight it. See also Armstrong interview, December 19, 1965, 129.

105. Mary Anderson, "The Plight of Negro Domestic Labor," *Journal of Negro Education* 5 (January 1936), 71; Phyllis Palmer, *Domesticity and Dirt: Housewives and Domestic Servants in the United States, 1920–1945* (Philadelphia: Temple University Press, 1989), 131–33.

106. Abraham Epstein, "The Social Security Act," *Crisis* (November 1935), 338, 347.

107. NAACP Papers, Microfilm, Part 1, Reel 9, March 11, 1935, 1680.

108. *Senate Resolution Preliminary Report, 1941*, 5, 8. Rep. Jerry Voorhis of California made the same argument a few years later when he argued for extending coverage on the grounds that "at present those not covered are paying in higher prices, at least the major portion of the employer's contribution to the OASI of those that are covered. I do not think I need to explain that . . . those people in the population who are not covered by the act pay the same prices as those that are and those prices reflect at least a part of the employers' contribution to the taxes that support those who are covered." House, *Hearings on Amendments to the Social Security Acts of 1946*, 308.

109. NAACP Papers, Microfilm, Part 1, Reel 2, Minutes of the Board of Directors, February 11,

1935, 1674. Among the Advisory Council members appointed to study the question was Lucy Randolph Mason, who, however, quit the council in its early days. At the committee's request, officers of the NAACP conferred with Abraham Epstein. Part 1, Reel 10: Resolutions of 28th Annual Conference of NAACP, Detroit, June 29–July 4, 1937; Resolutions, 30th Annual Conference, July 1, 1939; Resolutions, of 31st Annual Conference, June 18–23, 1940.

110. Louis Resnick to Mr. Altmeyer, March 23, 1937, File 720, Box 239, Entry 20, PI 183, Central File, RG47, NARA. Resnick warned Altmeyer that "the excluded groups are to be made acutely conscious that they have been 'discriminated against' in provisions of the Social Security Act, and that the American Federation of Labor, in promoting the passage of this law, sought to provide coverage only for groups that are definitely within the ranks of organized labor." See also Wilbur J. Cohen to Thomas C. Blaisdell, March 9, 1937, ibid.

111. Adam Clayton Powell, Jr. to John G. Winant, February 23, 1937, File 721.1, Box 238, Entry 20, PI 183, Central Files, RG47, NARA.

112. August 30, 1938, File 011.1, Box 133, Executive Director's Files, RG47, NARA.

113. For example, Walter Campbell to Mrs. John Moore, March 19, 1937, File 721.1, Box 240, Entry 20, PI 183, Papers of the Social Security Board, Central File, RG47, NARA; and see esp. the April 14, 1937, memo from Robert Huse to members of the Social Security Board informational service, instructing them how to answer inquiries with regard to exclusion of coverage under the old age benefits provisions of the Social Security Act (ibid.).

114. Cohen to Altmeyer, memo, November 1, 1938, File 720, Box 237, Central Files, RG47, NARA.

115. The staff of the Social Security Board summed up its problems with including the excluded groups in a memo presented to the Advisory Council on November 5, 1937: "The Problem of Extending Old-Age Insurance to Cover Classes Now Excluded," File 025, Box 9, Chairman's Files, RG47, NARA. Its reasoning affirms and extends that of its chair, Arthur Altmeyer. See Altmeyer to Miss E. Pangle, February 25, 1937, and Wilbur J. Cohen to Thomas C. Blaisdell, March 9, 1937, both in File 720, Box 237, Central Files, RG47, NARA.

116. Advisory Council Minutes, December 11, 1937, morning session, 21.

117. Ibid., February 19, 1938, afternoon session, 19–25; the five-million figure comes from Wilbur J. Cohen to Thomas C. Blaisdell, memo, March 9, 1937, and excludes unpaid family labor.

118. Advisory Council Minutes, October 22, 1938, morning session, 37, 44, 6, 42–44.

119. *Hearings on Social Security Act Amendments of 1939*, 2328–29; Brown asserted his position that coverage for farm and domestic workers begin "as soon as administratively possible" and then responded to committee pressure by suggesting that he "would not be disappointed if the legislation were not enacted at this time" (1279).

120. Altmeyer to Robert Doughton, chair, House Ways and Means Committee, May 29, 1937, in File 721.1, Box 240, Entry 20, PI 183, Central Files, RG47, NARA. This file is full of letters objecting to efforts to extend the exclusions to a great variety of food-processing workers; see esp. Altmeyer to John W. McCormack, May 2, 1940.

121. Oscar Powell to the Hon. Harry Woodring, December 16, 1939, File 721.32, Box 240, Entry 20, PI 183, Central Files, RG47, NARA.

122. Rae Needleman, "Are Domestic Workers Coming of Age," *American Federationist* 46 (October 1939), 1070–75.

123. *Senate Resolution Preliminary Report, 1941,* 4–5.

124. House, *Hearings on Amendments to the Social Security Acts of 1946,* 308–9. On the resurrection of Townsend, see testimony of Rep. Victor Wickersham of Oklahoma, in favor of it, ibid., 96; and for the opposite perspective see the testimony of John Corson, a former director of the Bureau of Old-Age and Survivors Insurance, House, *Hearings on the Social Security Act Amendments of 1949,* 1966.

125. House, *Hearings on Amendments to the Social Security Acts of 1946,* 315–18; and see testimony of M. Albert Linton, representative of the Joint Committee of Social Security of the American Life Convention and the Life Insurance Association of America, arguing that increasing the tax without extending coverage would be unwise because "the amount paid by the employer does enter into his cost and he probably adds it on to the cost of his product and therefore it represents something that is being paid now by the people who are not covered under Social Security, and they should not pay through the general revenues, when they are not getting coverage" (430).

126. Draft of Marion Folsom article for *Atlantic Monthly* attached to a note dated December 21, 1948, File 095, Box 26, Office of the Actuary, General Correspondence, 1946–60, RG47, NARA.

127. House, *Hearings on Amendments to the Social Security Act of 1946,* 543–45.

128. Ibid., 345 (Hostetter), 359 (Ligren).

129. House, *Hearings on the Social Security Act Amendments of 1949,* 2183.

130. Testimony of Miss Lucille Lewis in behalf of the National Board of the YWCA, Washington, D.C., ibid., 2185.

131. Altmeyer, ibid., 1084.

132. Plunkett, ibid., 544, 543–44. Questions about the unfairness of excluding workers who had worked in covered jobs during the war emerged repeatedly in these hearings (114, 360, 544). They reemerged in 1949: see the testimonies of Edgar G. Brown, director, National Negro Council, Washington, D.C., and Clarence Mitchell, labor secretary of the NAACP, House, *Hearings on the Social Security Act Amendments of 1949,* 1878, 2144.

133. House, *Hearings on Amendments to the Social Security Act of 1946,* 360, 418.

134. Ibid., 361.

135. House, *Hearings on Social Security Act Amendments of 1949,* 2516 (Burns), 1591, 1587 (Miller). Miller's testimony also favored maternity insurance and lowering the widow's pension age to sixty.

136. House, *Hearings on the Social Security Act Amendments of 1946,* 359.

137. Testimony of Ruth Ligren, ibid., 360.

138. Johnson, ibid., 418.

139. Testimony of Helen Hostetter, ibid., 343.

140. *Old Age Insurance for Household Workers,* Women's Bureau Bulletin no. 220 (Washington, D.C.: GPO, 1947), 2–3, 11, 17.

141. House, *Hearings on the Social Security Act Amendments of 1949,* 1212; testimony of Herman Eberharter, ibid., 1506.

142. House, *Hearings on Amendments to the Social Security Acts of 1946,* 210–11.

143. For example, representatives of the Baltimore Urban League, the YWCA, and domestic

workers themselves testified for coverage during House, *Hearings on the Social Security Act Amendments of 1949*, April 21, 22, and 26, 1949, 2183–85. These were summarized by the Social Security Administration's Division of Research and Statistics; see UD/Entry 11, Division of Research and Statistics, General Correspondence, 1946–50, RG47, NARA.

144. U.S. Congress, Senate, *Hearings before the Committee on Finance on H.R. 6000, Social Security Revision, 1949*, 81st Cong., 2d sess., part 2 (Washington, D.C.: GPO, 1950), 1185; hereafter, Senate, *Finance Committee Hearings on Social Security Revision, 1949*.

145. Ibid., 1292.

146. House, *Hearings on the Social Security Act Amendments of 1949*, 1245.

147. "Information on Position of Women's Organizations Regarding Coverage of Domestic Service by Old-Age and Survivors Insurance," submitted to House, *Hearings on Social Security Act Amendments of 1949*, 2328–29.

148. Ibid., 1243.

149. Wilbur J. Cohen and Robert J. Meyers, "Social Security Act Amendments of 1950: A Summary and Legislative History," *Social Security Bulletin* 13 (October 1950), 3–14.

150. See Achenbaum, *Social Security: Visions and Revisions*, 38–39; and Derthick, *Policy Making for Social Security*, chs. 10–15 for details of these changes, as well as for the debate over the addition of disability insurance in 1956.

151. Jay Iglauer, Advisory Council Minutes, February 18, 1938, morning session, 14; and "Description of Proposed Plan AC-12," 6.

152. Advisory Council Minutes, October 22, 1938, morning session, 5.

153. Walter Fuller, ibid., February 19, 1938, afternoon session, 11–12. Fuller was president of the Curtis Publishing Company of Philadelphia.

154. Advisory Council Minutes, February 19, 1938, afternoon session, 11, and April 29, 1938, morning session, 25.

155. Senate, *Finance Committee Hearings on Social Security Revision, 1949*, 1361.

156. Advisory Council Minutes, February 19, 1938, afternoon session, 13, April 29, 1938, morning session, 27, and October 22, 1938, morning session, 4.

157. Advisory Council Minutes, February 19, 1938, afternoon session, 11–12, and April 29, 1938, morning session, 23; Advisory Council, *Final Report*, 16.

158. See, for example, the Senate debate on the proposal, *Congressional Record—Senate*, July 13, 1939, 9011, where the failure to give men extra benefits unless their wives were also sixty-five came under harsh attack.

159. *Senate Resolution Preliminary Report, 1941*, 9, endorsed the idea of sixty as the age for female retirement, as did a 1947 Advisory Council to the Senate Committee on Finance that included Marion Folsom, Albert Linton, and Douglas Brown, who had served on both of the earlier Advisory Councils. Finally, President Harry Truman, running for reelection in 1948, included it among the benefits he endorsed for his Democratic Party platform that year, and in 1949 he made it part of his legislative package. Cohen, *Retirement Policies under Social Security*, 28–29.

160. House, *Hearings on Social Security Act Amendments of 1949*, 1590. When a compromise age of sixty-two was agreed on in 1955, the insurance industry, which opposed a lower age, challenged the benefits to men, arguing that 50 percent of the wives of sixty-five-year-old men were younger than sixty-two. Testimony of Edward H. O'Connor, manag-

ing director, Insurance Economic Society of America, U.S. Congress, Senate, *Hearings before the Committee on Finance on HR 7225, Social Security Amendments of 1955*, 84th Cong., 2nd sess. (Washington, D.C.: GPO, 1956), 481; hereafter, Senate, *Finance Committee Hearings on Social Security Amendments of 1955*.

161. House, *Hearings on Amendments to the Social Security Act of 1946*, 546–547.

162. House, *Hearings on Social Security Act Amendments of 1949*, 1991.

163. Senate, *Finance Committee Hearings on Social Security Revision, 1949*, 1366. The CIO's representative did not disagree: Emil Rieve, chair of the CIO Social Security Committee, president of the Textile Workers' Union of America, and a labor representative to the Advisory Council, favored "reducing the age of permissive retirement" for women workers as well as for wives, widows, and mothers because "the average wife is somewhat younger than the husband is.... When the husband reaches 65 really he cannot retire, because his wife is not entitled to her share of his retirement, because she is not 65 years of age yet.... By reducing the age for women, they could probably retire when the men reach the age of 65" (1257).

164. Senate, *Finance Committee Hearings on Social Security Amendments of 1955*, 499. Cruikshank estimated that if the age were lowered to sixty-two, benefits would go to 800,000 additional women: 300,000 women workers, 300,000 wives of retired workers, 200,000 widows, and 3,000 dependent mothers of deceased workers.

165. Testimony of Eveline Burns, Senate, *Finance Committee Hearings on Social Security Revision, 1949*, 1299. Burns supported lowering "the age of retirement to 60 for wives and widows" but not for the primary beneficiary—which "should be 65 for both men and women." All workers, in her mind, deserved the same treatment, regardless of sex. And, in Burns's judgment, good policy would encourage people to keep working as long as possible. By 1955, the NCL had modified its position and testified in support of lowering the age for all women; Senate, *Finance Committee Hearings on Social Security Amendments of 1955*, part 2, 529.

166. Statement of Mrs. James W. Kideney, chairman, Legislative Program Committee, AAUW, Senate, *Finance Committee Hearings on Social Security Amendments of 1955*, part 3, 1052; the AAUW had earlier taken a gender-neutral position with regard to men retiring, questioning the need to have either men or women retire from the workforce at a particular age; cf. House, *Hearings on Social Security Act Amendments of 1949*, 1541. The National Federation of Business and Professional Women's Clubs took by far the strongest position. See testimony of executive director, NFBPWC, Olive Huston, House, *Hearings on Social Security Act Amendments of 1949*, 1595–96, 1599: the differential would "establish a dangerous pattern for private business, both in its own pension funds and in the mandatory retirement age which it may set." However, note the response of Sen. Thomas Jenkins of Ohio, who told Huston, "You have been the first woman, at least, who has especially expressed an opposition to this change or reduction from 65 to 60 years of age for women" (1597). The NFBPWC took the same position in 1955, testifying that the organization "vigorously opposes any legislation which would lower the retirement age for women only" because "it is well known that a discrimination or difference which is first imposed on a voluntary basis quickly becomes, in custom and in fact, an arbitrary and binding straitjacket"; Senate, *Finance Committee Hearings on Social Security Amendments of 1955*, part 1, 231.

167. Testimony of Alex F. North, treasurer of the Allen Bradley Co. of Milwaukee, Wisc., House, *Hearings on Social Security Act Amendments of 1949*, April 26, 1949, 2390; testimony of Edward H. O'Connor, managing director. Insurance Economics Society of America, Senate, *Finance Committee Hearings on Social Security Amendments of 1955*, part 2, 480–82. The Catholic Church opposed reducing the retirement age for women on the grounds that it would create pressure to reduce the age for men, and thus threaten the whole Social Security system by pressing it to reduce the age for both "to 60 or 55"; testimony of Rt. Rev. Msgr. John O'Grady, secretary, National Conference of Catholic Charities, Senate, *Finance Committee Hearings on Social Security Amendments of 1955*, part 3, 907.

168. Graebner, *History of Retirement*, 221. When asked, Altmeyer suggested that while he supported lowering the age at which women were eligible for benefits, he gave disability benefits a higher priority; House, *Hearings on the Social Security Act Amendment of 1949*, 1243.

169. Ibid., 1598. Huston continued: "I think, as business-women, we look at it as a business proposition; that we are establishing an account on which we can have a return. If kindness enters into it, then we are going into another field."

170. Ibid., 1598–99.

171. Wilbur J. Cohen and Fedele F. Fauri, "The Social Security Amendments of 1956," *Public Welfare* 14 (October 1956), 188–89; the net result was to make some 300,000 working women, 300,000 wives of retired workers, and 200,000 widows eligible for immediate benefits. Senate, *Finance Committee Hearings on Social Security Amendments of 1955*, 14.

172. From 1.2 million to 4.8 million; Ella J. Polinsky, "The Position of Women in the Social Security System," *Social Security Bulletin* 32 (July 1969), 15.

173. *New York Times*, June 8, 1939. An earlier editorial had noted that some of the increased costs would be covered by "tax contributions from persons not now included" (December 19, 1938).

174. Advisory Council Minutes, February 18, 1938, afternoon session, 46.

175. See, for example, the comments of Theresa McMahon, ibid., morning session, 8.

176. Cf. testimony of Linton, House, *Hearings on Amendments to the Social Security Act of 1946*, 433; also Sylvester J. Schieber, *Social Security: Perspectives on Preserving the System* (Washington, D.C.: Employee Benefit Research Institute, 1982), 29.

177. Advisory Council Minutes, February 18, 1938, afternoon session, 46.

178. McCormack questioning Altmeyer, House, *Hearings on the Social Security Act Amendments of 1939*, 2176.

179. Nancy Cott, *Public Vows: A Political History of Marriage in the United States* (Cambridge: Harvard University Press, 2000).

180. Robert J. Myers, *Social Security*, 2d ed. (Homewood: Richard D. Irwin, 1981), 240–41.

181. Joseph A. Pechman, Henry J. Aaron, and Michael K. Taussig, *Social Security: Perspectives for Reform* (Washington, D.C.: Brookings Institution, 1968), 84–85; see also the discussion in Derthick, *Policymaking for Social Security*, 261.

182. Schieber, *Social Security*, tables 1–6; Polinsky, "The Position of Women in the Social Security System," 19.

183. The proposal for each spouse to have a share in the other's benefits comes from Huston. See also Polinsky, "The Position of Women in the Social Security System," 4.

184. Margaret Mead and Frances Balgley Kaplan, eds., *American Women: The Report of the President's Commission on the Status of Women and Other Publications of the Commission* (New York: Charles Scribner's Sons, 1965), 140. The precedent came from federal government pensioners, who could retire with pensions after thirty years of service, then take Social Security-covered jobs for ten years and draw both pensions.

185. U.S. Congress, House, *Executive Hearings on the Social Security Act Amendments of 1961 on H.R. 4571, Social Security Amendments of 1961*, 87th Cong., 1st sess. (Washington, D.C.: GPO, 1961), 112; hereafter, House, *Executive Hearings on Social Security Act Amendments of 1961*.

186. Ibid., 148, Noah M. Mason of Illinois speaking. The position that this provision was "a plan to ease the unemployment problem" was also taken by the National Association of Manufacturers. See testimony of John E. Carroll, chairman of the Employee Health and Benefits Committee, National Association of Manufacturers, U.S. Congress, Senate, *Hearings before the Committee on Finance on H.R. 6027, Social Security Benefits and Eligibility of 1961*, 87th Cong., 1st sess. (Washington, D.C.: GPO, 1961), 20: "Unemployment is a problem which should be called by its right name and solved by appropriate measures." Hereafter, Senate, *Finance Committee Hearings on Social Security Benefits of 1961*.

187. House, *Executive Hearings on Social Security Act Amendments of 1961*, 148; cf. 146.

188. Ibid., 149.

189. Ibid., 33–34, 114. The issue was also raised by the Chamber of Commerce, Senate, *Finance Committee Hearings on Social Security Benefits of 1961*, 37, 40, and E. Russell Bartley, director of industrial relations, Illinois Manufacturers Association, ibid., 117.

190. House, *Executive Hearings on Social Security Act Amendments of 1961*, 35, 114.

191. Ibid., 39.

192. Testimony of John E. Carroll, Senate, *Finance Committee Hearings on Social Security Benefits of 1961*, 15, 20.

193. House, *Executive Hearings on Social Security Act Amendments of 1961*, 17.

194. Martha W. Griffiths, "Sex Discrimination in Income Security Programs," *Notre Dame Lawyer* 49 (February 1974), 534.

195. *Weinberger v. Wiesenfeld*, 420 U.S. 636 (1975), 652.

196. Ibid., 645, 647.

197. *Califano v. Goldfarb*, 97 S.Ct. 1021 (1977), 1023. Justice William J. Brennan for the Court.

198. *Califano v. Webster*, 430 U.S. 313 (1977).

199. *Califano v. Goldfarb*, 1028.

## Chapter 4

1. *Breedlove v. Suttles*, 302 U.S. 277 (1937), 282.

2. *Kahn v. Shevin*, 416 U.S. 351 (1974); quoted, "Reply Brief for Appellants," Docket no. 73–78, U.S. Supreme Court, October term, 1973.

3. *In re Lockwood*, 154 U.S. 116 (1894); see Joan Hoff, *Law, Gender, and Injustice: A Legal History of U.S. Women* (New York: New York University Press, 1991), 182–84, 247–49.

4. *Reed v. Reed*, 404 U.S. 71 (1971); *Phillips v. Martin Marietta Corp.*, 400 U.S. 321 (1971); and *Frontiero v. Richardson*, 411 U.S. 677 (1973), which came perilously close to declaring sex a suspect classification.

5. *Kahn v. Shevin*, 353–54, 355.

6. The most insightful discussion of the nineteenth-century conflict is in Linda Kerber, *No*

*Constitutional Right to Be Ladies* (New York: Hill & Wang, 1998), ch. 3. For a useful analysis of *Kahn v. Shevin*, see John D. Johnston, "Sex Discrimination and the Supreme Court, 1971–1974," *New York University Law Review* 49 (November 1974), 661–73.

7. This history is documented in Boris I. Bittker, "Federal Income Taxation and the Family," *Stanford Law Review* 27 (July 1975), 1389–463. Bittker's work was prefigured by that of Randolph Paul, *Taxation in the United States* (Boston: Little, Brown, 1954); Oliver Oldman and Ralph Temple, "Comparative Analysis of the Taxation of Married Persons," *Stanford Law Review* 12 (1960), 585–605; and Douglas Y. Thorson, "An Analysis of the Sources of Continued Controversy over the Tax Treatment of Family Income," *National Tax Journal* 18 (1965), 113–32. See as well Grace Ganz Blumberg, "Sexism in the Code: A Comparative Study of Income Taxation of Working Wives and Mothers," *Buffalo Law Review* 21 (1972), 49–98; Edward J. McCaffery, *Taxing Women* (Chicago: University of Chicago Press, 1997); and the pioneering work of Carolyn Jones, "Split Income and Separate Spheres: Tax Law and Gender Roles in the 1940s," *Law and History Review* 6 (Fall 1988), 259–309.

8. *Breedlove v. Suttles*, 357, 360. "Like classifications based upon race, alienage, and national origin," Brennan argued, classifications based on sex "too often have been inexcusably utilized to stereotype and stigmatize politically powerless segments of society."

9. Quoted in Bittker, "Federal Income Taxation and the Family," 1400.

10. The best general summary of U.S. income tax history is John F. Witte, *The Politics and Development of the Federal Income Tax* (Madison: University of Wisconsin Press, 1985); see also Paul, *Taxation in the United States*. For the development of women's legal status as persons in tax law, see Randolph E. Paul and Valentine B. Havens, "Husband and Wife under the Income Tax," *Brooklyn Law Review* 5 (1936), 241–71; and Jeannette Anderson Winn and Marshall Winn, "Till Death Do We Split: Married Couples and Single Persons under the Individual Income Tax," *South Carolina Law Review* 34 (1983), 829–83. For the complexities of the wife's position with regard to property law, see Blanche Crozier, "Marital Support," *Boston University Law Review* 15 (1935), 28–58.

11. Lawrence H. Seltzer, *The Personal Exemptions in the Income Tax* (New York: National Bureau of Economic Research, 1968), 50.

12. Winn and Winn, "Till Death Do We Split," 831; McCaffery, *Taxing Women*, 29–30. Witte, *The Politics and Development of the Federal Income Tax*, 77–78, notes that from 1913 to 1915, the threshold for paying taxes was so high that only 2 percent of wage earners had to file returns. This changed rapidly during World War II, when individuals with incomes of $750 per year, about 75 percent of wage earners, became eligible to pay taxes. The best summary of this debate is in Bill Ratchford, "Joint Family Returns in the Federal Income Tax," *Bulletin of the National Tax Association* 27 (February 1942), 133–41.

13. Groves, *Federal Tax Treatment of the Family* (Washington, D.C.: Brookings Institution, 1963), 62; Jones, "Split Income and Separate Spheres," 303, fn. 118, estimates that the numbers of marital partnership returns filed reached a high of 244,670 in 1930, then declined for most of the depression, bouncing back to 261,470 in 1937 and increasing steadily thereafter.

14. This is documented at length by Jones, "Split Income and Separate Spheres," 274–93.

15. *Lucas v. Earl*, 281 U.S. 111 (1930).

16. *United States v. Robbins*, 269 U.S. 315 (1925).

17. The Treasury took four states to court to test this proposition. See Paul Bruton, "The Taxation of Family Income," *Yale Law Journal* 41 (June 1932), 1172–94, and the discussion in McCaffery, *Taxing Women*, 37–45.

18. *Hoeper v. Tax Commission*, 284 U.S. 206 (1931), 212, 216, 215.

19. *Lucas v. Earl*, 281 U.S. 111 (1930).

20. Paul and Havens, "Husband and Wife under the Income Tax," 264.

21. The Supreme Court definitively upheld the community property interpretation in *Poe v. Seaborn*, 282 U.S. 101 (1930). Several commentators have noted that this decision sits uncomfortably with other tax decisions that also considered who had the benefit of the taxable property (generally conceded to be the husband). The Court's refusal to take use into consideration in this case, and the consequent clarity of the decison in denying the Treasury's desire to aggregate income for tax purposes, have led at least one commentator to note that the Court's effort to defend states' rights was as much to defend personhood as to protect property. See Paul Trigg, "Some Income Tax Aspects of Community Property Law," *Michigan Law Review* 46 (1947), 1.

22. McCaffery, *Taxing Women*, 29–57, illustrates differences in payments when income is split and under aggregate income.

23. U.S. Congress, *Revenue Revision, 1934: Hearings before the House Committee on Ways and Means*, 73d Cong., interim, 1st and 2d sess., December 15, 1933 (Washington, D.C.: GPO, 1934), 111; hereafter, *Revenue Revision, 1934*.

24. Ibid.

25. This is not a universal point of view. See Louise Dulude, "Taxation of the Spouses: A Comparison of the Canadian, American, British, French, and Swedish Law," *Osgoode Hall Law Journal* 23 (Spring 1985), 69–85.

26. *Congressional Record—House*, February 16, 1934, 2659.

27. *Revenue Revisions, 1934*, 642.

28. Ibid., 643, 642–43.

29. Statement of Rep. William Lemke, U.S. Congress, *Community Property Income Hearings before a Subcommittee of the House Committee on Ways and Means on H.R. 8396*, 73d Cong., 2d sess., May 1–7, 1934 (Washington, D.C.: GPO, 1934), 313; see also *Revenue Revisions, 1934*, 126, 639.

30. Memorandum brief submitted by Charles E. Dunbar Jr., U.S. Congress, *Revenue Act of 1941: Hearings on H.R. 5417 before the Senate Committee on Finance*, 77th Cong., 1st sess., 1941, 1585.

31. In addition to *Poe v. Seaborn* and *Hoeper v. Tax Commission*, the following were among the cases repeatedly cited in the congressional defense of the rights of women: *Arnold v. Leonard*, 273 S.W. 799 (Tex. 1925); *Hopkins v. Bacon*, 282 U.S. 122 (1930); *Wright v. Hays' Administrator*, 10 Tex. 130 (1926); *Martin v. Moran*, 32 S.W. 904 (Tex. Civ. App. 1895 no writ); *Watson v. Harris*, 130 S.W. 237 (1910); *Davis v. Davis*, 186 S.W. 775 (1916); *Knowlton v. Moore*, 178 U.S. 41 (1900). In light of these cases, Senator Connally told House members that they would be unwise to change the law "for the reason if we adopted it now and went along 2 or 3 years and then the Supreme Court should hold it unconstitutional, there would be millions of dollars of refunds with great administrative costs, and a great amount of accounting in the amount going back"; *Revenue Revisions, 1934*, 639. See also, ibid., 124–25, and *Congressional Record—House*, February 19, 1934, 2804–8.

32. *Revenue Revision, 1934*, 641; and see ibid., 127, 631.

33. Ibid., 126–27.

34. Ibid., 641.

35. *Congressional Record—House*, February 19, 1934, 2808–9.

36. Henry Morgenthau Jr. to "My Dear Mr. President," May 21, 1937, File: Taxes, Box 16b, President's Secretary's File, FDR Library. The charges were included by FDR in his June 1, 1937, message to Congress. "Income Tax Avoidance," *Tax Policy* 4 (August, 1937), 1–3; U.S. Congress, *Tax Evasion and Avoidance, Hearings before the House Committee on Ways and Means*, 75th Cong., 1st sess., August 9–10, 1937 (Washington D.C.: GPO, 1937).

37. The idea of a proportional tax was first proposed in 1934 in response to a House Committee report. This history is captured in ibid., 3–4.

38. Ratchford, "Joint Family Returns in the Federal Income Tax," 34–35. The Senate Finance Committee proposed to amend the bill to tax community property income to the spouse who earned it. A floor vote (242–160) defeated the provision, and it was finally withdrawn in the Senate without a vote. The Senate did manage to add an amendment that made alimony a tax deduction for the payer and taxable income for the recipient, a clause whose passage testified to the shift in tax responsibility on the breakup of the family unit. See Roy D. Blakey and Gladys Blakey, "The Revenue Act of 1941," *American Economic Review* 31 (December 1941), 813.

39. The 1924, 1926, and 1928 tax codes included provisions for earned income credits. They had been dropped in 1930, theoretically in deference to the need for revenue, but their elimination was consistent with widespread efforts to discourage married women's wage-work during the depression years. See Paul, *Taxation in the United States*, 179.

40. See, for example, Roswell Magill, *The Impact of Federal Taxes* (New York: Columbia University Press, 1943), 44–72, written at the height of the debate. Magill, then a professor of law at Columbia, argues for the equity of a provision that "makes *her* pay more income tax than she used to pay in light of the increased taxable capacity of the couple" (72, emphasis added).

41. *Revenue Revision, 1934*, 641; see also the comments of Rep. Morgan Sanders of Texas: "If you can group them [these taxes] under the head of the husband and wife, then why not include all of the children? Why not group the entire family?" *Congressional Record—House*, February 19, 1934, 2808.

42. Rep. John Costello of California, *Congressional Record—House*, August 1, 1941, A3704.

43. Harley Lutz, letter to the editor, *New York Times*, July 6, 1941.

44. "Re: Joint Income Tax Returns," *Independent Woman* 21 (May 1942), 155: see also the columns of Godfrey Nelson, especially "Joint Tax Return and Its Problems," *New York Times*, July 6, 1941.

45. *Congressional Record—House*, July 31, 1941, A3688, reprinting a letter from Jules B. Jeanmard, Bishop of Lafayette, to Rep. Vance Plauche of Louisiana.

46. The Rev. Theodore Savage, president, Greater New York Federation of Churches, letter to the editor, *New York Times*, July 21, 1941.

47. Memorandum from Leonard E. Read, general manager, Los Angeles Chamber of Commerce, to Chambers of Commerce and Trade Associations, June 28, 1941, in National Woman's Party Papers, 1913–74, Reel 71 (Microfilm Corp. of North America). Read continued, "It would be difficult to conceive of a proposition capable of inflicting greater social and moral damage to this country than the one under consideration."

48. Arthur Krock, "A New Penalty on the Marital State," *New York Times*, July 4, 1941.
49. Catherine Curtis, National Director of Women Investors of America, letter to Hon. Robert Doughton, chair, House Ways and Means Committee, June 26, 1941, *Congressional Record—House*, August 1, 1941, A3716. The distinguished jurist Roscoe Pound weighed in as well. See "Pound Scores Tax Plan," *New York Times*, July 21, 1941, reporting Pound to have declared that it would be unjust to make people who refused to avail themselves of a divorce pay a higher tax. To accept separate returns where husband and wife were living apart would "obviously run counter to the settled policy of maintaining the institution of marriage." "Those who have been divorced," wrote Krock in "A New Penalty on the Marital State," "or have refrained from marriage for selfish reasons, or who cohabit on a 'free love' basis, will pay millions less to the government than married couples."
50. Godfrey Nelson, "Problems Posed by Joint Returns," *New York Times*, July 20, 1941.
51. *Congressional Record*, August 1, 1941, A3755. He goes on to: "Let us not destroy this relationship that has built this country up both morally and financially. Let us not invade states' rights and their organic laws nor pass discriminatory measures that would invade the due-process rights of individuals.... There are many other ways of producing the revenues necessary for our present program other than those that will demoralize and lower our present Christian civilization and probably degrade the sacred institution of marriage."
52. Ibid., August 4, 1941, A3764.
53. The figure comes from McCaffery, *Taxing Women*, 31.
54. Some sense of the dramatic escalation that occurred is provided by Jones ("Split Income," 294), who estimates that in 1940 some seven million families were subject to taxes; by 1945, that number had increased to forty-two million.
55. *Congressional Record—House*, July 17, 1942, 6325.
56. Ibid.
57. Stuart Piebes, letter to the editor, *New York Times*, July 23, 1941. See Henry Dorris, "Women Warn of More Divorces with Enforcing of Joint Returns," *New York Times*, March 26, 1942, quoting Judge Sarah Hughes of Dallas testifying against the proposal: "We have the anomalous situation of one department of the government crying out for more women workers and another department saying 'if you dare we will penalize you because you are married.'"
58. "Tax Bill Improved," *New Republic*, August 11, 1941, 172.
59. Alice Kessler-Harris, "Gender Ideology in Historical Reconstruction: A Case Study from the 1930s," *Gender and History* 1(Spring 1989), 31–50; see also Lois Scharff, *To Work and to Wed: Female Employment, Feminism, and the Great Depression* (Westport: Greenwood Press, 1980), and Winifred Wandersee, *Women's Work and Family Values, 1920–1930* (Cambridge: Harvard University Press, 1981).
60. Krock, "A New Penalty on the Marital State"; and the discussion in McCaffery, *Taxing Women*, 340–41.
61. U.S. Congress, *Hearings on Revenue Revision of 1942 before the House Committee on Ways and Means*, 77th Cong., 1st sess., March 3, 1942 (Washington, D.C.: GPO, 1942), 1340–41; hereafter, *Revenue Revision, 1942*.
62. *Congressional Record—House*, July 17, 1942, 6322.

63. *Revenue Revision, 1942*, 1340.
64. Florence Seabury, letter to the editor, *New York Times*, May 25, 1942; see also the unsigned editorial, "Re: Joint Income Tax Returns," *Independent Woman* 21 (May 1942), 155.
65. "Willkie Joins Fight on Joint Income Tax," *New York Times*, March 23, 1942.
66. "Tax Bill Improved," *New Republic*, August 11, 1941, 171.
67. Rep. John M. Costello, *Congressional Record—House*, August 1, 1941, A3703.
68. Dorris, "Women Warn of More Divorces."
69. By 1942, an astonishingly broad coalition of women's organizations opposed mandatory joint tax returns. In addition to the National Woman's Party and the National Federation of Business and Professional Women's Clubs, which had long testified against the mandatory joint return, an array of other organizations normally at odds with these two now joined in uneasy coalition to defeat the proposal. They included the NWTUL, the General Federation of Women's Clubs, the National Negro Business and Professional Women's Clubs, the National Association of Women Lawyers, and the American Association of University Women (by now ERA supporters). Among the major national women's groups, only the League of Women Voters remained supportive. As nearly as I can determine, the National Consumers' League remained neutral on the issue. The coalition was reported in the *New York Times*; see "Women Plan to Fight Joint Tax return: Miss Kenyon, Miss Donlan Direct Drive," May 31, 1942.
70. *Revenue Revision, 1942*, 1235–36.
71. Dorris, "Women Warn of More Divorces."
72. "Mrs. Roosevelt Backs Joint Income Return," *New York Times*, June 9, 1942. Krock quotes Eleanor Roosevelt to the effect that the system is unfair to a husband or wife who supports the family alone, because the dual providers get off with a lower tax; "Mrs. Roosevelt's Conversion to Joint Tax Return," *New York Times*, June 9, 1942.
73. Alice Manning, "Congress Upholds Women's Rights," *Independent Woman* 20 (September 1941), 276.
74. Caroline Lexow Babcock to Mrs. F. C. Gurley, July 15, 1941, Reel 71, NWP microfilm. The letter continues, "It was framed when the common law prevailed everywhere in this country and the courts have ruled that as far as the Constitution is concerned the women of today have no status except that granted them by the common law, with the one exception of the 19th Amendment which grants them votes. Congress is therefore free to do about it as it pleases as far as the women citizens of this country are concerned, and we cannot appeal to the Constitution as men can."
75. Something of the political excitement generated by the opening is suggested in the following letter from Edna (Peggy) Capewell to Caroline Babcock, January 23, 1942, Reel 72, ibid.: "Then I recall Mrs. Wiley saying the next time the Congressmen asked for help on the 'combined income tax' we had better tell them to fight their own battles if they couldn't stand by us afterwards. I notice it is up again. What are we going to do about it...? If they call on us we surely have the 'power' in our hands now, let them vote ERA out of Committees favorably at once, and out of Congress for State action, and then we will help them for they have already been shown that we can and will do it when we want to. Caroline it seems we have them in the hollow of our hands... if we just press in on each group hot and heavy and show no mercy." See also Anna Kelton Wiley to Alice Paul, July

31, 1941, Reel 71, ibid.: "The country is seething now with antagonism to the joint income tax returns for husbands and wives. It is doing us a lot of good. People who never sided with us before begin to see the light"; and Mrs. Harvey Wiley to Hon. Robert Doughton, July 8, 1941, ibid.

76. February 2, 1942, Reel 72, ibid.

77. Mrs. Harvey Wiley to Hon. Robert Doughton, July 8, 1941, Reel 71, ibid.

78. "Joint Tax Return Fought by Women," *New York Times*, January 27, 1942.

79. *Congressional Record—House*, July 17, 1942, 6322.

80. *Congressional Record*, August 1, 1941, A3715, reprinting a letter from Cathrine Curtis [*sic*] national director of Women Investors of America: "It will destroy the independence of women and wipe out benefits of wills, trust funds, individual property ownership and legacies. It will return women, free-born American women, to the primitive status of being the chattels of their husbands" (3716).

81. "Tax Bill Improved," *New Republic*, August 11, 1941, 172.

82. John M. Costello, *Congressional Record*, August 1, 1941, A3704.

83. William Stratton of Illinois, ibid., July 21, 1941, A3532.

84. William Wheat of Illinois, ibid., August 8, 1941, A3839. Feminist Edith Nourse Rogers offered similar sentiments: "If the mandatory joint income tax return which the committee inserted in the bill in secret sessions behind closed doors without giving the women of the country any opportunity to voice their opinions becomes law, married women in the United States will be returned to the old common-law status of chattels of their husbands, the position married women have occupied in Europe for centuries"; *Congressional Record*, August 1, 1941, A3715.

85. "Mandatory Joint Tax Returns: Views of the Nation's Press," *U.S. News*, July 25, 1941, inserted by Clinton Anderson of New Mexico, *Congressional Record*, July 22, 1941, A3546.

86. Anna Kelton Wiley to President of the Senate et al., July 1941, Reel 71, NWP microfilm; and see Rep. Bolton's comments, *Congressional Record—House*, July 17, 1942, 6322.

87. See Bittker, "Federal Income Taxation and the Family," 1411–12; Jones, "Split Income and Separate Spheres," 302–4. At the time the 1948 split-income provision passed, similar measures were on the agenda in Massachusetts, Indiana, and New York.

88. Statement of Robert Silberstein, representing the National Lawyers' Guild, U.S. Congress, *Hearings before the Senate Committee on Finance, on H.R. 4790, Reduction of Individual Income Taxes*, 80th Cong., 2d sess., March 1–10, 1948 (Washington, D.C.: GPO, 1948), 272, 404; hereafter, *Senate Tax Reduction Hearings, 1948*. Among many articles, see "Trend toward Income Splitting Law Rolls Up Popular Approval," *Business Week*, December 27, 1947, 22–24; Robert Yoder, "How Nine States Beat the Income Tax," *Saturday Evening Post*, May 24, 1947, 23; "Spread of Income Splitting," *U.S. News*, September 12, 1947, 44–45.

89. Testimony of Paul Foley, *Senate Tax Reduction Hearings, 1948*, 279.

90. Rep. Bertrand W. Gearhart, *Hearings before the House Committee on Ways and Means on Revenue Revision, 1947*, part 2, 80th Cong., 1st sess. 890; hereafter, *Revenue Revisions, 1947*.

91. "Community Property States," *New York Times*, May 31, 1947; testimony of Albert Reeves, *Revenue Revisions, 1947*, 880, 884; testimony of Mr. Martin, ibid., 894. For a superb dis-

cussion of the fearsome possibilites conceived by the legislators of common law states as they imagined the consequences of converting to community property status, see Jones, "Split Income and Separate Spheres," 283–87. Jones notes the threats of greedy and manipulative wives, bankruptcy for husbands, and forced divorces.

92. Tax experts had begun to propose a split-income solution shortly after the war ended. See Stanley Surrey, "Family Income and Federal Taxation," in National Tax Association, *Proceedings of 39th National Conference* (1946), 357, and "The Tax Treatment of Family Income," reprinted in *Revenue Revisions, 1947*, 846–74.

93. Richard Goode, "Federal Tax Legislative Activities in 1947," *National Tax Journal* 1 (1948), 72–73. For the following history, see Groves, *Tax Treatment of the Family*, ch. 4, and Paul, *Taxation in the United States*, 494–98.

94. "Division of Family Income—A Tax Red Herring," *Commercial and Financial Chronicle*, December 4, 1947, 1.

95. "New Support for Tax Splitting," *Finance Week*, June 27, 1947, 45. There were exceptions, of course. Harley L. Lutz called it a "scheme to defeat more fundamental revision of the individual income tax"; "Division of Family Income—A Tax Red Herring."

96. *Revenue Revisions, 1947*, 884.

97. Ibid., 887.

98. Ibid., 885.

99. Bernard B. Smith, "Divorce Is Cheaper than Marriage," *Harper's Magazine* 195 (September 1947), 232–33; John S. McClellan, "Where You Pay Less Income Tax," *American Magazine*, January 1948, 36–37, 146–47.

100. Some analysts later argued that shifting the tax basis from the individual to the family unit "was never publicized prior to the enactment of the 1948 Act"; Douglas K. Chapman, "Marriage Neutrality: An Old Idea Comes of Age," *West Virginia Law Review* 8 (1985), 341. Lawrence Zelenak, "Marriage and the Income Tax," *Southern California Law Review* 67 (1994), 343, suggests that the rationale for the joint return "that a couple acts as an economic unit by pooling its resources" was developed "only as an after-the-fact rationalization." The evidence offered here suggests the opposite. It was the deeply rooted belief in this assumption that permitted Congress to override objections of the community property states.

101. *Revenue Revisions, 1947*, part 2, 848.

102. Ibid., 888.

103. Testimony of Paul Foley, *Senate Tax Reduction Hearings, 1948*, 278, 282.

104. Stanley Surrey, "Federal Taxation of the Family: The Revenue Act of 1948," *Harvard Law Review* 61 (July 1948), 1108; and see *Revenue Revisions, 1947*, part 2, 897.

105. Ibid., 1109; and see, for example, the communications of the General Federation of Women's Clubs to the House Committee on Ways and Means, *Revenue Revisions, 1947*, part 2, 914–17.

106. These figures come from: U.S. Department of Labor, *Bureau of Labor Statistics, Labor Statistics from the Current Population Survey* (Washington, D.C.: GPO, 1998), table 2; U.S. Department of Labor, *Handbook on Women Workers: Trends and Issues, 1993* (Washington, D.C.: Women's Bureau, 1994), 4–5; Phillip N. Cohen and Suzanne M. Bianchi, "Marriage, Children, and Women's Employment: What Do We Know?" *Monthly Labor Review*, December 1999, 22–31.

107. U.S. House of Representatives, Committee on Ways and Means, *Internal Revenue Code of 1954, Report to Accompany H.R. 8300*, 83d Cong., 2d sess., House Report no. 1337 (Washington, D.C.: GPO, 1954), 5.

108. Ibid., 30.

109. U.S. Senate, Finance Committee, *Legislative History of the Internal Revenue Code of 1954*, Senate Report no. 1622, 83d Cong., 2d sess. (Washington, D.C.: GPO, 1954), 35–36; United States Code Congressional and Administrative News, *Internal Revenue Code of 1954*, 83d Cong., 2d sess. (St. Paul: West Publishing, 1954), 83.

110. Typescript, "February 28, 1961, Discussion with Trade Union Women," Box 529, Esther Peterson Collection, Schlesinger Library, Radcliffe College.

111. "Arguments over these issues": see, for example, George F. Break and Joseph A. Pechman, *Federal Tax Reform: The Impossible Dream?* (Washington, D.C.: Brookings Institution, 1975), 32–34; Douglas Y. Thorson, "An Analysis of the Sources of Continued Controversy over the Tax Treatment of Family Income," *National Tax Journal* 18 (June 1965), 118–23; and Joint Committee on Taxation. "The Income Tax Treatment of Married Couples and Single Persons," prepared for House Ways and Means Committee and Senate Finance Committee, April 2, 1980 (Washington, D.C.: GPO, 1980), secs. 4, 5. For number of couples paying marriage penalty, see Chapman, "Marriage Neutrality: An Old Idea Comes of Age," 343. In 1995, the Congressional Budget Office estimated the number at 42 percent, or twenty-one million couples, and the average penalty at $1,380 per return. At the same time, twenty-five million couples (51 percent of all joint returns) got a marriage bonus. "Congress Vows to Renew Debate on 'Marriage Penalty,'" *Wall Street Journal*, December 30, 1997.

112. Pechman and Engelhardt, "The Income Tax Treatment of the Family," 9. By 1977, fourteen of twenty-four OECD countries allowed individual income taxation. See Harvey Brazer, "Income Tax Treatment of the Family," in Henry J. Aaron and Michael J. Boskin, eds., *The Economics of Taxation* (Washington, D.C.: Brookings Institution, 1980), 274.

113. Pamela B. Gann, "Abandoning Marital Status as a Factor in Allocating Income Tax Burdens," *Texas Law Review* 59 (December 1980), 3. Powerful analyses of the inequities of family taxation also came from Brazer, "Income Tax Treatment of the Family," and "Note: The Case for Mandatory Separate Filing for Married Persons," *Yale Law Journal* 91 (1981), 363–81.

114. U.S. Congress, *Tax Treatment of Single and Married Persons Where Both Spouses are Working: Hearings before the House Committee on Ways and Means*, 92d Cong., 2d sess., March 1992 (Washington, D.C.: GPO, 1992), 96–97.

115. U.S. Congress, *Hearings before the Joint Economic Committee . . . on the Economic Problems of Women*, 93d Cong., 1st sess., July 24, 1973 (Washington, D.C.: GPO, 1973), 221.

116. *Mapes v. United States*, 576 F.2d 896 (Ct. Cl. 1978).

117. Marjorie Kornhauser, "Love, Money, and the IRS: Family, Income-Sharing, and the Joint Income Tax Return," *Hastings Law Journal* 45 (November 1993), 63–111.

118. Statement of June E. O'Neill, director, Congressional Budget Office, "Marriage and the Federal Income Tax," House Ways and Means Committee, February 4, 1998, http://www.cbo.gov/showdoc.cfm?index=322&sequence=0&from=5; Richard W. Stevenson, "Senate Approves Tax Cut to Help Married Couples," *New York Times*, July 19, 2000; and see, for example, Virginia Postrel, "The U.S. Tax System Is Discouraging

Married Women from Working," *New York Times*, November 2, 2000, and Linda Waite, "Staying Married and Paying a Price," *New York Times*, October 12, 2000.

## Chapter 5

1. Ronald W. Schatz, *The Electrical Workers: A History of Labor at General Electric and Westinghouse, 1923–1960* (Urbana: University of Illinois Press, 1983), 122, 125.

2. Dominick V. Daniels of New Jersey, *Congressional Record—House*, August 10, 1970, 28035.

3. National Council of Jewish Women to Committee on Political and Civil Rights, March 8, 1963, Box 10, File: Committee on Political and Civil Rights, President's Commission on the Status of Women Collection, John Fitzgerald Kennedy Library, Boston; hereafter, PCSW Collection.

4. These figures come from U.S. Department of Labor, *1975 Handbook on Women Workers*, Women's Bureau Bulletin no. 297 (Washington, D.C.: GPO, 1975), 16–18, 27.

5. Carolyn Ware provided a clear exposition of this conundrum in her background paper for the PCSW. See typescript, "Background Memorandum on the the Status of Women," Folder 831, 11–16, Esther Peterson Collection, Schlesinger Library, Radcliffe College. For more on the 1950s, see Joanne Meyerowitz, ed., *Not June Cleaver: Women and Gender in Post-War America, 1945–60* (Philadelphia: Temple University Press, 1994).

6. Anonymous writer to Miss Alice Paul, May 28, 1956, File 3, Box 17, RG–21 001: Legislation Department Records, The George Meany Memorial Archives (GMMA).

7. On the September 1945 incident, see Ruth Milkman, *Gender at Work: The Dynamics of Job Segregation by Sex during World War II* (Urbana: University of Illinois Press, 1987), 131–32.

8. Dorothy Sue Cobble, "Recapturing Working-Class Feminism: Union Women in the Post-War Era," in Meyerowitz, *Not June Cleaver*, 57–83; Lisa Kannenberg, "The Product of GE's Progress: Labor, Management, and Community Relations in Schenectady, New York, 1930–1966," Ph.D. diss., Rutgers University, 1999; Dennis Deslippes, *Rights Not Roses: Unions and the Rise of Working-Class Feminism, 1950–1980* (Urbana: University of Illinois Press, 2000); Nancy Gabin, *Feminism in the Labor Movement: Women and the United Auto Workers, 1935–1975* (Ithaca: Cornell University Press, 1990); and Daniel Horowitz, *Betty Friedan and the Making of the Feminine Mystique: The American Left, the Cold War, and Modern Feminism* (Amherst: University of Massachusetts Press, 1998).

9. I am indebted to Christina Florin and Bengt Nilsson for introducing me to this idea. They elaborate it in " 'Something in the Nature of a Bloodless Revolution': How New Gender Relations Became 'Equal Status Policy' in the 1960s and 70s," in Rolf Torstendahl, ed., *State Policy and Gender System in the Two German States and Sweden, 1945–89* (Uppsala: Department of History, 1999), 11–78. Florin and Nilsson point out that attention to "equality" as a general principle is quite a different matter from attention to gender equality, which requires an examination of, and threatens to reformulate, fundamental institutions. For the United States, see Elizabeth H. Wolgast, *Equality and the Rights of Women* (Ithaca: Cornell University Press, 1980).

10. Single mothers got the same benefits as all other mothers; fathers received financial incentives to take some parental leave; an extensive, community-centered child care network was created; and an individual income tax was adopted in 1971. Still, occupational

segregation remains high, though the wage gap is narrower than in most Western industrial countries. See the discussion of these issues in Diane Sainsbury, *Gender, Equality, and Welfare States* (Cambridge: Cambridge University Press, 1996), part 2.

11. The positions of the Women's and Children's Bureaus on maternity leaves and the terms of the ILO Convention can be found in File: 6–2–9–3, Box 67, Entry 10, RG86: *Records of the Women's Bureau*, National Archives and Records Administration (NARA). See also testimony of Frieda Miller, U.S. Congress—House, Hearings before the Committee on Ways and Means on H.R. 2893 on the Social Security Act Amendments: Old Age, Survivors and Disability Insurance, 81st Cong., 1st sess., (Washington D.C.: GPO 1949), 1587.

12. National Manpower Council, *Womanpower: A Statement by the National Manpower Council with Chapters by the Council Staff* (New York: Columbia University Press, 1957), 350. The same commission concluded that there was little sentiment for child care for working mothers. We cannot know the truth of either statement, but both influenced policy at the time.

13. See the discussion in "Transcript of Proceedings, May 18, 1962," 30–38, File: Committee on Social Insurance and Taxes, Box 4, PCSW Collection.

14. National Manpower Council, *Womanpower*, vii, 328, 329.

15. Ibid., 343, 53. The report is riddled with this assumption; for example, "the charge that women workers generally are the objects of discriminatory practices is now not made with the same regularity or intensity as in the past" (343).

16. Ibid., 53.

17. Eileen Boris, "'You Wouldn't Want One of 'Em Dancing with Your Wife': Racialized Bodies on the Job in WWII," *American Quarterly* 50 (March 1998), 77–108.

18. Hugh Davis Graham, *The Civil Rights Era: Origins and Development of National Policy* (New York: Oxford University Press, 1990), 42. Graham offers the most comprehensive account of the political negotiations surrounding the executive order and the creation of the committee, 29–43.

19. Ibid., 39.

20. Esther Peterson, typescript, "Ch. 6: Status," 27, Folder 41, Peterson Collection.

21. Katherine Ellickson, typescript, "The PCSW: Its Formation, Functioning, and Contribution," January 1976, 2, Folder 831, Peterson Collection.

22. Peterson, "Ch. 6: Status." See also Ann Campbell, Second Oral History Interview with Esther Peterson, January 20, 1970, Oral History Collection, JFK Library, where Peterson describes the Women's Bureau as "almost a negative influence ... with an attitude like hurry up and get this out of the way" (60). See as well Ellickson "The PCSW," 5.

23. Campbell, Second Oral History Interview with Esther Peterson, 56. The clarification is a written addendum to the oral history transcript, February 19, 1979, in which Peterson recalls the timing of their strategy. She locates the moment as "before we had the other executive orders relating to employment."

24. Secretary Arthur Goldberg, draft of memo to the President, March 29, 1961, Folder 833, Peterson Collection. In the same file, see the new rough draft, April 11, 1961. In November, the group was still tinkering with the commission's name. At first they labeled it "The Presidential Commission on the Legal Status of Women." Then they shifted to "Commission on Women in American Democracy" before they moved to "President's Committee

to Promote Full Opportunity for Women." They considered "President's Committee on the Status of Women" before settling finally on "Commission." The name changes reflect not only the agony of decision making but also the subtle distinction embedded in the search for women's relationship to citizenship. "Status of women" in a sense justifies the removal of the concept of citizenship from the document. See esp. memo from Peterson to the Secretary, December 11, 1961, Folder 837, Peterson Collection.

25. Margaret Mead and Frances Balgley Kaplan, eds., *American Women: The Report of the President's Commission on the Status of Women and Other Publications of the Commission* (New York: Charles Scribner's Sons, 1965), 207.

26. Issued on the same day, December 14, 1961, the press release included a vague assertion that "a mere statement supporting equality of opportunity must be implemented by affirmative steps to see that the doors are really open for training, selection, advancement, and equal pay" and promising that individual merit would be the criterion for opportunity in government jobs, as opposed to ordering nondiscrimination for employees of federal contractors. Cf. "Statement by the President on the Establishment of the President's Commission on the Status of Women," File: Commission on the Status of Women, Box 93, President's Office Files, JFK Library.

27. Mimeo, "Summary of May 5, 1961, Meeting: National Women's Organizations and Women's Bureau Staff," 3, Folder 833, Peterson Collection.

28. Ware, "Background Memorandum," 16–17.

29. For an excellent account of the careful construction of the commission to exclude most advocates of the ERA, see Cynthia Harrison, *On Account of Sex: The Politics of Women's Issues, 1945–1968* (Berkeley: University of California Press, 1988), 146–54.

30. Campbell, Second Oral History Interview with Esther Peterson, 57.

31. Ibid., 58.

32. Peterson did not regret this choice, which she had at first thought of as a "small price to pay," and later welcomed Boddy as someone who had rendered "a very valuable service because she kept bringing us back to reality as to where people were" (ibid., 59–60).

33. The purpose of the Hayden Rider was to allow exceptions that could protect women.

34. Mrs. Samuel Brown, typescript, "Statement before the Committee on Civil and Political Rights of the President's Commission on the Status of Women," March 8, 1963, 4, File: Committee on Civil and Political Rights, Box 10, PCSW Collection. Brown represented the National Council of Jewish Women.

35. Harriet Pilpel, Transcript of Proceedings, Committee on Civil and Political Rights, May 28, 1962, 106, Box 11, PCSW Collection. For a sense of the continuing confusion in this committee, see the comments of Edith Green (12–13), Marguerite Rawalt (60), and Frank Sanders (155). See as well the long discussion on women in jury service in the same committee on August 24, 1962, ibid.

36. Transcript of Proceedings, PCSW, June 16–17, 1962, 115–16, Box 4, PCSW Collection.

37. Pat M., undated memo to Mrs. Peterson, 2, Folder 936, Peterson Collection.

38. Peterson to Wilbur J. Cohen, Drafts and attached Memo from M.W. to Esther, April 29, 1964, Folder 1083, Peterson Collection.

39. Typescript, "Substance of Recommendation," Document no. 7, February 8, 1963, 3, Committee on Protective Labor Legislation, Folder 2, File: Meetings, Box 3, PCSW Collection.

40. S. A. Wesolowski, Transcript of Proceedings, Committee on Protective Labor Legisla-

tion, June 6, 1962, 72, Box 13, PCSW Collection. Wesolowski, an executive of a Manchester, New Hampshire, knitting mill, continued in this vein for several minutes: she came by this weakness "naturally, by nature, woman has these responsibilities in living, where the man doesn't have the same ones. The woman has to bring her family up. She bears children; or we would have no society" (74). Other committee members agreed with him.

41. Ibid., the final report of the Committee on Federal Employment Policies and Practices offered an example of such positive treatment, explaining women's failure to achieve labor market success as follows: "The lack of social pressure on a woman to achieve monetary success or fame, plus a tendency, either inborn or socially developed, to seek work that expresses her concern for others and her need to give of herself, often leads to highly constructive activities that do not bring public recognition." See "Typescript of Final Report of Committee on Federal Employment Policies and Practices," August 1963, 66, Box 7, PCSW Collection.

42. Committee on New and Expanded Services, "Interim Report," typescript, February 8, 1963, 1, File: Meetings, Folder 2, Box 3, PCSW Collection.

43. Pat M., undated memo to Mrs. Peterson, 1, Folder 936, Peterson Collection.

44. A. C. Stevens to Margaret Mealey, January 17, 1963, Folder 908, Peterson Collection. Stevens had threatened to resign before, claiming that he was "not convinced that exploitation of women in industry constitutes such a great social evil today" and that he did not have strong convictions about the status of women. Stevens to Mr. James J. Reynolds, November 8, 1962, ibid.

45. Aiken to Esther Peterson, March 15, 1963, Folder 936, ibid.

46. Typescript, "Remarks of Willard Wirtz before the Conference on Employment Opportunities for Women," September 24, 1962, 7, File: 12–14, Box 2, PCSW Collection.

47. Many of the elements in this discussion are documented in the minutes of the first PCSW meeting, February 12–13, 1962, Document 18, 5–6, Folder 855, Peterson Collection; see as well typescript, "Problems in Connection with the Domicile of a Married Woman," March 6, 1963, 1–8, Committee on Civil and Political Rights, Document 7, PCSW Collection.

48. Transcript of Committee on Protective Legislation meeting, March 18, 1963, 25–26, File: Committee on Protective Labor Legislation, Box 13, PCSW Collection. The quotes in the discussion that follows are drawn from this meeting, 25–41. See as well the transcript of the June 29, 1962, meeting of the Committee on Social Insurance and Taxes, 159–69, File: Committee on Social Insurance and Taxes, Box 14, ibid. By 1961, New Jersey, Rhode Island, and California provided cash benefits for maternity leave under their temporary disability insurance programs for workers.

49. For this committee discussion: Transcript of meeting of the Committee on Political and Civil Status of Women [sic], August 24, 1962, 33, 89–99, File: Committee on Political and Civil Status of Women, Box 11, PCSW Collection.

50. Ibid., 99.

51. Typed transcript, "Washington Reports to the People," July 29, 1962, Folder 850, Peterson Collection.

52. Doris Boyle in Committee on Protective Labor Legislation, transcript of proceedings, June 6, 1962, 75, Box 13, PCSW Collection.

53. See, for example, Transcript of Proceedings, Committee on Social Insurance and Taxes, June 29, 1962, 54, Box 14, PCSW Collection.

54. Pat M., undated memo to Mrs. Peterson, 3, Folder 936, Peterson Collection. This position was ultimately the one that the Committee on New and Expanded Services also came to. Its "Interim Report," dated February 8, 1963, stated: "Conditions should be such that, for example, if a woman is the head of the family she will not be forced to seek gainful employment while her children are young" (1). File: Meetings, Folder 2, Box 3, PCSW Collection.

55. Typescript, "Remarks of Vice President Lyndon B. Johnson, before the Conference on Employment Opportunities for Women," September 24, 1962, 5. File: General, Box 4, PCSW Collection.

56. Bookbinder routinely represented Secretary of Commerce Luther Hodges. Transcript of Proceedings, PCSW, June 16–17, 1963, 108, File: General, Box 4, PCSW Collection.

57. Oral interview with Lyndon Baines Johnson, by David G. McComb, October 31, 1968, 3–4, University of Texas, Oral History Project, LBJ Library. Johnson was still in office at the time.

58. Miss Ketchin, Transcript of Proceedings, Committee on Protective Labor Legislation, June 6, 1962, 110, Box 13, PCSW Collection.

59. Transcript of meeting of the Committee on Social Insurance and Taxes, June 29, 1962, 160, PCSW Collection.

60. Transcript of Proceedings, PCSW, April 9, 1962, 62–63, File: General, Box 4, PCSW Collection.

61. Transcript of Proceedings, Committee on Civil and Political Rights, April 9, 1962, 64, Box 11, PCSW Collection.

62. Transcript of Proceedings, Committee on Protective Labor Legislation, June 6, 1962, 30, Box 13, PCSW Collection. The first speaker is Dorothy Keyserling; the second, Esther Peterson.

63. Exchange between Edith Green and Harriet Pilpel, Transcript of Proceedings of the Committee on Civil and Political Rights, May 28, 1962, 47, Box 11, PCSW Collection.

64. Esther Peterson to Kitty Ellickson, February 21, 1963, Folder 912, Peterson Collection.

65. "Problems of Negro Women," in Mead and Kaplan, *American Women*, 219. See also, President's Commission on the Status of Women, Consultation on Minority Groups, Transcript of Proceedings, April 19, 1963, passim and 18–20, Box 3, PCSW Collection; hereafter, PCSW Minority Consultation.

66. "The Negro Woman's College Education," March 1962, in typescript memorandum, "The Negro Woman," 1, Folder 912, Peterson Collection.

67. Daniel Patrick Moynihan to Mrs. Peterson, March 26, 1963, 1, ibid.

68. Ibid.

69. PCSW Minority Consultation, 30, 22 (Dr. Inabel Lindsay of Howard University), 18.

70. Ibid., 35. Deborah Gray White takes Height to task for being too conservative in this regard, arguing that she might have confronted the idea of matriarchy as earlier black women had confronted deleterious comments about their family lives. But in the context, it is not clear that Height and others would have seen the framework as negative. Deborah Gray White, *Too Heavy a Load: Black Women in Defense of Themselves, 1894–1994* (New York: Norton, 1998), 201.

71. See discussion surrounding comments of Mrs. Viola Hymes, president, National Council of Jewish Women, Transcript of Proceedings, April 9, 1962, 57–58, Box 4, PCSW Collection.

72. Transcript of Proceedings, Committee on Protective Labor Legislation, June 6, 1962, 141, Box 13, PCSW Collection.

73. The first speaker is Norman Nicholson, an executive at Kaiser Industries; Transcript of Proceedings, Committee on Government Contracts, April 4, 1962, 64, Box 12, PCSW Collection.

74. Ibid.

75. Mead and Kaplan, *American Women*, 119.

76. Ibid., 49.

77. For background on Murray, see her autobiography, *Song in a Weary Throat: An American Pilgrimage* (New York: Harper & Row, 1987), esp. ch. 29; and Linda Kerber, *No Constitutional Right to Be Ladies: Women and the Obligations of Citizenship* (New York: Hill & Wang, 1998), 185–99.

78. Pauli Murray to General Counsel, ACLU, August 15, 1962, File 875, Box 49, Pauli Murray Collection, Schlesinger Library, Radcliffe College. Harrison, *On Account of Sex*, 126–37, provides the fullest account of Murray's efforts to use the Fourteenth Amendment to develop a compromise with the forces advocating an ERA. See as well Murray's own account in *Song in a Weary Throat*, 348–53.

79. Pauli Murray, Typescript, "A Proposal to Reexamine the Applicability of the Fourteenth Amendment to State Discriminatory Policies on the Basis of Sex per se," 1, File: Committee on Civil and Political Rights, Box 10, PCSW Collection.

80. The Supreme Court refused to acknowledge sex as a reasonable classification in many of the cases discussed above, including *Muller v. Oregon*, 208 U.S. 412 (1908) and *Breedlove v. Suttles*, 302 U.S. 277 (1937). See also John D. Johnston Jr. and Charles L. Knapp, "Sex Discrimination by Law: A Study in Judicial Perspective," *New York University Law Review* 46 (1971), 675–747; and Kenneth L. Karst, "'A Discrimination so Trivial': A Note on Law and the Symbolism of Women's Dependency," *Ohio State Law Journal* 35 (1974), 535–57.

81. Murray, "A Proposal to Reexamine the Applicability of the Fourteenth Amendment," 8 ff., Murray was convinced that such a distinction would not disturb protective labor laws. In response to a query from Katherine Ellickson, October 4, 1962, File 876, Box 49, Murray Collection, Murray wrote on October 13, 1962, "My position on labor legislation, protective in nature, is that it should not be disturbed" (ibid.).

82. Pauli Murray and Mary O. Eastwood, "Jane Crow and the Law: Sex Discrimination and Title VII," *George Washington Law Review* 34 (October 1965), 233, 235, 238.

83. Murray, "A Proposal to Reexamine the Applicability of the Fourteenth Amendment," 8; the following material is drawn from 18, 22–23, 34.

84. Dorothy Kenyon to Board of Directors, ACLU, March 28, 1963, File 878, Murray Collection; Kenyon to Pauli Murray, April 4, 1963, File 878, ibid. For more on the relationship between Kenyon and Murray, see Kerber, *No Constitutional Right to Be Ladies*, 185–99.

85. Transcript of statement by Mrs. Samuel Brown, March 8, 1963, 4, Box 10, PCSW Collection. Phoebe Morrison to Pauli Murray, January 14, 1963; Pam to Pauli Murray, January 16, 1963; Freund to Esther Peterson, March 11, 1963; unsigned letter to Pauli Murray,

January 21, 1963 (Murray's response to "Dear Thacher," January 30, 1963, reveals its author); Pauli Murray to Ellickson, March 20, 1963, and Ellickson to Murray, March 29, 1963; all in File 877, Murray Collection.

86. These proposals can be found in Mead and Kaplan, *American Women*, 210–14.

87. Margaret Hickey (public affairs editor of the *Ladies Home Journal*), Transcript of Proceedings, June 16–17, 1962, 129, File: General, Box 4, PCSW Collection.

88. Mead and Kaplan, *American Women*, 200, 202, 204.

89. Murray, *Song in a Weary Throat*, 348.

90. For discussion of political debates preceding passage, see Harrison, *On Account of Sex*, 89–105; for meanings, see Alice Kessler-Harris, "The Double Meaning of Equal Pay," in Kessler-Harris, *A Woman's Wage: Historical Meanings and Social Consequences* (Lexington: University of Kentucky Press, 1990), 81–112.

91. William H. Davis, chairman, NWLB, to Frances Perkins, June 4, 1943, File: Equal Pay, 1943, Box 385, RG86, NARA.

92. Testimony of Lewis B. Schwellenbach, *House Hearings before Subcommittee no. 4 of the Committee on Education and Labor on HR 4273 and HR 4408, Bills proposing Equal Pay for Equal Work for Women and for Other Purposes*, 80th Cong., 2d sess., February 9–13, 1948, (Washington, D.C.: GPO, 1948), 79; hereafter, House, *Equal Pay Hearings, 1948*.

93. Women were 90 percent of all workers in one third of the leading occupational categories for women. U.S. Department of Labor, *1965 Handbook on Women Workers*, Women's Bureau Bulletin no. 290 (Washington, DC: GPO, 1965), 91–92.

94. Paul Burstein, *Discrimination, Jobs, and Politics: The Struggle for Employment Opportunity in the United States since the New Deal* (Chicago: University of Chicago Press, 1985), 22.

95. House, *Equal Pay Hearings, 1948*, 69.

96. This phrase is from Peter J. Frelinghuysen of New Jersey, *Congressional Record—House*, May 23, 1963, 9196. The following discussion of the floor debates relies on the same source. Quoted: Thompson, 9196–98, Frelinghuysen, 9197; Goodell, 9197–98; Florence Dwyer of New Jersey ("justice, fairplay and equity"), 9200; and see James G. Fulton of Pennsylvania, 9194; Kelly, 9202; John H. Dent of Pennsylvania, 9200; St. George, 9193; William F. Ryan of New York, 9212.

97. Campbell, Second Oral History Interview with Esther Peterson, 53. Clearly agitated, Peterson continued: "How do you define equal, you see? If you have work of comparable character—but equal, then you get down to identical, and she really wrecked us.... She was really a negative force on the bill.... They supported the equal rights amendment but not the equal pay bill."

98. Edith Green of Oregon, *Congressional Record—House*, May 23, 1963, 9199.

99. See, for example, William F. Ryan of New York, who hoped that Congress would enact "a comprehensive measure to eliminate discrimination in employment," or Massachusetts's Harold Donohue, who rejected the idea that a woman "because of her very nature ... should not be given as much money as a man for similar work"; both ibid., 9212.

100. Ibid.

101. Ibid.

102. Ibid., 9205.

## Chapter 6

1. Among the several very good accounts of what happened in the congressional debates, see esp. Hugh Davis Graham, *The Civil Rights Era: Origins and Development of National Policy, 1960–1972* (New York: Oxford University Press, 1990); Cynthia Harrison, *On Account of Sex: The Politics of Women's Issues, 1945–68* (Berkeley: University of California Press, 1988); Patricia G. Zelman, *Women, Work, and National Policy: The Kennedy-Johnson Years* (Ann Arbor: UMI Research Press, 1982); and Jo Freeman, "How 'Sex' Got into Title VII: Persistent Opportunism as a Maker of Public Policy," *Law and Inequality: A Journal of Theory and Practice* 9 (March 1991), 163–84. For informative and original explorations of the addition of sex as part of a deliberate strategy, see Carl M. Brauer, "Women Activists, Southern Conservatives, and the Prohibition of Sex Discrimination in Title VII of the 1964 Sex Discrimination Act," *Journal of Southern History* 49 (February 1983), 37–56; and Caruthers Gholson Berger, "Equal Pay, Equal Employment Opportunity, and Equal Enforcement of the Law for Women," *Valparaiso University Law Review* 5, no. 2 (1971), 333–37. For an alternative view, see Cynthia Deitch, "Gender, Race, and Class Politics and the Inclusion of Women in Title VII of the 1964 Civil Rights Act," *Gender and Society* 7 (June 1993), 183–203.

2. Esther Peterson interview with Paige Mulhollan, November 25, 1968, 32, Lyndon Baines Johnson Library. Edith Green, Democratic congresswoman from Oregon from 1952 to 1971, repeated the thought several years later when, during congressional hearings on discrimination against women, she commented that she had voted against the amendment to add sex to House Title VII "because I thought it was a gimmick to water the bill down and to really defeat the Civil Rights Act." U.S. Congress, *Hearings on Discrimination against Women before the Special Subcommittee on Education of the House Committee on Education and Labor, on S. 805 and H.R. 16098,* 91st Cong., 2d sess., part 2, July 1 and 31, 1970 (Washington, D.C.: GPO, 1970), 669; hereafter House, *Hearings on Discrimination against Women, 1970.*

3. *Congressional Record,* February 8, 1964, 2577. For an example of the Party's strategy, see the testimony of Maud Younger, congressional chairman of the National Council, Woman's Party, Washington, D.C., U.S. Congress, *Hearings before the House of Representatives Committee on Labor on S.158 and H.R. 4557: Thirty Hour Week Bill,* 73d Cong., 1st sess., April-May 1933 (Washington, D.C.: GPO, 1933), 745–749.

4. This exchange is reproduced from the Rules Committee Hearings in Zelman, *Women, Work, and National Policy,* 60–61.

5. Prior to 1964, sex discrimination was not prohibited in federal equal employment opportunity bills, though it was excluded in a few states, notably New York and Wisconsin. Paul Burstein, *Discrimination, Jobs, and Politics: The Struggle for Equal Employment Opportunity in the United States since the New Deal* (Chicago: University of Chicago Press, 1985), 22.

6. Carrie Donald's comments on Brigid O'Farrell's and Suzanne Moore's "Unions, Hard Hats, and Women Workers," in Dorothy Sue Cobble, ed., *Women and Unions: Forging a Partnership* (Ithaca: ILR Press, 1993), 103. For a persuasive interpretation of these sensibilities, see Barbara Ehrenreich, *The Hearts of Men: American Dreams and the Flight from Commitment* (New York: Anchor Press/Doubleday, 1983).

7. Martha Griffiths, "Women and Legislation," in Mary Lou Thompson, ed., *Voices of the New Feminism* (Boston: Beacon Press, 1970), 112–13.

8. Pauli Murray and Mary O. Eastwood, "Jane Crow and the Law: Sex Discrimination and Title VII," *George Washington Law Review*, 34 (December 1965), 238–39.

9. *Congressional Record—House*, May 23, 1963, 9199.

10. Donald Allen Robinson, "Two Movements in Pursuit of Equal Employment Opportunity," *Signs* 4 (Spring 1979), 414. But in fact the 1963 House equal employment opportunity hearings produced an interesting exchange between Sen. Harrison Williams of New Jersey (testifying for a new bill) and Rep. Dave Martin of Nebraska, who challenged the removal of the word *sex* from this version of the bill. Williams, fumbling in response, said he would add *sex* if Martin would then vote for the bill, and then retreated in confusion to the following statement: "Well, we have the equal rights amendment. The women in some departments are in a favored position. Some of us wonder if they want to lose that position. Certainly, on equal pay, I agree with you." U.S. Congress, House, *Hearings on Equal Employment Opportunity before the General Subcommittee on Labor of the Committee on Education and Labor, H.R. 405 and Similar Bills*, 88th Cong., 1st sess. (Washington, D.C.: GPO, 1963), 19; hereafter House, *Hearings on Equal Employment Opportunity, 1963*.

11. *Congressional Record—House*, February 8, 1964, 2579, 2580.

12. Peterson added, "As it happened, it didn't, and I was wrong." Peterson interview, 32. See Zelman, *Women, Work, and National Policy*, 58, on the absence of grassroots support.

13. *Congressional Record—House*, February 8, 1964, 2581.

14. Ibid., 2583.

15. Quoted, ibid., 2582; Zelman, *Women, Work, and National Policy*, 4–5, argues that all of the women were ERA supporters. Note, however, that Kelly, *Congressional Record—House*, February 8, 1964, 2583, says she is not for the equal rights amendment.

16. Freeman, "How 'Sex' Got into Title VII," 174–75.

17. The quotes in this paragraph come from *Congressional Record—House*, February 8, 1964, 2583–2584. See 2580, 2581, and 2584 for additional racist cites. For a full discussion, see Brauer, "Women Activists, Southern Conservatives, and the Prohibition of Sex Discrimination," 50–53.

18. The quote is from James Russell Tuten of Georgia. According to Brauer, ibid., 53, most nonsouthern Democrats voted against the amendment. Southerners and Republicans supported it in a 168–133 vote.

19. *Congressional Record—House*, April 8, 1964, 7217; for a full discussion, see Susan Gluck Mezey, *In Pursuit of Equality: Women, Public Policy, and the Federal Courts* (New York: St. Martin's Press, 1992), 43.

20. Pauli Murray, *Song in a Weary Throat: An American Pilgrimage* (New York: Harper & Row, 1987), 356.

21. For the political development of the EEOC, see Graham, *The Civil Rights Era*, 211–32; see also Zelman, *Women, Work, and National Policy*, ch. 6, and Harrison, *On Account of Sex*, 185–96.

22. "Roosevelt Finds Sex Discrimination in Jobs Is Big Problem; Appoints Seven Key Aides," *New York Times*, July 21, 1965.

23. "8854 Job Discrimination Charges Filed with EEOC in First Year," typescript, in File: Draft Papers on Title VII, Box 959, Esther Peterson Collection, Schlesinger Library, Radcliffe College. Equal Employment Opportunity Commission, *First Annual Report*, 90th

Cong., 1st sess., House Document no. 86 (Washington, D.C.: GPO, 1966), 58–59. Mezey, *In Pursuit of Equality*, 39, says that in the first five years, there were 52,000 charges of discrimination. The EEOC recommended that 35,445 be investigated, and of these one quarter were charges of sex discrimination, half were based on race, and the rest religion and national origin. The figures of 1,400 in the first hundred days etc. come from Graham, *The Civil Rights Era*, 228. In contrast to these large figures, Roosevelt told a November news conference that "only about 15 per cent or 400–500 of the complaints the commission has received so far deal with sex discrimination" and emphasized that it would be primarily occupied with problems of race discrimination. "New Guidelines on Job Sex-Discrimination Recognize Some Exceptions but Limit Them," *Wall Street Journal*, November 23, 1965.

24. King Carr to Mary Keyserling, October 26, 1964, and Mary Dublin Keyserling to N. Thompson Powers, November 5, 1964, Folder 1083, Peterson Collection.

25. For some of these voices, see Dorothy Sue Cobble, "Recapturing Working-Class Feminism: Union Women in the Postwar Era," in Joanne Meyerowitz, *Not June Cleaver: Women and Gender in Postwar America, 1945–1960* (Philadelphia: Temple University Press, 1994), 57–83; and Dennis Deslippe, *Rights Not Roses: Women, Industrial Unions, and the Law of Equality in the United States, 1945–1980* (Urbana: University of Illinois Press, 1999).

26. This and the following figures come from EEOC, *First Annual Report*, 39–45, 64. All told, the EEOC counted 2,432 sex discrimination complaints between July 1, 1965, and June 30, 1966, out of a total of 8,854 complaints received.

27. Interview with Alfred Blumrosen, June 17, 1999, tape in author's possession. Zelman, *Women, Work, and National Policy*, 94.

28. U.S. Congress, *Hearings before the Joint Committee on Economic Problems of Women*, 93d Cong., 1st sess., part 1, July 1973 (Washington, D.C.: GPO, 1973), 129.

29. "Roosevelt Finds Sex Discrimination in Jobs Is Big Problem; Appoints Seven Key Aides," *New York Times*, July 21, 1965.

30. "De-Sexing the Job Market," *New York Times*, August 21, 1965; and see John Herbers, "For Instance, Can She Pitch for Mets?" *New York Times*, August 20, 1965, and Esther Peterson's letter of response, "Discrimination Faced by Women Workers," *New York Times*, September 3, 1965, in which Peterson invokes needs rather than rights. "Twenty-six million women are in the work force. One out of three workers is a woman. Women work for the same reasons men do—because they must work to support themselves and their dependents." See the excellent account of these early days in Graham, *The Civil Rights Era*, 211, 213ff.

31. "Sex and Nonsense," *New Republic*, September 4, 1965, 10.

32. U.S. Congress, House, *Hearings on Equal Employment Opportunity, before the General Subcommittee on Labor of the House Committee on Education and Labor, H.R. 8998 and 8999*, 89th Cong., 1st sess., June–July 1965 (Washington, D.C.: GPO, 1965), 34–35, 41–42, 105; hereafter, *House EEO Hearings, 1965*.

33. Ibid., 62–63 (Fowler); "Male-type jobs" and the paragraph-ending quote, John H. Dent of Pennsylvania, 47.

34. Ibid., 63.

35. Phyllis A. Wallace, ed., *Equal Employment Opportunity and the AT&T Case* (Cambridge: MIT Press, 1976), introduction and part 4.

36. The addition of this clause to the introduction to the "Proposed Guidelines on Discrimination Because of Sex" is documented in "Insert for 100 Days' Report," typescript, undated, in Minutes, October 27, 1965, 6A, and in the appendix to Minutes, Commissioners' Meeting no. 46, November 16, 1965, Office of the Secretariat, EEOC.

37. David W. Zugschwerdt to the Commission, July 9, 1969, Envelope 8–15–69, EEOC. The new "Guidelines on Discrimination Because of Sex," 29 C.F.R. Section 1604, are attached to this memo.

38. Monroe W. Karmin, "New U.S. Commission Plans Big Push to Open More Posts to Negroes," *Wall Street Journal*, October 13, 1965.

39. Elizabeth Shelton, "Title VII Will Referee Sex by Common Sense," *Washington Post*, November 23, 1965.

40. C. A. Burford to EEOC, July 14, 1965, in Minutes, September 9, 1965, EEOC.

41. "Insert for 100 Days' Report," typescript, undated, in Minutes, October 27, 1965, 6A, EEOC. "Digest of Legal Interpretations Issued or Adapted by the Commission, July 2, 1965–October 8, 1965," typescript, November 23, 1965, EEOC.

42. EEOC, *First Annual Report*, 40.

43. "Insert for 100 Days' Report," typescript, undated, 7–A, in Minutes, October 27, 1965, EEOC.

44. Testimony of George Fowler, *House EEO Hearings, 1965*, 64; in its November 1965 guidelines, the EEOC explicitly rejected marital status as a grounds for refusing a job to a woman.

45. Complaint, Case no. 6–6–5759 (LA 6–9–9), charge filed June 6, 1966, 12, Envelope 6–20–68, EEOC. The airline also claimed that inferior customer service and difficulty in arranging flight schedules would result from employing married women. See also Commissioner's Charge Case no. AT6–9–603 (6–8–6975), charge filed August 16, 1966, 4, ibid., where the airline admitted that its "no-marriage restriction was imposed to avoid the stress on home and family life which would be caused by the absence of married stewardesses from their homes." The same airline did not fire male cabin attendants, pilots, and so on for marriage.

46. Ibid., 9. The argument that women's traditional roles could in fact justify occupational discriminations continued. In August of 1968, a U.S. district court held that a man was not entitled to relief from the draft because women were excluded from it. Rather, women were still entitled to "special recognition" on the historical grounds that "if a nation is to survive, men must provide the first line of defense while women keep the home fires burning." *United States of America v. James St. Clair*, 291 F. Supp. 122 (1968), 125.

47. Case no. 5–10–2439, 4, and Richard Berg to Gordon Chase, March 31, 1967, both Envelope 4–5–67, EEOC.

48. Alfred Blumrosen, *Modern Law: The Law Transmission System and Equal Employment Opportunity* (Madison: University of Wisconsin Press, 1993), 94. Blumrosen quotes *Quarles v. Phillip Morris, Inc.*, 279 F. Supp. 505 (E.D. Va. 1968), 516, to the effect that "Congress did not intend to freeze an entire generation of Negroes into discriminatory patterns that existed before the act."

49. EEOC, *First Annual Report*, 40. The first Title VII case that made its way to the Supreme Court involved this issue and held for the EEOC: *Phillips v. Martin Marietta Corp.*, 400 U.S. 542 (1971). See the discussion of this case in Ruth Bader Ginsburg, "Gender and the Constitution," *University of Cincinnati Law Review* 44 (1975), 1–42.

50. Clifford Alexander to Ramsay Clark, August 21, 1967, Envelope 8–30–67, EEOC.

51. U.S. Department of Labor, *1975 Handbook on Women Workers*, Women's Bureau Bulletin no. 297 (Washington, D.C.: GPO, 1975), 11, 17ff.

52. EEOC, *First Annual Report*, 42–43.

53. Minutes, Commissioners' Meeting no. 100, May 19, 1966, 13, EEOC.

54. Minutes, Commissioners' Meeting no. 101, May 25, 1966, 8, EEOC.

55. Minutes, Commissioners' Meeting no. 122, August 17, 1966, 5–6, EEOC.

56. Summary Report, Minutes of Commissioners' Meeting no. 105, June 27, 1966, 1, EEOC. The formal response, which went to the bank's director of public relations, closed with the caveat that "it is fairly common practice for women to remain on the job through the fifth or sixth month of pregnancy, and it would seem to us, therefore, that requiring a woman employee to cease work after the fourth month might well be unreasonable."

57. EEOC, *First Annual Report*, 40–41. The Supreme Court finally settled the issue in the landmark case of *Cleveland Board of Education v. LaFleur*, 414 U.S. 632, 639, where it agreed that mandatory maternity leave rules violated the Fourteenth Amendment.

58. Equal Employment Opportunity Commission, *Second Annual Report*, 90th Cong., 2d sess., House Document no. 326 (Washington, D.C.: GPO, 1968), 44.

59. EEOC, *First Annual Report*, 6–7; typescript, "8854 Job Discrimination Charges Filed with EEOC in First Year," Folder 959, Peterson Collection.

60. Minutes, Commissioners' Meeting no. 46, November 16, 1965, 4, EEOC. In one case against a large tobacco company, the respondent acknowledged separate seniority lists and admitted that "tradition alone is a factor in its classification of the job in question as a male job." The EEOC subsequently upheld the complainant's charges. Case no. 6–4–4066, Envelope 5–4–67, EEOC.

61. *Federal Register* 33, no. 38 (February 24, 1968), 3361; see *Diaz v. Pan American World Airways, Inc.*, 442 F.2d 385 (1971). Fairness was at issue once again when female cabin attendants approached the EEOC claiming that they had been terminated for reasons of age. Once again the EEOC found cause for their complaints, ultimately forcing the airlines to drop these requirements. See Case no. 6–6–5762 (SF 6–12–57), filed June 6, 1966.

62. To follow the conversation among the commissioners, see Minutes, Commissioners' Meeting, no. 25, September 21, 1965; no. 26, September 22, 1965; and no. 92, April 19, 1966, EEOC. Graham, *The Civil Rights Era*, ch. 8, has an excellent summary of the role of various commissioners in the debates.

63. Minutes, Commissioners' Meeting no. 93, April 20, 1966, 5, EEOC; and see the discussion at the previous meeting, April 19, 1966, 6–8.

64. *Congressional Record—House*, June 20, 1966, 13689. Griffiths went on to attack EEOC executive director Herman Edelsberg for defending EEOC inaction on sex by claiming "that the sex provision of Title VII was a 'fluke' and 'conceived out of wedlock.' The Press in focusing on odd or hypothetical cases has fostered public ridicule which undermines the effectiveness of the law and disregards the real problems of sex discrimination in employment."

65. *Proceedings of the 20th UAW Constitutional Convention*, May 16–21, 1966, 7, 9.

66. Black members included Coretta Scott King, Phineas Indritz, and Anna Arnold Hedgeman, as well as Pauli Murray. Judith Hennesee, *Betty Friedan: Her Life* (New York: Ran-

dom House, 1999), 102–4; Ruth Rosen, *The World Split Open: How the Modern Women's Movement Changed America* (New York: Viking, 2000), 78–88.

67. Clarenbach and Friedan to Wirtz, April 9, 1967, File: Government: 1964–5, Folder 584, Peterson Collection. Daniel Horowitz, *Betty Friedan and the Making of the Feminine Mystique: The American Left, the Cold War, and Modern Feminism* (Amherst: University of Massachusetts Press, 1998), 277–78, argues that Friedan's radical background suggests a deeply rooted sympathy for black civil rights and predisposed her to piggyback race onto sex. See also Harrison, *On Account of Sex*, 197–98.

68. Edith Green to Stephen Shulman, February 14, 1967, File: EEOC, Box 12, Edith Green Papers, Oregon Historical Society; hereafter, Green Papers.

69. Typescript, "EEOC Issues Guidelines on Classified Advertising, Rules Separate Male-Female Ads Illegal," June 20, 1968, Envelope 6–20–68; Minutes, Commission Meeting no. 188, June 2, 1968, EEOC. The vote was three to two. Vice Chairman Luther Holcomb (he and Samuel Jackson were the only remaining members of the original five commissioners) dissented, as did Vincente Ximenes. Jackson, Chairman Clifford Alexander, and Elizabeth Kuck approved.

70. Equal Employment Opportunity Commission, *Third Annual Report*, 91st Cong., 1st sess., House Document no. 91–107 (Washington, D.C.: GPO, 1969), 14–15.

71. Minutes, Commissioners' Meeting no. 204, June 20, 1968, 1, EEOC.

72. Equal Employment Opportunity Commission, *Fifth Annual Report*, 92d Cong., 1st sess., House Document no. 92–98 (Washington, D.C.: GPO, 1971), 12.

73. Mrs. Martin J. Walters to President Renny, October 28, 1964, Folder 1083, Peterson Collection. The name has been changed. The operative Supreme Court decision is *Goesaert v. Cleary*, which held that states could draw "a sharp line between the sexes with regard to employment"; 335 U.S. 464 (1948), 466.

74. Minutes, "Conference on State Protective Legislation," 3, Envelope 8–31–66, EEOC.

75. Edmond M. Boggs to Luther Holcomb, August 23, 1966, ibid.

76. Marjorie D. Tibbs to Herman Edelsberg, June 8, 1966, ibid.

77. EEOC, *First Annual Report*, 43, 64; "New Guidelines on Job Sex-Discrimination Recognize Some Exceptions, but Limit Them," *Wall Street Journal*, November 23, 1965.

78. Charles Horsky to Esther Peterson, January 17, 1966, Folder 583, Peterson Collection.

79. Esther Peterson to Mary Keyserling, March 1, 1965; Keyserling to Peterson, March 23, 1965; and Peterson to the Secretary, undated memo (probably early April 1965), 1, all Folder 1084, Peterson Collection.

80. Ibid., 2.

81. Typescript, flier on the letterhead of the National Consumers' League, January 1967, Folder 657, Peterson Collection.

82. "AFL-CIO Comment on Minimum Wage and Maximum Hours Legislation for Women to Subcommittee on Protective Labor Legislation," mimeographed memo, November 27, 1962, Folder 908, Peterson Collection. The 1965 AFL-CIO convention unanimously approved a resolution on women workers that stated in part, "The AFL-CIO continues to afford general support to state labor standards legislation and believes that appropriate safeguards under such laws are not inconsistent with equality of employment opportunities for women." Resolution no. 195, *Proceedings of the Sixth Constitutional Convention of the AFL-CIO*, San Francisco, December 9, 1965, 378.

83. For example, see Olya Margolin to Andrew J. Biemiller, August 5, 1966, and Biemiller to Margolin, August 9, 1966, File 22, Box 55, RG21–001: Legislation Department Records, The George Meany Memorial Archives (GMMA); Kenneth Meiklejohn to Esther Peterson, January 2, 1968, ibid.; Andrew J. Biemiller to Richard P. Sears, September 18, 1969, ibid.; and Office of the President, Communications Workers of America, to All Local Presidents, July 22, 1966, Folder 959, Peterson Collection.

84. Dolores Doninger to Mr. George Meany, August 14, 1972, File 5, Box 10, RG21–001, GMMA.

85. Kenneth Meiklejohn to Esther Peterson, January 2, 1968, and policy statement attached, File 22, Box 55, RG21–001, GMMA.

86. Andrew J. Biemiller to Ms. Dolores Doninger, May 15, 1972, File 10, Box 17, RG21–001, GMMA. As late as 1970, Myra Wolfgang, vice president of the Hotel, Restaurant, and Bartenders' Union, was quoted by *Business Week* to the effect that "the equality it may achieve may be equality of mistreatment"; "Women's Liberation Counts a Victory," June 13, 1970, 99.

87. Typescript, "Title VII and State Protective Laws: Draft-Working Paper," February 2, 1967, 1, 5, 6, Folder 959, Peterson Collection.

88. The case inside NOW was best made by Marguerite Rawalt. In her capacity as general counsel, she wrote a powerful amicus brief on behalf of three female plaintiffs pleading to have the California Labor Code invalidated. The argument attacked directly the Court's position that women were not persons under the meaning of the Fourteenth Amendment, by pointing to other decisions that had held the right to work as "the most precious liberty man possesses" and a liberty of which women, like men, could not be arbitrarily deprived. If the right to liberty were inalienable, then it followed that state legislatures could not take it away, even if "some women wish to have such limits imposed on them." The brief is reprinted in House, *Hearings on Discrimination against Women, 1970*.

89. Commissioners' Meeting no. 46, November 16, 1965, 3, Envelope 11–16–65, EEOC. The commissioners also worried about equal pay laws, but in the event, these proved to be a far less significant problem than the equal treatment and occupational segregation issues raised by protective labor laws. For some of the thinking, see "Problems Which May Require Solutions in Administering Title VII of the Civil Rights Act in Complaints of Discrimination on the Basis of Sex," unsigned typescript, November 5, 1964, Folder 1083, Peterson Collection; and John Herbers, "U.S. Warns States against Sex Bias," *New York Times*, November 23, 1965.

90. "Conference on State Protective Legislation," typescript, June 16, 1966, 3, Envelope 8–31–66, EEOC.

91. EEOC, *Second Annual Report*, 45.

92. Anne Draper to Tom Harris, Don Slaiman, and Andrew Biemiller, September 6, 1966, File 22, Box 55, RG 21–001, GMMA.

93. "Title 29—Labor," *Federal Register* 33, no. 38 (February 24, 1968), 3344.

94. *Bowe v. Colgate-Palmolive Co.*, 272 F. Supp. 332 (1967), 334. Mary Eastwood, "The Double Standard of Justice: Women's Rights under the Constitution," *Valparaiso University Law Review* 5 (1971), 292–94, describes the tortuous route taken in a class action suit against North American Aviation, Inc., which denied women jobs that might occasionally require

overtime work with premium pay. The case, originally filed in October 1966, was bounced from court to court until, finally, a federal appeals court decided that the precedent set in *Muller v. Oregon*, 208 U.S. 412 (1908), was worth revisiting. See *Mengelkoch v. Industrial Welfare Commission*, 437 F.2d 563 (9th Cir. 1971). A three-judge court finally held for the women.

95. EEOC, *Second Annual Report*, 44.

96. *Rosenfeld v. Southern Pacific Co.*, 293 F. Supp. 1219 (November 1968), 1224. The court held that the California law in this instance directly conflicted with Title VII and that the state law must yield.

97. *Weeks v. Southern Bell Telephone and Telegraph Company*, 408 F.2d 228 (1969), 235–36.

98. *Cheatwood v. South Central Bell Telephone and Telegraph Company*, 303 F. Supp. 754 (1969), 758; hammering another nail in the coffin of sexual stereotyping, Chief Judge Frank Johnson Jr. added that "Title VII surely means that all women cannot be excluded from consideration because some of them may become pregnant" (759–60). In 1970, a New Jersey court dismissed that state's prohibition on female bartenders as serving no public purpose; *Paterson Tavern and Grill Owners' Association, Inc., v. Borough of Hawthorne, New Jersey*, 57 N.J. 180, 270 A.2d 628 (1970). In 1971, the Supreme Court finally held sex to be an inappropriate classification. See Ginsburg, "Gender in the Supreme Court: the 1973 and 1974 Terms," in Philip Kurland, ed., *The Supreme Court Review* (Chicago: University of Chicago Press, 1975), 1–4.

99. Memorandum: Office of the General Counsel to the Commission, July 9, 1969, 10, Envelope 8–15–69, EEOC.

100. Memorandum, Elizabeth J. Kuck, Commissioner, to Marie D. Wilson, August 14, 1969, ibid.

101. Rosemary Pringle, *Secretaries Talk: Sexuality, Power, and Work* (London: Verso, 1988); Rosabeth Moss Kanter, *Men and Women of the Corporation* (New York: Basic Books, 1977).

102. Horowitz, *Betty Friedan and the Making of the Feminine Mystique*, 230–31.

103. *Congressional Record—House*, June 20, 1966, 13689–90.

104. Daniel Patrick Moynihan, *The Negro Family: The Case for National Action* (Washington, D.C.: GPO, 1965), 29.

105. For the background and flavor of the controversy, see the introduction and essays in Lee Rainwater and William L. Yancey, *The Moynihan Report and the Politics of Controversy* (Cambridge: MIT Press, 1967). Pauli Murray vigorously and persistently opposed the negative implications of the Moynihan Report for the educational and employment opportunities of black women; see Pauli Murray to Editors, *Newsweek* magazine, September 4, 1965, Folder 582, Peterson Collection. Murray testified against the harmful effects of assumptions about black matriarchy at House, *Hearings on Discrimination against Women, 1970*, part 1, 336.

106. In 1967, Senator Abraham Ribicoff and Wilbur Cohen, then undersecretary of Health, Education, and Welfare, sparred as to the number of job training programs. Cohen estimated that there were "at least five, six or seven separate types of training programs." Ribicoff put the number at eleven. Of these, only one, the work experience program created by the Economic Opportunity Act of 1964 on the theory that exposing welfare recipients to work would provide an incentive to leave public assistance, had a significant proportion of women (just over half). See the discussion in U.S. Congress, Senate, *Hearings on the Social Security Amendments of 1967 before the Committee on Finance on H.R. 12080*, 90th Cong., 1st sess., part 1, August 22, 1967 (Washington, D.C.: GPO, 1967), 261ff; hereafter, Senate, *Hearings on Social Security Amendments of 1967*.

107. "A Matter of Simple Justice," report of the President's Task Force on Women's Rights and Responsibilities, April 1970, reprinted in House, *Hearings on Discrimination against Women, 1970*, June 1970, 63; and see the dialogue between Edith Green and Pauli Murray on these issues, ibid., 374.

108. Ibid.

109. Senate, *Hearings on Social Security Amendments of 1967*, September 20, 1967, 1633 (Ferebee), 1555 (Wyman). As historian Joanne L. Goodwin has pointed out, early interventions provided just enough income for a mother to support her offspring, but not necessarily enough to keep her out of the paid labor force altogether; *Gender and the Politics of Welfare Reform: Mothers' Pensions in Chicago, 1911–1929* (Chicago: University of Chicago Press, 1997). See also Linda Gordon, *Pitied but Not Entitled: Single Mothers and the History of Welfare, 1890–1935* (Cambridge: Harvard University Press, 1994).

110. Testimony of William Robinson, representing the National Council of Churches of Christ in the USA, Senate, *Hearings on Social Security Amendments of 1967*, 1729.

111. For an analysis of the racialized and gendered content of legal thinking around this time, see Judith Olans Brown, Lucy A. Williams, and Phyllis Tropper Baumann, "The Mythogenesis of Gender: Judicial Images of Women in Paid and Unpaid Labor," *UCLA Women's Law Journal*, 6 (Spring 1996), 457–539. A scathing condemnation of the gendered content of such thinking can be found in John D. Johnston Jr. and Charles L. Knapp, "Sex Discrimination by Law: A Study in Judicial Perspective," *New York University Law Review*, 46 (1971), 675–747.

112. Senate, *Hearings on Social Security Amendments of 1967*, part 3, September 20, 1967, 1633.

113. Ibid., 1557, and see part 2, 1127: Long was bothered by his sense that women who were "drawing welfare money to stay at home have to be provided with a top paid job, that they have to be trained so they can be the top secretary in your office.... You know somebody has to do just the ordinary everyday work. Now if they don't do it, we have to do it. Either I do the housework or Mrs. Long does the housework, or we get somebody to come in and help us, but someone has to do it, and it does seem to me that if we can qualify these people to accept any employment doing something constructive, that that is better than simply having them sitting at home drawing welfare money...." The Long quotes are from 1556–57, 1651, 1547, and 1652.

114. Ibid., 1662.

115. Ibid., 1637.

116. *New York Dept. of Social Services v. Dublino*, 413 U.S. 405 (1973), 427. Only Justice Brennan joined the dissent.

117. "Draft Program Memorandum: Affirmative Enforcement," typescript, October 2, 1966, Envelope 10–4–67, EEOC; typescript: "Elimination of Discrimination by Affirmative Government Action," July 1968, Envelope 4–14–69, EEOC.

118. David L. Stebenne, *Arthur J. Goldberg: New Deal Liberal* (New York: Oxford University Press, 1996); Harrison, *On Account of Sex*, 145–46.

119. For example, Esther Peterson, whose commitment to opposing the ERA had stemmed from her desire to protect the interests of poor women, wrote to Labor Secretary Willard Wirtz in the early spring of 1967 to urge that, in light of the support of women's groups, he include sex as a basis of discrimination within all executive orders forbidding discrimination on government contracts. Wirtz declined. See Zelman,

*Women, Work, and National Policy*, 115. This is also one of several incidents to which Peterson alludes when she compares her rather uncomfortable relationship with Wirtz to her excellent association with his predecessor, Arthur Goldberg; Peterson, *Restless: The Memoirs of Labor and Consumer Activist Esther Peterson* (Washington, D.C.: Caring Publishing, 1995), 139–40.

120. "Draft Program Memorandum: Affirmative Enforcement," typescript, October 2, 1966, 2, Envelope 10–4–67, EEOC.

121. House, *Hearings on Discrimination against Women, 1970*, part 1, 322.

122. Over the span of twenty years, state and federal courts slowly evolved a definition of discrimination that took account of biology and cultural roles. When it articulated this stance in its 1987 decision, it brought into focus some fundamental tensions inherent in women's full participation in the labor force and propelled a reexamination of some basic assumptions around which Americans have tended to agree. These include the meritocratic paradigm that has traditionally legitimized workforce opportunity, the meanings and salience of gender difference, and the validity of firmly held notions of individual rights.

123. House, *Hearings on Discrimination against Women, 1970*, 343.

124. Jonathan S. Leonard, "Women and Affirmative Action," *Journal of Economic Perspectives* 3 (Winter 1989), 61.

125. House, *Hearings on Discrimination against Women, 1970*, 688.

126. See Johnston and Knapp, "Sex Discrimination by Law: A Study in Judicial Perspective." The underlying myth structure in the judiciary is illuminated in Brown, Williams, and Baumann, "The Mythogenesis of Gender: Judicial Images of Women in Paid and Unpaid Labor."

127. Elizabeth Shelton, "Women Charge Federal 'Runaround,'" *Washington Post*, July 27, 1970.

128. House, *Hearings on Discrimination against Women, 1970*, part 2, 94–95.

129. Biemiller to Bayard Rustin, April 23, 1970, File 2, Box 10, RG21–001, GMMA.

130. Ginsburg, "Gender and the Constitution," 10; *Phillips v. Martin Marietta Corp.*, 400 U.S. 321 (1971). In December of the same year, the Court finally agreed that women belonged in the Fourteenth Amendment. In *Reed v. Reed*, 404 U.S. 71 (1971), it decided that a mandatory selection of a male estate executor over a female arbitrarily deprived women of protection under the equal protection clause.

131. Cf. Graham, *The Civil Rights Era*, 412.

132. "Working Wives: Revolution in American Family Life," *U.S. News and World Report*, November 17, 1969, 95–96.

133. Citizens' Advisory Council on the Status of Women, *Report of the Task Force on Social Insurance and Taxes*, April, 1968, 77, 75, 116.

134. Ibid., 21, 44. The task force included an appendix (51–52) that disputed the claim that pregnant women were abusing the system by claiming to be willing to return to work when their real intent was to remain at home.

135. Ibid., 22–24, 12, 47–49.

136. Ten years later, not quite half of all men and just a little more than half of all women believed that discrimination barred women's access to good jobs.

137. Comments of Roman C. Pucinski of Illinois, *Congressional Record—House*, April 29, 1970, 13525.

138. Quoted in Graham, *The Civil Rights Era*, 397–98. This at a moment when a third of all federal jobs, but only 2 percent of top jobs, were held by women.

139. House, *Hearings on Discrimination against Women, 1970*, 617.

140. Ibid., part 1, 413.

141. "Women's Liberation Counts a Victory," *Business Week*, June 13, 1970, 98.

142. "A Matter of Simple Justice: Report of the President's Task Force on Women's Rights and Responsibilities," reprinted in House, *Hearings on Discrimination against Women, 1970*, 38.

143. *Congressional Record—House*, April 29, 1970, 13524–25.

144. House, *Hearings on Discrimination against Women, 1970*; the Green quotes that follow are from 369, 376, 2, 669.

145. Ibid., 429. Green returned to this theme repeatedly: see 497, 579, 626–27, 672.

146. Ibid., 618, 621, 662, 667–68, 670. For more on the possibillity that prejudices based on race are much more deeply rooted than prejudices based on sex, see Pamela Trotman Reid and Susan Clayton, "Racism and Sexism at Work," *Social Justice Research* 5, no. 3 (1992), 249–68. The Special Task Force on Women's Rights and Responsibilities also noted bitterly that "being female is not considered as much of a handicap as belonging to a minority group, despite economic data clearly indicating the contrary"; "Report of the President's Task Force," in ibid., part 1, 62.

147. Ibid., 636, and see 621.

148. Testimony of Preston M. Royster, Equal Employment Opportunities officer, HEW, ibid., 655–56. In these attacks, Representative Albert Quie of Minnesota occasionally joined Green. "The greatest discrimination in this country is against the blacks, so maybe they need to have a woman," he suggested. Royster (apparently black), answered: "I am not sure that is really true. I think the protests over discrimination are more vocal by the blacks than other groups, but I would suggest that discrimination against women is equal." Quie's response: "At least they selected you to fill your position. Maybe they need a woman to look after women. We have a little difficulty understanding them." All quotes, 656.

149. Ibid., 656; see also Marguerite Rawalt, "The Equal Rights Amendment," in Irene Tinker, ed., *Women in Washington: Advocates for Public Policy* (Beverly Hills: Sage Publications, 1983), 49–78.

150. Eastwood, "The Double Standard of Justice," 282.

151. House, *Hearings on Discrimination against Women, 1970*, 328–82, quotes from 328–29, 331. For more on Murray's position in this period, see Pauli Murray, "The Liberation of Black Women," in Thompson, *Voices of the New Feminism*, 87–102, and "The Rights of Women," in Norman Dorsen, ed., *The Rights of Americans: What They Are and What They Should Be* (New York: Pantheon Books, 1971), 521–45.

152. *Congressional Record—House*, August 10, 1970, 28005.

153. Ibid., 28025, Joel T. Broyhill of Virginia speaking. And see the comments of Dominick V. Daniels of New Jersey: "We have clung to the comfortable belief that a woman's exclusive and rightful place is in the home" (28035).

154. Ibid., October 12, 1971, 35802, James V. Stanton of Ohio speaking.

155. Ibid., August 10, 1970, 28019.

156. This and the following quotes are from Esther Peterson to Martha Griffiths, October 12, 1971, Folder 1634, Peterson Collection. Organized labor did not vote to support the ERA until October 1973—after the amendment had gone to the states for ratification.

## Epilogue

1. Judge John Nordberg, "Memorandum Opinion and Order," *Equal Employment Opportunity Commission v. Sears, Roebuck and Co.*, in the U.S. District Court, Northern District of Illinois, Eastern Division, January 31, 1986, 64, 66, 101.

2. *Equal Employment Opportunity Commission v. Sears, Roebuck & Company*, 839 F.2d 302 (7th Circuit, January 14, 1988), 29, and dissent by Cudahy, 112–13, 114.

3. Vicki Schultz, "Telling Stories about Women and Work: Judicial Interpretations of Sex Segregation in the Workplace in Title VII Cases Raising the Lack of Interest Argument," *Harvard Law Review* 103 (June 1990), 1749–838; Ruth Milkman, "Women's History and the Sears Case," *Feminist Studies* 12 (Summer 1986), 375–400.

4. A year and a half later, another circuit court decided a similar case for the plaintiffs, explicitly rejecting the conclusion in *Sears*. See *EEOC v. General Telephone Company of Northwest, Inc.*, 9th Circuit, September 12, 1989, 11239; and see *Johnson v. Transportation Agency, Santa Clara County*, 480 U.S. 616 (1987).

5. U.S. Congress, *Hearings before the Joint Economic Committee, Congress of the United States, on the Economic Problems of Women*, 93d Cong., 1st sess., part 1, July 10, 1973, 1, 3; hereafter, *JEC Hearings, 1973*. Aileen C. Hernandez complained that it was "unfortunate that the men are not present because I feel that we are telling you something that you already know, and it might have done the other members of the Joint Economic Committee some good to have been here this morning" (128).

6. Ibid., part 2, 230 (Blumberg), 300 (Bell), 274 (Ball/Griffiths), 341, 344 (Dahm). Dahm noted that 1.7 million domestics were still excluded from the system, as were 700,000 farm workers and 8 million state and local government employees (342).

7. Ibid., 272, 343.

8. John D. Johnston Jr., "Sex Discrimination and the Supreme Court, 1971–1974," *New York University Law Review* 49 (November 1974), 659.

9. *Cleveland Board of Education v. LaFleur*, 414 U.S. 632 (1974).

10. *Kahn v. Shevin*, 416 U.S. 351 (1974); *Schlesinger v. Ballard*, 419 U.S. 498 (1975).

11. Thurgood Marshall, "Reflections on the Bicentennial of the United States Constitution," *Harvard Law Review* 101 (November 1987), 13.

12. Council of Economic Advisors, *Economic Report of the President* (Washington, D.C.: GPO, 1973), 90.

13. *JEC Hearings, 1973*, part 1, 67, 117.

14. "Women's Liberation Counts a Victory," *Business Week*, June 13, 1970, 99.

15. *JEC Hearings, 1973*, 66, 67, 342.

16. National Manpower Council, *Womanpower* (New York: Columbia University Press, 1957), 343.

17. Joan Williams, "Deconstructing Gender," *Michigan Law Review* 87 (February 1989), 813–20.

18. *Johnson v. Santa Clara County Transportation Agency*, 480 U.S. 616 (1987); quoted, 632. Melvin Urofsky, *Affirmative Action on Trial: Sex Discrimination in Johnson v. Santa Clara* (Lawrence: University Press of Kansas, 1997), provides an excellent overview of the history of the case.

# Index